The Economics of Transition

From Socialist Economy to Market Economy

MARIE LAVIGNE

First published 1995 by
MACMILLAN PRESS LTD
Houndmills, Basingstoke, Hampshire RG21 2XS
and London
Companies and representatives
throughout the world

ISBN 0–333–52730–5 hardcover
ISBN 0–333–52731–3 paperback

A catalogue record for this book is available
from the British Library.

10   9   8   7   6   5   4   3
04   03   02   01   00   99   98

Copy-edited and typeset by Povey–Edmondson
Okehampton and Rochdale, England

Printed and bound in Great Britain by
Creative Print and Design (Wales), Ebbw Vale

THE ECONOMICS OF
TRANSITION

Contents

List of Tables, Boxes and Figures

Tables

Boxes

Figures

Preface

'Until recently the world was divided into the first, second and third world. The notion of the second world is now losing its substance. What remains is a huge amount of debris and ruins which is a combination of the first and third worlds: by its aspirations and longing to create a democratic political system and prospering market economy it relates to the first world, a part of which it would like to become; however, by the state of the economy and the types of national and social problems it often resembles the third world.' (Vaclav Havel, President of the Czech and Slovak Federal Republic, 4 September 1991, Prague, opening speech of the International Forum for Culture and Democracy)

Since the Berlin Wall was breached on 9 November 1989, the former socialist countries have remained on top of the agenda in the Western media, not only because of dramatic political developments such as the anti-Gorbachev coup and the collapse of the USSR in 1991, or because of the lingering state of war in the former Yugoslavia and in parts of the former USSR. Economic developments make headlines as well. The transition to the market arouses public interest out of proportion to the share of these countries in the world economy. Western governments, firms, international organisations and ordinary citizens, are eager to keep informed, to understand, to help, to advise, to trade, to invest, to be involved in one way or another.

At the same time, after several years of transition, frustrations and even a kind of fatigue develop in the West. Though transition to the market is now acknowledged as a longlasting process which might extend to a whole generation, structural transformation seems very slow. While growth has resumed in Eastern Europe, there are only a few signs of the possible ending of a protracted recession in Russia. Along with this gloomy assessment, the West increasingly feels the impact of the East, in many ways. East and West are now parts of the same world. In the past, following the usual international classification, one could divide the world into three parts: the developed market economies, or, in the parlance of the East, the capitalist world; the 'second' world of the centrally planned economies, which used to call itself socialist; the Third World of the developing economies. Now there is just an economic division between rich and poor countries. There is no longer a systemic division. The market economy has won. What is the price of this victory? Will the Western model succeed in the East? Will the rich Western countries be able to go on supporting the South and at the same time pull the East up to their average level of development? What does this imply in terms of assistance, market liberalisation, and increased immigration? Are our recipes and programmes really suited for the transition process? If these programmes do not work as they should, is the model to be blamed?

Much has already been written on transition. Reports, conference materials, collective books, guides for businessmen, and scholarly articles in specialised and non-specialised journals, have flourished. It is fairly impossible to follow this surge in the literature, and to avoid being overtaken by events. It looks therefore provocative to offer a textbook by one single author on such a fast-moving subject. The purpose and the approach need to be clarified.

The author of this book has been studying Soviet and Eastern European economies for over thirty years. Thus, I belong to the professional world of what used to be called 'sovietology'. This profession is feeling very frustrated lately. Since the beginning of the transition many new experts have come into the field, from various backgrounds, mainly from an experience in developing countries. Many of the former 'sovietologists' have lost credibility, because none of them had predicted that the system would collapse when it did, or the way in which a collapse would occur, and also because they were suspected of bias due to their involvement in the study of a now dead system. Personally I do not feel guilty of lack of foresight. We all were wrong: both those who year after year predicted that the system was bound to collapse, and those, more cautious, who thought it might go on muddling through for many years. Many of us believed that the system might last longer if reformed, and we had even devised the categories of 'modified' or 'reformed' planned economies. The sudden end of the system took everybody by surprise, as well as the radical shift to the market, which excluded any 'third way'. Does this mean that we may now dispense with any understanding of the past? The present transition process has no historical equivalent or precedent, such as the situation of the Western European countries after the Second World War, or the evolution in the developing countries. The transition is burdened with the legacies of the past. This past has to be assessed, especially as history is being rewritten due to new information and new statistical data now available. Slowly, 'the figure in the carpet' reveals itself. Knowledge of the past helps to undestand the inertia of the present. History also evidences that the fruit was rotten, through dozens of signs that we know how to decipher only now; thus the present provides us with keys to explain the past.

This book is concerned with economics. Is there such a thing as 'transition economics'? In the past there was a wide debate in the profession as to the relevancy of mainstream economics to the analysis of centrally planned economies. Whatever the answer in theory, in practice it was very difficult to use any sophisticated econometric model for lack of reliable data. Now there seems to be a wide consensus on the theory. In the East, while communism has been discarded politically, and even outlawed in some countries (for instance, in the Czech Republic), economists and policy-makers alike endorse the fundamentals of neo-classical economic science. Their Western advisers eagerly support this attitude, especially as the standard adjustment and stabilisation packages which they recommend are based on the same theoretical assumptions. I believe that the disillusions in the transition process will lead to a more complex approach, closer to the 'political economy' concept. This concept is generally considered ..ith suspicion both in East and West. It is reminiscent of Marx, more than of Ricardo. It suggests at best a reluctance, at worst an inability to use mathematical formalisation. Beyond such simplifying views, one may find an inspiration in new approaches such as the institutionalist one, and in the combination of economics with political science and history. The last chapter of this book explores these alternatives approaches.

This book is also the outcome of a personal involvement. I have been travelling in East Central Europe and in the USSR since 1964. I have witnessed the first year of the transition in Prague in 1990–1. I have many personal friends in all these countries. Therefore I cannot look at the transition from a mere scholarly point of view. I want the transition to succeed, and I sense all the sorrows and pains associated with this process, which looked so exhilarating in the beginning. I have a special thought for my Russian friends. Not only are they facing the damages and losses resulting from the past regime, which they had to bear for so long; and not only, in their own private lives, are they looking back at their wasted years, and anticipating an uncertain and difficult future for their children. But also, they are explicitly or implicitly burdened with a collective guilt for what their leaders have imposed upon others. Their native motherland has vanished; its name is associated with infamy, and glorious memories are wiped out. The 900 days during which Soviet Leningrad resisted the enemy sink into oblivion while St Petersburg is born again. Transition is irreversible: nobody wants the communist past to be revived, but should all of it be doomed?

Finally, let me add a few methodological notes. The book is divided into two parts, the fist one dealing with the past of the centrally planned economies under 'real socialism', the second exploring the transition in progress. Central and Eastern European countries, together with the former USSR, are mainly considered here; other experiences are mentioned but not elaborated upon.

The book is targeted for students in economics, political science, and history of Eastern Europe. Though designed for undergraduates and not requiring a preliminary acquaintance with the subject, it may also be used on advanced courses as an introduction to transition economics. For teachers and graduate students, a guide for further reading provides opportunities for a deeper investigation. The book is also meant for the general public wanting a simple and clear approach to the complex issues of the transition to the market. It does not pretend to convey detailed information on all its aspects for all the countries under review. This is why, contrary to almost all the books devoted to this topic, no country studies are presented. The purpose is to offer basic and comprehensive guidance to the essentials, so that the reader may use what he/she already knows about the past of this area, sort out the huge volume of information brought to him or her by the media day by day, and follow up on his/her own through further reading.

A book on such a topic cannot be definitive. The process analysed is transitory by definition. People and governments in the East have to go through and out of transition; international organisations, states, and experts in the West are busy helping, advising, monitoring, and observing the process. The ultimate aim is not to create a new type of society, a new system. The East wants to rejoin the developed West where it stands. To reconstruct a market economy is, however, a long and complex task: we know where we start from, we believe we know how to get there, but we cannot know exactly what the outcome will be. The story is still open-ended.

*   *   *

I could not have written this book (as well as the shorter French book on which the present volume elaborated and expanded, *L'Europe de l'Est, du plan au marché*) without various favourable circumstances such as fruitful contacts and discussions in several research centres in the beginning of the transition. I would like to acknowledge the research support of the European University Institute (1988), of the Bundesinstitut für internationale und ostwissenschaftliche Studien (BIOST) in Cologne (1989), of the Averell Harriman Institute at the Columbia University and of the Institute for East–West Studies (IEWS) in New York (1990). I had the great privilege of being appointed by the IEWS as the director of its Central European branch, the European Studies Centre in Prague (1990–1), and this gave me the invaluable opportunity of witnessing the first steps of transition in a former communist country, as well as the privilege of working with a team of people enthusiastically dedicated to assisting the transition process. I was asssociated for two years (1991–3) with the Programme for Strategic and International Security Studies of the Graduate Institute for International Studies in Geneva. With the support of the French Ministry of Education and of my university, I organised in 1992 an international 'summer school' on the transition to the market which again allowed me to develop exciting intellectual contacts.

I cannot formally express my gratitude to all the friends, colleagues, specialists and institutions who actually helped me in devising this book, gathering the material, and clarifying my ideas. I earnestly apologise for not mentioning everybody toward whom I have an intellectual debt. Among the few names I want to mention, I shall begin with two dear friends of many years, with whom I have repeatedly discussed the issues of feasible or unfeasible socialism, and who both died in 1994: Alec Nove, Emeritus Professor at the University of Glasgow and father of the British sovietology, and Aleksandar Vacic, the head of the Division for Economic Analysis and Projections at the Economic Commission for Europe of the United Nations in Geneva. Several friends agreed to read the manuscript and to comment; I am especially grateful to Joel Dirlam, Marvin Jackson, Viktor Kuznetsov, Harriet Matejka. and Mario Nuti, for their attention and their remarks. All conclusions and remaining errors are mine.

Pau, France   MARIE LAVIGNE

I

The Past: Real Socialism

1 The Bases of the Socialist Economic System

We have chosen to call the former *socialist* countries as they usually called themselves, rather than 'Soviet-type', 'centrally planned', or 'command' economies, or other designations sometimes preferred by scholars. This is not just a matter of semantics. Using the wording 'socialist' may involve the writer into conflictual issues. As does Kornai (1992, p. 10), we have decided to keep the phrase by which the system referred to itself. In this sense we deal with 'really existing', or 'real', socialism (a wording coined by dissidents in the 1970s, such as Rudolf Bahro), as opposed to 'ideal'. Our aim is 'to empirically examine actual economies and their behaviour' (Pryor, 1985, p. 3). Why then keep the word 'socialist' which has been extensively used in a normative sense? Because it is impossible to describe this system without stating its ideological and normative foundations. The task is not an easy one. There has never been an economic theory of really existing socialism, though some definitions have been offered (Sutela, 1994).

Is it possible to define features common to all the countries which belonged to the 'socialist economic system', from the 1930s in the USSR up to the collapse of the system in 1989–90, from Eastern Europe to China and Cuba? Three criteria are usually quoted. First, in such a system, economic life was under the control of a single party, whether or not the party was called communist. Second, the economic institutions were based upon collective, or state, ownership of the basic means of production. Third, compulsory central planning was the main coordinating mechanism, with an increasing but still subsidiary role devoted to market instruments.

From this it is sometimes inferred that the party ruled everything, that people did not own anything, and that the plan commanded all economic decisions. Even in a science-fiction novel, such mechanics are inconceivable. The principles define the foundations of the system, not its real operation. They are intimately linked with an ideology, Marxism-Leninism, which was revised and adapted in each country by the individuals and elites in power. This intimate linkage explains why these principles have been totally rejected by the new governments in all countries where a political 'revolution' occurred at the inception of transition.

THE PARTY CONTROL OF THE ECONOMY

In all socialist countries the party controlled the economy. For historical reasons the party sometimes appeared as the dominant element in an 'alliance' or 'front' of parties. It often called itself communist, but in about half of the socialist countries other denominations were used, such as the Socialist Workers' Party in Hungary, the Polish United Workers' Party, the Party of Labour in Albania and North Korea. In Yugoslavia, to distance itself from the Soviet regime, the party had chosen to call itself a 'league' of communists. These variations made really no substantial difference in the basic concept of the leading role of the party.

The Ideology

Some differences existed, however, in the interpretation of the Marxist-Leninist doctrine, even beyond the Soviet-Yugoslav rift in 1948, or the Sino-Soviet schism in 1961. In fact, the ideology of the 'really existing socialism' had little to do with Marx or Lenin, from which only a few standard quotations were borrowed. It was a set of norms and codes of speech and conduct, which were defined by the leaders, and were not subject to discussion or critique. Any person entitled with some authority or responsibility had to comply with the codes and to refer to the official doctrine. Thus the smallest divergence from the code was significant, and generations of Western 'kremlinologists' became very apt at deciphering the meaning of these variations. Actually, while 'socialism' was still an ideal for the Western left, nobody believed in the ideology of 'real socialism' in the East; moreover, nobody was supposed to believe, as long as the official behaviour conformed to the party standard. Breaches were tolerated as long as they remained hidden, but always remained subject to penal liability. In the economic field, parallel to the 'official economy' described in textbooks, a 'shadow' economy developed, as a safety valve to the official system, but was never officially acknowledged.

Such a status of the dominant ideology helps us to understand what occurred in this field immediately after the transition. There was a massive rejection of the words 'communism' and 'socialism', and of anything associated with these words, such as social democracy (and probably even 'social' security, which is an oblique reference to socialist values: the reluctance to consider it a priority is not only due to the lack of resources to finance it). In some countries not only the communist party but also the communist regime was formally outlawed (as was the case, for instance, in the Czech Republic, by a law of July 1993). The communist parties had to find a new denomination to remain legal; none of them nowadays has a clear doctrine other than the opposition to the new majorities – not excluding tactical alliances once back in power.

The Nomenklatura

The leadership of the party was often associated with the *nomenklatura*, a Russian word which became internationally the symbol of communist privileges. In fact the institution allowed the party to control all the high-level appointments. For instance, all executive positions in the economic sphere, from the government members to the enterprise managers, were mentioned on special lists (hence the word *nomenklatura*, coded list). Any appointment on a listed position had to be approved by the relevant party organ, for instance the Central Committee for a minister, the city committee in the case of the director of a local enterprise. The word *nomenklatura* ultimately qualified all the party cadres entitled with political power and economic responsibility, and benefiting from privileges such as the right to shop in special stores.

The party itself was a hierarchy. At the lowest level, in the enterprises, the collective farms, and more generally in all local economic units, the party cells had to ensure that the management was complying with the political instructions from above. The local or regional party authorities had often to settle disputes that occurred between the enterprises, or those that occurred between the enterprise and the state administration, for example a ministry. On each decision level, the party was above all other authority and ruled in last resort. This system was particularly sophisticated in the Soviet Union, due to the immensity of the country and the federal structure of the state. This explains the disastrous disorganisation which occurred there once the party system collapsed. No other authority could any longer keep the economy together. The seemingly powerful state bureaucracy derived its legitimacy from the party alone, and revealed itself helpless once the party was outlawed in the economy.

At the level of the state, the party organs had pre-eminence over the governments and the parliaments in fixing the main lines of economic policy, approving the macro-economic plans, determining the regional or sectoral policy, deciding upon the share of consumption and investment within the domestic product. They have also launched all the economic reforms. However, the party usually had no specific apparatus to deal with economic questions. The only exceptions were the party administration in the USSR under Khrushchev, in Romania under Ceausescu, and the Asian communist parties. The overall party control usually operated indirectly, through political intervention in other bodies.

The Economic Administration

The communist regime is indeed often equalled with a pervasive state bureaucracy. The Soviet model was imposed after the Second World War in Eastern Europe. A large number of sectoral and functional agencies were set up. Functional agencies, such as the Planning office, the office of Prices, the Investment Bank, the Labour office, had to implement the kind of coordination tasks which the market realises spontaneously in capitalist economies. For instance, the offices of Prices were fixing wholesale and retail prices. In market economies, whenever price agencies exist, they do not fix prices; they just have to check that prices are determined by the market in conditions of fair competition. Most typical were the agencies for 'material and technical supplies', which performed the task of linking together buyers and sellers in the production and distribution process. When there is no free inter-enterprise market, the state has to bring together the suppliers of means of production and the users of these goods, and to ensure that the contracts comply with the provisions of the plan, by issuing selling and purchase state orders for machinery, intermediate goods and spare parts. In the USSR, this agency was called *Gossnab* (state supply administration) and employed about one million workers by the end of the regime. Its collapse severed inter-enterprise links before new ones could be established through the market.

Along with these coordination tasks, the state bureaucracy was also managing the enterprises, often exerting a 'petty tutelage' on them. This was done through branch ministries, more or less numerous according to the countries. In the USSR there were about sixty of them in the beginning of the 1980s. In some Eastern European countries the state bureaucracy had been revamped and simplified along with the reforms in planning and management. However, party control remained, in a modified form, as we shall see in Chapter 3.

Local Government

Is a communist system compatible with strong local governments? In principle this should be the case. The USSR was born as the Republic of Soviets, i.e. of elected councils of people's representatives. In fact, the local soviets have always had only limited economic and political power. The big enterprises were managed directly from Moscow, through federal ministries and central party organs. The lack of a genuine economic base in the regions is also an explanation for the chaos in the former Soviet Union. Once the system collapsed, the republics and regions were left with huge unmanageable industrial giants on their territories, which were meant to supply a large range of customers or users all over the country, and operated often with 'imported' labour from other republics, mainly from Russia.

There was a brief attempt at reviving local authorities in the economic field. In the USSR and elsewhere in Eastern Europe, in the beginning of the 1960s, regional economic agencies (called *sovnarkhozy* in the USSR) were set up to break the power of the branch ministries. This was an initiative by Khrushchev to get rid of the Stalinist administration; the outcome was to substitute the 'parochial spirit' of the local administration to the 'petty tutelage' of the ministries, and the experiment was dropped everywhere. In China, however, the provinces had always had extensive economic rights, which were only occasionally cut during recentralisation campaigns in the 1960s and the 1970s.

Self-Management

One should expect a socialist regime to grant large management rights to the workers, who are the collective owners of the means of production. According to the communist ideology, the party itself is merely the vanguard of the workers' class. Actually only Yugoslavia organised all economic activity on the basis of direct self-management since 1950. In other socialist countries formal arrangements for worker participation in management have operated through various institutions and mainly through the official trade unions, which were considered as the 'transmission belts' of the party. This worker participation always remained very indirect. More politically active workers' councils emerged occasionally during periods of crisis, such as 1918 in Russia, 1956 in Poland and Hungary, 1968 in Czechoslovakia, and 1980 in Poland (where they were supported by the unofficial trade union *Solidarnosc*). They have been crushed or rendered ineffective.

The official trade unions had quite significant functions, but not in the sphere of management. They were mass organisations encompassing almost all the workers, unlike the party, which always remained an elite organisation with a membership amounting to a share of the total population comprising between 6–7 and 12–15 per cent. The trade unions were active in guaranteeing job security, and effectively opposing redundancies. In most countries they were also managing social security at large, and hence were perceived as welfare organisations providing, along with social security benefits proper, also free vacations, semi-free housing, gardening plots, etc. In the transition process they were discarded as supporters of the communist party; they have yet to be replaced in their social functions.

Self-management has collapsed as a form of economic operation and as a doctrine. Its weaknesses were patent in Yugoslavia, where it remained in force until the end of the regime (Uvalić, 1992, p. 207). The system led to inefficiencies and corruption, fuelled inflation, and generated disguised private ownership and inequality. In the other post-socialist countries, self-management ideals were soon identified with hidden communism, and workers' participation schemes were rejected as inefficient compared with genuine capitalism. Employee ownership was often banned from privatisation blueprints. The failure of self-management in the East is probably in turn jeopardising any attempts to implement it in the West beyond the existing scattered and imperfect experiences.

COLLECTIVE OWNERSHIP OF THE MEANS OF PRODUCTION

In all socialist countries except Yugoslavia, 'socialist' ownership of means of production was established. Consumer goods have never been socialised, and could even be transmitted by heritage. However, the ownership of consumer goods was called 'personal', as 'private property' was considered a capitalist concept. In addition the access to consumer goods, especially durables, was rationed for economic–systemic reasons, because demand was always in excess of supply, and through administrative regulations.

Socialist Ownership

As a rule in all socialist countries, large-scale productive assets were state property, in industry, domestic trade, and services (transportation, banks, insurance companies), following waves of nationalisation in the wake of the revolutions that had established the new regimes. In Yugoslavia the concept of 'social' ownership was introduced in 1950 as a distinctive feature of the self-managed system. The assets did not belong to the state, nor to the workers, but they were the property of the nation as a whole. This fuzzy concept was never clearly specified and only generated confusion in the legal definition and economic management of property rights in Yugoslavia.

In agriculture, socialisation mainly took the form of collectivisation through the compulsory establishment of cooperative farms. Land itself was seldom nationalised: the USSR and Mongolia were exceptions. In most Eastern European countries only large landowners were expropriated, and their property distributed to the peasants in the early stages of the land reform (see Chapter 2). Land was later turned to cooperatives for an indefinite use period: this emerged as a big problem when transition began and it became obvious that many, if not most, of the potential claimants on land had either left the country or become city-dwellers.

In the USSR the collectivisation was conducted through terror during the period 1928–36 and led to the constitution of *kolkhozy* (from the Russian *kollektivnoe khozjajstvo*, i.e. collective farming), while a part of the agricultural sector was organised in *sovkhozy* or state farms (from the Russian *sovetskoe khozjajstvo*, or Soviet farming). There were differences in principle between these two types. Legally the *kolkhozy* were cooperatives, managed by an elected chairman and a general assembly of members endowed with decision-making and income-sharing rights. The *sovkhozy* were state farms managed like state industrial enterprises, by an appointed director. Whereas the *kolkhozniki* were members of the cooperative and were supposed to divide among themselves the revenue of the farm once all costs were covered and all obligations toward the state met, the *sovkhozniki* were wage-earners like industrial workers. The *sovkhozy* were originally established as technically more advanced, specialised farms, and also as the model of a more socialist type of farming. It was expected that in the long run the *kolkhozy* would transform into *sovkhozy*. This never happened, but the differences between the two types of farming became gradually smaller, especially when both types were merged into large-scale agro-industrial complexes, managed on the model of the big state enterprises.

In Eastern Europe state farming never gained great extension, and large-scale cooperatives were the dominant format. However, like these in the USSR, these cooperatives also evolved toward a state-like management. They were very large units; they farmed between 3,000 and 25,000 hectares of land, and they were increasingly involved in industrial activities.

Non-Socialist Ownership

Non-socialist ownership in the production sector was to be found mostly in agriculture. In two countries, i.e. Yugoslavia and Poland, cooperative farms were abolished almost from the outset, in 1953 in Yugoslavia in the wake of abandoning the Soviet model, in 1956 in Poland due to the strong political protest of the peasants. In these two countries private agriculture was conducted on over 80 per cent of the arable land. However it was considered as ideologically inferior to a socialist type of farming. For this reason private farms were discriminated against in terms of severe limits on total acreage farmed and supplies of equipment or materials; they were indirectly controlled by the distribution network. Private farming was managed on a family, non-capitalist type, with backward organisation and low performance.

In all other countries, peasants were allowed to farm a family plot for their own use, and to sell their produce, at free prices, on the city markets which were called in the USSR '*kolkhoz*' markets'. They had specific property rights including the ownership of the house and the use of a narrow strip of adjacent land, plus the right to a limited number of cattle, all of which was subject to administrative regulation and political control, and could not hence be likened to genuine 'private' property. The family plot had three basic functions: to alleviate the political resistance to collectivisation; to provide fresh produce and meat to the cities and thus to supplement the deficient state supplies; and to serve as an excuse for the state not to guarantee that people employed in the cooperative sector would actually be paid for their work. In some countries and especially in Hungary the family plot system evolved into a genuine quasi-private system within the cooperative, with extended rights to the peasants based on contracts with the cooperative.

Outside agriculture there remained sometimes a small private sector in the form of small retail trade and handicrafts, for instance in the German Democratic Republic.

Within the state sector, a semi-legal or illegal 'parallel' or 'shadow' economy developed in all socialist countries. This is one of the most harmful legacies of the past, which is heavily constraining the transition process. The shadow economy was based on corruption and pilfering or large-scale stealing of state property. Its operation implied a close cooperation between the 'mafia' and the party *nomenklatura*. It did not encounter social disapproval, first because everybody tried to benefit from its spillovers be it on any small scale, second because despite the ideology, ordinary citizens never really cared for the state property which was rather perceived as belonging to nobody. Sometimes this 'second' economy is now assessed as a valuable experience of the market, and the only one successful, in the former centrally planned economies. In fact it had quite disastrous consequences. It contributed in shaping an image of successful business as linked with crime. It helped the former members of the *nomenklatura* to initiate very early privatisation to their sole benefit. It provided organised crime with power, financial and material means, and networks which established it as one of the main social forces following the transition. Thus, it may be seen as the most damaging outcome of the state ownership based on the political monopoly of the party.

CENTRAL PLANNING

When one does not wish to label 'socialist' economies as such, one generally calls them CPEs, centrally planned economies. The plan is a coordination mechanism opposed to the market. Strictly speaking, a plan is a set of techniques for determining what future action should be taken to achieve given objectives with a maximum coherence and efficiency. In a socialist economy, the plan is mandatory and not indicative. It encompasses the economic activity overall. The decision-makers are political authorities (such as the party hierarchy, and the state administration subordinate to the party). Its implementation is controlled and subject to legal and political sanction; the plan is imposed on a large number of executive bodies such as ministries and departments, enterprises, local agencies.

Defined as a 'mechanism', or as a set of 'techniques', the central plan was considered as an instrument enabling the management of everything under socialist ownership and party control. In the 1960s, when the performance of the planned economy seemed to falter, the party authorities tried to reform the mechanism through introducing some elements of the market. This reforming approach overlooked the point that the market and the plan were not compatible, not just because of their mechanisms, but because of the system of which central planning was a part, based upon the power monopoly of the party.

Planning Techniques

The planning procedures covered different time-spans (five years, one year, one quarter, one month). The most important plan from the point of view of its binding nature was the yearly plan. The planning process went through several stages. Technically the core of it was the drafting of 'material balances'. The method has been developed under Stalinist planning and used in all socialist countries. A balance is a table identifying sources of supply and uses for individual products or product groups. It shows domestic internal production on the supply side, and its domestic uses (intermediate outputs, investment, consumption) on the uses side. As the two sides of this table can only be made equal fortuitously, the balance is achieved through internal iterative adjustments (increase in production, cuts in intermediate or final uses), and only then through foreign trade (imports increase resources on the supply side; exports provide a use for excess production). Table 1.1 gives an example of a simplified scheme of balance. The balances were drafted first for the material inputs (raw materials, fuels, agricultural goods, semi-manufactured intermediate goods), then for machinery and equipment, and finally for manufactured consumer goods.

Table 1.1   *Simplified scheme of material balance*

Resources		Uses	
1. Domestic production	1,000	1. Inputs used for production	500
2. Imports	200	2. Investment	250
		3. Consumption	150
		4. Exports	300
Total	1,200	Total	1,200

These figures are conventional. Data are measures in kind, in physical units such as tonnes, metric metres, etc.

For example, let us suppose that this balance deals with coal. The units would then be (thousands of) tonnes. On the left side, domestic production is calculated on the basis of the capacities of production, such as the number of fields and pits already operated or to be put into operation during the planned period, minus the capacities to be closed during that period. The planner uses technological coefficients to determine how much a given pit may produce during the planned period (year, month, five-year period, etc.). These coefficients are always estimated for optimal conditions of operation, i.e. the plan is 'taut'. Hence, if the possible production has been overestimated, the planned uses cannot be covered, which has in turn consequences on the whole production chain. On the right side, the various uses of coal are estimated for the whole planned period. One may need coal as an input (as fuel for power stations, as material for the chemical industry, etc.); one may use it for final consumption, both collective (to heat hospitals, schools, state buildings) and individual (when coal is bought by the people for heating purposes); one may want to replenish the state reserves in coal. Once this process is completed the balance is adjusted through foreign trade. Here coal is both exported and imported, with a net export position.

In the Soviet Union during the Stalinist period their number exceeded 18,000. The procedure was iterative. Once the planner had finished a first 'round' he had to redraft the whole set of balances, because unexpected users' needs in the manufacturing process led to a reformulation of the balances ahead. The process was never convergent, for many reasons: first, one never had time enough to refine the calculations; second, the methodology was crude; and third, the initial data were always biased.

The last reason is crucial. As long as economic data (such as physical output, capacity of production, initial stocks) are used at a same time as initial information for the planner and as the basis for assigning tasks to an enterprise and for evaluating it, the enterprise, which is the initial information giver, will cheat on the figures. And thus, there will be a cumulative process by which initial biases will propagate; corrections made on the spot will not restore a true picture. In fact, plan orders are largely determined and written by those who are to implement them, but not according to a deliberate process of decision-making sharing. Cheating is a built-in feature of the system.

A Non-Reformable System

Are there conditions under which a central planning system may function efficiently? The answer is probably yes: in a situation of war or similar circumstances. There have to be few key priorities, strictly defined, and the plan has to be implemented under a quasi-military discipline. Western democracies have briefly experienced such situations. The USSR was a comparable case from the beginning of central planning in the early 1930s, until 1945. Even then the planning process did not operate efficiently: not all goals were met, except for a few priority sectors, and the achievements went along with a huge waste of human and material resources.

Later on, when the Soviet economy became more diversified, as the Eastern European economies did after the war, the amount of planned items increased, and controlling of plan implementation became increasingly difficult. The first wave of reforms in the planning and management system followed in the 1960s, so as to improve the declining growth performance of the planned economies. All these reforms failed, because the basic principle of planning remained untouched: the units and agents subject to the planning process had to prove that they had successfully implemented the plan, for which they had provided the data embodied into the compulsory indicators to be fulfilled.

Only after the collapse of the system was it clearly understood that the system was not reformable. It was not a question of decentralising the planning process, as long as there remained a controlling political authority to whom one had to report. Nor was it a question of refining the planning methods. Restoring mathematical methods applied to planning, rediscovering linear programming for the drafting of an optimal plan (i.e. maximising an objective function under constraints) could not improve the outcome because, however loosened, the plan remained a binding order based on political priorities.

This is not to say that the plan could effectively regulate the economic activity overall. Even under totalitarian regimes, the plan was unable to control it in every detail; later on, when most of the centrally planned economies shifted into a bargaining-type, or manipulated, economy, with decentralised units trying to influence the political authorities, central control was less and less effective. However the voluntarist ideology remained. The party still claimed to ultimately keep the economy in tutelage. The combination between such an ideology, and the increasing complexity of economic life, leading to contradictions among multiple target and performance indicators, gradually became unsustainable.

Here again there is a negative legacy. The plan was linked with the party to such an extent that the transition governments rejected any concept of a plan, even indicative, even strategic, even drafted and implemented within decentralised and really autonomous enterprises. 'Plan' will be a dirty word for a long time.

Plan versus Money

In the beginning of the Soviet regime money was considered as an anachronism and a symbol of capitalism. Later, when planning was introduced, the targets or 'indicators' were set in kind. The metric tonne became the most used unit, not only for commodities such as coal, steel, wheat, etc., but also for manufactured goods such as machinery. Money was used when it came to aggregate the material balances into a global macro-economic balance, but only as a unit of account.

Attempts to reconcile money and plan emerged within the reforms aiming at introducing 'market-and-money instruments', to use the Soviet parlance, so as to enable a better fulfilment of the plan. However, though 'market-like' notions such as prices, profit, monetary policy, credit, etc. were increasingly used, the wording was misleading. Money was not playing an active role in the economy: prices were administered, plan targets still privileged the volume of output, the survival of the enterprise did not depend on its profits but on its aptitude to negotiate the plan targets with the political authority. The Central Bank which issued money and which also was the single credit institution – the so-called 'monobank' – performed mainly accounting functions. Its extended network of branches surveyed the implementation of the plan at the enterprise level. Each enterprise had an account in the local branch and had to use it for all its payments. Conversely, individuals could only have a savings account and had to use only cash in banknotes or coins for their payments. Separate circulation of cash and non-cash money allowed for a separate control of enterprise and consumer spending, the ultimate aim being the strict implementation of the plan. Thus, though planning procedures are not technically incompatible with money, the Soviet-type centrally planned system excluded money from any significant influence on the economy. This too has a strong impact on the transition: though there were currencies and banks, the operation of money categories was by and large a *terra incognita* for the new leaders in the transition countries.

2 History

The ideal-type presented in the first chapter was not meant to describe how the socialist economic system appeared and evolved, but to stress its most permanent features which transcended time and space. This chapter will show how it came into existence and extended to a relatively large number of countries.

This book mainly deals with the countries which belonged to the 'Soviet model': the USSR itself and, after the end of the Second World War, the people's democracies in Europe. The latter comprised a sub-set of six countries, from north to south: the German Democratic Republic (GDR), Poland, Czechoslovakia, Hungary, Romania, and Bulgaria. These countries, though applying increasingly distinct models of planning and management, nevertheless remained in the framework of the Soviet model. They formed with the USSR the core of what was called 'the Soviet empire', and belonged to an international economic organisation called Comecon, or CMEA (Council for Mutual Economic Assistance), which embodied the Soviet control on the international economic relations of the area. In Europe, two other countries initially followed the same model, then broke the link: these were Yugoslavia and Albania. Yugoslavia defined itself in 1950 as a self-managed society. Albania chose to join the Chinese camp in 1961 in the Sino-Soviet dispute, and later on, in 1977, also broke up with China. Despite its rupture with the USSR, it remained the last case of the Stalinist model until the collapse of the regime in 1991.

Several developing countries adopted the socialist path: China, Mongolia, North Korea, Vietnam and Laos in Asia, Cuba in America. Mongolia, Cuba and Vietnam joined the CMEA; China and Korea developed a different kind of socialism.

All these countries called themselves socialist and in some cases would deny the same denomination to the others, like the Albanian regime to which the Soviet-type countries were 'ex-socialist' or revisionist. In addition, many Third World countries were at one point or the other engaged on a 'socialist path of development', or 'socialist-oriented'. But they never reached the end of the path so as to become fully-fledged socialist.

Though this chapter deals with history, the purpose is not to add one more assessment of the past to the many existing. It is rather to better understand the present by looking at the past with a new glance. Why did the Soviet model collapse so quickly following the beginning of the transition process? Why is economic transition to the market well under way in Asian socialist countries while communism remains as an ideology and a political regime? Can one derive lessons for the transition from the beginnings of socialism?

THE USSR: THE STALINIST MODEL

There was never in twentieth century history a case of transition to socialism without violence, i.e. without a revolution or a war. In all cases there was a violent breach with the past. The first one occurred in Russia. The October Revolution was for decades celebrated in the communist world as the beginning of a new era which would bring happiness to the world along the lines of Marx in the *Critique of the Gotha Programme* (1878): 'when all the springs of social wealth will flow in plenty and when the society will be able to write on its banners: from each according to his abilities, to each according to his needs'. Such a society was to be built in two stages. The first one was building socialism. This stage was officially reached in the USSR in 1977, for the sixtieth anniversary of the Revolution. The new Constitution which was adopted in October of that year stated that the Soviet Union was an 'advanced socialist society', from which one could move to the next stage, building the communist society. In fact, even the first stage was an ideological fantasy. The shift was from a rather primitive capitalism to a planned partocracy labelled 'really existing socialism' by its dissidents. The stages of this evolution are briefly described in Box 2.1.

The Beginnings: From War Communism to the NEP and from NEP to Stalinism

The November 1917 Revolution (October according to the Russian calendar) brought to power the majority faction (in Russian, *bolshevik* meant those retaining the majority) of the Russian workers' social-democrat party, under the leadership of Vladimir Lenin.

The revolution

Was this first 'transition' inevitable, from autocratic tsarism to communism? In February 1917, another transition was initiated, by the 'bourgeois' Revolution which launched the Provisional government, based on a parliamentary democracy and on a market economy with a strong role devoted to the state, not just to deal with the war, but also to complete industrialisation (which had heavily relied on foreign and state capital until then) and to conduct an agrarian reform, in a country where over 80 per cent of the population lived in the country. Why was is necessary to wait almost seventy-five years to see a pluralistic democracy and a market system implemented?

Box 2.1 *Chronology of the USSR*

- 25 October (7 November) 1917: beginning of the October Revolution (the Bolsheviks seize the Winter Palace in Petrograd); they proclaim all power to the Soviets (the councils of delegates of workers, peasants, and soldiers);
- 26 October (8 November) 1917: the private property on land is abolished; the 'Land Decree' declares the land national property;
- 14 (27) December 1917: nationalisation of private banks;
- 21 January (3 February) 1918: all foreign debts are repudiated (nullification of the 'Russian loans');
- 3 March 1918: the peace of Brest-Litovsk is signed with Germany and ends the war; the treaty will be renounced by Russia in November 1918;
- 22 April 1918: nationalisation of foreign trade, which become a state monopoly;
- 28 June 1918: large-scale industry is nationalised;
- 1918–1920: period of 'war communism' (the economy is managed in a military way; cities are supplied by compulsory deliveries imposed on the peasants; money nearly disappears and most of the transactions are conducted in kind);
- 29 November 1920; nationalisation of industry as a whole is decreed;
- March 1921: the New Economic Policy (NEP) is launched: compulsory deliveries of food products are abolished, and replaced by a tax in kind; trade of any kind is authorised; small-scale industry is denationalised;
- 12 October 1921: the State Bank (*Gosbank*) is officially created;
- 30 December 1922; establishment of the Union of Soviet Socialist Republics (USSR):
- 1922–1924: currency reform through nearly two years of circulation of parallel paper currencies, the *sovznak* ruble and the *chervonets*;
- 20 January 1924: death of Vladimir Ilyich (Ulyanov) Lenin, the founder of the Russian bolshevik party; Josif Vissarionovich (Dzhugashvili) Stalin who was secretary general of the party since 1922 begins to build his one-man power on the party and the state;
- Law of 29 June 1927 on 'state industrial trusts', which is the basis of the legislation on state-owned enterprises;
- December 1927: the NEP ends; the first five-year plan 1927/28–1931/32 is launched;
- 1928–1932: mass collectivatisation of agriculture;
- 1935: beginning of the Stakhanovite movement, named after the coal-miner Stakhanov who managed to achieve an output fourteen times greater than the norm;
- 1937–1938: Stalin 'purges' the Army, the Party and the state administration; terror extends to the whole society;
- 22 June 1941: German forces invade the USSR by violation of the Nazi–Soviet pact of 1939; human war losses amounted to at least 20 million people;
- 9 May 1945: the Soviet soldiers seize Berlin; this date is officially the end of the war for the USSR;
- June 1947: announcement of the Marshall plan of assistance to the reconstruction of Europe; participation in the plan is offered to Eastern Europe, which rejects it on Stalin's instructions;
- January 1949: the Council for Economic Mutual Assistance (CMEA or Comecon) is created by the USSR, Bulgaria, Hungary, Poland, Romania and Czechoslovakia;

- May 1955: the Warsaw Pact is signed by the same states, plus the German Democratic Republic (GDR);
- 5 March 1953: Stalin dies; Nikita Khrushchev becomes First Secretary of the Party;
- February 1956: XXth Party Congress; de-Stalinisation begins;
- October 1964: Khrushchev is ousted and replaced by Leonid Brezhnev as first secretary of the Party and by Alexander Kosygin as prime minister;
- 1965: the Kosygin economic reform is launched;
- 1979: a minor economic reform is launched for industry;
- May 1982: a large-scale food programme is launched so as to restructure the agricultural sector and to provide food self-sufficiency to the USSR;
- November 1982: death of Leonid Brezhnev, who is replaced by Yuri Andropov; a campaign to increase discipline in industry is launched;
- February 1984: death of Andropov, who is replaced by Konstantin Chernenko;
- March 1985: death of Chernenko, replaced by Mikhail Gorbachev, who starts a campaign for economic recovery based on anti-alcoholic measures, a commitment to a sharp acceleration in growth so as to counteract the so-called 'stagnation' of the Brezhnev period; in politics, *glasnost* or 'transparency' of political and public life is proclaimed;
- 1986: launching of an economic restructuring package, called *perestroyka*, which is more radical than any previous reform; private property is indirectly admitted (through the 'leasing', or *arenda*, contract in agriculture, the 'cooperatives' in industry and services); very quickly a general disorganisation develops in the economy and the society, threatening the state institutions;
- January 1991: *de facto* disintegration of the CMEA;
- 19 August 1991: a coup against Gorbachev fails; Yeltsin takes the power in Russia; the USSR gradually disintegrates;
- December 1991: the Commonwealth of the Independent States is established among all the former Republics of the USSR, except the three Baltic States and Georgia; the USSR ceases to exist.

This failure may be partly explained by the weakness of the Provisional government. But the main impulse was the seizure of power by a party organised on a military style and inspired by the communist ideology; the circumstances of the world war and the civil war that followed, and the desperate situation of the economy, helped to strengthen the grip of the party and to develop its monopoly. In the economic field, Marxism revisited by Lenin led to the party taking over the 'commanding heights' of the economy, using the state apparatus. Thus the basis for the socialist ownership of the means of production was set. Land, banks, industry, and foreign trade were nationalised in 1917–18. The third foundation of a socialist economic system was established more than ten years later, when in 1928–9 planning became the main controlling device of the economy.

How should one look at the 'war communism' period in 1918–20 (Malle, 1985)? Some historians see it as at the first experience of fully-fledged communism, when state property was forcibly established along with an overall state control on production and distribution. Others point out that terror and military discipline went along with economic collapse and country-wide chaos, and that the measures taken were a desperate attempt to cope with the situation and to survive, i.e. to ensure food supplies for the cities through requisitioning in the country, which triggered peasant riots. Probably 'both factors played a role and reinforced each other' (Nove, 1992, p. 75). The debate on the nature of 'war communism' is not just intellectual. It has an impact on how the New Economic Policy (NEP) is seen.

The NEP

Was the NEP, or New Economic Policy, launched by the communist party in March 1921, the first experience of a transition from socialism to capitalism? Much later, during the *perestroyka* years (1986–91) the NEP was often invoked as an example. The answer should be no. The transition was meant to lead from a militarised communism to the first stage of socialism, with a strategic retreat during which temporary concessions would be made to the market principles. Thus, capitalism was partly restored in the small and medium-size industry, which was denationalised. Some forms of mixed economy were implemented on a relatively modest scale, such as concessions of mining fields to foreign companies, and leasing of nationalised enterprises to private capitalists. Large enterprises were kept in state ownership, but with a market-type management. They were gradually merged into state-controlled trusts which were the harbingers of the huge industry-wide 'branch' monopolies which developed later. Requisitioning was abolished and replaced by a tax in kind which allowed individual peasants (who provided most of the agricultural production) to retain the rest of their produce for their own consumption and for sale on the urban markets. Finally, over the years 1922–4, the currency was stabilised, which put an end to several years of hyperinflation and flight from money. The currency stabilisation was achieved through a quite unprecedented method. The paper currency introduced by the Bolsheviks, the *sovznak* (Soviet token), depreciated at an accelerated pace since the end of war communism, and in June 1922 it was decided to introduce a parallel paper currency, the *chervonets*, which was backed by gold and supposed to be equivalent to the pre-revolutionary 10-ruble unit. Both currencies co-existed in 1923 and early 1924, until the sovznak was driven out of circulation in March 1924, and a new stabilised ruble became the sole currency, following an exchange of banknotes. This experience was very often discussed in Russia in 1992 and 1993 as a possible way of ending hyperinflation and monetary disorder.

During the years of *perestroyka*, there was an extended debate on the nature of the NEP. Was it really a deliberate strategic retreat, the ultimate aim being to build full communism? Or could it have been a longlasting process leading to a stable mixed economy? Such questions were hotly discussed by the end of the 1980s. Only if the answer was yes to the second question could the NEP provide a suitable gradualistic model for transforming the Soviet economy. Indeed, some of the fascinating intellectual debates during the NEP could point to such an answer. But again, it was a political move, the seizure of total power by Stalin in 1929, that determined the course of the events by putting an end to the NEP and its promises.

The Stalinist Era

Was Stalin really necessary? This is the title of a famous book by Alec Nove (1964). What would have been the development of Soviet socialism without Stalin? In any case Stalin shaped the system. He had been secretary general of the party since 1922, eighteen months before Lenin's physical death. He ruled the party when Lenin was no longer able to speak and act; he put an end to the NEP after defeating Trotsky, in 1926, and Bukharin, in 1929. From then on the ideological monopoly of the party was blended with the sole power of a leader.

The Stalinist model was based on three principles. A heavy industry base was to be built so as to ensure growth. This could not be achieved without forcibly extracting the surplus created in agriculture, which acted as a justification for collectivisation. Five-year planning was launched as a mobilising force, as well as an instrument for controlling the economy.

The great industrialisation debate

The Soviet industrialisation debate (Erlich, 1960) was in fact a debate over agriculture. Clearly agriculture was the single source of surplus (primitive socialist accumulation, as Preobrazhensky called it). How to increase this surplus through a suitable agrarian policy? How to channel it into industry?

In 1927, the Soviet agriculture was very little socialised. Nationalisation of land was pure fiction. Cooperatives accounted for less than 1 per cent of the sown area. Most of the farms were small in size, and following the abolition of requisitioning peasantry shifted to a subsistence-type economy. The 'right-wing' opposition led by Nikolai Bukharin contended that one should base the development of industry on a political alliance (*smychka*) between urban workers and peasants on which NEP itself was built. Peasants, especially middle and 'rich' peasants (the notorious *kulaks*; see definition in Nove, 1992, pp. 103–4), should be encouraged through market incentives to produce and sell more. The government would thus be able to export grain and to import the machinery needed for industrialisation, while agriculture would provide industry with raw materials to manufacture, and food to process, so as to feed a growing-in-size urban labour force. In turn, industry would help agriculture to modernise, through sales of equipment, fertilisers and industrial consumer goods. Then the conditions might be ripe for the socialisation of the country without scaring the peasants.

The left-wing opposition did not believe in the *smychka*. Its leaders, Lev Trotsky and Eugen Preobrazhensky, advocated a forcible collection of the surplus through taxes in kind, non-equivalent exchange (i.e. high prices for industrial goods sold to the peasants and low prices paid for their produce, changing into deliberate policy the 'price scissors' crisis which had developed in 1923–4), and forced cuts in supplies of consumer goods to agriculture.

For political reasons Stalin used the debate so as to get rid of his political opponents. First the left opposition was defeated in 1926–7. Later the arguments of the left served to defeat the right-wing opposition in 1929, and the collectivisation could be launched (Davies, 1980).

The mass collectivisation through terror

The immediate aims of collectivisation were twofold. The first one was to liquidate the *kulak* as a class, as they could not be won over, and to base the political support of the regime in the country on the poor and middle peasants regrouped in cooperatives. From the beginning of collectivisation, therefore, anyone reluctant to join a collective farm was labelled a *kulak* and deported. The second aim was to increase procurements for the cities so as to force and support industrialisation.

The consequences of this type of collectivisation were manifold. Peasants resisted collectivisation by slaughtering livestock. The Soviet animal husbandry never really recovered, and still in 1940 remained under its 1928 level. Millions of peasants died, due to the physical elimination of the peasants considered as *kulak*, and to the famine which developed in 1933 as a consequence of the forced procurements policy. A large share of these deaths occurred in Ukraine, which still fuels the resentment of the Ukrainians against the Russians.

Finally, though it may seem not so tragic a consequence compared to the sufferings of the people, the mass collectivisation terror led to the political discrediting of the cooperative as an institution in all the ex-communist world: perhaps not for ever, but at least for a long time. People tend to remain in cooperatives for job security and social security reasons; governments want to get rid of them because of political aversion. In transition countries, the only politically acceptable and economically feasible way of agricultural management is thus small family farming, because capital is lacking to develop large-scale capitalist farming. It will take a very long time to overcome this rejection of the cooperative as such, including the various models experimented with in Western countries such as food-processing, marketing or supply cooperatives, which are still unconsciously identified with the Stalinist *kolkhozy*.

In the USSR, mass collectivisation was officially completed by 1935, when the model statute of the kolkhoz was adopted. Before that, the MTS (Machine and Tractor Stations) were set up in 1931, not only to supply the cooperatives with machinery and spare parts but also to control them politically. Though the MTS were turned into repair and maintenance stations after Stalin's death, without explicit political functions, the *kolkhozy* were never really able to control their technical capital, and this also explains much of their inefficiency.

The state sector was made of *sovkhozy* which were supposed to represent the highest model of socialist agriculture. *Sovkhozy* did not develop very much however, mainly because they were costly (the peasants had to be paid a fixed wage, as in industry, while the *kolkhoznik* was supposed to get a share of the *kolkhoz* revenue, if any, once the procurement obligations had been met).

Planning

Already in 1920 a first concept of an all-embracing economic plan had been drafted under the misleading name of GOELRO (State plan for the electrification of Russia), which was in fact a long-term development plan, already using the 'balance' method. This plan was never actually implemented.

Stalin turned planning into a political undertaking, not only by making it compulsory, but also by mobilising all the party propaganda for its implementation. The first five-year plans were meant to achieve a 'leap forward' in heavy industrialisation, through large increases in output of electricity, raw materials, metals and heavy machinery. The first three five-year plans fixed unrealistically high targets which were never met, but there was a dramatic rise in the production of the heavy industry (see Chapter 4). Operational annual planning only began in 1930 for 1931.

The Stalinist model was adjusted to the war effort and post-war reconstruction requirements, by becoming still more dictatorial. Stalin himself decided to theorise it in a series of articles, published in pamphlet form in 1952, as *Economic Problems of Socialism in the USSR*. The pamphlet stressed, among other things, that the Marxian 'law of value' did not apply within the production sector. Stalinism did not disappear with the death of its founder in 1953 despite the ideological 'thaw' which occurred in the late 1950s, and the reforms that followed. It permeated economic activity as well as political life. Among its main sequels in the conscience and behaviour of economic agents one may mention the shunning of any individual initiative, the formal compliance with the political will expressed by the authorities, the cult of the overfulfilment of the plan, and the pervasive cheating and biasing of means and achievements.

Post-Stalinism

Stalinism and the cult of the personality of Stalin were officially abolished in 1956. Three leaders played a dominant role as heads of the party and, since Brezhnev, of the state: Nikita Khrushchev (1953–64), Leonid Brezhnev (1964–82) and Mikhail Gorbachev (1985–91), not to mention the shorter terms of Yuri Andropov (1982–4) and Konstantin Chernenko (1984–5).

In an erratic style, Khrushchev launched economic reforms which were to be extended but also paralysed by his successor. His merits were significant. He put an end to the terror; he denounced Stalin's crimes in his famous 'secret report' to the XXth Congress of the party (1956); he allowed for a cultural and intellectual 'thaw'; he alleviated the situation of the peasants for the first time since collectivisation; he permitted a renaissance of economic thought. He promoted the first economic experiments which were to inspire the Brezhnev–Kosygin reforms. The Western world was sympathetic to these reform ideas, which were expressed in a theoretical form by an economist, Yevsey Liberman, in the famous article published in *Pravda*, 9 September 1962: 'Plan, Profit, Premium'. This article triggered a huge literature, in the USSR and in the West, on the combination plan–market and its viability.

In the next chapter the reforms that followed will be discussed at more length. Due to the action of Khrushchev, the Soviet Union emerged from totalitarian Stalinism. But Khrushchev did not, any more than his successors, breach the monopoly of the communist party which granted him legitimacy. He instructed the other party leaders in Eastern Europe to repress all movements that put this monopoly in jeopardy (in 1953 in GDR, 1956 in Poland and Hungary). He strengthened the role of the party in the Soviet economy by doubling the state economic administration with a specialised party administration at each organisational level. Thus he maintained the legacy of Stalinism while ending the worship of the individual who had founded and embodied this regime.

THE CREATION OF THE PEOPLE'S DEMOCRACIES IN EUROPE

After Europe was split up between East and West at the Yalta Conference (February 1945), Eastern Europe was in the orbit of the USSR. But not only Soviet tutelage and the Red Army established the communist power in this region. The war and the resistance to Nazi occupation had strengthened the local communist parties. In most countries, just after the war, leftist, non-communist movements were struggling in favour of a democratic transformation of their countries. Before the Second World War, only Czechoslovakia was a democracy in the Western sense. All the other Eastern

European countries had been ruled by dictatorships for most of the inter-war period. Czechoslovakia was also a developed market economy, a feature shared with Eastern Germany which became ruled by the Soviets in 1945, until its transformation into a fully-fledged state, the GDR, in 1949. The rest of Eastern Europe was much less industrialised, and had been hit by the pre-war depression and by unemployment. About 60 million peasants in Eastern and Central Europe had been subject to a quasi-feudal rule; after the war they demanded a land reform, expropriation of the big landowners and the redistribution of land among the peasants.

The First Measures

Should these countries have remained in the orbit of Western Europe, one may imagine the pattern of their post-war transformation. There would have been a land reform, most likely nationalisations of industrial enterprises belonging to wartime collaborationists (as in the case of the firm Renault in France), and of 'natural' monopolies such as railways, energy carriers, mines and public utilities; the governments would have been of a dirigist type.

Indeed, nationalisations began before the communists seized the power in Eastern Europe. Even before the end of the war the workers had established their control on the enterprises abandoned by their owners as the Soviet troops advanced, in various self-management experiences. The new governments, within which the communist parties shared the power with others, proceeded to nationalise first the property recovered from the enemy or confiscated to the collaborators, and only then large-scale industry. The former owners, except the collaborationists and the ex-occupying forces, were compensated, unlike what had happened in Soviet Russia. This explains why after 1989 the transition governments which decided to compensate the victims of nationalisations, or to restitute property in kind, chose to include only those who had suffered from communist national-isations *stricto sensu*. Such a principle for establishing compensation rights entailed huge procedural difficulties and legal disputes, which in turn delayed privatisation. In addition this principle virtually excluded Jewish people (or their heirs) from any compensation, as their property had been confiscated by the occupying forces and then nationalised in the first wave.

In the country areas, the estates of the great land-owners were confiscated and redistributed to the peasants, with an extreme fragmentation of holdings. Re-concentration soon began. Cooperatives pooling agricultural labour and equipment were installed, especially in those countries which had already had a cooperative experience before the war, such as Bulgaria, Czechoslovakia and East Germany.

The Shift to the Soviet Model

In two countries, Albania and Yugoslavia, the communist rule was established without the help of the Red Army, without any democratic transition following the national liberation. In both cases the Stalinist model was immediately implemented. Both countries left the Soviet orbit as we have seen (see Table 2.1); Albania was to retain the Stalinist model until the very end of communism.

In the other countries, after the communists seized power, mass nationalisations began and were completed very quickly, in four or five years (1948–52) except in the GDR where a sizeable industrial private sector continued to exist until 1972. In some countries (Hungary, Poland, and the GDR) a small-scale handicraft and retail trade private sector remained. Collectivisation in agriculture was on the whole less brutal than in the USSR. Administrative and police coercion was nevertheless often employed, and the negative impact of these procedures led the authorities to relax their pressure in the middle of the decade 1950–60 – only in Poland did the government decide to stop collectivisation altogether in 1956. By the beginning of the 1960s the collectivisation was completed, and the cooperative was the dominant model of farming. The state farms remained very limited in terms of their share of arable land, which nowhere exceeded 10 per cent.

Planning emerged much later. In fact Eastern Europe had no consistent planning system until the early 1960s. Long-term development was monitored through investment programmes. Current economic activity was politically controlled according to short-term voluntarist policies.

Nevertheless Eastern Europe followed the 'Soviet model' very closely. The communist party had a political monopoly. The authorities controlled the production capacities in a centralised way. The strategy of economic development gave priority to heavy industry, even in those countries which had a diversified industrial structure before the war (Czechoslovakia and the GDR).

Was Yugoslavia a Different Model?

Of all the features just mentioned Yugoslavia retained only the first one. The 'League' of Communists was a communist party. The fact that Tito broke with Stalin and declared the regime non-aligned, and also the economic and social trends in the country, created an illusion of commitment to democracy and to the market. Self-management became a foundation of the regime in 1950. However, the very vague concept of 'social' ownership really meant in practice ownership by the state, though without the legal institutions of state property. This concept only made things more difficult when the transition began in 1990 and when moves were made to privatise what did not belong to anybody; in some cases it was

Table 2.1   *The beginning and end of the socialist economic system*

Country	Beginning of the socialist regime	End of the regime or present state
Russia/USSR	October 1917 Revolution; nationalisations, 1917–18; launching of mass collectivisation, 1927–9; introduction of five-year planning, 1928→	December 1991: founding of the Commonwealth of Independent States. January 1992: beginning of the transition to a market economy in Russia.
Mongolia	A people's democracy is proclaimed in 1924. 1940–60: nationalisations and collectivisation.	1991: beginning of multipartism and of the transition to the market.
Yugoslavia	1945: the People's Front wins the elections; a Soviet-type economic system is announced. 1946–8: mass nationalisation and collectivisation.	1948: Tito breaks with Stalin. 1950: self-management becomes the basis of the Yugoslav socialism. 1965: instruments of a market economy are introduced. 1991: break-up of Yugoslavia.
Albania	1946: the people's democracy is proclaimed. 1961: break-up with the USSR; Albania chooses a 'Chinese way' of development.	1991: anti-government demonstrations; elections won by the communist party. 1992: new elections; a non-communist government is formed.
Eastern Europe	Between the end of 1945 and 1948: the communists win the elections. Feb. 1948: Communist coup in Prague. Between 1946 and 1949: mass nationalisations; introduction of central planning. 1948: collectivisation begins; stopped in 1956 in Poland.	Poland: first non-communist government in Sept. 1989. Hungary: beginning of multipartism in 1990. Czechoslovakia: 'velvet revolution' in Nov. 1989. Romania: end of the Ceausescu regime in Dec. 1989. Bulgaria: free elections in 1991. 1990–2: beginning of the transition to the market.
East Germany	Oct. 1949: the Soviet zone becomes a people's democracy, the German Democratic Republic (GDR). 1950–52: large-scale nationalisations and collectivisation. August 1961: the Berlin Wall is erected.	9 November 1989: the Berlin Wall is breached. July 1990: monetary and economic union with Federal Germany. October 1990: Germany is unified in a single State.
China	Oct. 1949: the people's democracy is founded. 1949–52: nationalisations, setting-up of people's communes.	During the 1980s: the political line is hardened (massacre of the students on Tian An Men square, 1989) while the economy is moving gradually towards the market.
Vietnam	1945: a people's democracy is established in the North. 1976: the socialist republic of Vietnam is proclaimed following the end of the war and the reunification.	During the 1980s and early 1990s: communist rule remains, a market economy gradually emerges.
Cambodia	1975–6: Khmer Rouge Revolution; the country is renamed Kampuchea. 1979: Vietnam takes control of the country.	1991: an agreement of national reconciliation is signed. 1993: free elections; chaotic development of a market economy.

Laos	1975: founding of the people's democracy.	During the 1980s and early 1990s: same trend as in Vietnam.
North Korea	1948: founding of the people's democracy. 1950–3: Korean war ending with the permanent division between North and South; a Stalinist-type economy develops in the North.	1991: reunification begins to be discussed; no significant change in political or economic trends within the regime.
Cuba	1959: revolution conducted by Fidel Castro; founding of the socialist republic of Cuba.	No evolution toward a puralistic democracy or a market economy; limited openness toward the world economy.

Sources: For Eastern Europe: Geoffrey Swain and Nigel Swain, *Eastern Europe since 1945*, London and Basingstoke: Macmillan, 1993; for the non-European socialist countries: Jeffries (1993).

necessary to first nationalise social property in order to clarify property rights. Planning no longer existed after the early 1960s, but markets were nevertheless controlled, especially for means of production.

Since the break-up of the country in 1991, the ex-Yugoslav republics have been pitted against each other in nationalistic and ethnic conflicts. The story of Yugoslavia is one of deception. The Western European left was thrilled by the self-management experience, which fulfilled utopian dreams. Third World ideologists valued the non-alignment of the country until it became obvious that Yugoslavia sided with the developing world so as to benefit from commercial and political privileges. Idealists were frustrated, and free marketeers very happy, with the opening to foreign investment, and with the operation of something resembling a wild market economy, at the end of the 1960s. Everybody underestimated the communist nature of the regime, quite authoritarian though localist, and hence necessarily compromised in regional conflicts.

THE VARIANTS OF THE SOCIALIST MODEL IN THE THIRD WORLD COUNTRIES

Why have only a few Third World countries embraced the communist regime? Why did this regime survive much more lastingly than in Europe?

China was the first case. Mao Zedong brought his party to power in 1949. The regime was supported by the USSR until 1961, though the building of socialism proceeded until 1958 slower than had been the case in the USSR; it became more radical in 1958, just when Khrushchev was loosening the system in the Soviet Union. In a nutshell, one can summarise the evolution of Chinese socialism as a series of vacillations. Totalitarian collectivisation through people's communes, and an unrealistic 'Great Leap Forward' in the 1950s were followed by some liberalisation in the early 1960s, then by the fanatical Cultural Revolution in 1966. Less dramatic vacillations followed in the 1970s. The turn towards a more radical reform was taken in 1978, with a specific mixture of an increasingly strong private sector co-existing with a traditional state sector, increasing autonomy to the provinces, macro-economic regulation replacing planning, and all this topped by the unflinching political control of the party (Lemoine, 1986).

The other socialist regimes in Asia have more lastingly remained under Soviet influence, especially in the case of Mongolia which was a landlocked country almost enclaved in the USSR, and became socialist in 1924. In North Korea and North Vietnam, the building of a socialist regime was heavily influenced by war (Korean war starting in 1950, various Vietnam wars from 1947) and by the strong personality of the first leaders (Kim Il Sung and Ho Chi Minh). The militarised economic system established in North Vietnam, based on mandatory planning and the quest for food self-sufficiency, was extended to the reunified South in 1976, to Laos, and to Cambodia which Vietnam controlled since 1979. Like China, the Vietnamese regime introduced a strongly market-oriented reform in 1986 without relaxing the party control on the economy and society.

The Cuban regime was shaped by the leadership of Fidel Castro who conducted the 1959 revolution and since then remained at the head of the party, and by the impact of the cold war and of the US boycott which put the Cuban economy under Soviet sole influence.

Many other countries in the Third World were at one time or another on 'a socialist path of development' after the end of the colonisation era in 1955 (the year of the Bandung Conference). Usually these were countries under a one-party rule, which introduced land reforms, conducted more or less extended nationalisations, mainly to control their natural resources, initiated some planning, and were assisted by the USSR and subsidiarily by the Eastern European countries. An exhaustive list would yield more than twenty countries, most of them in Sub-Saharan Africa but also in Asia (Indonesia before 1965; Burma; Afghanistan after 1979; Iraq; Syria; South Yemen), and in America (Nicaragua in 1983). These countries were called, in the socialist countries' parlance, 'socialist-oriented' (Lavigne, 1988). What prevented them being considered as socialist? The vacillations of the economic policies and regulations suggested that their commitment to socialism might be reversed. The parties in charge almost never were communist ones; Afghanistan is an exception, but in this case the communist party was not credible because it was imposed by the Soviets. Socialist-oriented regimes were often established in Muslim countries. The Islamic doctrine proved to be a powerful barrier against communism, and the fundamental incompatibility between these two ideologies has been later underlined through the emergence of Islamic integrism: a lesson which should be kept in mind when looking at the transition in ex-Soviet Central Asia.

3 The Reforms: Experiences and Failures

How did the one-party, one-property, one-plan system operate in practice? Before Stalin's death the question was hardly relevant. The Soviet Union had been living in war-like conditions, preparing and conducting war, then recovering from it, and was protecting itself against the 'capitalist encircling'. All economic failures could be attributed to these exceptional circumstances.

The political thaw following the death of Stalin triggered a first wave of reforms in the USSR and in Eastern Europe. Another wave followed in the 1960s, to which many supplements and corrections were added, without success. *Perestroyka* in the USSR was the last attempt.

Why did all these attempts fail? There was a widespread awareness that it was impossible to plan and control millions of human activities from the centre, that state ownership had to be managed by people who felt economically, and not just politically or legally, responsible for it and interested in the outcome. Why did it take such a long time to acknowledge the failures? In other words, why was the system non-viable and why did it nevertheless survive for so many years? All these questions are asked and answered for the 'Soviet-type' socialist countries in Europe, excluding non-European countries, and, in Europe, Albania and Yugoslavia.

THE APPARENT LOOSENING OF THE PARTY CONTROL

As we have seen in the previous chapter, Khrushchev perceived the need for reforms. He tried to relax the overcentralisation of the economy, by replacing the powerful industrial ministries inherited from the Stalin period by regional economic agencies, the *sovnarkhozy* (see Chapter 1). In doing so he merely shifted the 'petty tutelage' of the ministries to the 'localism' of these agencies, and the reform was in fact gradually nullified even before his ousting in 1964. Similarly, in Eastern Europe and especially in Hungary and Poland (already the forerunners) blueprints for a more decentralised management of the economy were developed. When the movements toward political liberalisation were repressed in Eastern Europe, following the Soviet intervention in Budapest in 1956, the reform projects in the economic field were stifled as well. Khrushchev went even so far as to press for a supranationally centralised system of planning in the framework of Comecon in 1962, which could never be implemented due to the active

29

(Romania) or passive (other Eastern European countries) resistance of his partners.

This first wave of aborted reforms yields two lessons. The first one is that no reform was viable if this led to questioning the leading role of the communist party in each country, and of the Soviet party in the region. The second lesson, which was not so obvious at that time, is that any reform complying with the first principle could indeed achieve a great degree of liberalisation in the economic field, without meaning that the regime was fundamentally modified. The normalisation which followed the Czechoslovak reform of 1967–8 – the 'Prague Spring' – epitomises the first lesson: the experiment was stopped when the Soviet party understood that the Czechoslovak party had lost control. At the same time in 1968 the 'new economic mechanism' was launched in Hungary. It did not meet with substantial objections from the Soviet party leaders, even when it proceeded much further in economic management liberalisation than the Prague blueprint of 1967. Here was the illustration of the second lesson.

New Relations between the Centre and the Enterprise

It was a decline in the rates of growth that prompted the search for a reform blueprint. While in the 1951–6 period in almost all countries there was a two-digit annual percentage growth of the national product (see Table 4.1 in the next chapter), after 1956 growth rates declined steadily, well into the next decade. A political decision was then made: the enterprises should get new incentives so as to work better, without any altering of the foundations of the system. The socialist enterprise should be induced to implement the plan more efficiently, not by compulsory orders or by sanctions, but through appropriate incentives. This should be achieved without abandoning central planning or central control on the economy.

Almost in all countries these reforms concentrated on the industrial sector, and only in Hungary was the agricultural sector considered as a priority for reform as well.

Obviously, for the enterprise to react to new stimuli, it needed more autonomy and more room for manoeuvre, so that alternative strategies could be implemented. The need for autonomy was amply proclaimed, but never actually satisfied. The enterprise remained in most countries subordinate to industrial ministries; in all countries it was kept under control of the party. There were oscillations in the policy, from more to less decentralisation, and vice versa. There were also conflicts between the party authorities and the enterprises. However one must not forget that the party officials, the high-level cadres of the economic administration, and the enterprise executives belonged to the same *nomenklatura*, and shared the same material and political privileges.

A Limited Autonomy

The reforms shared similar features in all the countries, despite sometimes marked differences in their scope. Officially their aim was to grant more autonomy to the enterprises.

(a)   In Eastern Europe the number of *the branch ministries* was reduced – in the Soviet Union the streamlining of the central administration, though on the agenda, could never be implemented before the Gorbachev era. In Hungary, for instance, the cut went so far as to suppress almost all central ministries. However, the relevant control functions were often transferred to the central departments of the suppressed ministries.

(b)   The *mandatory character of the plan* was relaxed. The number of compulsory indicators was cut, even to zero in the case of Hungary. But the party system remained unchanged, and through that channel the authorities could always intervene in the enterprises' management.

(c)   Only the *large enterprises* got more freedom of manoeuvre. The smaller units remained technical divisions of the big enterprises, and had no autonomy whatsoever. Large enterprises were themselves merged into even larger complexes called industrial associations or unions, which were endowed with some of the functions held by the ministries. In the GDR these complexes were called *Kombinaten* and were vertically integrated, from the raw-material base up to the distribution of the final processed product. In Poland the so-called 'big economic organisations' which were formed in the beginning of the 1970s helped to decentralise the management of the economic units, and later, after 1975, were used to reinforce central control. The Hungarian trusts were also vested with administrative functions, which loosened in the 1980s. In the less reformed countries, the industrial *centrale* (Romania), or state economic amalgamations (Bulgaria), or *koncerny* and associations (Czechoslovakia) retained control functions on their lower components until the end of the system.

(d)   Even in the most favourable cases, the autonomy of decision-making never extended to the *investment* sphere. Here it was limited in three different ways. First, the central plan was always dealing with new investments, in creating new enterprises, and in developing infrastructures such as transport, communications, energy distribution. Second, in the case of investments within existing enterprises, the decision-making power of the enterprise was in fact hampered by the difficulties in the supply of investment goods, which in most cases remained allocated centrally. Finally, in most countries investment was basically financed out of the budget, and the enterprises had very limited funds for self-financing. Long-term investment credit was used in some countries, including the USSR, and developed in Hungary on a large scale. Even in this last case, the process meant that the National Bank of Hungary, a 'monobank' financing all the economic activity in the country, in effect controlled the enterprises.

One may thus question the very concept of 'autonomy of the enterprises'. The enterprises were still obeying orders. True, they were increasingly writing down these orders themselves, and discussing their commitments with the political authority. The command economy was becoming a bargaining economy (Kornai), or a manipulated economy (Fallenbuchl).

These processes have sometimes been likened to the Western lobbying practices. The stakes and the positions of the partners were however totally different. The socialist enterprises, or their coalitions, did not aim to get additional markets or to realise additional profits, like the lobbies in a capitalist economy. They wanted to preserve power positions, which were measured in terms of control on resources: how to get higher allocations of investment goods, how to be permitted to hire more workers, so as to supply a greater volume of output. The party authorities alike wanted to steer input and output flows. This was in essence a Stalinist framework; but now, negotiation replaced command.

The Illusions of Participation

Workers' participation, in terms of power-sharing, was high on the agenda of the reformers. In all countries some scheme was devised to enrol workers into a more active involvement in planning and management. There was a contradiction here: self-management, Yugoslav style, was still considered with suspicion. The party authorities were strongly opposed to that form of self-management, which was again evidenced when in 1980 in Poland the dissident trade union *Solidarnosc* pushed a self-government scheme forward. The martial law in December 1981 put an end to the endeavour.

It was not possible either to resurrect the Stalinist-type of workers' stimulation through Stakhanovite-type policies. The Stakhanovite movement was born in 1935 (see Box 2.1, Chapter 2) when a coal-miner managed to rationalise his work so as to get a dramatic increase in his output. This was a political way of mobilising the workers for a higher productivity; the 'heroes' of such stories were politically selected individuals; their performance was set beforehand, and obtained through better supplies of equipment and through help of aides. The Polish film director Andrzej Wajda showed this process in his excellent movie *The Man of Marble* (1976). In the 1960s, collective performance had to be promoted, not just in output, but in management. In the USSR there were thus 'brigade contracts' whereby groups of workers within an enterprise pledged themselves to achieve a series of performance indicators, both physical and financial, while the management committed itself to provide the required supply conditions for them to be able to do so. Official trade unions took part in these schemes. Hungary went so far as to establish enterprise councils with a large workers' representation, which had to elect the director of the enterprise.

However, all the efforts made to associate unions or workers to the management of the enterprises remained formal. The workers were less than enthusiastic, which is quite understandable: if the enterprise has no real autonomy outside its political links with the authorities, why share this helplessness with its executives?

A DWINDLING OF THE STATE OWNERSHIP MONOPOLY?

'Everything belonged to the state' is a widely accepted cliché, but state (or, in fact, party) ownership was never exclusive. Other forms of collective property were to be found along with it. State property itself gradually eroded in the wake of the reforms. We have to grasp its essence to understand why the transition is nowadays so difficult.

State Ownership

Let us sum up some of the features of the state enterprises. They were managed by members of the *nomenklatura*. They were much bigger than comparable enterprises in the West, in terms of the number of employees for example. Often, especially in the Eastern European countries, only one enterprise or two manufactured a given good. They were subordinate to some administrative body but they could bargain over the directives they received. Finally, there was a hierarchy according to a branch criterion. It was much preferable to be director, engineer, worker, in an enterprise belonging to the military–industrial complex than in light industry. This complex included not only defence industries but almost all heavy industry in general, i.e. the mining, fuel, steel, machine-building, and automotive industries. The privileges of the executives, and the wages and bonuses of the employees were higher. In addition, these industries were advantaged in the planning procedures, and got better supplies, attracted better quality workers, than the light industries manufacturing consumer goods. Three features of this industrial structure have to be discussed at more length.

  (a) The standard *industrial structure* in a socialist economy has very often been described as 'monopolistic' or 'oligopolistic'. This is, strictly speaking, a misconception. A monopoly or an oligopoly is a particular kind of market, defined by the number of sellers facing the buyers. Here we have no market at all. Hence we cannot use the same phrases. This is not just a matter of terminological accuracy. Failing to understand how the socialist 'monopolies' worked led to illusions and difficulties during the transition: the illusion that such entities could respond to market signals in ways described by the microeconomic standard theory; the illusion that they might be controlled by some kind of 'anti-trust' policy borrowed from market economy regulations; the difficulties of dismantling these big units.

For the same reason – the absence of a market – one cannot apply standard concentration analysis to the large socialist firms. Only by approximation can one speak of the industrial associations in the East as cases of horizontal concentration, or of East German combines as examples of vertical integration. The socialist 'trusts' were not the result of mergers, or expansion and entry into new markets, as both goods markets and capital markets were controlled. They were the outcome of a political–administrative decision not based on competition or market criteria such as profitability. They were used to relay the central orders to the constituent units. This situation also explains why the conglomerate form of the external expansion of the firm was not to be found in the East. Such a structure did not fit the sectoral division of the economic administration, and would have implied the existence of a fully-fledged capital market. The socialist enterprises were not allowed, even in their limited range of autonomy in the field of investment, to expand in sectors different from their main scope of activities. They were however allowed, and even encouraged, to carry on 'complementary' activities with their 'spare' capital and human resources. This was indeed often the case, in the USSR, in the enterprises belonging to the military–industrial complex, which used to manufacture various consumer goods in addition to their main output.

(b) In contrast to market economies, there was a *lack of small and medium enterprises*. We have already seen that within the huge state firms and amalgamations the smaller units had no autonomy whatsoever. Outside these firms, there were simply no such units. In this sense, the socialist oligopolies could not be compared to market oligopolies with a fringe of subcontractors, maintenance units or suppliers, such as is found, for instance, in the Western automobile industry. Such activities were 'internalised'. Each big firm or amalgamation developed such units or workshops within its own structure, so as to protect itself against shortages or defects in the supply of these goods and services. There was no specialisation in the supply of spare parts and components; self-sufficiency was the rule, which entailed large inefficiencies. In each enterprise, so-called auxiliary activities absorbed a large share of the workforce, and no economies of scale could occur because there was no pooling of these activities. Thus we may understand why privatisations stalled in the beginning of the transition. It was very difficult to privatise these giant enterprises as they were, and de-monopolisation was required; but there was no clear criterion on how to split them. On the other hand, one could not begin with privatising the small and medium enterprises, as these were very scarce in the industrial sector, the only significant exception being Hungary at the end of the 1980s.

True, there were smaller state units in the consumer services sector: restaurants, hotels, retail trade outlets, repair services, more generally all household commercial services. But very often they were part of chain stores or establishments. They were also totally dependent on wholesale 'monopolistic' suppliers.

(c) The last feature is the *multi-faceted nature* of the large socialist enterprises. They were not just production and management units. They had political, administrative and social functions. The director was appointed by the political authority on the basis of the 'one-man rule'. This Stalinist principle (*edinonachalie* in Russian) endowed the director with wide powers but ensured that he was politically accountable to the party. The 'red executives' (Granick, 1954) were politically reliable, often technically competent, but had no management skills in the Western sense. They had to perform a number of administrative tasks as medium-level directing organs. They also were the heads of social communities which might compare to the big family enterprises in early capitalism, and they could be likened for instance to the ironworks lords in France in the beginning of the century. They provided their workers not only with a salary and a guaranteed job, but also with a full set of additional benefits such as housing, kindergartens, vacation centres, enterprise restaurants and stores offering staples and various consumer items at reduced prices, and sometimes health care services as well. The official union played a substantial role in managing these social benefits. This amounted to a large social protection system of a paternalist type; the 'father' here was the communist state, above the manager who acted as its representative.

Here is one of the big dilemmas of the post-transition period. The economies in transition need a modern industrial structure with large firms surrounded with small and medium enterprises. But they cannot just keep the ex-communist large firms, simply privatising them and turning them into market 'monopolies' or 'oligopolies' by virtue of renaming them. They must first be dismantled and restructured again, so as to rescind their previous features.

Cooperative Ownership

In the years preceding the transition, the status of the cooperative sector increasingly became very close to that of the state sector, along with the growing concentration of collective farms and their evolution into agro-industrial complexes. The political control on the (formally elected) management was always quite stringent because peasants were traditionally considered with suspicion by the communists. However, like the big state firms, and perhaps even to a greater degree, the cooperatives provided a social protection framework to their workers, taking into account that the social security regulations were extended to the peasantry later, and in a less complete form than to the urban workers.

Within the cooperatives, a quasi-private sector developed, mostly through contracts between the management and the peasants, whereby the latter performed definite tasks for the cooperative, such as fattening up livestock or grow specific produce, while the cooperative would provide seeds, fertilizers, feed, young animals to breed. An entrepreneurship spirit developed in the cooperatives as well as among their members, especially in Hungary where 'co-ops' came to own hotels and night-clubs.

These features explain at the same time why the post-transition governments were impatient to dissolve the cooperatives as strongholds of the communist system, and why the peasants were not so eager to leave the protection which the cooperatives provided, so that even when new legal rules organised the dismantling or the transformation of the cooperatives, they were not applied in actual fact.

Non-State Ownership

This section deals with the legally operating non-state economy. The parallel or shadow economy activities will be dealt with in the next section as it rather resorts to the perversion of central planning by the black market.

The private sector proper remained marginal until the end of the system. It was almost non-existent in the industrial sector, except in Hungary. In this country it was, so to say, incorporated into the state sector, through a specific institution called 'enterprise economic work partnership', established in 1982. It could be likened to the contract system in the agricultural cooperatives: the workers pledged themselves to undertake a specific task for their own enterprise, in their usual workplace and with the regular equipment and materials belonging to the enterprise, but after hours and on a sub-contracting basis. Their firm could thus escape the rather stringent rules on wage increases, as members of the 'partnership' were not paid as wage-earners but as sellers of a service. The experience showed that both productivity and profitability were much higher than in the normal workshop – not surprisingly as the employees were 'hoarding' their forces for these jobs. This form of hidden privatisation was also applied in the USSR under Gorbachev.

The family plot within the agricultural cooperatives (i.e. in the USSR and in Eastern Europe except Poland where there were no cooperatives) was almost everywhere promoted in the framework of the reforms, except in Romania. In 1985 the share of the family plots in total arable land was between 3 per cent (in Czechoslovakia and the USSR) and 15 per cent in (Hungary). Their share in agricultural output was much higher, up to 34 per cent in Hungary; for some products such as potatoes, vegetables, fruit, poultry, eggs, it was much higher still (Lhomel, 1990). The family plots performed apparently much better, which has often been attributed to the sheer superiority of private versus collective farming. This is a misinterpretation. The family plot was a part of the collective farm. It used the cooperative's equipment, seeds and fertilisers, either legally on a contractual basis, or by pilfering. The family plot was labour-intensive at the expense of the cooperative; the peasants spared their effort for their own plot. This was especially obvious in the harvest periods, when urban workers were compulsorily sent to the country to help the peasants and found out that most of the latter were busy on their own plots. This is not to say that the peasants benefited from the system unduly. But if one looks on the family plot as a quasi-private form of ownership, as an enterprise it operated in artificial, non-market conditions. Demand was guaranteed because of the shortage of agricultural goods on the state market, itself due to inconsistent planning and to artificially low prices for food products. The peasants did not have to worry about the usual financial constraints faced by market economy peasants (how to get and repay bank loans for instance). Low public transportation prices allowed them to travel long distances to sell their produce. The case of Georgian producers selling tomatoes and flowers on the Moscow market is well known; true, in this case to get on crowded planes with a large shipment required bribery, and hence strengthened the 'Caucasian mafia' which was later to derive high benefits from the transition. Family plots looked succesful, but they were not quasi-markets. The family plot institution partook of the global system proper to Soviet-type economies.

COMBINING THE PLAN AND THE MARKET

In the mid-1960s the phrase 'combining central planning with market instruments' was very popular. The Eastern reformers used it to express their commitment to a greater efficiency of the system, and to some openness to Western concepts. In the West it was hailed as a step toward capitalist methods. The failure of all attempts to 'combine' the plan and the market exemplifies the economic non-feasibility of socialism, which is basicly due to its political foundations. Though the principles of the reforms seemed sensible, the implementation led to a stalemate whatever the variants. The only successful outcome was the soaring parallel economy, a perverse combination of black market and central planning.

The Principles

The market was supposed to assist planning by introducing more efficiency. It was understood as a set of recipes which had allowed capitalism to flourish, of which the most successful was the principle of profit maximisation. By reading Western textbooks, open-minded economists found that according to the neo-classical theory, whenever an economic agent maximises his own interest, with all economic agents behaving in the same way on all the markets, one gets an optimum, that is the maximum output associated with the complete utilisation of all available resources. As mathematical economics had been rediscovered, and re-established in the USSR in the late 1950s, under the leadership of Nemchinov, Kantorovich and Novozhilov, this could also be expressed in terms of linear programming, as the solution of a problem of maximising a production function (or minimising a cost function) under input (or output) constraints (Kantorovich, 1959, 1965). At the same time, the procedure allowed the determination of scarcity prices for inputs and outputs.

This indeed looked an ideal world. The idea of reconciling the interests of all members of society with the interests of the society as a whole seemed perfectly compatible with the socialist ideal of increasing the welfare of the people. The mathematical backing of the theory granted it scientific respectability irrespective of any system. A crucial point was however overlooked. It was assumed that the 'common good' of the society as a whole could be defined by the central planner, that is by the party. The law of the market was to be applied, which meant that supply had to adjust to demand; however demand was equated to the needs of the consumers and the producers as they were expressed in the plan.

In the West the reforms revived the discussion over market socialism, theoretical foundations of which will be discussed in the last chapter of this book. The reformers in Eastern Europe and in the USSR did not refer to market socialism (except in the short-lived Prague Spring experience), and following the repression of the Czechoslovak reform after 1968 the phrase remained even taboo almost until the end of the system. However in the West the reforms were hailed as a genuine rapprochement between socialism and capitalism. The thesis of a convergence between both systems was expressed as early as in 1961 by the future first Nobel prize laureate in economics (1969) Jan Tinbergen. Each of the systems would improve in borrowing the best elements of the other; capitalism and socialism would gradually converge towards a mixed socio-economic system (Tinbergen, 1961). Another sign of this misinterpretation of the reform trend was the fact that the Nobel prize in economics was awarded in 1975 to Leonid Kantorovich, though the laureate had always been very keen on presenting himself as a mathematician, not as an economist, and dismissed all perception of his work as supporting the idea of market socialism.

Indeed this misperception was strengthened by the fact than in the East the reformers claimed that the market instruments should be used in two crucial fields, price determination and assessing the efficiency of investment. At first glance one could expect that the two principles to be applied in the management of the enterprises, that is greater autonomy *vis-à-vis* the Centre and profit maximisation, would allow for rational price fixing and investment decision-making. But as we have seen earlier, nothing really changed either in the political subordination of the enterprise to the party authorities, or in the dominance of state property. In such conditions market instruments were stifled.

The Stalemate

Though some progress was made in the way prices were determined, in the incentive system which should have induced profit maximisation, and in the choice of investment criteria, the reforms came to a deadlock because market coordination could not operate.

(a) In the field of *price-fixing*, prices were supposed to guarantee a 'normal' profit to 'well-managed' enterprises according to the Soviet reform blueprint. The concept of a 'normal' profit was never really clarified, either as to the definition of the profit ratio (various formulas were suggested, the profit being related to full costs, or to wages only, or to the value of productive assets), or as to the magnitude of the ratio. The enterprises were supposed to be 'well managed' when they complied with the plan commands. Even though they were supposed to take part in the drafting of these orders, in form of 'counter-plans' as in Russia, or even when plan orders were formally abolished altogether as in Hungary, the enterprises had always to seek approval from the authorities.

Prices were to be 'liberalised' but in fact remained centrally fixed in most cases. Only in Hungary did liberalisation reach significant proportions, but was never complete. In other countries 'rationalisation' of prices was sought instead. This meant that prices were set by a special administrative agency, according to various formulae based on a cost-plus principle. For some categories of goods, price-fixing was more flexible, and used price brackets or ceiling prices; a very small share of the prices could be fixed directly by the enterprises. This was the procedure for wholesale prices. Retail prices were a matter of social policy and were either heavily subsidised for essential goods, or much higher than the costs of production for 'luxury goods' such as cars, many items of clothing, footwear, and various household appliances. The differences between wholesale prices and retail prices were either covered from the state budget as subsidies or accrued to the budget in the form of the turnover tax, and there was no automatic relation between the two categories of prices.

The resulting prices were not market prices. They were not, and could not be, influenced by domestic competition, not only because the wholesale prices were centrally controlled, but also because of the concentration of the economic units. External prices had no impact either. There was no automatic repercussion on the domestic prices through the exchange rate as the domestic economy was isolated from the outside by a functional autarky, the instruments of which were foreign trade planning, state monopoly of foreign economic relations, and currency inconvertibility (Holzman, 1974 and 1976; also see Chapter 5). In some countries a limited impact of foreign prices was deemed useful and actually organised in the beginning of the 1970s (Hungary and Poland). Even in this case, essential goods such as energy carriers and raw materials were largely excluded from repercussion, especially after the increase in world prices following the first oil shock in 1973, as the socialist countries were wary of importing external inflation.

(b) The *incentive mechanisms* aiming at profit maximisation were quite soon paralysed. The enterprise could not control profit-making because prices and costs were largely fixed independently of its action. Profit-sharing between the enterprise and the state budget was highly unequal; along various schemes the budget collected 70 to 85 per cent of the total net income of the enterprises. Profit-using was very limited though the need for more 'self-financing' was professed. The enterprise could not freely procure the goods allocated centrally, such as equipment, raw materials. In such conditions, the scope for decentralised investment was very narrow.

(c) For centrally planned investments, *efficiency calculations* were supposed to help the planners in their choices. Decisions to allocate investments to given branches or regions were political, as well as the choice of the macroeconomic investment rate. Most of the available resources were tied up in such choices. Efficiency criteria were used only for choosing between alternative solutions for getting the same outcome. The main criteria were the minimising of the pay-out period (the period required for returns from the investment to balance initial outlays), and a more refined approach introducing time-discount, along with using an internal rate of return to which the estimated profitability of the investment was compared. In this second approach, any investment with a profitability higher than the reference rate would be selected (see the entry by Ellman in Eatwell *et al.*, 1990). Such an approach is not unusual in Western business practice. But in the West, the reference rate is currently the rate of interest which is faced by the firm on the market. The interest rate could not play such a role in socialist economies. Even when investments were supposed to be financed mainly through bank credit, which was increasingly the case in Central European countries in the 1980s, the bank remained a monobank itself controlled by the authorities. The interest rate was merely an accounting device and could influence investment decisions only very marginally.

Could Any Reform Succeed?

It is only too easy now to answer negatively. Market coordination cannot go together with the monopoly of a party on the economy and the society. This could not be acknowledged openly but was implicitly taken into account. In the 1980s one had thus several variants:

(a) the *Hungarian* model, which included: a large decentralisation of decision-making; encouragement of private production activities;

price flexibility, coupled with international openness allowing the repercussion of external prices on domestic ones; regulation of the use of material and human resources through interest rates and taxes; some enterprise autonomy (limited by the high level of concentration) in the choice of suppliers and buyers. However the enterprises not only remained subject to political control, but also to frequent changes in policies and rules. This *ad hoc* regulation worked as a safety net as they could always be bailed out whenever the market indicators suggested they should be closed. It also generated a climate of uncertainty in the environment of the enterprise;

(b)   the *Polish* variant: it went very far in the direction of decentralisation and liberalisation in economic life, but the reform blueprint initially drafted with the contribution of the dissident union Solidarity was implemented by a military power born of the martial law of December 1981; this impaired the credibility of the reform both in the country and outside it;

(c)   conservative (as in *Czechoslovakia*), totalitarian (*Romania*), or technocratic (*GDR*) communist orthodoxy, with lip-service to the rhetoric of reform;

(d)   rather erratic economic experimentation with various reformist schemes, very often under the guidance and control of the Soviet Union (*Bulgaria*);

(e)   finally, the Soviet *perestroyka*, which went out of control, and which story belongs to the end of the system (Chapter 6).

Were the most far-reaching reforms at least a good introduction for the transition to the market? A full answer can only be given later. In some ways they were: Poland and Hungary immediately emerged as front-runners of the transition. At the same time it is easy to see how these incomplete reforms led to misunderstandings in the West and the East alike. Just because words such as prices, profit, interest rate, efficiency, and profitability seemed to mean something in the East one assumed that once all central controls were removed (which was presumed to be possible overnight) the market signals would lead to market-type automatic adjustments. It was not to be the case, and this would lead to bitter disillusions.

This is not to say that economic agents could not adjust to market-type signals. They could do so in a distorted way, which was the parallel or shadow economy.

The Pervading Parallel Economy

The parallel economy has sometimes been defined as a set of variously illegal or coloured markets, with shades going from almost white (official) to black (Katsenelinboigen, 1977). It ran parallel to the official economy but it belonged to the same system.

(a) The parallel economy was firmly established within the *party monopoly* itself, though the political and legal authorities were waging war against it. The material privileges of the *nomenklatura* made its members vulnerable to corruption as the beneficiaries of the privileges wanted to increase their standard of living; at the same time the *nomenklatura* cadres had the means to corrupt using their power positions. The mafia did not belong to the *nomenklatura* but used to bribe it, through buying judges, police officials, and the civil servants who could give access to any chunk of state ownership. As most of the resources were under public ownership this gave the mafia a much greater scope of activity than that of its Western counterparts.

(b) The parallel economy infiltrated the *state economy*. It would have been difficult to find anybody not practising it on any scale: moonlighting, use of state buildings, machinery, materials for personal needs, use of official positions to derive private advantages. It has to be mentioned that contrary to a rather widely accepted view in the West, the official positions procuring advantages need not be high-rank. A vice-minister could procure seats for sold-out performances in state theatres, but the cashier at the theatre window could do so as well, in a situation of chronic shortage generated by too low public prices.

The sheer mass of people involved in the second economy made it impossible to eradicate. Big crime was in some sense protected by such a number of accomplices. It is easy to see that the second economy, or shadow economy as it was also called, was not generated by the same reasons which' explain a similar behaviour in the framework of a market economy. Moonlighting in the West is due to the desire of the employer as well as of the worker to evade taxes or social security payments, or to dodge some legal regulations such as those on immigration and the right to work. Moonlighting in the East was due to the fact that most of the services, though being in short supply when provided by the state, could simply not be offered in a private framework. Even when it was legally possible, the suppliers of services were discriminated against in access to equipment and materials. Remaining within the state sector while filching and stealing was by far the most practical solution.

(c) The parallel economy operated within the *planned system*. Exactly like the official economy, it was an economy without money, or at least where money played a secondary role. The high-level mafia did not hoard money; it hoarded goods, or, what is tantamount in an inconvertibility regime, it hoarded foreign currency, whenever its members had access to foreign trade activities. As a rule this did not lead to ostentatious consumption. In such egalitarian societies as were the communist countries, wealth was immediately identified with 'speculation'; in police-controlled societies, it led to denunciation.

In the production sector, the parallel economy operated as well without money. Many of the operators acted not just in their own interest, but very often in the interest of their enterprise, to avoid deadlocks due to the rigidities of planning. When they acted in their interest it was not mainly to increase their profits or material benefits, but to strengthen their power within the system through overfulfilling the plan, or through increasing their material resources. Thus, in the USSR, emerged large hidden 'commodity exchanges': the directors of the state enterprises would use these organisations to swap equipment or materials so as to avoid the cumbersome official supply system. Later, during the transition, these organisations would come out in the open and merge with the remnants of the official allocating agencies to build rather efficient bartering corporations, which would now be used in the framework of a nascent market economy for 'spontaneous' privatisation.

Again, a parallel with the market economy illegal practices is in order. The parallel economy operators in the production sector did not bother to accumulate money. As there were no capital markets there were no associated economic delinquency: insiders' crimes did not exist in a literal sense, though of course insiders' positions within the system brought large advantages.

Central planning was helping the parallel economy in many ways. It allowed it to avoid the financial constraints of a market economy. The planning system generated the shortages through inadequate supplies and low prices for a range of basic goods. It allowed for unlimited opportunities of wasting and stealing public resources. The development of parallel activities eroded the moral sense of the population. The official ideology was obviously contrary to these activities while its representatives were involved in it. The people became used to a double language, and to a schizophrenic style of life. Everybody paid lip-service to the rhetoric of communism; everybody's everyday behaviour was the negation of this rhetoric.

4   The Performance

Is the overall performance of the socialist economic system to be considered as a total failure? Sometimes the system is credited for having brought an underdeveloped country, Russia, out of backwardness, be it at very high material and human costs. Could not another regime have achieved the same results at lesser cost? In Eastern Europe the Soviet model was introduced forcibly; it was not adapted, in any case, to those countries which were industrialised already before the war. The inefficiencies of the model became obvious as early as in the 1950s, triggering a 'treadmill' (Schroeder, 1979) of reforms. By the middle of the 1970s an open crisis developed and led to final collapse.

This is the story of a failure. It raises many yet unresolved questions. Can one really measure the performance of the system? For years the US Central Intelligence Agency reconstructed the Soviet statistics, considering them as exaggerating growth rates. Now the new Russian statisticians claim that the growth rates were actually lower, and deride the optimism of the CIA. Qualitative features are not easy to assess either. Was the lack of unemployment an advantage of the system or the sign of inefficiency? Shortages were obvious to any traveller. The actual level of consumption in households was much higher, especially taking into account social benefits. Again, was this a plus or a minus? Finally, how can we qualify the rampant or open crises in the socialist countries, which ended in the final crash?

THE STRATEGY OF GROWTH

The Soviet leaders liked to compare the performance of the country to the capitalist ones. Before the Second World War, Stalin claimed two-digit growth rates at the time of the Great Depression. After the war, in 1961 Khrushchev asserted that in the next twenty years the USSR would catch up with the United States and overcome them in terms of growth (XXIst Congress of the Communist Party). Was such a contention just preposterous bluster? We have to consider the aims, the professed strategy, the variants, the actual results. We shall begin with one of the most debated issues: the measure of performance.

The Measure of Performance

In the past, Western experts who used Soviet and Eastern European figures were suspected of lacking critical acumen. These data could only be distorted. When one used other figures recomputed in the West, there were usually large discrepancies among sources: not surprisingly, as the authors started from Soviet (Eastern) figures and derived theirs using different methodologies.

Table 4.1 compares the official growth rates published in the USSR and some alternative estimates for the national income (net material product) growth in 1922–85. It shows that official Soviet data are much higher than recomputed figures. If one assumes the recomputations to be more accurate,

Table 4.1   *The Soviet growth rates (1922–85): alternative estimates (annual rate of change of net material product,* in per cent)*

Years	Official figures	Western estimates	Alternative estimates
1922–40	15.3	5 to 6	8.5
1941–50	4.7	no reliable estimate	−0.6
1951–60	10.3	6.5 to 7.5	9.3
1961–70	7.0	5 to 6	4.2
1971–80	4.9	2.5 to 3	2.1
1981–85	3.6	2.0	0.6

* Net material product, or national income: this is the main aggregate in the Soviet national accounting system. Like the gross domestic (or national) product in the Western accounting system, it is a sum of values added, once the values of the inputs used in the production process have been deducted from the overall value of the production. But it does differ from the GDP or the GNP in three ways:

– it is net of the value of depreciation of the fixed assets;
– it is 'material' in the Marxist sense: the only items considered as material are the 'visible' goods, and services do not add to the national income except when they are attached to the supply of goods. For instance, freight transport generates a value added which is included in the national income, but not passenger transport. Such a distinction among 'productive' and 'non-productive' services has always been very difficult to apply. In addition it does not take into account a large number of services which are included in the Western definitions of GNP or GDP, such as education, health, administration, financial services, etc.;
– contrary to Western practice, it includes indirect taxes, as the latter are considered as the share of the net income accruing to the state, as distinct from the taxes paid out of the enterprise income. It might be called an aggregate 'at factor cost', and not at 'market prices'.

Sources: Columns 1 and 3: 'Stabilisation, Liberalisation and Reform', special issue of *European Economy*, no. 45, December 1990. For the alternative estimates, the quoted source refers to a Soviet source of 1990. Western estimates (column 2): compiled from various Western sources, including CIA estimates. The alternative figures are generally lower than the Western estimates, but only beginning from the end of Stalinism.

then the reliability of the official figures was greatest between 1951 and 1970, lowest during the Second World War, and again during the last years of the Brezhnev regime, which Gorbachev used to call the 'stagnation' (*zastoy*) years. Why such wide and fluctuating discrepancies?

'Wicked' figures

Were the Soviet statisticians (and emulating them, those from other socialist countries) cheating on purpose? Yes, without doubt, in many ways:

- Some data were never provided. Among the missing figures were those for everything related to defence, a number of demographic data (such as, for instance, the data on infant mortality or morbidity), social data (crime, accidents occurring in the workplace, natural or other disasters), economic data (there were no figures on the absolute magnitudes of prices and wages, except averages); financial data (many items, in addition to defence expenditures mentioned previously, were not reported), foreign trade data such as arms sales.
- The growth rates were exaggerated for various reasons. First, of course, the authorities wanted to show high growth rates. In Western practice as well, statistical offices may be induced by the authorities to display suitable figures; only this does not usually relate to growth. In France, for instance, the measurement of the price increases has often been a topic for disagreement between the unions and the government, because the increase in the price index triggered an increase in the minimum wage. In the same country and for political reasons, the level of unemployment was a matter of dispute between the government and the opposition in the beginning of the 1990s. Second, in socialist countries, enterprises were interested as well in over-reporting their output, as the overfulfilment of the plan triggered various bonuses. They were also interested in under-reporting the amount of their resources, so as to get more supplies or investment means, which would allow them to implement the output plan more easily. This kind of micro-economic cheating is not to be found in market economies, because the reporting enterprises have nothing to lose in reporting accurately, provided they are guaranteed that neither their competitors nor the tax officer will have access to the data. Third, and finally, the figures were biased because of wrong statistical methods. This has been amply discussed by Alec Nove (1987, 1992) and others. It was a particular case of the 'index numbers' problem. Over the period 1928–50 the growth rates were computed using as reference prices the 1926–7 prices. Statistically weighting an index with a remote base always shows higher growth rates than with recent reference prices; in addition, as the USSR was little industrialised in 1927, the new products which appeared later were

estimated at fictitious and high 1927 prices, exaggerating still more the growth rates.
- Agricultural figures were a special problem. Before 1953 all output data were grossly overestimated due to the fact that the harvest was recorded on a 'biological' basis, 'in the field'. Later the crop was recorded once harvested, but the numerous losses between the field and the consumer were never completely taken into account.

Were the Western figures better? Yes, because they gave lower and hence more credible estimates. But there were discrepancies among sources – not surprisingly, as the Western authors started from Soviet official figures on the physical output as their 'raw materials' (Nove, 1992, p. 430), and used various methods of aggregating and indexing, as well as different deflators. Western computations have already been criticised by the Soviet statisticians during the *perestroyka* period. The Soviet experts came to much lower estimates than the Western ones and especially than the CIA (Khanin and Selyunin, 1987, on the 'Wicked figures').

Is the full truth available now? In the West one often thought that statistical cheating was perfectly controlled and that the authorities had a kind of double accounting, with hidden files in some closed cabinet with the right and complete figures. Western experts gave credit to this feeling, especially as indeed, from time to time, some new data were disclosed, or some previous data corrected by the statistical offices. But the reality is much more worrying. When the transition began and when the statistical offices opened their books, along with calls for help to sort the data mess out, no hidden files were to be found. The system was lying to itself so as not to acknowledge its failures. Huge layers of economic history – to speak only of economics – remain unknown, and very little may be done to reconstruct what is missing.

Non-comparable data

It has always been near to impossible to compare Western and Eastern data on GNPs per capita. One had first to convert the main macro-economic aggregate used in the East, which was the net material product (NMP) (see Table 4.1), into a gross national (or domestic) product (GNP/GDP). To do so one had to estimate the value of the services to the people, which was not taken into account in the NMP. As many collective services in the East were provided for free, this added to the task. Then the aggregate in domestic prices had to be converted into a foreign currency (generally into dollars). This second step raised the problem of the suitable exchange rate. The currencies of the East were non-convertible and grossly overvalued according to the official rate. Other rates were computed and used, but in the same country there were multiple exchange rates according to product groups or according to the purpose for which they were used (commercial, and non-commercial rates). Finally, because of the autarky which isolated the socialist countries from the West, the structure of the relative prices was so distorted by comparison with the West that any aggregation was debatable.

The issue of relative prices deserves two further comments. First, price ratios would significantly differ in the East and in the West for the same goods. For instance, a car would cost much more in the USSR than in Western Europe in terms of oil, which meant either that cars were much more expensive in the USSR, or oil much less. This made the significance of a composite price index very questionable. Second, relative prices were very different, for the same pairs of goods, in consumer and in producer prices. In the West retail prices are roughly proportional to wholesale prices, and may be derived from the latter once one knows the VAT rate and the retailer's average profit margin. In the socialist countries, retail prices were decoupled from wholesale prices and were manipulated for policy reasons; thus there were hundreds of *ad hoc* rates of the turnover tax. As a result, any coherent calculation of an economically significant exchange rate was impossible.

This is why East–West GNP comparisons were so divergent according to the sources and methods. The World Bank itself never succeeded in reaching a widely accepted estimate, despite many years of efforts by a large team of experts (Marer, 1985). Table 4.2 provides an estimate for the year 1989. This table allows for a rough ranking of the socialist countries. There is not much significance in comparing Eastern European countries with middle-income market economies supposed to have a comparable GNP level (for example, South Africa and Hungary, or Romania and Panama). All problems have not been eliminated with transition. The vast divergence of the exchange

Table 4.2   *GNP levels: East–West comparisons (GNP per capita in dollars, 1989)*

| | | Formerly centrally planned economies | | | | |
Bulgaria	*Czechoslovakia*	*(GDR)*	*Hungary*	*Poland*	*Romania*	*USSR*
2,680	3,450	(5,000)	2,630	1,890	1,730	1,780

| | | Other middle-income economies | | | | |
Brazil	*Trinidad and Tobago*	*Portugal*	*South Africa*	*Mexico*	*Panama*	*Chile*
2,400	3,400	4,250	2,460	2,080	1,760	1,780

Sources: *World Bank Atlas 1991*; own estimates for the GDR.
For the USSR: *The Economy of the USSR, 1990*, joint report by the World Bank, IMF, OECD, and EBRD.

rates deriving from the initial devaluations and rates constructed on the basis of purchasing power parity also leads to biased comparisons (see Chapter 7).

Much time has been spent on statistics. Maybe too much attention has been focused in the past on disputes over figures. Such disputes expressed the frustration of Western experts and of the lay audience facing the opacity of the communist regimes. Indeed, in the West statistical reports are not always transparent, nor open. But there is a democratic debate over these issues. No debate was allowed in the East. To question data meant questioning the regime, its aims and strategies.

The Aim and the Model

The Soviet textbooks of political economy phrased the 'basic economic law of socialism' in terms which did not change much over time: 'satisfying increasingly better the growing material and cultural needs of the people by means of the constant development and improvement of the socialist production, on the basis of a high technical level'. The wording was slightly altered, but the definition remained basically the same since its formulation in the official *Manual of Political Economy* which was drafted under Stalin's supervision and published in Russian in 1954. The final aim was to satisfy the needs of the people. These needs were estimated and defined by the plan, that is by the party. To satisfy them one needed to increase output. Growth and qualitative improvement of the output required a voluntarist strategy, as distinct from the capitalist 'anarchy'.

The strategy applied in the USSR since the launching of the first Five-Year Plan in 1928 was based on a theory of reproduction, and on an industrialisation model.

The *theory of reproduction* was based upon a model developed by Marx in volume II of *Capital* to explain the crises of overproduction in the capitalist system. It was later reformulated by Lenin, then by Stalin. The theory shows that in a modern industrial economy the producer goods sector, which was called by Marx 'Department I', has to grow at a quicker pace than the consumer goods sector ('Department II'). This imbalance is due to the labour-saving character of technical progress, which increases the 'organic composition of capital' (the value of constant capital per worker, or capital–labour ratio; in Marxian terms constant capital means not just fixed capital, but also minimum working capital required for the needs of production). Productive potential exceeds the capacity of the market to absorb the product, which triggers crises.

This 'law of expanded reproduction' was significantly twisted by Marx's followers when applied to socialism. For Marx the law was independent from human volition, and had to lead to crises of over-producing; here lay the major contradiction of capitalism. For Stalin, under socialism such crises could not happen. In a socialist system demand does not set limits to growth, in contrast with capitalism where consumer demand has to be backed by the purchasing power of the wage-earners. The planning system has to respond to the needs of the people, which are increasing over time. Consequently the 'law of expanded reproduction' has to become a voluntarist rule. One has to invest more in Department I from the outset, so as to increase the productive potential in the long run. This will allow, in turn, an increase in production in Department II.

The rephrased theory thus implied that one generation (or more) would have to sacrifice itself so as to ensure the conditions of growth for its descendants. It was supplemented by an *industrialisation model*. In the initial phase of development a policy of *extensive growth* would be used, which would mean the following: increasing the numbers of industrial workers by forcibly displacing the agricultural labour force toward the industrial centres; building new plants, equipping them with new machinery; and developing untapped natural resources or new territories. Such a model was formulated by Stalin for domestic political purposes, to justify forced collectivisation that was meant to procure an agricultural surplus needed to finance the extensive development of the industrial sector. It was also used for international propaganda purposes, as it showed that a socialist country could be protected from crises, recession and unemployment, in the very years when the capitalist world was plagued by the Great Depression.

The growth strategy resulting from the model was based on several priorities: of investment upon consumption; of industry over all other branches; of heavy industry within industry; of the so-called productive (of material goods) sector, over non-productive activities (services). In addition, the 'capitalist encirclement' of the USSR and the requirements of war preparation led to the priority of a military–industrial complex. These priorities shaped the industrial structure in the USSR and later in Eastern Europe.

VARIANTS AND ALTERATIONS OF THE MODEL

All the socialist countries followed the Soviet model, including the developing ones for which it was still less adapted. We shall elaborate on the Eastern European trends at more length.

The Eastern European Variants

After the Second World War the USSR was in the position of imposing the Stalinist growth model on its satellites in Eastern Europe. It could claim that the strategy had been successful in allowing for the industrial take-off and for the victory in the war. The model was also an alternative to the economic policies for post-war reconstruction which were implemented in Western Europe, equally on a dirigist basis, often using planning methods and based on a rather extended public sector. Western Europe benefited from the Marshall Plan (since 1947), which had been offered to Eastern Europe, and actually accepted by Czechoslovakia, before the governments of these countries were urged by the Soviets to refuse it. The Soviet model thus appeared as a a counter-fire to the Marshall Plan (Swain and Swain, 1993, pp. 57–8).

The Implementation of the Model

The industrialist strategy was applied without any differentiation to all the people's democracies, even to those already industrialised such as Czechoslovakia and the GDR. In 1967, during the Prague Spring, two Czech economists, Jiri Goldman and Karel Kouba, established that the model was a source of inefficiency and imbalances; later this kind of critique could not be voiced (Goldman and Kouba, 1967). The Soviet model made Eastern Europe strongly dependent on Soviet supplies of fuels and raw materials. According to the requirements of extensive growth it implied an increasing use of natural resources which were abundant only in the Soviet Union, with a few exceptions for specific commodities (e.g. Polish coal, Romanian oil, etc.). This model also led to a hypertrophic development of the heavy industry in all Eastern European countries. For most of the goods produced by this industry the Soviet union offered a guaranteed market, which was a second cause of dependence. The next chapter will show how this double dependence shaped the mutual relations of the Soviet Union and Eastern Europe.

The implementation of the model was not always imposed by the USSR. In one instance at least it was a choice made against the wish of the Soviet leaders. For nationalistic reasons Romania began to break away from the Soviet Union at the end of the 1960s. When Khrushchev decided in 1962 that the Comecon countries should specialise according to their comparative advantages and hence suggested that Romania should supply its partners with agricultural goods, Romania refused to comply and asked for a Soviet credit to build the giant Galati steel-mill. The request was rejected and the Romanians nevertheless built the complex with Western credits. This was the start of the large scale steel industry in Romania, though the country lacked iron ore and energy resources (apart from oil). The West approved this defiant attitude of the Romanians (who often benefited from their opposition to the Soviets, especially in foreign policy matters; Romania was thus the first socialist country to be admitted to the IMF in 1972). The Soviets were right in stressing that it was irrational to develop a steel industry in Romania. This industry, disproportionate to the country's needs, allowed it to dump steel on Western markets before and mainly after the transition. One should add that large-scale steel investments were no less wasteful in other Eastern European countries. The main difference was that in Poland, Hungary, Czechoslovakia and Bulgaria they were supported by cheap (comparatively to world prices) Soviet supplies of iron ore and energy.

The Consequences of the Strategy

The policies followed in Eastern Europe had fairly convergent results. *Investment* quickly took a large share in the national income, rising from rather low levels in 1950 in all the countries (see Table 4.3). The highest level was reached around 1975; in that year investment amounted to a share of between 25 and 35 per cent of the national income. Initially most of it was directed toward the productive sector. Despite the fact that investment was by the end of the 1970s reoriented toward the non-productive sector (i.e., consumer services, infrastructure for health care, education, recreation and leisure), in 1985 the service sector at large still employed less than one-fifth of the labour force (one-eighth in Romania). The socialist countries were in this respect far behind the developed market economies where the services sector accounted for about 50 to 60 per cent of the labour force in the 1980s.

Within the industrial sector *heavy industry* benefited most from the growth strategy. It employed large numbers of workers. The most favoured branches in terms of investment were mining, the steel industry, heavy-machine-building, and the chemical industry. The industrial policy thus strengthened the lobbies of the military–industrial complex, the leaders of which formed the most powerful stratum of the *nomenklatura*.

The wave of reforms initiated in the mid-1960s entailed a change in strategy. Extensive growth was becoming too costly as its sources were drying up. There was no more available labour force to move from the country areas or to put to work: agriculture was beginning to experience a shortage of workers, and the levels of employment of women were about the highest in the world. Additional material resources were lacking as well. Even in the USSR, natural resources, which had been exploited very wastefully, were becoming scarce. New investment capacities could less and less easily be put in operation due to the already very high rate of accumulation. The GDR was the first country to decide upon an *intensive* strategy of growth, soon endorsed by the other countries. Intensive growth meant only the need for an increased productivity of labour and capital. One way of achieving it would have been to find the means to increase the productivity of the already existing capital. Instead, the main stress was put on *modernisation*, which meant a shift toward new branches embodying technical progress, such as the electronics industry, automation, and the nuclear industry. This new policy could benefit from the *détente* in East–West relations and the subsequent dramatic increase in East–West trade,

Table 4.3. *Structure of production in the socialist economies by sector and by final use, and structure of employment (1950–89)*

	Bulgaria	Czecho-slovakia	GDR	Hungary	Poland	Romania	USSR
Distribution of NMP (national income) by sector (in per cent)							
Industry, Construction:							
1950	43.4	71.2	53.1	55.4	45.0	49.4	63.6
1975	60.9	75.6	66.4	53.1	70.8	65.5	54.8
1989	69.8	70.3	70.6	57.8	59.9	67.0	54.8
Agriculture:							
1950	42.1	16.2	28.4	24.9	40.1	27.3	21.8
1975	22.1	8.7	10.9	21.2	14.8	16.6	17.1
1989	12.8	9.6	11.0	14.5	14.7	15.8	22.8
Transport, communications, commerce							
1950	10.1	10.6	17.2	17.1	nd	17.4	10.1
1975	16.6	11.9	19.8	24.8	12.3	16.2	18.9
1989	17.3	19.5	14.7	24.6	22.3	14.6	22.4
Other sectors of material production							
1950	4.4	2.0	1.2	0.6	nd	5.7	merged
1975	0.4	1.0	2.9	0.9	2.1	1.7	with
1989	0.1	0.6	3.7	3.1	3.1	2.6	services
Distribution of NMP between consumption and investment (in per cent)							
1950							
Consumption	80.0	83.0	91.0	77.0	79.0	nd	76.0
Accumulation*	20.0	17.0	9.0	23.0	21.0	nd	24.0
1975							
Consumption	67.0	71.0	78.0	75.0	66.0	65.0	73.0
Accumulation*	33.0	29.0	22.0	25.0	34.0	35.0	27.0
1989							
Consumption	82.0	83.0	78.0	78.0	60.0	75.0	77.0
Accumulation*	18.0	17.0	22.0	22.0	40.0	25.0	23.0
Distribution of employment by sectors in 1989 (in per cent)							
Agriculture	19.0	11.0	11.0	19.0	26.0	28.0	18.0
Industry and construction	46.0	48.0	49.0	30.0	37.0	43.0	40.0
Services	35.0	41.0	40.0	51.0	37.0	29.0	41.0

NMP: net material product (see Table 4.1 for definition)
nd = no data available
* Accumulation includes net investment, changes in inventories and the building up of state strategic reserves.
Source: *Statistical Yearbook* of the CMEA, 1971 and 1990.

which occurred in 1970–5. Eastern European countries and the USSR obtained large credits to buy Western machinery, and expected to repay these credits back by exporting the goods produced in the turnkey plants acquired from the West. The rhetoric of industrial cooperation epitomised this process. The oil shock of 1973 and the following Western recession was a major blow to these expectations. However, the policy of modernisation was pursued, with growing difficulties.

The contradictions of intensification

The Western recession was a convenient excuse for the stalemate of the intensification policies. These new industrial policies failed mostly because of internal contradictions.

- Priority to new sectors never led to a scrapping of the traditional ones. The military–industrial lobbies successfully resisted any weakening of the standard heavy industry. This industry was very energy-intensive, and became more costly to sustain in Eastern Europe when oil prices were raised within the CMEA in 1975. This led to a search for a maximal energy self-sufficiency, which implied a greater reliance on coal and had a disastrous impact on environment.
- Despite the official modernisation rhetoric, the link between innovation and its industrial application were very weak. The reforms could never counteract the built-in risk-aversion and hence innovation-aversion of the socialist managers, who preferred routine production that made the plan easier to implement and brought them more bonuses (Berliner, 1976).
- Export-competitive goods on Western markets were provided by mass production of intermediary goods (such as chemicals, steel products, textiles), and consumer manufactured goods of low quality. Incidentally, all these goods, which are not high-technology-intensive, are still the main export assets of the countries in transition. Though claiming that they wanted to develop high-technology goods, the Eastern European countries were very much behind not only the developed West, but also the newly industrialising developing countries.
- In the West, multinationals promote modernisation through intra-firm and intra-product trade. Eastern Europe lacked this powerful instrument. Despite continuing industrial cooperation with the West the socialist firms could not enter the networks of the Western multinationals, which used them mainly as sub-contractors. Thus technology transfers remained limited. One could only partly attribute these weak technological links to the Western Cocom-monitored (see Chapter 5) embargo on high-technology exports to the East, which no doubt played a role, adding to the inefficiencies of the domestic policies,

and to an almost complete lack of cooperation among the socialist countries in this field.

'Intensive growth' thus remained a propaganda concept. This concept was convenient in establishing both a continuity with the Stalinist period and a shift from the Stalinist model. It could be argued that the model had been appropriate up to a given moment in history but that it had to be abandoned at some point, though remaining within the same ideological framework. The Soviet Union also claimed that it could no longer sustain the original model despite its endowments in natural resources. However, the country was able to avoid any substantial change in industrial policy, despite the commitments of the authorities to modernisation: between 1973 and 1985 the enormous oil rent earned by the USSR (see Chapter 5) left the party leadership free to continue the wasteful use of resources. Significantly, the shift in policy occurred at the beginning of *perestroyka* in 1986, along with the fall in world oil prices.

The Non-European Variants

Cuba and the Asian socialist countries also adopted the Soviet model. This turned out to be still more disastrous than in Eastern Europe. However, such an error of strategy is not limited to the socialist world. Theories of development in market economies have also led to the advocating of strategies of industrialisation, and the dilemmas of balanced versus unbalanced growth were much debated in the 1950s. At that time most of the new independent countries launched 'industrialising industrialisation' strategies (to use the wording coined by François Perroux) coupled with strong state intervention. The orthodox socialist approach to industrialisation was not at odds with these currents of development economics, and in any case raised much fewer objections in the West than its forceful imposition on Eastern Europe.

In *Asia*, *North Korea* embarked under the leadership of Kim Il Sung upon an industrial programme based on the ideology of self-sufficiency (called *dzhuche*), helped however by raw materials and fuels imports from the USSR, which the country could pay for according to a clearing system of settlements. This system worked until 1990 and allowed North Korea to compensate its imports with its exports to the USSR; only the balance had to be paid for in hard currency, after a grace period. *Mongolia* had initiated a strategy of socialist industrialisation after the Second World War, concentrating on infrastructure, but was also developing light industry and the food industry. The country joined the CMEA in 1962 and in 1971 was given the status of a socialist developing country entitled to special assistance from the other CMEA members in the form of special credits and preferential prices. Consequently the country developed the areas in which its partners were most interested, mining and processing non-ferrous metals. In socialist *Vietnam*, industrial policy was subordinate to the needs of the war and heavily supported by the USSR. After the end of the war and reunification of the North with the South, Vietnam joined the CMEA in 1978 and diversified its strategy for development, in accordance with its CMEA partners' needs. Development of agriculture and food processing, with a special stress on tropical products to be sold to the European CMEA members, and of light industry, was added to the continuous expanding of mining and heavy industry (steel, cement industry). Withdrawal of the CMEA and of the Soviet aid by 1990–1 severely hampered economic growth.

China officially abandoned the Soviet model in the beginning of the 1960s, following the Sino-Soviet split and the end of the Soviet assistance. In fact the strategy had already been altered in 1958 with the 'Great Leap Forward'. According to this slogan, production had to grow at a quicker pace than in the take-off period, by 25 per cent annually instead of the 14 per cent achieved in 1953–8. The strategy was to be dualist. While big investments should be completed with modern techniques, new jobs should be created only in small enterprises located in the country, with a low capital-intensity. At the same time collectivisation was to be launched on a large scale through 'people's communes'. The Great Leap ended in an economic disaster in 1959–61, and entailed human losses estimated in the West at 60 million people. The cultural revolution floated a new slogan in 1966: 'to take agriculture as the basis and industry as the dominant factor'. Shifts of population from the country to the cities were stopped so as to fix people in the country. After Mao-Zedong's death in 1976 a new course towards reforms was taken in 1978. Here, too, modernisation was stated to be a main aim for industrial policy; it was to be sustained by foreign investment.

Cuba had launched in 1959 a programme of agricultural diversification that was meant to end the monoculture of sugar, and of balanced industrialisation, without priority to heavy industry. The US embargo in 1960, together with domestic policy reasons, impaired the implementation of this programme. In 1963 the priority was given to the growth of the output of sugar, which would condition the development of other sectors such as the mining and processing of nickel and cobalt, citrus production, later tourism, and the nuclear industry. This strategy could be successful only if Cuba could export sugar, and required support from the USSR. The first sugar agreement was signed between Cuba and the USSR in 1964 and renewed until the end of the Soviet system; similar, but less advantageous agreements were signed with the other Eastern European countries. These agreements allowed Cuba to export its sugar to the socialist bloc at subsidised prices against oil, machinery, and consumer goods, while letting the country sell sugar for hard currencies on the world market as well. The ending of these arrangements and particularly of the low-priced oil supplies from the USSR plunged Cuba into a deep economic crisis.

Non-European socialist countries have followed the Stalinist model with two specific features. First, it was not imposed on them in the same way. Most of these countries endorsed the model for ideological reasons, because of the commitment of their own leaders to their conception of Marxism, and 'nationalised' it (as in China with the Great Leap Forward, or North Korea with the doctrine of 'Tzhullima', the racing mythological war-horse). Second, in the case of the CMEA members and partly of North Korea, the continuation, with some diversification, of the strategy was very much dependent on Soviet and Eastern European aid. The ending of this aid in 1960 may have been a blessing in disguise for China, which was then forced to alter the model, albeit in an initially disastrous way. Assistance provided in the form of trade preferences and direct aid collapsed much later for the other countries, which had been inefficiently applying a model not adapted to their needs and economic profile for much longer.

THE CRISIS AND THE QUAGMIRE

Two distinct questions have to be answered. What was the nature of the crisis which hit the socialist countries in the 1970s and the 1980s, and could it be named a crisis to begin with? Was it the main cause of the final collapse of the system? Our contention in this book is that the economic situation was not the main reason for the failure of the system, though it certainly contributed to the collapse. This section will deal mainly with the socialist countries of Eastern Europe, and the USSR. The non-European countries followed a different pattern: they experienced economic difficulties as well, in part as a consequence of the withdrawal of assistance by the 'developed' socialist countries, without abandoning the political and ideological system.

The Economic Crisis

Table 4.4 gives the rates of economic growth in the Soviet Union and Eastern Europe since 1950. A similar trend is to be observed for all countries. Growth steadily decelerated, bouncing up a little in 1966–70 due to the initial impact of the reforms. The shift toward 'intensification' did not slow the deceleration. On the contrary, the trend toward deceleration and even an absolute decline of the NMP increased in the years just preceding the fall of communism (Figure 4.1).

Was this trend due to the impact of the Western economic recession following the first oil shock in 1973? A large literature had developed on this topic by the end of the 1970s (Neuberger and Tyson, 1980). This explanation is certainly true, among others, for the countries of Eastern

Table 4.4 *Growth rates in the Soviet Union and Eastern Europe, 1950–90 (annual change of NMP, in per cent)*

	Bulgaria	Czecho-slovakia	GDR	Hungary	Poland	Romania	USSR
1951–55	12.2	8.1	13.2	5.7	8.6	14.2	11.3
1956–60	9.6	7.0	7.4	6.0	6.6	6.6	9.2
1961–65	6.6	1.9	3.5	4.5	6.2	9.1	5.7
1966–70	8.7	6.9	5.0	6.7	5.9	7.7	7.1
1971–75	7.9	5.7	5.4	6.3	9.7	11.3	5.1
1976–80	6.1	3.7	4.1	2.8	1.2	7.2	3.7
1981–85	3.7	1.8	4.5	1.4	−0.8	4.4	3.2
1986–90	−0.5	1.0	−1.8	−0.5	−0.5	−3.5	1.3

Note: Official figures are used here. These figures exaggerate actual growth, as has been shown for the Soviet Union in the discussion over the measure of performance in the beginning of this chapter.

Source: *Statistical Yearbook of the CMEA*, editions of 1971 and 1986; ECE/UN, *Economic Survey of Europe in 1990–91.*

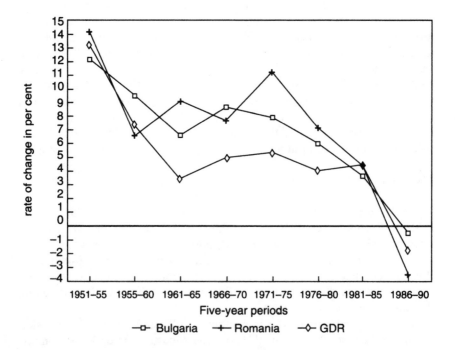

Figure 4.1(a)   *NMP: annual rates of change: Bulgaria, Romania and GDR*

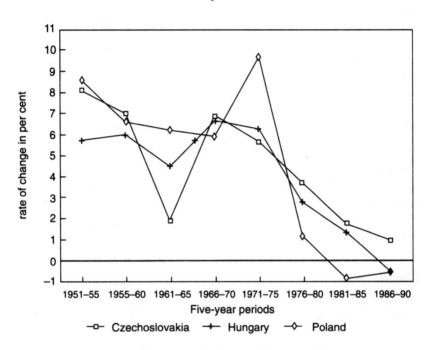

Figure 4.1(b)   *NMP: annual rates of change: Czechoslovakia, Hungary and Poland*

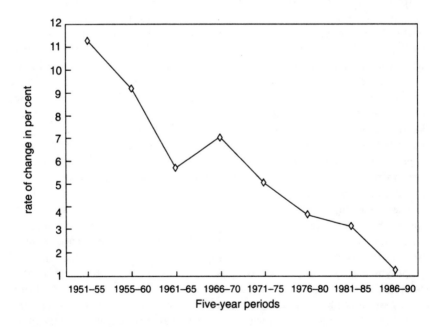

Figure 4.1(c)   *NMP: annual rates of change: USSR*

Europe, which were hit through the deterioration of their terms of trade with the West, the increase of their trade deficits and the surge of their indebtedness in convertible currencies. As was already mentioned, the USSR benefited on the other hand from the increase in world oil prices, to which has to be added two indirect consequences: the increase in the incomes of the oil-exporting countries allowed the USSR to expand its arms sales to these countries, and the rise in the price of gold (also partly provoked by the Soviet invasion of Afghanistan in 1979) provided the Soviet Union with additional gains from gold sales.

Comparing the impact of the oil shock on capitalist and socialist economies, Western observers were mainly focusing their attention on quantitative indicators. Among the domestic indicators, the most significant were, in addition to the deceleration or decline in growth, the rate of unemployment and the rate of inflation.

Quantitative indicators

(1) *Unemployment* did not exist in an open, measurable form. On the contrary, it was claimed in the East that these economies could face a shortage of manpower in the 1990s, due to unfavourable demographic trends. However, a large 'hidden' unemployment was to be found within the state enterprises, in the form of what Franklyn Holzman called 'over-full employment' (Holzman, 1976). Various reasons could explain why enterprises were induced to 'hoard' labour and to avoid lay-offs. Labour costs, though increased by taxes introduced in the course of the reforms, were not high enough to force enterprises to save labour. The main priority for socialist managers was to implement the output plan with least risk, and they knew that their enterprises would not disappear if their costs exceeded profits, because the bankruptcy laws were never applied even when they existed. All the hazards specific to central planning induced the managers to keep a reserve of manpower for various needs: to re-tool inadequate parts provided by the only supplier available according to the plan; to ensure repairs and maintenance, as there were no specialised services or subcontractors outside the enterprise; and to provide compulsory help to farms at harvest time. Very often a part of the manpower was just idle on the spot waiting for supplies to be delivered; when these finally arrived, all the workers were needed, working at full speed, to make up for the delay. It was often considered in the West that overmanning the enterprises was a deliberate policy to avoid unemployment. It was not – though full employment was indeed a goal. But the systemic features of central planning in fact had that effect, and the calls of the authorities for labour-saving practices by managers remained disregarded, even when the reforms were aiming at increasing productivity. A socialist manager was very much averse to job cuts, and this attitude survived after the transition.

(2) *Inflation* as a process of continuously rising prices did not exist until the mid-1970s in the socialist countries. In the pre-war history of the USSR and immediately after the war in people's democracies as well, there had been outbursts of hyperinflation, which were mopped up by currency reforms. Apart from such cases of revolution-driven or war-induced inflation, the official price indices in the socialist countries displayed a remarkable stability. Was it an advantage of the system? Were the indices truthful? Did the absence of visible inflation prove the lack of inflationary pressures?

In '*classical*' Soviet-type economies prices were fixed by price offices. Thus they were expected to be at any level the authorities wanted them to be. The level of prices would change only when the methods of price-fixing were modified, or when for one reason or another the authorities decided that some categories of prices for some kinds of goods had to change: for instance, when in 1967 the Soviet authorities resolved to end the undervaluation of a range of producers' goods and increased therefore their wholesale prices. In such a system there could however be *hidden inflation* (Nuti, 1986). Official indices were not reliable. In fact, though enterprises reported stable prices, they often imposed higher prices on their clients, for two reasons. First, they were in a position to do that because of their monopolistic situation and the shortages of producers' goods. Secondly, they were interested in doing so whenever the output plan was expressed in gross value, because a price rise made the fulfilment of the plan easier to report. Retail price indices also failed to show actual inflation because they did not take fully into account the movement of free prices on the *kolkhoz* markets.

In addition to hidden inflation, there was *repressed inflation*, a much wider phenomenon still. Though incomes were steadily rising, the supply of *consumer goods* did not follow, and the adjustment could not be made through price increases as the prices were fixed and stable for all the goods sold in the state retail trade. Unwanted savings would then increase, and thus the level of the deposits in the savings banks could be considered as an indicator of repressed inflation. Once transition to the market had begun, the amount of money in saving deposits caused great concern, as it was thought that this 'monetary overhang' could create large disturbances – in fact, it was very quickly wiped off by the post-transition inflation. Repressed inflation could also occur in the *producers' goods* sector, for identical reasons. Here the gap between the steadily rising investment funds expressed in money, and the limited supply of investment goods, led to unwanted delays in implementing investment programmes. The programmes were initiated because they were planned on the basis of the financial means available; they were stopped because of the lack of corresponding material resources. They remained uncompleted for a long time; this was called in the official statistics 'unfinished investments' and could also be used to measure inflationary pressures. Finally one should take into account the hidden costs of undermaintenance and obsolescence.

In the *modified* or *reformed* economies *open inflation* began to show. Several countries decide to implement a policy of true prices reflecting the levels of production costs, by cutting subsidies to the consumer. In some of these countries this policy could not be sustained politically. In Poland the increase in retail prices was delayed several times after unsuccessful attempts (in 1970 and in 1976, each time because of protests and demonstrations already monitored by the dissident union Solidarity). It could be imposed only in 1982, after the Martial Law was put in force, and prices then rose by over 100 per cent. In Hungary, on the contrary, a continuing policy of controlled price increases on consumer goods led to an inflation rate of between 5 and 9 per cent annually during 1976–86, and allowed for a significant reduction of the shortages. Other countries applied sudden and episodic price increases (in Bulgaria, Romania, Czechoslovakia).

Finally *imported inflation* appeared on a limited scale after 1973, when in Eastern Europe some countries introduced a limited repercussion of external prices on domestic prices, so as to make the enterprises sensitive to the world price increases for fuels and raw materials, and to provoke a less wasteful use of these resources.

Qualitative indicators

Quantitative indicators were used to compare the situation in the West and in the East but remained misleading as they did not represent the same realities in both systems. In fact the rampant crisis of the system showed through qualitative indicators, such as the growing shortages, the low morale of the workers and the lack of incentives which would increase the propensity to work, the rising crime, and the development of the shadow economy.

Could all this be termed a crisis? No, if 'crisis' is defined as a sudden break with a previous state. Yes, if it means a continuous disaggregation and debasement which cannot be stopped by any reform. What were the prospects? The most probable according to Western experts was 'muddling through' during an indefinite period; alternatively, collapse was only one of the envisioned outcomes, together with a radicalisation of the reforms, or a movement back to some reactionary and totalitarian variant.

The Assessment

Is the socialist model of growth to be credited with some positive outcome? Obviously it has been very wasteful in human and material resources; it failed to achieve modernisation and left all the countries lagging behind the developed market economies. Could things have turned out differently? Though valuable and serious studies evidence, for instance, how Czechoslovakia and Austria were growing apart in terms of economic performance, it is impossible to prove how Czechoslovakia would have fared under a different regime; we would have to suppose all other things equal, while obviously they would not have been equal because of all the conditions involved.

Again, one has to revert to qualitative criteria. Why, to begin with, did socialism attract people in the developing countries? The answer is that the socialist policies were perceived as able to overcome extreme poverty and famine, which they actually did in China.

In the more developed socialist countries of Eastern Europe and in the USSR, socialism generated a specific consumption structure. Basic needs were satisfied, on a qualitatively low level: people could feed themselves, get housed (be it by sharing flats with other families), have access to health care, education, public transport at a low cost. Huge subsidies to this kind of consumption led to acute shortages, and to numerous parallel ways of overcoming these shortages as there were no market-clearing prices, and no real market to begin with. At the same time 'luxury' consumption was held back. The supply of consumption goods and services suffered from the low priority granted to these sectors in the growth strategy. Everything offered to the consumer was shabby, and the selection of goods was very poor. Neglected maintenance of housing and public services (hospitals, schools, etc.) led to an extraordinary depreciation of investment in the consumer sector. There was a pervasive rationing system, not so much through open administrative rationing, but rather through queues induced by the permanent shortages, or through bureaucratic regulation of the access to some goods such as cars or housing.

In principle these were egalitarian societies. Incomes were not very much differentiated. What really differentiated the levels of consumption and the standards of living was political weight or position, which gave access to better supplies or services; or the opportunities of participating in the parallel economy.

A high degree of security characterised the socialist societies, 'from cradle to grave'. Jobs were implicitly guaranteed, and the citizens of these countries just could not understand that in a capitalist country people wanting to work could not get a job. The wide range of free or quasi-free services was not perceived as an achievement of socialismn, but rather as a set of mediocre and granted benefits. Looking at the capitalist world, large masses of people believed that if they were suddenly brought to that world they would be able to consume everything on display while retaining material security and reduced work standards proper to socialism.

There were no 'poor' in these societies, unless the whole population except the *nomenklatura* was to be ranged in this group. There were no wealthy either. Since transition began the privileges of the *nomenklatura* became better known. The residences for party members became hotels for foreign tourists; the living standards of the *nomenklatura* were complacently exposed in the media. According to Western European standards, their consumption opportunities did not exceed what is currently available in the West to medium-class households, though of course it was much over the ordinary people's standards in the East. Cases of pathological luxury such as the palaces of the Ceausescu family in Romania were exceptions. Any notoriously well-off style of living was suspected. *Nomenklaturists* and members of the mafia alike could never feel secure about their way of living, which had to be hidden and could end overnight for political or legal hazards.

5 International Economic Relations

'Bloc' autarky is usually seen as the main feature of the foreign trade behaviour of the Soviet-type socialist economies. The framework for these mutual relations was the Council for Mutual Economic Assistance (CMEA, or Comecon, the better-known English acronym), which had been founded in 1949. Relations with other socialist countries accounted for 60 to 75 per cent of the overall foreign trade of each of the Eastern European countries by the end of the 1980s. The share was 62 per cent for the USSR, and 40 per cent for Yugoslavia though the latter was not a Comecon member. Except for China, Asian socialist countries also mainly traded with other socialist countries (with shares comprising between 70 and 90 per cent of total trade), and so did Cuba.

Trade with market economies always remained lower than trade within the socialist world. East–West trade took off and soared during the 1966–75 decade. It was stimulated by the international *détente* and by the modernisation policies carried on in Eastern Europe. After 1975 these policies were deterred by the impact of the two oil shocks, and by the escalation of a new cold war following the Soviet invasion of Afghanistan (1979) and Martial Law in Poland (1981). Trade with the Third World was in principle based on a political solidarity with countries following a 'socialist path of development'. It remained marginal, and increasingly subordinate to the economic interest of the East.

Autarky did not just mean that the socialist countries sought to achieve self-sufficiency, nor that mutual trade among them accounted for the greatest part of their total trade. Their systemic features entailed a 'functional autarky' which we shall analyse first, before turning to its consequences.

'FUNCTIONAL' AUTARKY

The phrase was coined by Franklyn Holzman (1974). It explains a paradox. While the USSR, a large country endowed with all kinds of natural resources, could indeed afford self-sufficiency, none of the smaller socialist countries could have survived without trading, not only with socialist partners, but also with the capitalist countries. Thus these countries never were utterly closed; moreover, they moved toward an increasing openness in the course of the reforms. However, despite their efforts, they could never become fully-fledged members of the international economic system, which their market economy partners expressed by labelling them state trading countries. In fact, state trading was just a part of this functional autarky.

State Monopoly of Foreign Trade

State monopoly was equivalent in the area of foreign trade to state ownership of the means of production. It had been established in Russia in April 1918 in the wake of the first nationalisations. In its traditional form to be found in all socialist countries up to the beginning of the 1980s, it meant that specialised state organisations were handling all trade relations with all trade partners (including partners belonging to other socialist countries). These FTOs (foreign trade organisations) were attached to the ministry of foreign trade and/or to industrial ministries. They acted like a screen between the foreign partner and the domestic enterprise. With the former, they dealt on the basis of international prices and in foreign currencies (either convertible or non-convertible depending on the trade zone). With the latter, they dealt in domestic prices and currency. They usually specialised in products and groups of products. Each country had forty to sixty such FTOs. The Soviet FTOs were very large and powerful. For instance, Soyuzneftexport which traded in oil was the single largest oil exporter in the world.

The traditional organisation

Western exporters usually complained about the constraints which were imposed on them by the FTOs. In fact this kind of organisation also entailed substantial advantages, which became better perceived once the system started to erode. The constraints were numerous. One could not deal with the final buyer; one did not know from the outset which FTO should deal with a given transaction. Once the right FTO was identified, the negotiations lasted weeks or months and were conducted in a bureaucratic style. These constraints as well as the large size of the FTOs actually prevented small and medium type enterprises of the West from getting access to this market. Advantages were however numerous as well. The rules of the game were fairly steady. The FTOs acted as monopsonies; there was no need to look for many potential buyers. Corruption did exist, but not on a large scale as compared with Third World practices. The FTOs' agents had rather modest requests and feared political control. These agents, though bureaucrats, had a technical level of competence which impressed their partners. They also knew very well how to foster competition among the capitalist sellers who wanted to win them over; for the exporters who lost at this game it was of course a disadvantage, but the firm that won the deal could often count on the loyalty of its partners, as the FTOs liked continuity in business. Once signed, the contracts were implemented and the payments made promptly. But once all deliveries were completed, there was again a black hole; Western firms were often frustrated by not being able to follow the operation of the equipments supplied.

The alteration of the monopoly

The domestic reforms that started in the 1960s also entailed changes in the state monopoly of foreign trade. In Hungary and Poland, just before the beginning of the transition to the market, a number of enterprises could trade on their own account. The FTOs themselves were turned into trade companies, which could export and import a variety of goods and were no longer confined to a narrow range of products. They also could have representations abroad, and engage in foreign investment. In the other countries, the FTOs became increasingly linked with domestic enterprises, or even integrated as trade divisions of the latter. In the USSR the reform occurred later, in 1986 and 1988, and was more limited in scope. In all cases, whatever the reforms, changes were not substantial. The domestic enterprises shied from engaging directly in trade, especially with capitalist partners. They were not used to having to search for new markets; when they had to import they preferred to rely on the skills of the FTOs. In relations among socialist countries, the reforming countries had to align with the traditional ones, and in particular with the USSR. A Soviet FTO would never agree to negotiate with a Hungarian or Polish enterprise instead of a FTO. Thus the most advanced countries could never totally control the pace of their reform; in the foreign trade sector they had to take their mutual dependence into account.

Foreign Trade Planning

Foreign trade was planned as any other economic activity. Let us look again at Table 1.1. In the standard material balance for a given good, imports were to be found on the resources side, and exports on the uses side. Foreign trade was a residual instrument for adjusting the balance. If planned domestic resources appeared to be insufficient, and if it was not possible to increase growth or to save on domestic uses, imports were required. Ways then had to be found of increasing some exports, looking at all the cases where domestic uses of planned production could be curtailed.

This approach has two aspects. First, foreign trade is treated as an activity secondary to domestic trade. Second, imports are given priority over exports: a country is supposed to export only or mainly to pay for imports.

Both features have not always been well understood, especially as the socialist rhetoric tried to obscure them. The advantages of international specialisation in the framework of the 'international socialist division of labour' within Comecon were upheld, especially following the adoption of the 'integration programme' of 1971. From the point of view of planning, this did not mean a departure from the 'residual' character of foreign trade; it simply meant that specialisation requirements had to be integrated into domestic planning, either as excess production over the country's own requirements for the goods it was supposed to specialise in, or as a deliberate discontinuing of production for goods to be imported from others. Specialisation was thus internalised, but never wholeheartedly as each country feared that its partners might well not comply with the commitments to buy, or, worse still, to supply. Khrushchev had been aware of this reluctance, and had rightly, according to the logic of the system, pleaded for some supranational planning to overcome this 'trade aversion' (Holzman, 1974).

The priority given to imports was obvious during the first modernisation phase, in the early 1970s, when one could speak of an 'import-led growth' (Hanson, 1982). It was apparently breached when Eastern Europe had to shift policies due to its rising indebtedness. By the end of the 1970s the catchphrase became 'export dynamism'. This new priority was not to be likened to the pressure put on Western firms to 'export or perish'. In the latter case the need for competitiveness spurs *firms* on to conquer foreign markets; the socialist countries were constrained by the lack of foreign currency, which meant that *countries* had to export first so as to be in a position to import later (Wolf, 1988).

Inconvertibility of the Socialist Currencies

The issue of inconvertibility in the socialist system has been very much discussed in the West, not always accurately. Some misconceptions have to be dispelled first. The consequences of inconvertibility will then be assessed, as well as the measures taken to alleviate them within the system.

Definitions and misconceptions

The currencies of the Eastern European countries and of the USSR were not convertible, in the sense that they could not be purchased or sold against other currencies at a single exchange rate without restrictions and for all purposes. The implied definition in this statement is a very extensive one. Sub-categories of convertibility may be distinguished, such as internal convertibility (for the residents of the country, including the joint ventures) or external convertibility (for the non-residents only); convertibility for current account transactions only, or for all transactions including capital account ones. There are few countries in the world in which currency is totally inconvertible. It would imply totally closed borders. Even in Albania, which may be termed the most closed socialist country in the past, foreign tourists were allowed, in organised groups; they could change their currency into Albanian leks to buy the few goods there were to purchase on the market. In other words, the minimum degree of convertibility is external convertibility for non-residents and exclusively for tourist transactions.

The usual definitions take it for granted that the domestic currency is always convertible into goods – that there is real, commodity convertibility. As we have seen, this kind of convertibility did not exist in socialist countries. In the production sector it was restricted through the administrative system of allocation in kind; money could be 'converted' into goods if the plan provided for it. In the consumption sector various kinds of rationing, as well as the extensive system of free or quasi-free goods allocated within social consumption schemes, also prevented money being able to buy what could be available to the consumer: money could not freely buy houses, cars, domestic holidays, educational or health services. Commodity convertibility, at high prices, existed fully on the free *kolkhoz*-type market, but on a limited scale due to the marginal size of this market. One has to add that the domestic currency was even not convertible into itself. As was mentioned (Chapter 1, p. 13), there was a dichotomy between 'consumers' money' (usually available only in cash as individuals were not allowed to use cheques, or scriptural money in general), and producers' money (available in principle only in scriptural form; enterprises could use cash only to pay wages, and these payments were strictly controlled). This dichotomy originated from different principles for fixing consumer and producer prices (see Chapter 4, p. 39).

The reforms in Eastern Europe moved closer toward commodity convertibility, which was however never achieved: it would have implied a free market, liberalisation of domestic trade and of prices, indeed the end of central planning.

The Western businessmen operating in the East did not grasp all that. One thing hindered them in their trade with their Eastern European and Soviet partners, and this was the demand for compensation or barter. Such demands intensified when the indebtedness of the socialist countries began to increase. To sell their goods, exporters had to buy back anything that was offered, often such goods which were unexportable under normal conditions. Everybody then blamed inconvertibility: 'if these countries had a convertible currency they would not have to impose barter deals on us'.

The above argument is a macro-economic misconception. No country in the world is able to maintain a continuous trade deficit, except the United States of America whose currency is universally accepted as a world currency. All countries are very keen to restore their trade balance if it happens to be in deficit, and protectionist pressures result from this motivation. True, what is right at the macroeconomic level is not necessarily valid on the micro level. In a country with a convertible currency, imports and exports of a given firm do not have to balance as long as the overall trade balance is achieved. But in centrally planned economies the distinction between the micro and macro levels disappears or fades. Overall control is easier to achieve if each FTO is ordered to finance its assigned imports through equivalent exports by means of compensation.

The consequences of inconvertibility

Not only did inconvertibility hamper businessmen as exporters, or as partners in joint ventures willing to repatriate their profits or their capital in all cases when the joint venture did not generate convertible currency exports. It also reinforced the 'real' divide generated by central planning and FTOs between domestic and foreign activities. Inconvertibility went along with an official exchange rate which was a statistical unit of account used to convert foreign trade data expressed in various currencies, and a system of multiple exchange rates for various purposes. It had the following consequences:

- The planners had no means of selecting the best 'basket' of exports which would cover the required imports.
- There was no link between domestic and foreign prices. The latter could not influence the former in their overall trend, which was rather considered an advantage as it was a protection against imported inflation. They could not influence them in their structure either. The relative prices in the East were very different from the world relative prices. They were also significantly different among socialist countries. This is why, at the outset of the transition, convertibility was seen as a way of 'importing' a price structure close to the world prices. In the West as well, the price structures of the post-war European economies had been unified through liberalisation of trade and convertibility, and this example was often quoted.
- Though the domestic reforms should have created incentives for the enterprises to export on their own account, an overvalued domestic currency deterred them from seeking foreign outlets. This was partly remedied, through multiple exchange rates which aimed at stimulating the exports of selected products. But then a question remained unresolved: how to fix a proper exchange rate without freeing trade and lifting exchange restrictions?

Looking for a 'realistic' exchange rate

The reformers tried to find the 'right' exchange rate exactly as they had earlier tried to find the 'rational' price: they used sophisticated computations so as to provide proper signals to the enterprises and to the planners without introducing an actual market. Hungary and Poland set the pace (Liska and Marias, 1955; Trzeciakowski, 1978).

How does one find the right parity for the domestic currency? The different methods used amounted to estimating a purchasing power parity from a basket of exported goods. The value of a 'representative' basket where the exported goods were weighted according to their share in total exports was computed in domestic wholesale prices, and in foreign prices (the computation was made separately for the 'ruble' zone, and for the 'dollar' zone, i.e. for foreign trade conducted within Comecon in the unit of account of the organisation, and for trade in convertible currencies). The ratio of domestic to foreign prices yielded an exchange rate expressing the average amount of domestic costs required to earn one unit of foreign currency. A more refined computation was based on the marginal cost needed to acquire an additional unit of foreign currency.

Why was the calculated exchange rate not computed as a purchasing power parity for overall consumption, or GNP? First because the initial aim of such computations was to guide the export choices of the planners; second because the prices for many basic consumer goods were distorted by large subsidies differentiated according to the goods. Indeed, the exchange rate estimated from the general purchasing power parity (PPP) was substantially more favourable to the Eastern currencies than the exchange rate obtained from the specific 'export' PPP. Incidentally, this gap emerged in the early 1980s as a bone of contention between the World Bank and Hungary. The World Bank experts had estimated the GNP of Hungary using the general average PPP, which yielded a GNP per capita much over the upper limit of income allowing the country to benefit from World Bank loans as a developing country. The Hungarians contended that the specific PPP should be used, which put them under the critical benchmark. Their claim was accepted for political reasons, to demonstrate an international support for their reforms (King, 1991).

Though controversial, these computations were useful. They helped the planners in their choices; they provided incentives to the enterprises. But this was not convertibility. On the eve of the transition there were various rates to be found. In the USSR there was still an official, very much overvalued, exchange rate used only for statistical purposes. In the Eastern European countries the official rate geared to the Soviet ruble had been abolished in the 1980s, and replaced by a 'commercial' rate calculated as the average amount of domestic currency needed to earn a unit of foreign currency. Subsidies over this rate were used to promote exports, which amounted to using multiple exchange rates on a product-by-product basis. In the USSR, there were several thousands such multiple rates, called 'differentiated currency coefficients'. To this had to be added, in most countries, 'non-commercial rates' for transactions on services, and special tourist rates for foreign tourists. Hungary was undoubtedly the nearest to internal convertibility. Since 1976 it had abolished the official rate and introduced a single 'commercial' rate, which was unified in 1981 with the 'non-commercial' rate. Hungarian enterprises could buy foreign currency from the National Bank at the 'commercial' rate, provided they had enough domestic currency (forints); however, the Bank retained the monopoly for selling and buying foreign currency.

The quest for more accuracy in the field of foreign exchange was only directed to relations with the West. Intra-Comecon relations remained hardly affected, though they accounted for more than one-half of the overall foreign trade of the East. (See Figure 5.1; also Statistical Appendix, Table A.1.)

COMECON

International economic relations among socialist countries, and mainly within Comecon, not only accounted for most of their foreign trade, but also shaped the domestic economies by aligning the Eastern European countries on the Soviet model, and isolating them from the outside world.

How Comecon Worked

Originally the CMEA was a European organisation, created by Stalin as a response to the launching of the Marshall plan in 1947. The Communique on its creation (25 January 1949) was signed by the USSR, Bulgaria, Czechoslovakia, Hungary, Poland, Romania, and published in the party newspapers of these countries. Albania (1949) and the German Democratic Republic (1950) joined soon after. Albania unofficially left the organisation in 1961 when siding with China in the Sino-Soviet dispute. Legally, as the CMEA Charter did not have provisions allowing the expulsion of a member, Albania probably still could until 1990 have claimed its membership, surely a whimsical hypothesis . . . The organisation began to extend to non-European members in 1962 with the admission of Mongolia, a symbolic act designed to show that it was not confined to Europe and that it was meant to provide brotherly aid to underdeveloped socialist countries; Cuba was admitted in 1972 and Vietnam in 1978. No new member has been admitted since, and instead some applications were turned down, such as that of Mozambique in 1981 (Wiles, 1982).

Western journalists liked to call Comecon the 'common market of the East'. The Comecon was never a market, still less 'common'. Trade among its members was always negotiated and conducted bilaterally. Initially, the similarities in domestic structures of foreign trade planning and organisation imparted a substantial homogeneity to this trade, which began to alter only in the 1980s when reform trends started to diverge.

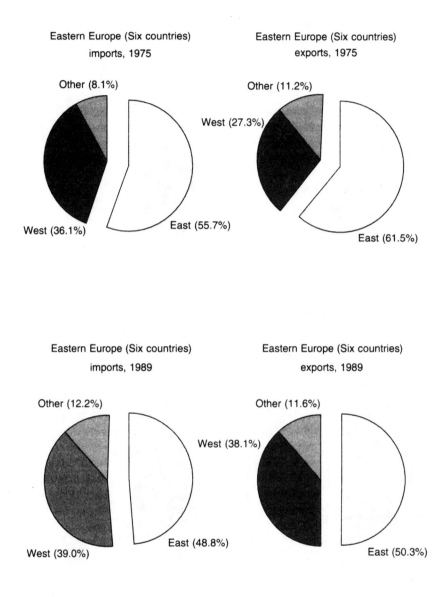

Eastern Europe (Six countries)
imports, 1975

Other (8.1%)

West (36.1%)

East (55.7%)

Eastern Europe (Six countries)
exports, 1975

Other (11.2%)

West (27.3%)

East (61.5%)

Eastern Europe (Six countries)
imports, 1989

Other (12.2%)

West (38.1%)

West (39.0%)

East (48.8%)

Eastern Europe (Six countries)
exports, 1989

Other (11.6%)

East (50.3%)

Figure 5.1 *Eastern Europe and the USSR: exports and imports by direction, 1975 and 1989 in percentage of overall trade*

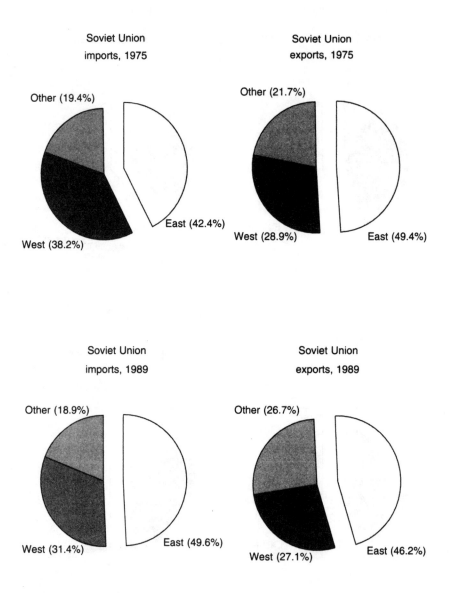

Figure 5.1 (cont.)
Note: 'East' refers to East European countries, members of the CMEA and the Soviet Union
'West' refers to Western European countries, North America and Japan

Source: See Appendix Table A1.

Trade

The operation of Comecon was confined to a few rules that were absurd but necessary, because in any trading system one needs to have *prices* for mutual trade, and a *currency* in which transactions are expressed and settled. In principle, according to the rules defined in 1958, but which became operational in 1964–5 only, intra-CMEA *prices* were supposed to be based on the world market prices calculated as an average of the five previous years, and fixed for a duration of five years. The intra-CMEA pricing rule resulted in terms of trade following the long-term trends on world markets, which since the end of the Korean War were disadvantageous to primary goods exporters and importers of manufactures. Thus the Soviet terms of trade with Eastern Europe had declined by about 20 per cent in 1958–70 (Hewett, 1974).

Following the first oil shock on the world market in 1973, it was decided in 1975 to revise the intra-CMEA prices every year, but to go on fixing them as the average of world market prices of the five previous years. Actually the rule applied mainly to primary goods, for which a 'world' price could be identified. Thus the increase in world oil prices was passed on intra-CMEA prices with a lag. Price-setting for manufactured goods resulted basically from bilateral bargaining.

Settlements were made in a unit of account called the 'transferable ruble', whose official rate of conversion into Western currencies was close to the official rate of the Soviet ruble. There were no actual payments between the member countries. The International Bank for Economic Cooperation (IBEC), which was set up in 1963 when this so-called system of multilateral settlements was agreed upon, kept the books for each country; the amounts of its trade transactions were reported as assets or liabilities, and in principle it should not have mattered whether a given country's trade was bilaterally balanced or not as long at it was balanced overall. In fact each country tried to avoid maintaining a surplus in any bilateral relation; as trade was planned in each country, and organised on a bilateral intergovernmental basis, there were no 'free' goods available to be sold or bought outside the system of trade agreements. Thus, a debtor position resulted in fact in an automatic credit from the IBEC; a creditor position could not be used for buying, and could not be converted into another currency, as the transferable ruble was neither convertible, nor, despite its name, transferable from one partner to another.

International specialisation

Comecon was thus a fake market. It was supposed mainly to ensure *coordination of the national plans*, but it never managed to achieve that task either. The conflict of interests between the USSR and its partners may be considered as the main reason why plan coordination never began, and indeed Khrushchev, and later Brezhnev, failed to involve the partner countries in any supranational scheme, though only Romania balked openly. In addition, technically it would have been impossible to achieve it. There was no concept of a coordinated plan, no methodology of constructing one. There were very few multilateral specialisation agreements, short of some branches such as car manufacturing, nuclear industry, or computers (Sobell, 1984). Each country was reluctant to give up self-sufficiency because it mistrusted its partners.

The pattern which eventually emerged in the 1970s and 1980s is said to serve the Soviet interests while being disadvantageous to Eastern Europe. Is it really so? Yes, if by that we mean that the USSR could get large supplies of some finished goods (Hungarian Ikarus buses, Bulgarian forklift equipment, GDR railway wagons, Polish ships, Czechoslovak nuclear equipment) or parts (for instance for the Lada car, these parts being manufactured in each of the Eastern European countries in return for finished cars). But these goods were of a poor quality by Western standards, and the Soviet Union repeatedly complained about this. The Eastern European countries complained as well, arguing that goods manufactured to accommodate the Soviet needs were unexportable to the West. Should the Soviet Union be held responsible for the fact that it allowed its partners to dump on its market large quantities of otherwise unsaleable goods? This is a very common argument nowadays, on the grounds that the inefficient production structure of Eastern Europe originating from the Soviet pressure in the 1950s, which had imposed the Stalin-type 'extensive' growth model, actually made the East dependent on the Soviet supplies of raw materials and on the Soviet market for sales of goods processed with these materials. But then, who won?

How the East was Won

In the previous section we have seen that Comecon was just non-existent as an economic body: it was neither a market, nor a supranational instrument of planning. Had it any reality whatsoever?

Once more, we have to go back to the foundations of the system. Behind Comecon the communist party's monopoly was to be found, along with the dominant role of the Soviet party. The Warsaw pact (signed in 1955, to counteract NATO) expressed the same monopoly in the area of international security politics, and had indeed supranational military powers. While in the economic sphere Comecon itself was powerless, it was supplemented by summit informal 'conferences' of the heads of the communist parties, which always met just before crucial decisions to be taken by Comecon on its structure, charter, or orientations. In addition, Brezhnev used to hold successive bilateral meetings with his counterparts during vacation time, in a Crimean resort, to discuss economic as well as political issues.

Did that mean that political domination served the economic interests of the USSR? Whatever the intentions of the Soviet Union, the answer is no. This issue has been one of the most debated in the sovietological literature. Already in the early 1960s, in a several-year-long debate with Horst Mendershausen, Franklyn Holzman had proved that the USSR was not systematically discriminating against its CMEA partners through the prices which it charged them (by comparison with selling prices to the West) or the prices it paid them (by comparison with the prices paid to the West) (see Holzman, 1962 and 1965; Mendershausen, 1959 and 1960). The debate re-emerged in the 1970s, and after 1973 and despite the changes in the price mechanism made in 1975 the Soviet price for oil appeared to be much lower in CMEA trade than in trade with the West. The comprehensive econometric study by Marrese and Vanous (1983) showed that the particular pattern of Soviet export *and import* prices with the CMEA led to substantial losses for the Soviet Union in terms of forgone gains from trade with the West. Also, the study sought to evidence that such losses were a permanent feature of Soviet trade with the CMEA, and that they had only been exacerbated after the rise in world oil prices in 1973. What was significant here was not that the Soviet price for oil was lower than the world price (and remained so until 1985), but that the relative price of Soviet oil in terms of Eastern machinery was structurally much lower than the world oil price relative to Western machinery, once an adjustment was made for the low quality of Eastern goods. Table 5.1 summarises the issues of the 'subsidy debate'.

The authors felt that they had to explain such findings, especially because the amount of the Soviet 'subsidy' or 'indirect transfer' was so large, and because it did not fit with the traditional picture of the Soviet Union as the political leader of the bloc. The answer was then that the USSR was granting subsidies for 'unconventional gains' such as political and ideological allegiance and military security.

Eastern European authors have never agreed upon the existence of such transfers. The few of them who entered the debate argued that the level of prices was not a substantial issue. One had to look, they said, at the substance of the CMEA mechanism, which was in the long run detrimental to all partners because it perpetuated an obsolete production structure and isolated the CMEA countries from the world economy (Köves, 1983).

Thus Comecon was a negative-sum game: everybody had been losing. It no longer makes sense in elaborating on the various projects aiming at improving its mechanisms. The last project was launched in 1988, not just by coincidence at the same time as the drafting of the Single Market within the EEC. It provided for a 'unified socialist market'. But then it was already too late to save the Comecon, or too early to envision a new kind of union

Table 5.1   The issues of the 'subsidy debate'

Years	Price of Soviet oil sold to CMEA[1]	Terms of trade of the Soviet Union in trade with CMEA[2]	Balance of trade of the Soviet Union with the CMEA countries[3]	Variations of oil supplies to the CMEA countries	Overall impact (apparent subsidy)[4]
1960–73	>	–	+	increasing	+
1974	<	–	–	increasing	+
1975–85	<	+	+	increasing	+
1986–7	>	+	–	increasing	=
1988–9	>	+	–	increasing slightly	–
1990	>	–	–	decreasing	–
1991	=	+	– (deficit decreasing)	falling	–

1.   > = over world price (at the official exchange rate transferable rouble/dollar)
   < = under world price
   = on the level of world prices
2.   + = increasing terms of trade (prices of Soviet exports to CMEA grow faster than prices of Soviet imports from the CMEA)
   – = decreasing terms of trade (prices of Soviet exports to CMEA grow slower than prices of Soviet imports from the CMEA)
3.   + = surplus of the Soviet Union
   – = deficit of the Soviet Union
4.   'Apparent' means that dynamic losses of Eastern Europe (for instance, a distorted structure of economic activities, or the isolation from Western markets) are not taken into account.
   + = positive 'subsidy' from the Soviet Union to the CMEA countries
   – = negative 'subsidy'
   = overall impact impossible to ascertain
   (In all cases, with the 'official' exchange rate of the transferable rouble to the dollar.)

Sources: The literature on the 'subsidy debate' and in particular Marrese and Vanous (1983); Köves (1983); Holzman (1985); Desai (1986); Brada (1988 and 1991).

among Eastern European market economies. The blueprint of the 'unified market' thus not only failed to be implemented, it was totally discarded. The 45th session of the CMEA in January 1990 decided upon a quasi immediate shift to 'world prices' and settlements in hard currencies. The 46th session (June 1991) formally put an end to the organisation, whose legacy however would endure much longer.

TRADE AND COOPERATION WITH THE CAPITALIST WORLD

The world as seen by the socialist countries was divided up on an ideological basis. Socialism was pitted against capitalism. Capitalism in itself was not a homogeneous whole. Developing countries were meant to have priority, and among them the 'socialist-oriented' countries, initially called 'the countries following a socialist path of development', until too many of them had turned back on that path, such as Ghana, Indonesia, Egypt, Somalia and others. Finally, by political order of closeness, came the capitalist developed countries, which however were economically most significant to the East.

The South: A Costly Partnership

Were the socialist countries exploiting the South, or helping it? The commonly accepted view in the West is that East–South relations were just a variety of the North–South relations. Both displayed the same commodity pattern. The socialist countries were purchasing primary products at conditions which were not more favourable to the South in terms of prices or guaranteed outlets. They were selling manufactured goods, mainly equipment which could not have been sold to the West and was not adapted to the needs of the South. Nobody has forgotten the notorious case of the Soviet snow-ploughs sold to Guinea, back in the 1960s (Lavigne, 1988, p. 102).

Trade, not aid

Let us elaborate a moment on these snow-ploughs. They exemplify the routines of central planning and their impact on trade. In this case, snow-ploughs were part of a shipment of locomotives. In the USSR locomotives are always supplied with snow-ploughs in front. The Soviet plant had got an order to deliver the locomotives, from the FTO which was dealing with Guinea. It fulfilled the order, without any contact with the ultimate buyer, and was paid in rubles as if the goods were sold to a domestic buyer. It was not the least interested in what happened next: if the snow-ploughs were of no use, just take them away, no need to fuss!

In quantitative terms, East–South trade remained marginal. It never accounted for more than 1 per cent of world trade. It was concentrated on a small number of countries in the South. The ten top partners accounted for 65 to 80 per cent of total trade, the most consistent ones over time being Egypt, India, Iraq, Iran, and Libya. Imports were driven by the Eastern needs for raw materials, oil, food products, including grain in the case of the USSR. Prices paid were in line with world prices in all cases they could be computed. Often Eastern imports from the South were used to repay trade and cooperation credits extended in kind, allowing Third World countries to buy Eastern machinery, and to realise big projects such as dams and power stations, steel mills, oil refineries, cement plants, developing of the mining industry. The big puzzle here was the amount of Soviet arms sales. There was a 'residual' between the amount of the overall Soviet exports to the Third World and the identified exports, in the range of 50 to 60 per cent of the Soviet sales to the South. This 'residual' was supposed to hide arms exports; the issue absorbed considerable effort from many Western experts, and was never completely clarified.

Initially the settlements between the East and the South were made mostly in clearing; by the end of the 1970s trade agreements had moved toward hard currency settlements except for Third World socialist countries and a few other exceptions, and trade with the South became thus a non-negligible source of hard currency for the East.

The major contention of the socialist countries was that trade in itself should be considered as an assistance, in particular because it was linked with cooperation that helped the South to industrialize and hence to develop.

A controverted assistance

Was this type of assistance really adapted to the South's requirements? Western experts denied it. The following points have been stressed:

- Aid was small as a percentage of the GNP. The most favourable figures computed in the West yielded shares of between 0.1 and 0.25 per cent, lower than the average share of the Western ODA (official development assistance) in Western countries' GNP, which was 0.35 per cent in the 1980s.
- Aid was small when compared to the Western ODA; it amounted to 10 per cent of it in 1985.
- Aid was extended on harder terms than Western ODA and contained very few grants. Eastern countries acknowledged that but contended that grants were a way for the West to get rid of its surpluses, and did not really help the South to start helping itself (the famous motto 'don't give thy poor neighbour a fish, teach him how to fish' was quoted *ad nauseam*).
- Aid was economically tied because it was in most cases granted in kind on credit, in the form of supplies of equipment and technical assistance by Eastern experts; the recipients could not choose and had to use low quality and inappropriate equipment.
- Aid was politically tied as it benefited above all the developing socialist countries: Cuba, Vietnam, Mongolia and Cambodia absorbed 70 per cent of total aid in the 1980s. When the socialist-oriented countries (Afghanistan, Ethiopia, Angola, Mozambique, South Yemen) were

added the share was 85 per cent. The political bond was enhanced by the fact that the USSR was by far the largest donor, extending over 85 per cent of the total.
- This aid was directed mainly toward the building of a heavy industry, and induced the recipient countries to follow the socialist strategy of development, which turned out to be a wrong choice. Third World countries were also persuaded to increase their state sector and adopt a planning system if they wanted to get socialist aid.

This critical assessment was largely justified, though the USSR tried to fight the arguments put forward. In 1982, a large political offensive was launched in the UN, when the Soviet delegation claimed that its assistance amounted to 1 per cent of its GNP, without any serious evidence for it. Whatever the figures and the claims, the USSR, and ranking second the GDR, assisted such countries which without their help would have got no assistance at all. This was the case of the socialist Third World countries; following the collapse of the USSR and of the GDR, Cuba, Vietnam, Mongolia and some other 'client' countries were to experience great difficulties.

In addition, the USSR probably helped the Third World more than it wished. Data disclosed in 1990 have shown that the indebtedness of the developing countries toward the USSR, recomputed in dollars, amounted overall to over $66 billion, to which one had to add the transferable ruble debt of the developing *socialist* countries, of over 58 billion in dollar equivalent (*Izvestia*, 1 March 1990; comment in Lavigne, 1991, p.371). These figures may be inflated; in any case, most of it will not be recovered, though some agreements were later concluded with individual debtors such as India.

Which party was really less developed?

Should the East have helped the South at all? It was implicitly assumed that the Eastern European countries and the USSR were, if not 'rich' countries (a categorisation they indignantly discarded, particularly during the debate on the New International Economic Order in the 1970s), at least more developed than the Third World countries. In the USSR, at the end of the Gorbachev period public opinion had already begun to balk at the budgetary expenditures for assistance to the Third World: 'rather Baku than Kuba', the saying went.

The communist ideology required that the East should help the South; assistance was necessary so as to prove that there was an alternative to capitalism. The collapse of communism reversed the situation. Now, together with the South and in competition with it, the East is asking for assistance and getting it.

Such an inversion of roles prompts a question: What is under-development? Eastern Europe is poorer than the oil-exporting countries following the oil shock, and less technologically advanced not only than the newly industrialising countries of South East Asia but also than Malaysia, India or Brazil. Russia has natural resources and has achieved high-tech buildup in the military sphere but lags behind in civilian technology probably even more than Eastern Europe. The GDR, the 'jewel' of socialist Eastern Europe in terms of industrial development, turned out to be in need of an overall scrapping of its industrial capacities. Human capital is the only asset which seems to remain: the level of education and training of the population is the distinctive feature in comparison with the Third World, and even in this matter, South East Asia or Latin America offer the same advantages.

Eastern European countries in transition are not prepared to accept identification with the Third World. Communist propaganda was unfailingly supporting the demands of the Third World to capitalist countries and sided with them in international fora. It consistently upheld anti-racist attitudes, while the general attitude of the public was rather hostile to Third World nationals. The people in the East had very little experience of living with racial minorities due to the small number of immigrants, if one excepts foreign students mainly from Africa, or occasional parties of workers as temporary migrants, mainly from Cuba and Vietnam. The collapse of communism engulfed anti-racist values as well. The countries in transition emerged as the new bastions of racism: ethnic tolerance is one more casualty of this story.

East–West Relations: War or Peace?

Has *détente* favoured East–West trade? The usual understanding is 'yes'. East–West trade soared with the emergence of détente, of which the first political sign was the trip to Moscow by General de Gaulle in 1966, and the most significant the German–Soviet treaty of 1970. It declined in the 1980s along with the new tensions with the USSR on Afghanistan and Poland. Actually this is an over-simplifying view. East–West economic relations always were what they are now, after the transition: an economic necessity for the East, a political asset to the West with few economic advantages and some very serious economic drawbacks.

Trade and détente

The East–West rhetoric obscured the fact that East–West trade has strictly followed the economic trends; it has prospered in periods of sustained growth, it has declined in periods of recession. The rhetoric culminated with the first Conference on Security and Cooperation in Europe (CSCE) which ended in 1975. Thirty-four European countries from East and West endorsed a Final Act signed in Helsinki. The economic 'basket' of the CSCE fostered trade and cooperation 'among countries with different economic and social systems', and hence the spirit of Helsinki became mentioned in all toasts and celebrations following the signing of trade agreements and contracts. East–West trade was also used politically in the West. Through 'linkage' or 'leverage' policies the West, and especially the United States, attempted to influence the USSR so that it would authorise emigration of the Soviet Jews, leave Afghanistan, allow the democratic process to unfold in Poland.

In fact East–West trade strictly adjusted to the economic interests of both parties. Trade flourished when these interests coincided. This happened at the turn of the 1970s when the Eastern countries decided to step up modernisation, and when the Western firms found a thriving market for the sale of turn-key plants. Even following the first oil shock, trade was still booming for some time, because Eastern countries' borrowing allowed the Western banks to recycle petro-dollars, and because the Western partners were confident that the USSR would never let its 'brother countries' down: this was the famous 'umbrella theory', which definitively faded out when Poland in 1981, then Romania in 1982, asked for rescheduling of their official debt to the governments.

The USSR, though it was the country most responsible for the political tensions that had developed in the end of the 1970s and the beginning of the 1980s, successfully expanded its Western trade. Here again the economic interests of the USSR and the West coincided. The USSR needed equipment to develop its energy resources and thus go on benefiting from the high price of energy carriers. It was the last large-scale buyer of equipment in the world when there was no longer a market due to the recession. Western Europe needed the Soviet oil and especially natural gas. The USA administration tried in 1981 and 1982 to block both the Western European sales of pipes and equipment for the Urengoy gas pipeline linking Western Siberia with Western Europe, and the purchase of gas by the major EC countries, and lost on both counts. At the same time, President Reagan in April 1981 recalled the grain embargo imposed on the USSR in January 1980 by his predecessor President Carter as a sanction against the Soviet invasion of Afghanistan, because the interests of the US farmers as grain exporters were in line with the Soviet interests as buyers. Soviet–West trade dramatically collapsed only in 1986, when the political climate had improved following Gorbachev's accession to power, while world oil prices had plummeted, which deprived the USSR of a large share of its hard currency gains.

All these developments show that political events, however dramatic, did not affect East–West trade as much as economic trends did. Could East–West trade have developed much more in the absence of any systemic barrier? Probably not. Lasting non-systemic constraints hindered this trade, and still do.

The limits to East–West trade

Western businessmen complained about *systemic* constraints such as inconvertibility, the monopoly of foreign trade, state ownership, central planning, red tape and political-bureaucratic interference, and restrictions in setting up joint ventures. All these were serious obstacles, along with the impact of the 'bloc' autarky which implied that the Comecon members were supposed to seek suppliers within the bloc first. Even for large Western enterprises the approach of the Soviet and Eastern European markets was not easy, and always remained rather 'exotic'. The systemic barriers acted as protectionist tools. The socialist countries either had no tariffs or did not use them except as bargaining instruments when they began to be admitted to the GATT. A tariff can work, i.e. prevent a domestic buyer from purchasing an imported good, only on two conditions: (i) if the importing firm has genuine autonomy in deciding what to buy and from whom; (ii) if the domestic prices of imported goods are linked with the external prices. Neither of these conditions existed, or existed only partly, as we have seen above in discussing state monopoly of foreign trade and inconvertibility.

The pervasive impact of these systemic barriers led to the conclusion that if and when they were lifted, trade with the West would expand. This was indeed the case, especially as intra-Comecon trade collapsed much quicker than expected, and was partly reoriented to the West (see Chapter 9). But the *structural* limits remained as they were. Here one has to differentiate the USSR from Eastern Europe. The USSR was a huge market for equipment and machinery; it sold commodities needed by the West, of which few (such as non-ferrous metals and aluminium exports, for instance) could hurt Western producers . For the West, Eastern European countries were not as attractive as the USSR. They were smaller markets; as suppliers they could only offer 'sensitive' intermediate goods, such as steel, textiles, chemicals, and food products, because most of their manufactured goods were not adapted to the Western demand and of too low quality (Table 5.2 and Figure 5.2). Their exports to the West were often contained by anti-dumping procedures; they were accused of selling at prices inferior to the 'normal value' of the goods in GATT's wording, and they could not argue on the basis of their actual domestic prices because they were treated as state trading countries, with artificial costs and non-convertible currency. As will be seen later (Chapter 9) not much of this changed even after the transition.

Could the socialist countries have enhanced their competitiveness? They claimed it would have happened, had not the West erected a *strategic embargo* against them, depriving them of access to high technology. Embargo surely existed in the form of the unofficial CoCom (Coordinating

Table 5.2 *Eastern Europe and the USSR: commodity composition of trade with the West in 1990 (in per cent of total trade)*

	Exports to the West		Imports from the West	
	Eastern Europe	Soviet Union	Eastern Europe	Soviet Union
Commodity groups				
Primary products	28.5	23.1	15.1	23.6
of which:				
Food	16.9	2.4	10.0	20.2
Raw materials (excluding fuels)	5.1	8.9	4.3	1.9
Mineral fuels	10.7	56.5	3.2	0.7
of which:				
Oil	5.6	40.6	2.1	0.7
Gas	0.1	11.7	no imp.	no imp.
Manufactures	60.0	14.4	79.9	74.1
Semi-manufactures	21.4	9.5	22.2	22.9
of which:				
Iron and steel	7.2	2.6	2.8	6.3
Chemicals	9.3	4.4	14.4	11.9
Machinery and transport equipment	13.6	3.4	41.3	42.5
of which:				
Road vehicles	1.6	1.6	4.0	1.5
Transport equipment	6.8	1.0	11.2	10.9
Specialised machinery	4.8	0.7	21.5	24.1
Industrial consumer goods	25.0	1.5	16.5	8.7
of which:				
Textiles	3.4	0.4	6.4	1.9
Clothing	9.8	0.0	1.9	1.1
Total	100.0	100.0	100.0	100.0

Note: As seen from the table, the share of sensitive goods (food products, iron and steel, chemicals, textiles and clothing) amounted to 46.6 per cent of Eastern European exports on the eve of the transition.
Source: Computed from the data given in *ECE/UN, Economic Bulletin for Europe*, vol. 44, December 1992, p. 67.

Committee), established under the aegis of the United States and located in Paris in an annex of the US Embassy. The list of the commodities subject to embargo has been widened or scaled down according to the intensity of the Cold War. It reached its highest extension in the 1950s, then was reduced in stages until the late seventies and was again expanded in the early 1980s. Since 1949 CoCom had monitored Western exports of high technology to the East. But CoCom was rather more an excuse for the East failing to

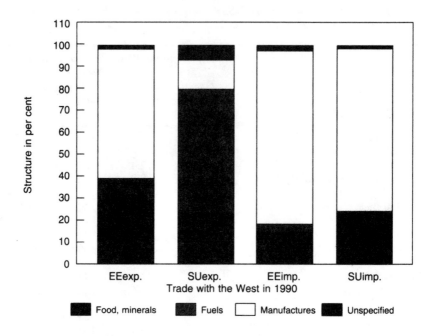

Figure 5.2(a)   *Eastern Europe and the USSR: commodity composition of trade*

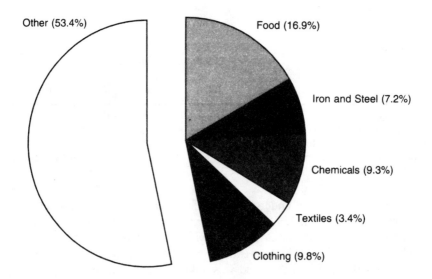

Figure 5.2(b)   *Eastern Europe: exports to the West, 1990: share of sensitive products*

control technical progress. The system itself blocked modernisation and innovation. For the West, the strategic embargo was a guarantee that everything had been done to prevent the USSR and its satellites from expanding militarily or economically, or, later on, to sanction them for their international misbehaviour. CoCom indeed survived the transition for a few years, and went into voluntary retirement in March 1994. A new organisation no longer directed against the former Soviet bloc is expected to replace it in the future. Meanwhile, national controls on high technology sales remain, with a focus shifted to specific developing countries.

II

The Present: Transition in the Making

6 The End of the System

Why did the system collapse? Why did it collapse so quickly following the first jolt? In the 1980s it had become commonplace to predict that the system could not go on like this and was doomed. However, everybody was taken by surprise, even those who anticipated the ultimate outcome. I remember listening in 1990 to a lecture by Janos Kis, the Hungarian former dissident philosopher involved in political action after the beginning of the transition: 'Anyone who'd tell me to-day that a year ago he predicted what would happen is a liar. Anyone who'd tell me to-day that he knows where we are going to stand one year from now is a charlatan.'

Everybody now proffers his or her interpretation of the collapse. One may explain it as a combination of accident and necessity; of domestic and external causes; of economic and political determinants; as influenced by the West or as due to developments within the socialist system; as mainly attributable to Soviet policies or as imputable to Eastern European actions. Is it relevant to ponder on the causes, once everybody has agreed that the process is irreversible? Yes, and not just to please academics' longing for rationale. Understanding the causes may help to discern the directions of the transition process and its difficulties, and also to explain why non-European countries show a different pattern.

I believe that politics unlatched the process. The socialist economic system as it existed had been failing for a long time but might have gone on 'muddling through' indefinitely. Politics also explains why violence and war sometimes erupted, while elsewhere the process was softer. In any case a political event marked the beginning, whether we consider it the breach of the Berlin Wall on 9 November 1989 or the Polish elections bringing to power the first non-communist majority on 4 June 1989 – which was also the day of the shooting on Tiananmen Square that ended the students' Beijing Spring.

THE CAUSES OF THE COLLAPSE

What collapsed was the 'really existing socialism' whose foundations were analysed in Chapter 1. Only three years after the October Revolution, in 1920, Ludwig von Mises, the Austrian neo-classical economist, had predicted that the system could not work. Yet the Stalinist model strengthened and was imposed upon Eastern Europe after the war. With some changes it lasted for over four decades more. Then it crumbled with incredible speed. Why?

The Roots

If one looks at the way the actually existing socialism operated, once the political terror was lifted following Stalin's death there were plenty of reasons explaining why the system should collapse; but it didn't; so the question is, what made the system last?

Inherent economic flaws

For more than thirty years the communist leaders have been warning that the system was working inefficiently and that reforms were needed, with the well-known phrases about 'improving planning and management', 'increasing productivity', 'shifting to an intensive growth policy'. Western experts agreed on the inefficiency symptoms; they disagreed on the feasibility of a reform.

The following symptoms, or imperfections as they were usually called in the Eastern official parlance, were usually mentioned:

- growth was declining;
- productivity of labour and capital was low; output per worker was decelerating over time, and output per unit of fixed assets dramatically declined, especially after the mid-1970s;
- technical progress was implemented slowly, even when available, and the lag with the West was growing;
- the military buildup was absorbing a large part of the GNP, especially in the USSR where the CIA estimates put it in the range of 16 per cent in the 1980s;
- in the USSR, the agricultural sector remained backward despite gigantic investments, and could not provide food self-sufficiency;
- the standards of living and consumption were mediocre.

Such a state of affairs was explained by policy errors, and also by the external environment, of which the components were: the oil shocks (in the case of Eastern Europe this had entailed foreign trade deficits and a growing indebtedness: in the case of the USSR it had, on the contrary, created a bonanza that had dispensed with serious reforms); the Western recession that had made access to Western markets more difficult. The external political environment of the post-*détente* era was quoted as well. The Eastern analysts underlined the stiffening of high technology export controls; the Western experts stressed the military buildup in the USSR which increased the share of military expenditures in the budget and the GNP and prevented any improvement in the consumption level.

By 1985, just before the accession of Gorbachev to power, the Western experts offered several scenarios, referring to the trends that were then observed (cf. Chapter 3):

- continuing inadequate reforms as in the USSR, leading to stagnation or to an open crisis;
- the strengthening of conservative trends in the GDR and Czechoslovakia, with only cosmetic reforms leaving the central planning system intact; the system seemed more viable here due to a better standard of living than anywhere else in the East, and to better conditions for modernization sustained by powerful industrialist lobbies;
- market-oriented reforms in Hungary, Poland and to a lesser degree in Bulgaria, stopping short of actually introducing the market and discarding the plan and the bureaucracy;
- the status quo, for atypical cases such as the 'communism in one family' in Romania, where the populace was amazingly to Western eyes enduring the hardships imposed on it by the regime. Albania could be ranked among the last remnants of the Stalinist regime as well;
- finally, uncertainty in the case of Yugoslavia, a fake market economy, just enough committed to reforms to benefit from IMF packages, politically controlled by a very authoritarian party whose power was challenged by national–ethnic disputes; an expert aptly named it 'feudalised socialist mercantilism' (Rusinow, 1989, p. 59).

The global outlook, or most probable baseline scenario, has been summed up by the late Ed Hewett, exactly as most of his colleagues would have viewed it (Hewett, 1989, p.4): 'some reforms, and some changes in policy, both of which have a positive effect on performance; but nothing bold or terribly decisive. It amounts to "muddling through" with sufficient flexibility to avoid the most treacherous pitfalls, but with sufficient conservatism so that the more dramatic possibilities for improving the situation remain unexplored.'

Obviously there are many good reasons for explaining *post factum* why the system could only collapse. Among many others, a synthetic exposition may be found in Easterly and Fisher (1994). Both authors deride the very 'mistaken' assessment expressed in *The Soviet Economy: Toward the Year 2000* (Bergson and Levine, 1983), according to which there was scope for reform and resumption of growth in the USSR. They contend that the clue to the Soviet collapse must be found in the systemic inability to substitute capital for labour: thus, while capital was growing, labour force per unit of capital was not declining, and hence the rate of return to new investment had to decline to a level of near zero by the mid-1970s. Apart from the fact that this looks like a rather trivial explanation (besides, the point had been made earlier, and the authors pay tribute to Martin Weitzman for it; they claim that recently available data make it the more convincing), we still remain with the question: why did the collapse occur *so late?*

Political and social causes

The economic situation in itself could not explain why the whole system collapsed at a given point. Are, then, specific social and political reasons to be found?

It is not enough to say that the society had lost any trust in the regime. This had happened long ago. Communism did not represent moral values any more. The corrupted ruling class was despised; people saved their forces and efforts for themselves, and any attempt to 'mobilise' them for the socialist sector could only misfire.

Western influences are sometimes put forward to explain the collapse of communism. The masses began to have an idea of a 'civil society' and aspired to it. Again, this was not new. They had developed an idealised image of Western society through travelling to the West and from Western tourists, TV, and radio broadcasts. All these channels were not so easy to get to, but all the more effective. What spark set the fire ablaze?

The Start

The socialist economic system rested upon the monopoly of the party. Hence a breach in this monopoly triggered the collapse. It had to happen in the USSR. Whatever their disputes, the communist parties were linked by their solidarity for survival. When the legitimacy of the Soviet communist party was allowed to be questioned in the USSR, and when the Soviet party renounced support of that legitimacy in the 'brother' countries, any spark could set the fire. That happened soon after Gorbachev came to power.

Perestroyka

Though the last stage of the Soviet reform, called *perestroyka* or re-structuring, raised immense hopes, it is not very relevant now. The economic programme launched by Gorbachev was remarkable for its weaknesses.

(1) Two blunders were made at the start in 1985–6. First, the proclaimed anti-alcoholic campaign was fighting just one sign of public loss of morale; it incensed the people, generated crime, made speculators richer and the state poorer. Second, the catchphrase of 'stepping up growth' was strongly reminiscent of Stalinist parlance. Of course the external and internal situation had deteriorated: the people felt that it was only too easy to invoke at the same time the bad harvest of 1985, the Chernobyl catastrophe of 1986 and the fall in world oil prices, to demand an exceptional effort.

(2) *Perestroyka* was announced in 1985, really launched in 1987, and stopped short of any radical change. In 1987 the enterprises got more rights

but remained under central command through the so-called 'state orders' which were central planning in disguise. Private ownership was not legally acknowledged. So-called 'individual activities' were supposed to be a substitute for private enterprise; their scope was very limited. The new law on cooperatives (1988) offered greater opportunities to entrepreneurship but these were mainly used in the services sector to launder mafia money. The leasing contract (*arenda*) in agriculture did not motivate the small minority of would-be farmers on their own, who dreaded a reversal in policy and the hostility of the other peasants. Endless administrative restructuring that was meant to simplify bureaucracy in fact created additional red tape.

(3) Ineffectual as it was, *perestroyka* however managed to destabilise the Soviet economy and to create an open crisis situation in 1989. While prices remained fixed, inflationary pressures mounted, and the word 'overhang' became largely used to denote the gap between effective demand and available supply at fixed prices. The budget deficit was increasing, and rationing was being introduced in the big cities. At the end of 1989 the first stabilisation and reform blueprint was made public. This programme drafted by the minister in charge of reform, the economist and academician Leonid Abalkin, was to be followed by many others (see next chapter, Box 7.1).

(4) *Perestroyka* did not imply abandoning either socialism as an ideology, or the party monopoly, though Gorbachev undertook to massively replace the party cadres. Western economists strongly criticised the concept of 'regulated market socialism' which expressed that stance.

Glasnost

Glasnost is a political concept that is hard to render in one word. Usually it is translated in English as 'openness' (Nove, 1992, p. 395) or 'public disclosure' (Lapidus, 1991, p. 141), with authors however feeling that it should be explicated. Thus it is described as 'a freeing up of access to information, the gradual erosion of censorship, and the progressive elimination of taboos on subjects that had previously been impossible to discuss in the mass media' (Dallin and Lapidus, 1991, p. 3), or 'encouragement of more open expression in public communication in order to mobilise support for the reform programme' (Remington, 1991, p. 97), or 'freedom of criticism, discussion and publication' (Nove, 1992, p. 396). In the field of economics *glasnost* had an immediate impact on the overall performance of Soviet workers. Their already low productivity went on decreasing as they were increasingly immersed in reading the papers and watching the television during working hours. Political pluralism was introduced in 1990 and the party's monopoly on power was ended explicitly in February 1990. However its implicit ideological monopoly was ended only in 1991, following the failed 19 August *coup* against Gorbachev. It is not so easy to date the moment when Gorbachev decided that the Soviet party would no longer interfere with the political changes in the brother countries' parties. In any case the process began with a double abstention. The Soviet party did not condemn the so-called 'Round Table' negotiations, which opened in February 1989, between the Polish leadership and the opposition represented by Lech Walesa, the president of Solidarity. It did not block the progress toward multipartism in Hungary which had begun in the first months of 1989. The transition could start.

Is this analysis exaggerating the 'Gorbachev factor'? One may also turn things differently. The Soviet communist party was no longer interested in its economic domination in Eastern Europe because the situation in the USSR had become economically and politically critical. The communist power then collapsed in Eastern Europe because it derived its legitimacy from the USSR, beginning with the countries – Poland and Hungary – where this power was already most eroded.

THE FIRST STEPS OF THE TRANSITION: CENTRAL EUROPE

Table 6.1 shows the stages of the political revolution in Eastern and Central Europe, which preceded economic transition. While in Part I we have merged all these countries in the phrase 'Eastern Europe', from now onwards we are going to differentiate among groups. One country will shortly go out of our focus. This is GDR, which has been absorbed into the Federal Republic of Germany. The first circle of the transition comprises three countries of Central Europe: Poland and Hungary, soon joined by Czechoslovakia following the 'velvet' Revolution in November 1989. The second circle includes the Eastern European countries proper, a designation which we prefer to that of 'Balkans': Romania, Bulgaria, Albania, parts of the former Yugoslavia, to be joined in 1993 by Slovakia. (See Table 6.2 for the new geopolitical picture of the former communist Eastern Europe.) The case of the USSR will be discussed in the next section devoted to the final collapse of the socialist system.

The GDR: A Merger

The GDR was a symbol of maximum communist rigidity, and also of what could be called a 'success story' within the communist camp. It lost its political and economic identity less than one year following the breach of the Berlin Wall (9 November 1989), first when the economic and currency union was implemented on 1 July 1990, then when the political union was decreed on 3 October 1990. The GDR became the five new provinces, 'Neue Länder', of united Germany. The area faced the same stabilisation and restructuring problems as the other countries. The German government swiftly moved on the stabilisation front (in fact the currency union was the most radical instrument of macroeconomic policy) and on privatisation. The latter was tackled by an *ad hoc* institution, the *Treuhandanstalt*, a state-owned holding company whose task was to restructure and sell East German assets or else to close the enterprises down, a process to be completed by end-1994. The Western part of the country devoted more effort to this task and many more funds than the total assistance made available to the remaining countries in transition. Apart from the financial burden, the material losses were huge: a large share of the productive capacities were simply dismantled as obsolete and harmful to the environment. Human costs were to be large as well: while the GDR population had one of the highest activity rates in the world (the share of working population to total population of working age was over 80 per cent in 1989), the rate of unemployment had already reached 10 per cent of the labour force in 1991. The developments within the New Länder are not going to be elaborated upon hereafter. The GDR is no longer a state, and it is no longer part of the East. Its transition has been a unique experience. Two lessons may be derived from this experience for the other countries in transition. First, even with favourable conditions such as extensive access to finance and expertise, the transition was painful for the East Germans: many lost their jobs and suffered a decline in their standard of living. Second, the transition process bypassed them: they did not take the decisions, and a very small part of the assets in their region could be recovered by them in the short run. The East Germans thus shifted from the paternalistic rule of the communist state to the paternalistic control of the capitalist state-and-business establishment.

The PHARE Countries

In July 1989, during the Summit of the G-7 (the group of the 7 most industrialised countries in the world), it was decided to empower the Commission of the European Communities with the coordination of assistance to Poland and Hungary. At a time when the transition was not yet perceived as irreversible, the purpose was to strengthen the commitment of both countries to building democracy and a market economy. The Commission then launched a programme called PHARE. (PHARE is originally a French acronym meaning: Pologne, Hongrie, Assistance à la Restructuration Economique. It may easily be transposed into English: Poland, Hungary, Assistance to the Restructuring of the Economy). Both countries were clearly designated as the most advanced in their progress toward these aims. In 1990 other countries were added to the PHARE list: Czechoslovakia, Bulgaria, Yugoslavia, later Romania. The first two recipients of the PHARE aid kept their lead, at least in terms of total assistance received. Czechoslovakia claimed to be part of the leading group

Table 6.1 The stages of the political revolution in Central and Eastern Europe, 1989–91

Countries:	Bulgaria	Czechoslovakia	GDR	Hungary	Poland	Romania
Stages of the political revolution:	January 90: the leading role of the CP is abolished	November 89: the students and the people demonstrate against the regime (the 'velvet' revolution)	9 November 89: breaching of the Berlin Wall	October 89: multipartism is accepted by the party	September 89: first non-communist government	December 89: overthrow of the Ceaucescu rule; a national salvation government is formed
	June 90: free parliamentary elections		April 90: first non-communist government headed by L. de Maizière	March-April 90: the non-communist opposition wins the elections	December 90: election of Lech Walesa as Head of State (the only case of a direct election by the people in the countries in transition)	May 90: the National Salvation Front wins the parliamentary elections and Ion Iliescu is elected president of the Republic
	August 90: election of a non-communist president as head of state Zh. Zhelev	June 90: the non-communist parties win the parliamentary elections	July 90: economic monetary union with the FRG October 90: political union with the FRG	August 90: a non-communist head of state, Arpad Göncz, is elected	October 91: first free parliamentary elections	
	October 91: the non-communist opposition wins the elections to the Parliament		December 90: first legislative elections in unified Germany			

Official launching of the economic reform:					
February 1991: price liberalisation devaluation of the lev	September 90: adoption of a 'scenario of economic reform'	Beginning in July 90: economic and monetary integration within Germany	1989–90: continuation of the reforms already under way	January 90: launching of the first 'shock therapy big bang' (macroeconomic stabilisation, liberalisation of prices and trade, small-scale privatisation)	April 1991: the first reform programme, prepared as an IMF-agreed package, is launched (price liberalisation, stabilisation)
October 1991: beginning of the small privatisation	January 91: launching of a 'big bang' type stabilisation programme; beginning of the small privatisation through auctions		February 91: stabilisation programme agreed with the IMF; continuing reform not embodied in a programme document		August 91: law on privatisation

Table 6.2   *The countries of Central and Eastern Europe: official names, population and territory*

Official name of the country	Area (thousand sq. km)	Population (in millions, 1990)
Republic of Albania	28.7	3.2
Republic of Bulgaria	110.9	8.9
Czech and Slovak Federal Republic	127.9	15.7
divided since 1 January 1993 into:		
the Czech Republic	78.9	10.3
the Slovak Republic	49.0	5.3
Republic of Hungary	93.0	10.5
Republic of Poland	312.5	38.0
Republic of Romania	237.5	23.2
Socialist Federal Republic of		
Yugoslavia	255.8	23.8
since 1991–2 divided into:		
Federal Republic of Yugoslavia	88.4 (S)	9.9 (S)
(Serbia[1] + Montenegro)	13.8 (M)	0.8 (M)
Republic of Croatia	56.5	4.8
Republic of Slovenia	20.3	2.0
Bosnia-Hercegovina	51.1	4.5
FYROM[2]	25.7	2.0

[1] Including its two autonomous provinces, Vojvodina and Kosovo.
[2] Former Yugoslav Republic of Macedonia. The country would like to call itself Republic of Macedonia, but Greece and Bulgaria, which both have a large Macedonian minority, oppose this move.

in 1990, and indeed each of the three countries signed the so-called 'Europe' agreements on the same day, 16 December 1991, becoming thus 'associated' with the EC. They did not carry on transition with the same methods, at the same speed, with the same outcomes. What united them was their geographic position in Central Europe, their resolve to return 'back to Europe' as soon as possible, in line with their complete break with their communist past.

(1)   The first steps on the way to the market had been made by *Hungary*, still under the communist rule. A bankruptcy law was enacted in 1986, though hardly implemented in the following years. A two-tier banking system had been introduced in 1987. The National Bank of Hungary (NBH) retained the right to issue money and perform the regulatory functions of a central bank. Several big commercial banks emanating from the dismantling of the NBH lending directorates and regional departments were extending credit to the economy, along with new, smaller commercial banks which were set up by enterprises, local governments, and cooperatives, some them including the participation of Western capital. In 1988 the Company Law

provided for creating joint stock companies, and in 1989 the Transformation Law allowed state enterprises to convert themselves into such companies. By 1988, all forms of ownership were legally on the same footing: state, cooperative including non-agricultural activities, private (with an upper limit of 30 persons employed in private enterprise since January 1988), and foreign (with 100 per cent foreign ownership permitted since 1 January 1989). In 1985–7 the economy was suffering from slow growth, low productivity, a growing rate of inflation and a large current account imbalance coupled with a rising debt service. In January 1988 Hungary introduced an austerity programme with the approval of the IMF. The programme was meant to curb domestic demand, to restore the budget balance and to generate a hard currency surplus in trade. At the same time a restructuring programme had been launched with the support of the World Bank, which was to provide funding for the implementation of a tax reform and for modernisation projects in agriculture and food processing. All the ingredients of a stabilisation-cum-transformation programme were already in place, under the aegis of a weakening and divided (among conservatives and a reform-minded majority) party.

(2) In *Poland* the situation was catastrophic in 1989. Unlike Hungary, the political situation had been clarified following the Round Table agreements concluded on 7 April between Solidarity and the communist government. On the economic front, the programme outlined in the agreements provided for institutional transformation, along with a reallocation of investment toward the consumer goods sector, and of budgetary expenditures toward social sectors such as housing. At a time when price control co-existed with inflation, no detailed macro-economic policy had been devised. However, inflation was swiftly moving toward hyper-inflation, for four reasons: a large budgetary deficit (due to growing subsidies on the one hand and tax laxity on the other, with state enterprises negotiating tax exemptions with the authorities); a huge external debt; a current account deficit; increases in incomes not matched by increases in supply. The minister of Finance of the new government formed in September, Leszek Balcerowicz, an economist and academic, launched on 1 January 1990 a stabilisation plan which was to become the symbol of the 'shock therapy'. The plan was drafted by a team of Polish experts with the help of Western advisers including the Harvard University economist Jeffrey Sachs. This plan capitalised on the popular support gained by Lech Walesa, the leader of Solidarity which had won the elections of September 1989, and on the unconditional commitment to the free market by the government.

(3) *Czechoslovakia* had not moved far on the road to transformation. The economy was still a standard centrally planned, state-owned and party-controlled economy. But the current economic situation was good. External accounts were balanced, the economy was growing slowly but there were no dramatic shortages and the level of consumption and living was perhaps still

higher than in the GDR. Prices were stable through price control, and there seemed to be no major inflationary pressures. The movement which had achieved the Velvet Revolution under the political and moral leadership of Vaclav Havel, the Civic Forum, seemed to have some margin of manoeuvre in launching a wide-scale, step-by-step restructuring programme rather than introducing drastic stabilisation measures. The economy was not over-heating and its main problems seemed to be how to modernise obsolescent industries and to free decision-making of enterprises once the tutelage of the party on the economy had ended. Nevertheless the 'shock therapy' model was chosen for reasons that will be detailed in the next chapter.

The *Eastern European* countries, *Romania, Bulgaria and Albania*, where reform started later and more hesitantly, share two features. They were less developed than the Central European ones. They remained for a longer time ruled by leaders close to the former political regime. Stabilisation programmes and transformation measures were launched later, in 1991–2, and hampered by lack of political consensus. Is there a link between a lower development level and the difficulties in breaking unequivocally with communism? The question may also be asked for Yugoslavia, where transition developed in the context of the civil war.

TRANSITION THROUGH BREAKING UP

Once freed from communism, the countries in transition sought to emancipate themselves from the links that kept them together in the past, and were only cemented by the communist party's monopoly. This happened both within the hard core of the communist bloc and within multinational states.

The Collapse of Comecon

Comecon and the Warsaw Pact organisation were dissolved almost at the same time in the middle of 1991. In both cases it was necessary to settle the legacies of the past, and decide whether something had to replace the former organisation.

The Warsaw Pact, created in 1955, was a military and political organisation. It deserves mention here only for the sake of comparison with what happened in the economic field. The main sequel of the Warsaw Pact was the need to repatriate the Soviet troops stationed on the territory of member countries. The repatriation schedule and the settling of the costs incurred were harder to negotiate than expected. Only in the case of the troops stationed in East Germany was the burden for both sides (the Soviet union and the ex-GDR) supported by one stakeholder, i.e. Western Germany. In all other cases, Central and Eastern European countries (except Romania, which did not have Soviet troops on its soil) had to restore the land and the buildings occupied by the armed forces at higher costs than expected. The Soviet Union, later Russia, had to provide for jobs and housing for the military back from Eastern Europe, while the country itself was in crisis. No new system of collective security replaced the Warsaw Pact. In fact Eastern and, yet more, Central European countries would have liked to become part of Nato or associated with it, exactly as they wanted to be economically reintegrated within Western Europe. To this claim a very oblique satisfaction was given, when in 1991 the secretariat of the CSCE was moved to Prague with symbolic functions.

Comecon had to be liquidated as well. The Western world almost unanimously hailed the phasing out of the organisation, until the drawbacks of the vacuum thus created became obvious, much later.

The legacies: debts and assets

Once the decision to dissolve Comecon had been taken in 1990, all that operated within the organisation or in parallel with it was dismantled. Bilateral and multilateral agreements and programmes became void. The fate of the CMEA *institutions* was however not the main problem. Compared with Western similar international organisations, the CMEA had not developed an overwhelmingly large bureaucracy. Of course, dismantling its committees, standing commissions and institutes has created redundancies, but the impact of these lay-offs is small compared with the impact of the domestic reforms. *Financial* matters were more difficult to settle.

In the beginning of 1990, there was within Comecon a net debtor, the USSR, and a net creditor, the GDR, *vis-à-vis* all the other members of the organisation. The USSR used to be a structural creditor until 1986. Over the years 1974–86 the USSR had accumulated a surplus of about 18 billion transferable rubles (TR) in its trade in goods with its partners, which was a benefit to them as it amounted to a credit with a zero rate of interest, the TR being inconvertible and non transferable, as was explained in Chapter 5. This surplus had apparently vanished by 1988. To begin with, it might have been much smaller (according to their statistics, the partner countries recorded a cumulated overall deficit of 11 billion TRs for the same period). In addition the USSR was in deficit (for a non-published amount) in trade in services. Finally a part of the surplus had been rescheduled (as was the case in relations with Poland). In any case in 1988–9 the USSR had already accumulated a debt of 6.5 billion TRs, and was again to be in deficit in 1990.

The settlement of the Soviet balances was reached through bilateral agreements with the partner countries. The first to be concluded was between the USSR and Hungary in 1990. It was an interesting exercise in cross-rates. The most favourable arrangement for the USSR's partners would have been to have their TR surplus converted at the official IBEC rate, over-valuing the ruble, which would have enabled them to get a large amount in dollars; that was what they claimed, though in the past they had implicitly discarded this rate when fixing their own commercial rates. For the USSR it would have been most advantageous to benefit from the cross-rate between the dollar and the ruble that derived from the Hungarian exchange rate for these currencies, and that strongly devalued the ruble, something the Soviets had criticised in the past. The negotiators settled for an average rate just in between both claims (see Table 6.3). Similar agreements were to be concluded with the other countries in the second part of l990. In fact, these agreements were all stalled in 1991. The Soviet Union and its partners disagreed on the outstanding amount of the debt, which had increased in the second half of 1990 and even in 1991. They also disagreed on the schedule of reimbursement, and on the interest rates. In addition, new claims on the USSR emerged in 1991 in relation to the Soviet military pull-out of Hungary, Czechoslovakia and Poland, as it was evidenced by the Eastern European countries that the damage caused by the Soviet troops to the environment, in addition to the other costs of the pull-out, was much greater than expected initially. As these new claims cannot be assessed quickly this issue is bound to add lasting uncertainty to the settlement of Soviet–East European claims. After the collapse of the Soviet Union itself end-1991, the Soviet liabilities were to be tranferred to Russia. Most of them were not yet settled by 1994. Arrangements were reached beginning 1995 with Poland and Hungary.

Table 6.3   *The collapse of Comecon: ruble/dollar cross-rates end-1989*

Bulgaria	Czech.	Hungary	Poland	Romania	USSR	IBEC
1.9	2.3	2.6	3.6	1.6	0.6	0.67

Note: The cross-rates express the value of one dollar in transferable rubles (according to the commercial exchange rates of the various CMEA countries). In the Soviet–Hungarian case, the most favourable arrangement for Hungary would have been to have its 800 million transferable ruble surplus converted into dollars at the official IBRC (the Comecon Moscow-based International Bank for Economic Cooperation) rate, close to the official Soviet rate, overvaluing the ruble (it would have got 1.2 billion dollars at the end-1989 IBEC rate). For the USSR it would have been advantageous to benefit from the Hungarian ruble/dollar cross-rate, which would have yielded a 310 million dollars debt. The perverse aspect of the game was that each negotiator would have gained if applying the rules set by the other one (of course for other purposes). The negotiators settled for an average rate of 1.09 ruble for one dollar, which provided Hungary with 734 million dollars (this sum was meant to offset future deficits with the USSR).
Source: Press reports.

The other country to have surpluses on all its partners was the GDR. Here the difficulties of a settlement were compounded by the effect of the currency union between the FRG and the GDR, and by the peculiarities of the East German trade accounting. The outstanding East German claims, to be claimed by unified Germany in hard currency, amounted to 10 billion transferable rubles at the beginning of 1991, i.e. to about 23 billion DM, of which 15 against the USSR, 2 against Poland, 1.7 due by Czechoslovakia, 1.3 by Hungary, 1.2 by Bulgaria and Romania each (ECE/UN 1991, p. 76). Is this debt ever to be repaid? In July 1991 the Federal Economy Minister of the ČSFR Vladimir Dlouhy declared in an interview with a Czech newspaper that more that 50 per cent of this debt should be written off ('How much do we owe Germany?', interview with *Mlada Fronta*, 19 July). This writing off may ultimately become a part of the German assistance to the East, a not too bad deal if one takes into account the fact that the united Germany has become the first trade partner of East Central European countries.

The new rules of the game

As we saw in Chapter 5, it was decided in 1990 to shift immediately to world prices and hard currencies in mutual trade. The emerging pattern of intra-CMEA prices, as anticipated at the beginning of 1990, was supposed to be much closer to the *relative* world prices, with an increase in the price of primary goods in terms of manufactures. A reversal was therefore anticipated in the Soviet balance with the East: instead of the deficits observed in 1988–9 and expected for 1990, it was thought the USSR would obtain a surplus in convertible currencies, which experts had put for 1991 in the range of 10–11 billion dollars. These assumptions were made prior to the increase of oil prices following the Iraqi crisis in August 1990, which significantly increased the expected Soviet surplus even in the event of a reduction in the quantities supplied.

The assumptions for what was going to happen in 1991 were based upon two hypotheses. The first one was that the new system of prices and settlements would actually work. The second was that apart from this basic change in the rules of the game, all other things would remain equal and in particular the commodity composition of trade. Eastern Europe would still be dependent on Soviet supplies of energy, and the Soviet enterprises would still ask for Eastern European machinery and consumer goods.

The *first assumption* proved wrong. The shift to world prices did not play a significant role in the regional trade after January 1991. Prices were not relevant in the past because arrangements in kind mattered more than prices, for systemic reasons embodied in domestic mechanisms as well as in the international ˇone. What happened once this international trade mechanism was dismantled? Trade in primary commodities proved to be

largely inelastic to prices. The Eastern European countries would have
bought more of Soviet oil had the Soviet Union supplied them, even at
higher prices than before – though their demand for energy decreased due to
the domestic recession in these countries. There is no evidence that the
Soviet Union has reduced its supply for price considerations. The cuts,
which reached one-third of the 1990 level according to the Economic
Commission for Europe (ECE/UN 1992, p. 88), have primarily been the
effect of domestic difficulties in the energy sector. They also result from the
general chaos in the country and the disruption of the former command
links, with sovereignty over natural resources being claimed by the
Republics and even by the direct producers.

Trade in manufactures appeared to be much more sensitive to non-price
determinants such as quality and performance than to price movements
(meaning that even very large cuts in Eastern European prices for machinery
would not necessarily dissuade Soviet buyers from seeking Western
suppliers). But even more, manufactured goods exports from Eastern
Europe to the USSR emerged as the major casualty of the new system of
settlements.

The *shift to settlements in convertible currencies* was a crucial component
of the new rules (Csaba, 1991). It was probably an illusion to believe that it
could be immediately implemented. The legacies of the past suggested that
transitory arrangements amounting to bilateral clearing in hard currency
might be sought. The situation as it developed in the second half of 1990 and
in the beginning of 1991 actually appeared very confused. Several bilateral
trade agreements were concluded between the Soviet Union and its partners,
providing for a transition period during which part of bilateral trade would
be conducted on the basis of 'barter packages' of goods specified in
'indicative lists' (ECE/UN, 1991, pp. 79–80). But, pressed by its economic
crisis, the Soviet Union had to secure hard currency from all its exports, and
allegedly 'was unable to pay' for its imports. Hence the collapse in imports
of manufactured goods from the East, which was indeed the major feature
of Soviet–East European trade in 1991, and reached 50 to 70 per cent
(according to goods) of the already depressed level of 1990.

The second assumption about what was to happen in 1991 was thus
equally wrong: not only was the shift to the new rules not realised, 'things
did not remain equal' as far as trade flows in volume and composition were
concerned. Trade collapsed overall, and still more for the Soviet imports
from Eastern Europe (manufactured goods) than for the Soviet exports (raw
materials).

The most obvious solution was to look for bilateral arrangements with
the Soviet Union and with the Soviet republics, particularly with Russia,
Ukraine, Bielorussia and the Baltic states. By the end of 1991, there was a
whole network of bilateral agreements and *ad hoc* arrangements involving,
on the one hand, Soviet and republican agencies, and on the other, Eastern

European governments, banks, and business associations. An increasing number of deals were negotiated directly on the enterprise level though it was very difficult to trace them. To go further supposed an orderly disintegration of the former USSR.

The Disintegration of the Multinational States

Before its collapse the communist system counted three federal states: the USSR, Yugoslavia and Czechoslovakia. None of these three structures, though very different, resisted transition.

The Yugoslav case

Yugoslavia is a puzzling case. From 1985 it was classified by the United Nations as a 'developing market economy'. It had no longer any of the standard features of a planned economy, except the most crucial one: the monopoly of power of the communist party. Though the political life was far from democratic, the aura of the self-management ideology and the reality of decentralisation gave Yugoslavia credibility in international public opinion. The Yugoslavs themselves hardly understood how their complicated self-managed system worked. An opaque terminology described it, such as the 'self-management communities of interest', which were supposed to manage the social services, and the 'basic organisations of associated labour', which were linked in 'work organisations' (enterprises) through 'self-management agreements'. In fact the whole system was operating through networks of localist interests. The six Republics (see Table 6.2) and the two autonomous provinces of the Republic of Serbia (Vojvodina and Kosovo) benefited from the dismantling of the federal powers in the 1960s and 1970s, and this was again wrongly perceived in the West as an example of decentralisation, identified with greater democracy. It looked at the end of the 1980s as if Yugoslavia did not need a 'transition' proper, but rather a structural adjustment programme. Indeed a long-term stabilisation programme had been adopted in 1983 with the support of the IMF but was not implemented. In 1988 a new stabilisation programme was drafted, but in 1989 the rate of inflation was over 1,200 per cent and social unrest in the form of strikes and political demonstrations was rising. The 'rich' Republics of the North (Slovenia and Croatia) no longer wanted to contribute to the development of the poorer ones. The Federal government and the party itself had lost popular support as facts about corruption and even huge financial scandals were revealed, such as the bankruptcy of the Bosnian food processing enterprise Agrokomerc in 1987 which shook the political and party establishment and evidenced the links between the enterprises, the banks, the local governments and the power.

The new Federal government which came to power in January 1989 launched in December a stabilisation programme which might be seen as an advanced version of the Polish shock therapy model, with the following measures: a restrictive monetary policy, wage control, the freeing of prices, cuts in budgetary spending, and convertibility of the dinar which was pegged to the DM. The party monopoly of power was abolished in January 1990 and the supremacy of self-managed social ownership was ended by a law on social capital in August 1990.

The programme failed due to the lack of political consensus among the Republics. Slovenia and Croatia began to move out of Federal, that is Serbian, domination throughout 1989 and 1990. Both Republics declared themselves independent in June 1991. At that time war had already begun. The disaggregation of the state was endorsed by the European Community which in 1992 recognised the independence of both states. The following story is one of ethnic war among, and within, the parts of the former Socialist Federative Yugoslavia, with an increasing involvement of the international community in words rather than in deeds. A 'normal' transition to the market could be pursued from 1992 onwards only by one of these parts, independent Slovenia.

The dismantling of the USSR

Western policy-makers and international organisations were taken aback by the disaggregation of the USSR, though many experts had long been warning about the looming burst of the Empire (Carrère d'Encausse, 1979). Gorbachev's international public image obscured the nationalistic and ethnic pressures, which first erupted in October 1987 into an open uprising in the High Karabakh, a little-known enclave inhabited by Armenians within the Republic of Azerbaidzhan. Centrifugal tendencies prevailed in efforts to rebuild a united community of nations.

Centrifugal tendencies. Very soon all the Republics and within them the ethnic minorities, whether or not endowed with a special regime during the Soviet period, began to claim various statuses (see Table 6.4) ranging from recognition, autonomy or sovereignty to independence. In 1989–91 all the former Soviet Republics declared themselves sovereign and/or independent, as well as the autonomous Republics in Georgia and Russia. The ethnic minorities began to claim some rights as well. According to the last census, in 1989 there were in the USSR 128 national minorities, and excluding those with less than 100,000 people they still amounted to fifty-six!

The West was not very happy with these centrifugal developments. As in the case of Yugoslavia, in the beginning Western governments and international organisations wanted to preserve some union. The Baltic countries were a special case as they had lost independence much later than

Table 6.4   *The former USSR and its successor states*

Name of the state	Area (thousand square km^2)	Population (1990, in millions)
Former USSR	22,403.0	288.6
Estonia[1]	45.1	1.6
Latvia	64.5	2.7
Lithuania	65.2	3.7
Russia (Russian Federation)[2]	17,075.4	148.0
Ukraine	603.7	52.0
Belarus	207.6	10.3
Moldova	33.7	4.4
Armenia	29.8	3.3
Georgia	69.7	5.5
Azerbaijan	86.6	7.1
Kazakhstan	2,717.3	16.7
Uzbekistan	447.4	20.3
Kyrgyzstan	198.5	4.4
Turkmenistan	488.1	3.6
Tajikistan	143.1	5.3

[1] Lithuania, Estonia, and Latva declared independence in 1990–1, and were all recognised by the international community following the coup of August 1991 against Gorbachev.
[2] The Baltic Republics, which were incorporated into the Soviet Union following the 1939 Molotov–Ribbentrop (Soviet-German) pact, were the first to declare independence, in March 1990 (Lithuania) and August 1991 (Estonia and Latvia). Eleven of the twelve remaining republics signed the CIS agreement on 21 December 1991 (see text). The remaining republic, Georgia, joined the CIS end-1993. The CIS is neither a federation nor a confederation and has no state attributes, though Minsk (capital of Belarus) is meant to serve as the 'capital', rather the coordinating centre, of the CIS.
Source: *World Bank Atlas.*

the rest of the Empire, and even in this instance it was felt that they should come to some understanding with the USSR, later with Russia.

In 1991 the Soviet economy was in deadlock. No federal economic programme was acceptable any more in the context of the conflict which opposed the president of the USSR Mikhail Gorbachev and the new president of Russia Boris Yeltsin, elected in June 1991. The anti-Gorbachev coup was at least partly triggered by the opposition of the old guard of the party against the union Treaty among the Republics which was ready to be signed on August 19, the day of the coup. The Republics were no longer paying their taxes to the federal budget. Some of them started to introduce their own currency. Inter-republican trade collapsed due to the general disorganisation of the economy and to autarkic tendencies which emerged in the form of custom duties, quantitative restrictions and embargoes resorted to by the Republics and even by smaller national units, down to individual cities. Privatisation could not be started as each Republic was claiming sovereignty on the assets located on its territory or even outside its boundaries.

The first recomposition attempts. The Russian president Boris Yeltsin attempted to rebuild a Commonwealth of nations, first between the 'Slavic' states (Russia, Ukraine, and Belarus which was the new name for Belorussia), then between all the new Independent States when eight other Republics decided to join the new grouping. The CIS (Commonwealth of Independent States) was officially formed on 21 December 1991 between all the former Republics except the Baltic States, and Georgia (which was to join later, in October 1993), and the USSR was officially dissolved nine days later. The CIS is neither a state, nor a federation, confederation or even a commonwealth (despite its name). It is a club of rather unwilling heads of state, engaged in conflicting relations (of which the most ominous oppose Russia and Ukraine over questions of nuclear security), and in variable coalitions.

Neither politically nor economically is the CIS heir to the USSR. The genuine heir is Russia, and this has been acknowledged by the diplomacy as Russia has moved into the former Soviet embassies and in the Soviet seats in international organisations. How Russia would be able to conduct its own transition while composing with its partners within the CIS appeared in the beginning of 1992 as the major challenge in the economic transformation in the former USSR.

The 'velvet divorce' in Czechoslovakia

This last case of a split within a state was a surprise. Nationalistic claims were considered in the West as non-existing in the Czech Republic and rather restrained in Slovakia. Federalism was indeed a Soviet creation following the normalisation process after 1968. But pre-war Czechoslovakia was an example of the few democracies in Central Europe, since the creation of the Republic in 1918, and until the partition of the state in 1939 forced by Germany. Was the split inevitable, beyond the devolution that had already occurred in 1990–2? The division between the Czechs and the Slovaks is rooted in historical, religious, ethnic and linguistic specifics, that are comparable to those which may be found in Western democracies, and that indeed sometimes lead to splits, especially when they are combined with inequalities in development and personal conflicts among politicians.

The Czech–Slovak break-up is thus rather atypical of the other cases of disintegration in the transition period. In these latter cases a common logic is to be found. The system had a centre which in the case of the USSR was Moscow and the Soviet communist party. The centre regulated inter-republican and inter-state relations through political influence. The autocephalous centre in Belgrade performed the same functions in communist Yugoslavia.

The collapse of the centres did not just induce chaos. Western experts tend to look at this situation as if the network of economic relations could be restored on new bases once the totalitarian power of the centre was gone. But communism did not eradicate national and ethnic tensions. It just stifled them and thus exacerbated them. It is impossible to tell when the disintegration will have gone far enough to allow for a recomposition. The restoration of the networks cannot be forced from the outside or the inside.

THE RESISTANCE TO TRANSITION IN NON-EUROPEAN SOCIALIST COUNTRIES

The non-European socialist countries managed their transition to the market in a very different way from the European ones, and also differed among themselves. Here are their particulars briefly summed up:

(1) The party remained in power; only in Mongolia were other parties admitted to participate in the elections held in 1990 and 1992. Except for that country, the communist party remains dominated by historic figures (Fidel Castro in Cuba), by family dynasties (in North Korea Kim Jong Il was the heir-designate to his father Kim Il Sung, and indeed moved into power when the latter died in July 1994), or by traditional oligarchies (in China and Vietnam).

(2) Except China, all these countries were linked with the USSR, either as members of Comecon (Mongolia, Cuba, Vietnam) or as recipients of assistance (all of the above plus North Korea and Laos). The severing of these links strongly disorganised these economies.

(3) In Vietnam, China and Mongolia the transition to the market has begun under the guidance of the party. Mongolia followed the Gorbachev model, then the Yeltsin model and shifted from a kind of *perestroyka* to stabilisation-cum-privatisation. In Vietnam and China, the reforms began at the end of the 1970s along similar lines in agriculture, on the basis of the so-called 'household responsibility system' in China and the leasing contracts in Vietnam, both allowing for large decision-making power extended to the family within a collective framework. It has dramatically improved the supply of food products. The private sector in industry and trade had been allowed to expand since 1979 in China,

1986 in Vietnam. The large state enterprises remain in public ownership and were still subject to central planning and bureaucratic control by the beginning of the 1990s.

(4) The opening of the socialist non-European economies to trade with non-socialist countries and foreign direct investment was both a boost to growth and an incentive to reform. In Cuba it was almost the only element of a reform.

The Soviet communist party has tried to impose the concept of a 'world socialist system'. This concept has collapsed as well. As was said in China in 1989, the year when the student uprising was crushed on Tiananmen Square, 'the centre of socialism has shifted to the East'. Is this specific socialism doomed as well? This may well be in the long run. In the meantime it is resisting substantial political changes. Tiananmen has been castigated in the West, but Western investors proved to be more confident in this system than in the uncertainties of the transition European style.

7 Macroeconomic Stabilisation

The transformation of the former centrally planned economies began in the two first 'PHARE' countries, Poland and Hungary. These two countries were the first in the transition to democracy, and also the first to benefit from the international community's involvement in the process of transition through assistance and advice.

As seen in the previous chapter, Poland was the first test case. The new policy-makers committed to the free market and their advisers rejoined in the feeling that a 'shock therapy' was needed immediately to stop hyperinflation, to cure the budget deficit, and to initiate structural reforms. This was the Polish 'Big Bang' launched on 1 January 1990 (see Gomulka, 1992). Similar packages were later devised for the other countries in transition, whatever their initial situation and their distinctive features. These packages basically applied the methods already experimented within developing countries, with an enthusiastic or half-hearted endorsement by the policy-makers depending on the domestic political setting.

It was expected that the stabilisation programmes would restore external and internal balances in the countries, and also bring about a recession, which would bottom out in the one or two years following the inception of the programme. Then, it was anticipated, the structural transformation could really develop.

What happened did not meet these expectations. Even in the most favourable cases, i.e. in Central Europe, though stabilisation achieved some successes, they were below the initial hopes of experts and policy-makers. The supply response either did not follow or was greatly delayed. Output fell more than anticipated. Structural changes have lagged everywhere. In Eastern Europe and in the former USSR, though commitments to the same packages have been expressed, the outcomes have been much worse than in Central Europe. True, in these less favourable cases the stabilisation therapy has not been fully applied, or has been managed amidst political struggles and internal disruption.

However, while 1992 was a year of deep disappointment, in 1993 there was a stir; Poland began to resume the growth path, and in 1994 other countries followed suit. How are these results to be explained ? Should one blame the proposed cure, or its implementation, or was it just the price to pay for getting out of decades of communism?

THE STABILISATION POLICIES

Stabilisation policy implies a package of measures, which are linked with the beginning of a structural reform. The agenda of the reformers has everywhere been based on a similar menu. But decisions had to be made as to the sequence and the speed of the chosen measures.

The Package

The stabilisation packages usually consisted of the following measures:

(a) *price liberalisation*, through the reduction of subsidies, and the deregulation of price fixing, going along with the *liberalisation of domestic trade*;

(b) *balancing the government budget* through increases in taxes (in particular, taxes on excess nominal wages have been introduced or raised, so as to fight inflation at the same time, see point (d), and cuts in government spending (beyond reducing of price subsidies);

(c) *a restrictive monetary policy* through an increase in the Central Bank interest rate so as to restore a positive real interest rate (in Poland new rates were even applied to old loans); a direct regulation of bank lending was also to be applied in most cases;

(d) *an incomes policy* aimed at stopping the inflation spiral (in Poland this was done through a weak indexation of the nominal wage during the first months of stabilisation, and a tax on wage increases in the state sector; in Czechoslovakia an agreement among the government, the employers and the unions determined both the desirable level of decrease in real wages and the permitted rate of increase in nominal wages; in Hungary increases in nominal wages were controlled through a tax on the wage bill, coupled with alleviations if the enterprise succeeded in cutting jobs);

(e) *foreign trade liberalisation* through the lifting of export and import licences, and the permission given to all enterprises to engage in foreign trade; tariffs, which were meaningless in the previous system of administered trade, at the same time became 'active' instruments of trade policy, and were lowered so as to express commitment to trade liberalisation; *current account internal convertibility* of the domestic currency (meaning that domestic enterprises and up to certain limits households were allowed to freely buy and sell foreign currency for current purposes; in Hungary and Poland a kind of internal convertibility had been introduced, with some limitations, before transition began; the Czech Republic is the only country that is moving toward full convertibility on capital account in 1995);

devaluation of the domestic currency bringing it down to the (black) market rate, with differences among the countries as to the subsequent determination of the rate of exchange.

Such packages are 'heterodox' stabilisation programmes that combine standard monetary and fiscal restrictions with several 'anchors' (Bruno, 1992, p. 752; ECE/UN, 1992, p. 43), which may bring to mind programmes applied in Israel or in Mexico. Typically stabilisation was anchored to nominal variables such as the rate of exchange and money wages, and to real variables (money supply and/or interest rate).

Structural measures aimed at creating a private market economy were simultaneously put on the agendas, including:

(f) launching the privatisation, and the dismantling of the former state monopolies;

(g) setting up a market environment through reform of the banking and financial sector and the tax reform;

(h) developing a social safety net meant to replace the former all-embracing protection system 'from cradle to grave', and also to cushion the impact of the austerity measures and of the structural transformation;

(i) initiating an industrial policy so as to identify the 'winners' and 'losers' in the industrial activities to be restructured; defining the activities in need of support and devising appropriate policies such as subsidies, protective tariffs, etc.; taking care of the environment, at least so as to stop the damage caused during the former regime.

Among the measures aimed at structural transformation, those under headings (f) and (g) had to be immediately launched or at least announced so as to add credibility to the stabilisation packages. The two last groups of measures were looked at as much less urgent in the first stages of the transition.

Tactical Choices

Once the strategy was defined, tactical choices had to be made. These choices raised hot debates in the beginning of the transition, which now seem rather irrelevant. The lack of experience of the policy-makers, coupled with the feeling that there was an optimal recipe to apply in order to move toward a market economy, may explain why the issues of sequencing, or of the choice between gradualism and shock therapy, were so extensively discussed.

The sequencing

Was there an optimal sequence to follow in the implementation of the stabilisation package? Considering the scope of the policies to be implemented, it seemed that the proposed measures should be introduced in some order, even if policy-makers were determined to move fast. A general consensus was reached on the point that stabilisation should precede structural transformation. However, the problem of credibility was seen as essential, so that even at an early stage announcements of systemic measures, such as a quick move toward privatisation and demonopolisation, were highly recommended by experts (see Nuti, 1991, and the survey by Jeffries, 1993, p. 336 ff.). In fact three issues have dominated the sequencing debate. They were related to the freeing of prices, to the liberalising of foreign trade, and to the financial sector reforms.

(1) The first issue in the sequencing debate was the *liberalising of prices*. There was widespread concern about a surge in inflation, beyond the expected initial jump once controls and subsidies were lifted. Because most of the producers and retailers were large state enterprises, it was feared that they would behave as 'monopolies' and tend to increase prices to the maximum profit level allowed by the market, at the same time increasing wages and thus fuelling an inflationary spiral (hence the taxation on excess wage increases). In addition, common knowledge on the socialist economies suggested that there was a very high 'monetary overhang' in the household sector due to repressed inflation and shortages, and that all this excess demand would pour in as soon as the prices were freed. Thus there was some argument over the issue of demonopolising first, before freeing the prices, and eliminating the overhang first as well. Both debates soon faded away. It became obvious that demonopolising could only go hand in hand with privatising and hence take time. Besides, as we saw in Chapter 3, large state-owned enterprises could not be likened to market-type monopolies. Their initial micro-economic adjustments in the transition context were survival-maximising rather than profit-maximising. Besides, the industrial state-owned enterprises lacked a global view of the market, especially of the consumer market. On the other hand, the monetary overhang was everywhere eliminated much more quickly than anticipated through the price hikes, which wiped out households' savings.

(2) The second issue in the sequencing debate was *foreign trade liberalisation*. The standard package implied the opening up of the domestic market along with a strong devaluation of the domestic currency, and a current account convertibility. This had at least four advantages. Firstly, price liberalisation would be automatically coupled with competition from abroad, which would prevent the domestic monopolies from too sharp increases in their prices. Secondly, the distorted price structure inherited from the past would be corrected by an 'imported' price structure reflecting

relative world prices. Thirdly, as an outcome of the devaluation, and provided a fixed or pegged exchange rate regime was selected, the exchange rate would provide a firm nominal 'anchor' for the stabilisation programme. Finally, a depressed exchange rate would deter imports, so that there would be no need for high tariffs at a time when more openness was required, if only to win the favours of the European Community (this fourth argument however contradicts the first: the higher the protection from devaluation, the less there is competition from abroad).

Despite these good reasons, the simultaneity of trade and price liberalisation has been questioned. It has been argued that excessive devaluation and excessive opening up of the economy exaggerated the initial price shock (Nuti and Portes, 1993), and that too early an exposure to external competition could devastate the domestic economy (McKinnon, 1992).

(3) The third debated issue relates to *banking and financial reforms.* Though such reforms belong to the phase of structural transformation, the standard instruments of monetary and fiscal stabilisation require a two-tier banking system, which would allow the Central Bank to influence the monetary creation by the commercial banks through an interest rate policy. They also require a well-functioning, modern tax system. If the budget deficit is to be reduced, not only must expenditures be cut, but tax collection must be improved, preferably with a new, sophisticated range of taxes combining direct and indirect taxation (Calvo and Frenkel, 1991), instead of the previous system where an arbitrary share of the enterprises' revenues was collected, with a large amount of bargaining over the payment. But if this is indeed a precondition to successful stabilisation, a full banking and tax reform might take too much time in view of the urgent needs of stabilisation.

In the course of the reforms, the debate over sequencing gradually became reduced to a few essential principles:

- Rather than the sequencing itself, the determination of the policy-makers to proceed with the announced measures was found critical, i.e. one moved from the issue of sequencing to that of *political credibility.* Thus the policies conducted in the Central European countries were opposed to those that were announced but not systematically implemented in Eastern Europe (Romania, Bulgaria) and in Russia;
- As it was obviously not possible to do everything at once, it was advocated that the policy-makers should move forward *along the whole front* of envisioned measures, so as to aim at stabilisation first and to introduce some piecemeal structural reforms needed to enhance the credibility of or to trigger the right responses from measures such as increases in the interest rate, or increases in taxes. To immediately aim at fine-tuning policies in economies characterised by rather primitive market conditions increasingly appeared as an illusion.

The speed of the transition: big bang versus gradualism

This issue, which was hotly debated in the first year of the transition and opposed the Polish and Hungarian cases, has lost much of its interest, as soon as it was recognised that stabilisation, when it is required, should be conducted swiftly, and that structural reforms can only be implemented over a number of years, because of the change in institutions and behaviour that such reforms require.

The origins of the debate stem from the difference between the initial situations of the first two countries to follow the path of transformation, Poland and Hungary (see previous chapter). Stabilisation was obviously required in Poland, which in 1989 was plagued by huge inflation coupled with shortages, by a large budget deficit and an unserviceable external debt (see Statistical Appendix, Table A.2). Hungary was also in need of stabilisation, but not with the same urgency. It had suffered from a high double-digit inflation since 1988, and the government budget had been in deficit since 1985, though the ratio of the budget balance to the GDP was improving. The foreign debt, which had been stabilised in 1982–3 due (already) to a stabilisation programme negotiated with the IMF, had again increased since 1985 and had become the highest in Eastern Europe in per capita terms, but Hungary went on servicing it and did not ask for rescheduling.

The issue was very soon influenced by Czechoslovakia stepping into the circle of the countries in transition, and debating over the proper programme to select amidst a very harsh political dispute between the right and left wings of the Civic Forum, the party that had won the first free elections in June 1990. The proponents of a free market represented by Vaclav Klaus, appointed minister of finance in 1990, advocated shock therapy, while the left wing of the Civic Forum, led by the political opponent to Klaus and minister of the economy during the first months of the transition, Valtr Komarek, favoured a step-by-step introducing of the market. The shock therapy model was selected and started on 1 January 1991, less out of necessity, since the macro-economic indicators were good (low inflation, low budget deficit, and very low foreign indebtedness), than as the expression of the political victory of the conservatives.

In fact similar packages were adopted in the three countries which initiated the transition. The same aims were set (to achieve external and internal balance) with the same instruments (a stringent monetary and fiscal policy). Though very close to standard IMF packages these measures were actually imposed by the governments which came democratically to power and which claimed full responsibility for their action, though acknowledging the role of Western advisers who had worked with the domestic economists (see Bruno, 1992, p. 743).

Why then oppose 'big bang' and gradualism? The answer is political. 'Big bang' or 'cold turkey' programmes express an intellectual and political commitment to a monetarist, neo-classical vision, along with a willingness to radically break away from the past. The big bang is a kind of insurance against any temptation to look for a 'third way' (any version of 'market socialism'). The launching of the 'shock therapy' used shock phrases such as the famous 'one cannot jump over a chasm in two leaps', a very inappropriate wording indeed as what was in question was more akin to climbing a steep mountain than crossing a chasm. The choice of the shock therapy meant that the new government excluded any move back to the past, and capitalized on the political and social consensus so as to impose drastic measures which would immediately lower the standard of living, with the promise of a quick recovery, instead of a muddling through. The governments of Poland and Czechoslovakia had precisely this profile. In both countries, the shock was embodied in instant measures such as freeing prices and cutting subsidies; it stopped at the door of the enterprises, as bankruptcies are not yet implemented on a large scale.

Conversely, the communist power had already collapsed even before 1990 through internal divisions and was totally discredited in Hungary, so that there was no need to exorcise it. On the other hand, the new coalition which came to power in 1990 was itself very divided and could not agree on a clear-cut programme; it was constrained by its electoral promises and by the firmly anchored feeling of the population that Hungary had been already for many years on the road to a market economy, and need not suffer the sacrifices endured by other countries. The IMF package was then retained, within the framework of a new stand-by agreement in 1991. It could not, technically, result in a 'shock' comparable to what was experienced in Poland and Czechoslovakia. Prices were already largely free, as well as foreign trade, and the forint was very near convertibility. Besides, Hungary had already undergone two experiences of IMF packages. There had been the early experience with an adjustment programme in 1982, the year when Hungary was admitted to the IMF. At that time, though meeting the requirements of the IMF as to its outcome, the programme was nevertheless conducted more with the help of centralised measures than with market instruments. While the IMF had then asked for the curbing of the aggregate demand, the reducing of domestic expenditure and the decreasing of foreign debt through a surplus in the current account balance of payments, the latter was achieved through cuts in investment and capital goods imports (not in consumption), and through export promotion accompanying successive devaluations of the forint (see Schuller and Hamel, 1985). Another IMF package was launched in 1988, and interrupted a year after because Hungary, already a largely decentralised 'semi-reformed' economy, was not sufficiently 'planned' to impose a stringent restrictive policy, and not sufficiently 'market' to rely on market macro-economic instruments.

To sum this up metaphorically, one could say that Poland and Czechoslovakia found themselves in the situation of heavy smokers being persuaded to quit their addiction at once and definitively, with all the traumatic consequences involved; while Hungary could say, paraphrasing George Bernard Shaw: 'implementing stabilisation is easy, I have tried it many times'.

That the whole issue is mainly a credibility problem may be evidenced from the fact that no transition government ever proclaimed itself gradualist. Hungary definitely applied a gradualist policy, with an undisputable continuity with the past reform trends, but its government never claimed to do that, and instead repeatedly declared itself committed to a quick transition to the market. In fact no single clear-cut package was implemented. The Hungarian stabilisation programme may be read through fiscal laws and what was made public from discussions with the IMF.

There was no theory of gradualism either. While shock therapy concepts were widely advocated for policy-making (see for instance, Sachs and Lipton, 1991; Winiecki, 1993a), there has been no specific plea for gradualism, only recommendations to the effect of softening the initial shocks whenever there had been an 'overshooting'. 'Gradualism needs a strategy' (Mizsei, 1993), and also a theory. It would be a sheer misconception to confuse gradualism with the evolutionary approach, which is nonetheless often done (see Chapter 10). This approach is a complex set of theses dealing with institutional and microeconomic developments, not with macroeconomic policies. Evolutionarists do not object to 'big bang' type stabilisation *per se*; they object to the assumption that the market is supposed to exist already when it does not (Murrell, 1992).

Finally one has to mention the cases when there was neither shock therapy (as in Poland, Czechoslovakia, or Bulgaria) nor implicit 'gradual-ism' (as in Hungary, Slovenia, Romania), but rather 'a shock without the therapy' (Ellman, 1992) as in Russia. The various successive programmes announced and partly launched in Russia in 1992–3 were based on a shock therapy concept (if only to please the IMF and Russia's creditors), but were altered due to political conflicts between parliament and government, or between the government, on the one hand, and the Central Bank, various lobbies linked with the previous *nomenklatura*, and the regional forces and lobbies, on the other. As a result the measures outlined were never fully implemented: prices were not fully freed, credit was not really tightened, nominal wages were allowed to outgrow inflation, and the convertibility of the currency was not implemented.

Anyhow, the stabilisation debate moved away rather early from the gradualist/shock therapy discussion. Soon after the beginning of the transition, the core of the debate focused on the question: why did stabilisation bring about so deep a recession? In 1994 a turnaround was to be observed for Central Europe, Albania, Romania and Slovenia, but still eluded the other countries in transition.

THE OUTCOME OF THE STABILISATION MEASURES

We review the distinctive features and outcomes of these programmes, and discuss the reasons why output fell to a much greater extent than expected.

The Main Features of the Stabilisation Programmes

The building blocks of the stabilisation programmes actually implemented are shown in Table 7.1. These are a combination of initial packages, changes due to domestic political events (new elections, change of government) or to external shocks (such as war in former Yugoslavia, the split of the Czech and Slovak Federal Republic), and alterations following agreements with the IMF. The former USSR is a special case. While the Baltic countries have embarked on stabilisation policies similar in design to those of Central Europe, most of the former Soviet space is struggling with problems resulting from the split-up of the country, the heavy legacies of the Communist past, and an erratic implementation of the reform packages. Most of the Western attention concentrates on Russia. Indeed what happens in Russia is bound to influence the whole area, especially as far as monetary and currency problems are concerned (see Chapter 9). In addition, outside Russia, market-based stabilisation policies are hardly experienced so far. Box 7.1 illustrates the vacillation of the Russian programmes.

Various forecasts have been made at the inception of the stabilisation programmes, by international organisations, or Western experts. Domestic governments have set targets in their programmes, with instruments to meet the targets, which are recalled in Table 7.2. The expected outcomes were the following: that inflation would decrease after a once-for-all sharp rise in prices following the ending of subsidies; that the budget deficit would be reduced; that the balance of payments situation would improve. Along with these positive effects a deterioration in real indicators was anticipated, with a drop in output, consumption and investment, but this was supposed to be a rather limited and short-lived phenomenon, with a quick recovery following the implementation of market-type policies.

Though actual outcomes differed, the general trend was in all cases a much bleaker picture than anticipated. Even when stabilisation was more or less achieved it remained fragile. Output declined much more than expected, and the start of recovery occurred later, even in Central Europe which offered the best prospects.

Table 7.1   *The building blocks of the stabilisation-cum-transformation programmes in Central and Eastern Europe, 1989–94*

Blocks of the transition	Hungary	Poland	Czechoslovakia (until 31 Dec. 1992)
POLITICAL REFORM: see Table 6.1			
PREVIOUS ECONOMIC REFORMS			
Type*	'New Economic Mechanism'	Reformed Soviet model	'Prague Spring' repressed, 1968
Dates	(1968; revised in the 1980s)	1966, 1973, 1982	Reformed Soviet model 1980–1
CONCEPT OF THE TRANSITION	'Gradualism'	'Shock therapy'	'Shock therapy'
MACRO-ECONOMIC STABILISATION	Restrictive monetary, budgetary and income policy launched by steps, 1990	Launched 1.1.1990; restrictive economic policy since then	Launched 1.1.1991; restrictive economic policy since then
PRICE LIBERALISATION	Gradual since 1975	January 1990	January 1991
DEMONOPOLISATION ('anti-trust' laws)	Anti-monopoly law in force as of January 1, 1991	Anti-monopoly office created in 1991	Law on the protection of competition (February 1991); Commercial Code (Jan. 92)
PRIVATISATION			
Restitution to former owners	Partial compensation	Very limited compensation	Yes (laws October 1990, February 1991)
Private ownership of land	Yes (June 1991)	Yes, since 1956	Yes (June 1991)
Small privatisation	Began in 1990	Began in 1989	Began in 1991 (law in Oct. 1990)
Large-scale privatisation	Began in Sept. 1990	Began in 1990	Law in February 1991
Main privatising institutions	State Property Agency (created in 1990); Hungarian State Holding Company (1992)	Ministry of Ownership Transformation (1990) usually called Ministry of Privatisation	Privatisation Ministries (Czech and Slovak) set up in 1990

Czech Republic (since 1 January 1993)	Slovakia (since 1 January 1993)	Bulgaria	Romania	Slovenia
See Czechoslovakia	See Czechoslovakia	Reformed Soviet model closely following Soviet changes (1965, 1979, 1987)	Specific centralised model (1967, 1979) deceptively called 'self-management'	Self-management Yugoslav style
Ultraradical reform continued	Previous policies with demagogy	'Shock therapy' concept; slow implementation	'Gradualism'	Erratic combination of 'gradualism' and radical reform
Restrictive monetary and fiscal policy	Restrictive monetary policy, budget balancing relaxed	Stringent monetary policy, not enough consistent fiscal policy	Lax credit policies, ineffective fiscal policy	Cautious and effective fiscal policy, tight monetary policy
Price controls covering about 5 per cent of GDP in 1993–4	Some prices (energy, rents) still controlled in 1993–4	February 1991; energy prices and rents still controlled in 1993–4	3 stages (Nov. 1990, April and July 1991). Controls reinstated in 1993	Gradual liberalisation since 1991
1991 law amended in line with EU regulations (1993)	1991 law amended in line with EU regulations (1993)	Law on the protection of competition (May 1991)	Law on unfair competition	Law on the protection of competition (1993)
See Czechoslovakia	See Czechoslovakia Law on restitution to churches (1993)	Yes (1991 – land, 1992 – other assets)	Limited (laws of 1991 and 1994)	Yes
See Czechoslovakia Completed in 1992 Second round in 1994	See Czechoslovakia Completed in 1993 Process stalled in 1993–4	Yes (1991 and 1992) Slow start in 1992 Law in 1992; voucher scheme in 1994	Yes (1991) Slow start in 1993 Begins in 1994	Yes Starts in 1993 Property Transformation Act (1992)
Czech Ministry of Privatisation, Fund of National Property	Slovak Ministry of Privatisation, National Property Fund	Privatisation Agency, State Fund for Reconstruction and Development	National Agency for Privatisation, (laws of 1990 and 1991), State Ownership Fund, Restructuring Agency (1994)	Agency of Privatisation, Development Fund

Table continued overleaf

Table 7.1 continued

Blocks of the transition	Hungary	Poland	Czechoslovakia (until 31 Dec 1992)
BANKING REFORM (creation of a double tier banking system)	Since 1987; banking laws end 1991	Since 1987–8	Since 1990; banking law, 1991
SETTING UP OF CAPITAL MARKETS (opening of a stock exchange)	Budapest Stock Exchange opened June 1990	Warsaw Stock Exchange opened April 1991	Prague and Bratislava Stock Exchanges opened in April 1993
SOCIAL PROTECTION SYSTEM			
Unemployment benefits (in per cent of average wages)	Yes (70% first year, 50% following year) reduced to 12 months in 1993	Yes (in % of the minimum wage)	Yes (65% of the wage during the 6 first months, 60% the following months)
Minimum wage	Yes	Yes (periodically revised)	Yes
Indexation of wages (on the price index)	Yes, in the state sector; since 1990 tripartite negotiation on a national level	Yes (coefficient 0,6 since May 1990)	Yes (indexation of the real wage)
OPENING UP THE ECONOMY			
Liberalisation of foreign trade (ending the state monopoly)	Complete in 1991	Complete in 1990	Complete in 1991
Single exchange rate	Since 1981	Since 1990	Since 1991
Internal convertibility	Since 1990 (de facto)	Since 1990	Since 1.1.1991
New laws on foreign investment	1989 amended in 1990	1988 amended in 1991	1988 law, amended 1992 Commercial code
Relations with international organisations:			
EEC (EU)	Association agr. (1991)	Association agr. (1991)	Association agr. (1991)
IMF	Membership in 1982	Membership in 1986	Membership in 1990
GATT	Membership in 1973	Membership in 1967	Founding member (1948)
External debt situation	Medium risk rating, no default	50% of the official debt has been forgiven by the Paris Club (April 1991)	Good rating

* Soviet model = reform based on some autonomy granted to state enterprises and on some market-type incentives, in the framework of a centralised planning system.

Czech Republic (since 1 January 1993)	Slovakia (since 1 January 1993)	Bulgaria	Romania	Slovenia
Czech National Bank + 25 commercial banks (not counting foreign banks)	Slovak National Bank + 17 commercial banks (1993)	Since 1987–90; banking laws 1991–2	Banking reform Dec. 1990, Banking laws April 1991	Banking independence October 1991, banking law Jan. 1993
Prague Stock Exchange (Apr. 93) RM Electronic trading system (periodic privatisation auctions)	Bratislava Stock Exchange (Apr. 93). RM-Slovakia trading system (periodic privatisation auctions)	Sofia Stock Exchange (Jan. 1992)	Bucharest Stock Exchange (1995)	Ljubljana Borza (1991)
Yes (reduced in 1993; max. duration 6 months)	Yes (reduced in 1993; max. duration 6 months)	Yes (for 12 months; about 60 per cent of average wage in 1992)	Yes (for 9 months)	Yes (max. duration 2 years)
Yes	Yes	Yes	Yes	Yes
Partial	Yes, partly	Yes, partly	Yes, partly (50 per cent)	Partial
Yes	Yes	Yes (1991)	Yes	Yes (1991)
Yes	Yes	Yes	in 1992	Yes (8 Oct. 1991)
Yes	Briefly suspended in 1993	Controlled	No	Yes
No	No	In 1991 (liberalised in 1992)	In 1990	Law of Oct. 1988 liberalised in 1993–4
Association agr. (Oct. 1993) Yes	Association agr. (Oct. 1993) Yes	Association agr. (March 1992) Yes (1990)	Association agr. (March 1992) Yes (1972)	Trade and coop. agre. (Nov. 1992) Yes (Jan. 1993)
Yes	Yes	No (observer status)	Yes (1971)	No
Good rating	Medium-risk country	High risk country Agreement with London Club (1994)	High-risk country	Good rating

Sources: General information on the reforms; the principle of the table and partly its construction are based on tables published in the *Economic Survey of Europe* in 1990–91 and in the following vols for 1991–92 and 1992–93 (Economic Commission for Europe, New York).

Box 7.1 *The reform plans devised for the USSR/Russia.*

A. The Soviet period (1987–91).

June 1987:   Blueprint of *perestroyka* (radical restructuring of economic management) adopted by the Communist Party.

November 1989:   Programme for transition to a mixed planned market economy (Academician and deputy prime minister Abalkin's programme).

May 1990:   Government programme to a regulated market economy (Prime minister Ryzhkov's programme).

August–September 1990:   Programme for a transition to a market economy (500-days programme), presented by a team working under the direction of Academician S. Shatalin.

April 1991:   Anti-crisis programme approved by the Supreme Soviet and presented by prime minister V. Pavlov.

June 1991:   Yavlinsky-Allison plan for transition to be implemented in five and a half years (G. Yavlisnky was one of the members of the Shatalin team; Graham Allison, a professor at Harvard University. Their plan was the basis of M. Gorbachev's discussions with the G-7 at the July 1991 Summit).

Abalkin Programme
Plan in three stages:
(a) 1990: stabilisation, legislation to be passed on market reform, first closures of non profitable enterprises.
(b) 1991–3: partial liberalisation of prices, development of markets.
(c) 1993–5: structural transformation, dismantling of monopolies, banking and financial reform, opening of the economy, partial convertibility of the ruble.

Shatalin Programme
Plan in 500 days:
(a) first 100 days (end-1990): stabilisation (reduction of budget deficit), beginning of denationalisation, unification of rate of exchange.
(b) 100–250 days: price liberalisation, strict financial controls.
(c) last 250 days: market stabilisation, privatisation, internal convertibility.
The Republics are offered an economic union with a single currency.

Yavlinsky Programme
Plan in 6½ years:
Very close to the Shatalin plan but proceeds immediately to price liberalisation, beginning of convertibility, tight fiscal policy, introducing of large-scale privatisation measures. Closely geared to foreign assistance.
Sequencing:
(a) mid-1991 to 1993: step-by-step stabilisation and price liberalisation; creation of legal and economic institutions of the market economy; privatisation;.
(b) 1994–7: structural adjustment.

B. The Russian reforms (1992–4)

The Gaidar–Yeltsin reform (January–February 1992 and later adjustments).

(a) *Building blocks*: Stabilisation Programme of 2 January 1992 and February 1992 Memorandum of Economic policy, prepared to win the approval of the IMF, actually granted in April 1992):

– Liberalising of prices as of 2 January 1992 (for 90 per cent of consumers' prices and 80 per cent of producers' prices). Prices of basic food items, medicines and rents remain controlled for the consumers, and energy prices for the producers.

– Liberalisation of domestic trade.

– Stringent monetary policy announced, based on high interest rates.

– Budget expenditures cuts (defence spending, subsidies).

– Minimum wage and pensions regulation; no incomes policy.

– VAT introduced first at a rate of 28 per cent, then lowered to 15 per cent.

– Privatisation programme to be started (decree of 29 December 1991).

- Single exchange rate to be introduced for the ruble at a fixed exchange rate, by April 1992. This rate would replace the official 'commercial rate', the various 'special' rates applied to the enterprises, and the interbank exchange market rate.
- Liberalising of foreign trade, except for energy carriers, the exports of which are to be regulated by quotas.
- Principle of close and liberalised economic relations between Russia and the former republics of the USSR.

(b) *Implementation in 1992–3*
- Implementation conducted first by a Gaidar-inspired government (Gaidar himself appointed prime minister in June 1992), then by the Chernomyrdin government, supported by the lobby of the 'industrialists', since December 1992.
- Political resistance to the complete freeing of prices and social pressure for wages increases (including minimum wages).
- Liberalisation of small-scale trade (street vending) completed though marred by racketeering and crime; large-scale retail trade and wholesale trade still monopolised.
- Lax monetary policy of the Central Russian Bank since mid-1992; negative real interest rates until end-1993.
- Budgetary targets not met; deficit rising from 1.5 per cent of GDP in first quarter to over 20 per cent by the end of 1992; substantial tax evasion.
- Multiple exchange rates until July 1992; then a unified rate is introduced but the enterprises still have to surrender part of their currency earnings at a special, less advantageous, rate; the single exchange rate is floating and grossly undervalued (average monthly wage expressed in US dollars is 8.9 in 1992).
- Limited trade liberalisation; discretionary licence system remains.
- Small privatisation conducted at a quick pace; large-scale privatisation beginning in October 1992 with a 'voucher' scheme. Land privatisation halted due to lack of a law on private property of land (the law is adopted only in October 1993).
- Monetary disintegration of the CIS area, and disruption of trade flows.

New Reform attempts and patching up of programmes (end-1993 to 1994)
- October 1993: Gaidar team back in power after Yeltsin's storming of the Parliament building; the building blocks of the 1992 programme are reassessed and tough monetary and budgetary polices are applied.
- December 1993: following the parliamentary elections and the defeat of the reformers, Gaidar and his team are pushed out of office; Chernomyrdin however continues the line of previous Gaidar monetary and budgetary policies.
- Monetary policy overshot, real interest rate reaches 8 per cent a month in April 1994.
- Budgetary policy fails target; ratio deficit/GNP exceeds 10 per cent during first quarter.
- July 1994; second phase of privatisation beginning.
- October 1994; some attempts at re-integration within the CIS; principle agreement reached at a CIS Summit to introduce a Payments Union and a Customs Union by 1997.
- 11 October 1994: the ruble depreciates by 27 per cent against the dollar; the government is reshuffled but the reform line is maintained.
- December 1994; the war against the Chechen Republic is declared; inflation regains momentum (the monthly rate reaches 16 per cent against 4.5 per cent in August) despite a sharp increase in the Central Bank interest rate; draft budget projects a deficit of 7.7 per cent of the GNP.

Sources: for the Soviet period, 'Stabilisation, Liberalisation and Devolution, Assessment of the Economic Situation and Reform Process in the Soviet Union', *European Economy*, no 45, December 1990; for the Russian reforms, press reports.

128

Table 7.2 The main instruments of the stabilisation programmes, 1990–4

Instruments	Hungary	Poland	CSFR (since 93: Czech Republic)	Bulgaria	Romania
Beginning of government programme	Various emergency programmes in 1990	1 January 1990	1 January 1991	1 February 1991	1 November 1990
Approved IMF stabilisation programme (date and duration)	20 February 1991 for 36 months superseded by arrangt of 15 Sept. 1993 (15 months)	5 February 1990 for 14 months then 18 April 91 superseded by arrgt of 8 March 1993 (12 months)	7 January 1991 for 14 months 17 March 1993 for 12 months	15 March 1991 17 April 1992 for 12 months each 21 March 1994 (12 months)	11 April 1991 for 12 months 11 May 1994 (for 19 months)
Degree of price liberalisation	90 per cent of prices free in 1991	90 per cent of prices freed on 1.1.90	85 per cent of prices freed on 1.1.91	70 per cent instantly freed; 84 per cent freed by mid-92.	80 per cent freed from Nov.90 to Nov.91
Exchange rate regime	Periodical devaluations; adjustable	Fixed, then crawling peg since Oct.1991; occasional devaluations	Fixed; stable since 1991	Managed float regime	April 1991: dual rate system (official fixed, interbank floating); Nov. 91: single rate floating
Initial devaluation (in per cent* of nominal rate)	January 1991 (plus 12.5)	January 1990 (plus 860 per cent over Aug. 89 rate)	January 1991 (plus 78.2 per cent over Aug. 90 rate)	February 1990 (plus 720 per cent over Jan. 91 rate)	November 1991 (plus 414 per cent over Oct. 90 rate)
Tax regime					
VAT**	Since Jan.88 (0; 6; 25); in 1993: 6; 10; 25; 1994: 10;15;20	Since July 93 0; 7; 22	Since Jan.93 0; 5; 23	Since April 1994 22	Since July 1993
Individual income tax**	0 to 40	20 to 45	5 to 47	0 to 40	6 to 45
Corporate income tax**	40	45	45	35	30 to 45

Real interest rate:					
Commitment	Rate > 0	Rate > 0	Rate > 0	Rate > 0	Rate > 0
Outcome	Rate slightly negative in 1991–3, then positive	Rate slightly positive in 1992 and in 1994	Rate slightly positive in 1991–3	Rate slightly negative in 1991–3	Rate continuously negative
Income policy	Wage bill tax to be applied on wage increases over a given rate; tripartite negotiations on nominal wage level; control system scrapped in 1993	Wage bill punitive progressive tax on excess wages in the state sector; relaxed in 1992; wage controls scrapped in 1994 and replaced with collective wage bargaining	Wage bill tax to be applied on wage increases over a given rate; tripartite negotiations on nominal wage levels; policy relaxed in 1992; controls reinstated in 1993	Wage bill tax to be applied on wage increases over a given rate; tripartite negotiations on wage levels; wage indexation and excess wage taxation lifted 92, reintroduced March 93	partial wage indexation
Anchors	Nominal: no Real: M	Nominal: W , f Real: M, i	Nominal: W , f Real: M , i	Nominal: W, M Real: no	No (implicitly: real W)

* Nominal rate expressed as an amount of national currency per unit of foreign currency.
** Rates expressed in per cent.
M = money supply; W = wages; f = exchange rate; i = interest rate

Notes: The table does not take into account the structural reform side of the programmes.
Sources: ECE, Economic Survey of Europe in 1992–1993; ECE, Economic Survey of Europe in 1993–1994; Bruno (1992); OECD country economic surveys; press reports.

The Achievements in the Monetary-Financial Field

The aims of the stabilisation programmes were to curb inflation, restore the fiscal balance and improve the external balance.

Inflation

In most of the countries *inflation* remains high. Czechoslovakia and, after the split, the Czech Republic displayed the best achievement with a steadily decreasing rate; however, the introduction of VAT in 1993 has led to a rebound of inflation, as in other countries that resorted to this measure (see Table 7.2). By 1994, the four Central European countries (Poland, Hungary, the Czech Republic and Slovakia), and Slovenia, had reached a stabilisation of the rate of inflation, with average annual rates ranging from 11 per cent (the Czech Republic) to 27 per cent (Poland) (see Appendix Table A.2 and Figure 7.1.) The Polish government symbolically expressed this stabilisation through a currency reform that came into force on January 1, 1995. A new zloty worth 10 000 times the old unit was issued, and at the same time a forecast of an inflation rate of 17 per cent for the year 1995 was made public.

Even in the countries which obtained the best results in fighting inflation, the annual rate remains over 20 per cent or close to it, except in the Czech Republic. All the other countries in transition display much higher rates, and may be classified into countries managing to keep this high inflation under control (Bulgaria), countries unable to reduce its rate (Romania) and countries that have moved into hyperinflation such as Russia and Ukraine.

Three questions have to be asked. Were the freed prices market-clearing prices? (In other words, is hidden inflation totally eliminated?) Why is inflation still so high? Were the policies wrong?

(1)   The sign of *effective market-clearing prices* has been the end of the shortages. In Poland, after the January 1990 big bang shortages disappeared almost overnight. The supply of the market improved significantly in Czechoslovakia and Hungary. Even when shortages still remained, as in Southern Eastern European countries and in the former CIS countries, the standard queues so representative of Soviet-type economies soon disappeared. Street vendors appeared everywhere, and so did Western imported consumer goods, be it at prices not affordable to the common citizen.

What is not quite clear is how these market-clearing prices were set. The standard explanation is that micro-economic actors behave like profit-maximising price-setters in a monopolistic structure of the market. We do not know of detailed studies on price fixing in transition. We presume that actual prices result from various influences. First of all, they are much more differentiated across each country than they used to be in the past, which expresses the emergence of fragmented local markets (except in the case when the former distribution channels are still in place and impose unified prices, or when these channels have been taken over by foreign retail

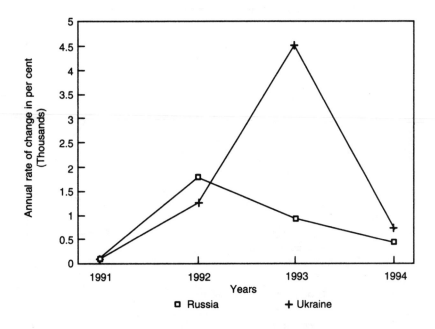

Figure 7.1(a) *Consumer prices, 1991–4: Russia, Ukraine (source: Table A.2(c))*

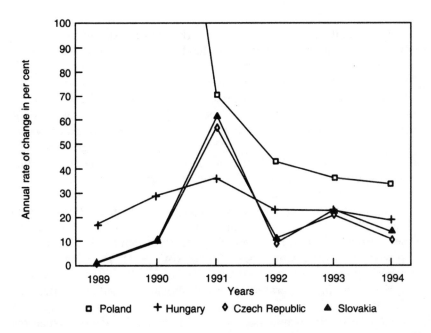

Figure 7.1(b) *Consumer prices, 1989–94: Central European countries (source: Table A.2(a))*

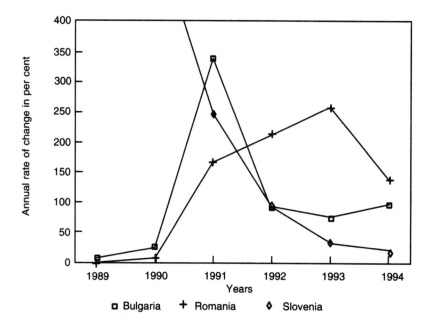

Figure 7.1(c) *Consumer prices, 1989–94: East South European countries (source: Table A.2(b))*

chains). Secondly, the black (or free) market prices existing prior to the transition influenced price-fixing in the beginning, before market-type adjustments were made when demand began to collapse after the wiping out of the monetary overhang in the household sector. Thirdly, due to the opening up of the economies the prices (absolute and relative) for foreign goods were fixed on the basis of the foreign prices, often with some 'overshooting', meaning that these goods soon became more expensive (in foreign currency terms) in the East than in the West. Foreign prices also influenced the levels and structure of the prices for tradable (exportable) goods. Finally, the price-makers (large industrial or retail enterprises) mostly set their own prices, exactly as they were doing when they were preparing their price proposals before approval by the planning or policy-making authorities in the past. Namely, they marked up their costs, adding to their current expenditures a percentage of profit more or less at random, up to what the market would bear (Menshikov, 1994). Typically, they did not adjust by trying to lower their costs, except for the few most successful enterprises. The price liberalisation shock did not immediately affect the inputs of the enterprises as the latter had large inventories (a standard feature of the former planned economies: see Winiecki, 1993b). When the inventories were slimmed down, adjustments in costs did not follow; the decrease in demand rather triggered a decrease in supply.

Price increases were not evenly distributed. When prices were freed, typically the food prices were the first to increase, due to the immediate curtailing of the large food subsidies. This precipitated a sudden increase in the share of food in the consumers' budgets, and a decline in overall demand which soon restored the market equilibrium. Next the prices for services increased, later and more gradually than food prices, because some public services were not deregulated immediately (e.g. rents, heating, public transport, etc.) (Szpringer, 1993). One has to remember that small privatisation began and expanded in the services sector, in areas where domestic prices had previously been totally preserved from foreign influence (such as personal services, catering). As prices were dramatically low in these areas, compared to world prices, there was a large margin for increase, which was successfully used by the 'new small entrepreneurs'. It was also, as Winiecki (1993b, p. 9) points out, very difficult to find equilibrium prices in this sector as the whole sector had been underdeveloped for so long, and as the suppliers had no experience of a market (short of what they might have learned in moonlighting, an activity very popular for many personal services). Thus sectoral inflation originating in the services sector may be longlasting, first because of the relative (to other sectors) growth of services, and second because of the initial indetermination of equilibrium prices in the field.

(2)   The continuation of *inflation* may thus be explained by structural factors. Other reasons have to be discussed.

On the *demand* side, inflationary pressure did not originate from the household sector. Monetary overhang in the household sector has everywhere been wiped out following the liberalising of prices, as has been seen. There was no wage-price spiral in most of the transition countries. Increases in nominal wages did not match price increases, due to income policies which were meant to sustain the monetary policy. It was expected, which proved right, that the under-development of the monetary system, and in particular the weak influence of monetary signals on state-owned enterprises, would require an additional 'anchor' in terms of nominal wages control. Such a control was ensured with the help of various instruments, such as a weak indexation of wages on price increases, taxes on excess wages, and contractual negotiation procedures among the government, the enterprises and the representatives of the workers (see Tables 7.1 and 7.2).

Indexation of nominal wages, be it weak, and the existence of contractual procedures certainly fuel inflationary anticipations. But some alleviation of the hardships of transition had to be promised to the masses. It may well be argued that instead of using the nominal wage level as an anchor, one should use the lowest *real* wage compatible with the macro-economic adjustment, and index the initial nominal value of this wage at the new prices, with a higher rate of protection (Nuti, 1991, p. 163). Using the nominal wage anchor even with a weak indexation may create self-sustaining inflation; if the rate of inflation is greater than expected when fixing the nominal target, it may lead (as was the case in Poland in 1990) to a drastic, unwanted drop in real incomes.

Supply-side factors explain the continuation of inflation even in countries which have been the most successful at containing it. The first one is the increase in *material costs*, in particular of energy. This increase was due to two factors: the loss of cheap energy supplies after the collapse of the CMEA and of the USSR, followed by the selling of energy – Russian oil and gas – at world market prices; the liberalising, be it belated, of domestic energy prices. Other material costs also increased, especially for imported inputs following the devaluations of the national currencies. The monopolistic behaviour of the state-owned enterprises certainly pushes prices up, not as a result of a market-type profit maximisation behaviour, but rather because these enterprises seek to maintain employment and to keep the movement of nominal wages as close as possible to the movement of prices. They have to comply with the above-mentioned income policies; they try to avoid lay-offs and hence they resort to part-time work and wages solutions.

(3)   In the view of the reformers and of their foreign advisers, the dominant explanation for inflation is the *excessive money supply*. This is why most of the countries declared themselves committed to a policy of positive real interest rates, which in several stabilisation packages constituted the main anchor of the stabilisation policy (as in Poland and Czechoslovakia), along with a money supply target (Table 7.2). During the first years of transition (1990–2), in most cases the interest rates remained negative, and at best fluctuated between − 3 per cent and + 1 per cent monthly in 1991 and 1992 (ECE/UN, 1993, p. 140); in 1993 they became positive in Central European countries, where inflation was under control, and negative elsewhere. Such a trend may certainly strengthen the monetarist views. Positive interest rates were indeed a major component of the targets negotiated with the IMF by Bulgaria and Romania in 1994 (stand-by agreements were reached with Bulgaria in April, and with Romania in May 1994). However, one may question the impact of high interest rates on inflation. Calvo (1991) shows that high interest rates may generate generalised bankruptcy which in turn brings back inflation. Also, high interest rates induce the main borrowers (the state-owned enterprises) to seek non-bank money, i.e. to increase inter-enterprise debts. When the latter reach a very high level the government is induced to inject money in the enterprise sector, and inflation soars again, which is what happened in Russia. Finally, interest rates are costs, that are passed on prices by monopolistic enterprises, and hence turn into factors of cost-push inflation.

Interest rate policy was usually combined with direct control of the money supply (through high obligatory reserve requirements ratios, and credit limits).

What about the causes of hyperinflation? The relaxation of the monetary policy is one explanation of hyperinflation in Russia, where the Central Bank in 1992 and in 1993 expanded loans to the enterprises so as to fight the accumulation of inter-enterprise credits, themselves very inflationary. To combat inflation, following the elections of December 1993 and despite the electoral defeat of the reformers (see Box 7.1), the Chernomyrdin government embarked on an extremely restrictive monetary policy, in order to get the approval of the IMF and unleash a tranche of a Systemic Transformation Facility (the new outfit created for countries in transition in April 1993), amounting to $1.5 billion, that had been withheld since September 1993, and which was released in March 1994. The commitment to the IMF included a rate of inflation of 7–8 per cent a month by the end of 1994, down from an average 20 per cent in 1993. Already in February–April 1994 inflation had come down to 8–9 per cent per month (dropping to 4.5 per cent in August). The *real* interest rate of the Central Bank was in April 1994 about 8 per cent monthly, an unheard-of magnitude in any country. It contributed to a drop in output which was of over 25 per cent in four months (January–April) as compared to the same period in 1993 (Nuti, 1994c). By the end of 1994 Russia had moved out of hyperinflation though the monthly rate of increase in consumer prices reached 16 per cent in December. It had survived a foreign exchange crisis in October, and vacillation in interest rate policy. But the Russian government had not yet been able to convince the IMF that it had suppressed another source of inflation, i.e. a lax fiscal policy.

Budgetary balance

Indeed a tight fiscal policy has been the second most important component of stabilisation packages. It is linked with monetary policy, since the main source of financing budget deficits is money creation. (See Figure 7.2.)

Mixed results have been obtained in the field of *budget deficits*. In general, fiscal imbalances tended to increase, for various reasons that reinforced themselves:

- The drop in output reduced budget revenues while increasing the need for social expenditures.
- Once the subsidies and the investment programmes were cut it was difficult to find additional ways of reducing expenditures; in the countries most plagued by deficits and in particular in the former CIS countries one little commendable way was to momentarily stop paying civil servants.
- Tax evasion, which already plagued the former system, grew and was increasingly difficult to track due to the inadequacy of the tax structure

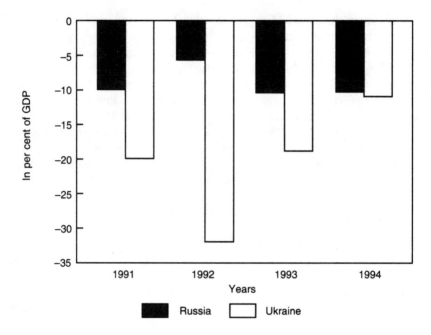

Figure 7.2(a)   *Budget deficit, 1991–4: Russia, Ukraine (source: Table A.2(c))*

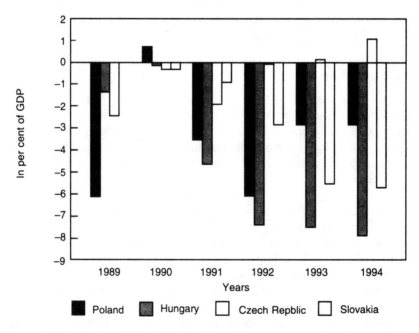

Figure 7.2(b)   *Budget deficit, 1989–94: Central European countries (source: Table A.2(a))*

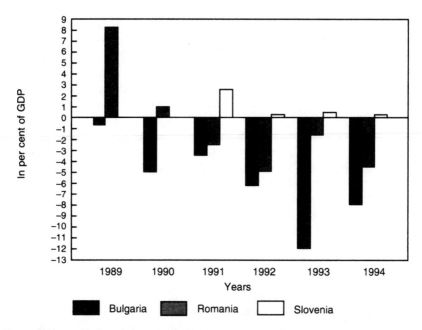

Figure 7.2(c) *Budget deficit, 1989–94: East South European countries (source: Table A.2(b))*

and instruments (this is the main reason why VAT was introduced in many countries – a measure that also fuelled inflation, in the form of one-time monthly outbursts). In Poland, the president himself confronted the Parliament in opposing the payment of income taxes in January 1995, arguing that the rates were too high.

Fine-tuning was very difficult to achieve, even in the countries displaying the best results. For instance, in mid–1991 the Czechoslovak government realised that the budget was showing a surplus much larger than the initial commitments, and had to increase government expenditures (a not quite sound move according to the IMF, as 'the budget surpluses reflected, in part, an artificial increase in enterprise profits stemming from inventory revaluations' (IMF, 1992, p. 66); as a result the deficit grew again. However, Czechoslovakia is the country which has managed to keep its budget deficit best under control. In Poland and Hungary the share of the deficit in the GNP exceeded in 1992 the ceiling target agreed with the IMF, for various reasons. One of them was the necessity of maintaining or developing social security financing, under the pressure of public opinion. The other important reason lies in the deterioration of enterprise performance and the tax evasion behaviour of the enterprises. As a result, both countries were unable to meet the conditionality requirements of the IMF. The subsequent agreements reached in 1993 with the IMF for both of these countries exemplify the dilemma of the policy-makers. Either the latter comply with the ceiling admitted by the IMF for the deficit/GDP ratio and are able to secure not only IMF financing but other credits from the international financial markets, in which case, however, the policy-makers are then confronted with an opposition which demands more public expenditures, especially in the social field. Or the policy-makers bow to the opposition, especially when elections are near, and lose international financing and credibility. The same dilemmas were faced in 1994 by Romania and Bulgaria.

As just noted, the way fiscal deficits were financed helped to sustain inflation. External finance was out of the question in most cases because of the existing indebtedness and the lack of credibility of the countries, and only Czechoslovakia seems to have occasionally resorted to this method. Non-monetary financing (i.e. borrowing on domestic financial markets, by issuing government securities) was also usually impossible due to the lack of development of the financial markets. In the countries which were able to do so (Hungary, Poland, to a lesser extent Bulgaria, and Russia in 1994) this had as a side-effect the reduction of credits available to the enterprises, because government bonds were preferred as less risky and more liquid than credits to the economy. Thus the main method of covering the budget deficit was borrowing from the Central Banks, which mechanically increased the money supply.

External stabilisation

In Eastern and Central Europe and even in Russia, the *external balance* situation improved significantly in the first years (1990–2) of the transition. In all countries exports to the West (and especially to Western Europe) steadily increased. This expressed both a reorientation of exports formerly directed to the CMEA region and particularly to the former Soviet Union, which collapsed in 1990–2, and the effect of the strong devaluation of the domestic currencies. The trade balances as well as the current account balances generally improved. But since 1993 an opposite trend is showing in some countries, as may be seen from Appendix Table A.2.

To understand these trends, one has to look at the exchange rate regime, at the reorientation of exports, and at the level of international indebtedness.

(1) The results of 1990–2 have been achieved through an *over-devaluation of the domestic currencies*. The promotion of exports may still require a continuing devaluation of the currency. This is why only a few countries have opted for a fixed rate regime (Poland between January 1990 and October 1991; Czechoslovakia; Estonia). A fixed exchange rate provides a nominal 'anchor' to the stabilisation programme and hence helps to curb inflation. It is essential that the stability of the new exchange rate be

credible. Otherwise people will expect repeated devaluations and this will provoke inflationary expectations as well. Thus the initial devaluation must be large enough to be credible, and subsequent inflation must remain contained so as to avoid an over-appreciation of the currency which would require a new devaluation. But then the initial devaluation may deter necessary imports, and induce wasteful exports (for instance, though Czechoslovakia certainly benefited from currency inflows associated with the tourist boom in 1991, it made domestic goods and services available to foreign citizens at unnecessary low prices). Calculations (see Table 7.3) show that the East European devaluations put the rate of exchange (expressed in units of domestic currency required to buy a unit of foreign currency) much below the purchasing power parity. This is also exemplified by the comparison of dollar wages in the countries in transition and in some developing countries. In 1990, the average dollar wage in Hungary and Poland was well below the average dollar wage in Paraguay or Thailand (Asselain, 1994, p. 837).

If inflation is nevertheless high, the currency soon becomes overvalued, which happened in Poland in 1991. The fixed exchange rate is no longer sustainable as the country suffers losses in competitiveness. Floating rates allow the balancing of demand and supply of the domestic/foreign currencies but induce sharp fluctuations of the nominal rate and feed inflationary expectations. They deter foreign investments, as prospective investors fear instability, unless a very predictable monetary and fiscal policy is conducted. However, this regime has been used in Russia, Bulgaria and Romania. The middle way is the crawling-peg regime (which was introduced in Poland in October 1991, while Hungary has a slightly different adjustable rate regime).

Are the currencies of the countries in transition overvalued or undervalued? All of them have been initially undervalued; yet most have appreciated in real terms, even the Russian ruble, as the rate of domestic inflation has been higher than the nominal rate of depreciation of the currency (Table 7.3 and Figure 7.3). Obviously it is very difficult to determine the equilibrium exchange rate here, not only because convertibility is not complete. Even if we had full convertibility, including that for capital transactions (a stage reached only in the Czech Republic in 1995), the underdevelopment of the capital market itself would lead to wrong signals. The standard models explaining how long-term rates of exchange are determined by the fundamentals are already unsatisfactory in the case of developed economies with sophisticated capital and monetary markets and a long experience in openness. We would suggest that in the conditions of the transition, a gradual narrowing of the gap between the current exchange rates and the purchasing power parities of the domestic currencies – without losses in competitiveness – would be a sign of a successful stabilisation-cum-transformation (Asselain, 1994).

Table 7.3 *Exchange rates, purchasing power parities and dollar wages in some countries in transition, 1991–1994*

	1990	1991	1992	1993	1994 (projection)
Poland					
Real ER (CPI-based), zl/$US 1989 = 100	101.4	69.1	674.2	64.9	63.7
PPP, zloty per $US	3165.4	5218.5	7168.5	9375.8	11833.5
Nominal ER, zloty per $US	9500.0	10576.1	13631.0	18145.0	22500.0
Ratio of official to PPR ER	3.0	2.0	1.9	1.9	1.9
Average monthly wage in $US	108.4	166	178.9	179.8	188.5
Real wage index (1989 = 100)	75.6	75.4	73.3	72.5	73.9
Hungary					
Real ER (CPI-based), ft/$US 1989 = 100	87.5	79.9	70.7	69.2	70.1
PPP, forint per $US	29.8	38.9	46.1	55.4	64.5
Nominal ER, forint per $US	63.2	74.8	79	92	110.4
Ratio of official to PPP ER	2.1	1.9	1.7	1.7	1.7
Average monthly wage in $US	212.7	240	282.2	295.4	301.5
Real wage index (1989 = 100)	96.3	88.6	87.4	84.1	100.0
Czech Republic					
Real ER (CPI-based), kc/$US 1989 = 100	119.7	120.5	108.2	103.8	100.0
PPP, koruny per $US	6.2	9.5	10.1	11.8	12.7
Nominal ER, koruny per $US	17.9	29.5	28.3	29.2	30.0
Ratio of official PPP ER	2.9	3.1	2.8	2.5	2.4
Average monthly wage in $US	188.4	136.4	164.0	204.5	226.7
Real wage index (1989 = 100)	94.2	71.9	79.3	82.3	85.0
Russia					
Real ER (CPI-based), R/$US 1989 = 100	92.9	149.8	1340.9	776.5	495.5
PPP, rubles per $US	0.61	1.33	21.88	217.0	850.0
Nominal ER, rubles per $US	0.58	1.74	170.7	928.3	2600
Ratio of official to PPP ER	0.9	1.3	7.8	4.3	3.1
Average monthly wage in $US	517.9	329.9	37.4	69.1	108.7
Real wage index (1989 = 100)	109	105.1	97.9	94.5	89.8

Notes: ER = exchange rate; PPP = purchasing power parity; CPI = consumer prices index.

Sources: *PlanEcon Report*, various country issues, 1994.

(2)   The improvements in current account balances achieved along with a *reorientation of trade* toward the West have been due to 'distress exports' of any commodity available toward the West, and facilitated by the agreements with the EC which liberalised trade for a large range of commodities. However the Europe agreements, which in 1993 involved six countries in Eastern and Central Europe (see Chapter 9, Table 9.3), do not concern sensitive exports such as agricultural goods, steel products, textiles; they do concern chemicals but with safeguard clauses. At the end of 1992 the European community imposed anti-dumping taxes on Eastern European steel exports. The mounting public concern in the West about the low-price imports from the East may endanger the growth of Central and Eastern European exports in the future, as the structure of trade has barely changed since the beginning of the transition, and as 'sensitive goods' represent over 50 per cent of total exports to the West. This is why the issues of the European Union's policy toward its associates are so crucial (see Chapter 9).

(3)   In most countries, the level of the *foreign debt* is a serious constraint. It is still very high in Hungary despite a decrease in the total amount and in the debt servicing ratio. With the exception of that country and of Czechoslovakia, net indebtedness rose in all countries. Poland obtained a 50 per cent reduction of its $33 billion official debt to governments in April 1991, in an arrangement with the Paris Club, to be implemented in two phases. A similar arrangement with the commercial banks (London Club) has been deadlocked by the inability of Poland to reach a final agreement with the IMF in 1992, and by the stopping of interest payments since Autumn 1989. In March 1994 a deal was reached with the London Club, by which the creditors agreed to slash the $13 billion commercial debt by 42.5 per cent. Another Eastern European country, Bulgaria, succeeded in signing a debt accord with its Paris Club creditors in April 1994 for the deferring of a $1.5 million official debt over 11 years, and with its London Club creditors in May 1994, providing for a 47.1 per cent reduction in the $8 billion commercial debt, which it had stopped servicing in 1989. Finally Russia, acting as the successor of the Soviet Union as regards commercial and official debt, obtained a rescheduling of $15 billion of its debt to the Western governments in April 1993, followed by another rescheduling agreement in June 1994. With commercial banks, Russia has negotiated several deferrals, but could not reach a comprehensive agreement until end 1994 because of its refusal to drop its 'sovereign immunity', that is to give its creditors unlimited claim over all state-owned assets as a guarantee for debt repayment.

Why is the debt status such a constraint for macro-economic stabilisation? This is because of the IMF role in the process. Macro-economic stabilisation packages were all agreed with the IMF even when they expressed the strategies and commitments of the national governments. Their implementation required international assistance or relief. In turn,

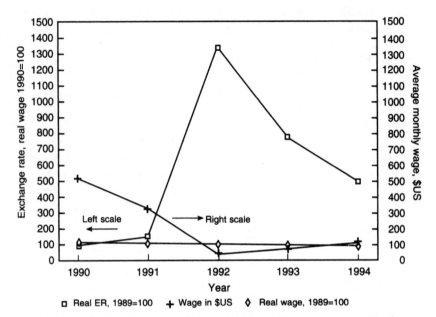

Figure 7.3(a)   *Real exchange rate index, real wage index, average monthly wage in $US, 1990–4: Russia*

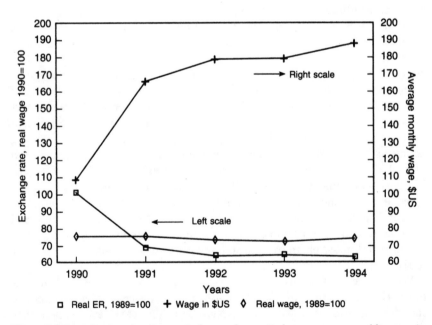

Figure 7.3(b)   *Real exchange rate index, real wage index, average monthly wage in $US, 1990–4: Poland*

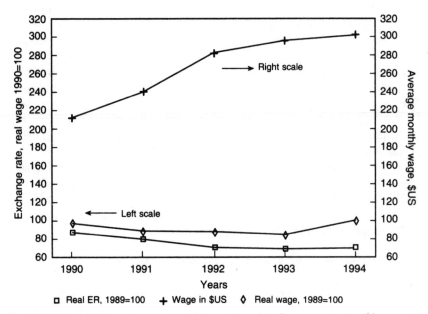

Figure 7.3(c) *Real exchange rate index, real wage index, average monthly wage in $US, 1990–4: Hungary*

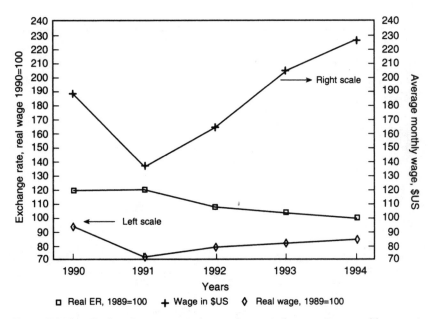

Figure 7.3(d) *Real exchange rate index, real wage index, average monthly wage in $US, 1990–4: Czech Republic*

international assistance in the form of debt rescheduling was granted by banks or governments only following the seal of approval of the IMF on domestic programmes. While these programmes were always quite stringent when drafted, their fiscal commitments were often reversed in budgetary votes by the legislative assemblies, leading to higher deficits than had been decided by the governments, mainly so as to increase social expenditures. The approval of the IMF was then withdrawn – and along with it prospects for debt agreements – until a new budget could be hammered out. In Russia, for instance, the 1994 budget was finally approved with a 9.6 per cent deficit (in relation to the GDP), which was below the IMF-set limit of 10 per cent.

Let us now turn to the real indicators. While the monetary and financial trends have been disappointing, though some successes have been achieved, real indicators have displayed a much gloomier picture. The deflationary policies conducted had the expected result of bringing about a recession, that was, however, unexpected in its magnitude.

The Achievements in the Real Field: The Fall in Output

By the end of 1992, three years after the beginning of transformation, output was still falling everywhere; a turnaround was visible only in Poland. Two years later the recovery was there, but limited and fragile (see Figure 7.4; also Statistical Appendix, Table A.2); and the pre-transition GDP levels were nowhere regained.

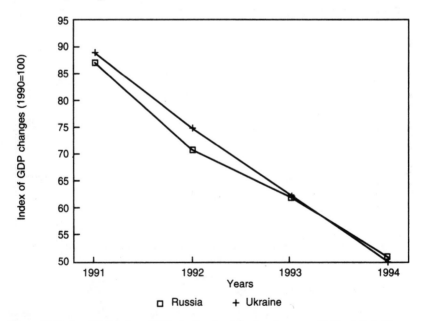

Figure 7.4(a) *GDP index, 1991–4: Russia, Ukraine (source: Table A.2 (c))*

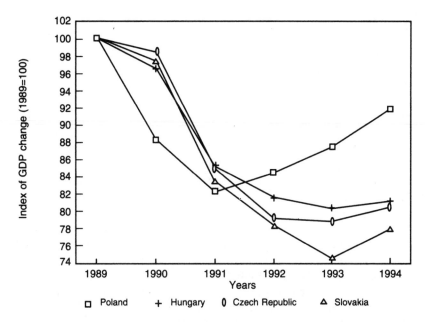

Figure 7.4(b) *GDP index, 1989–94: Central European countries (source: Table A.2 (a))*

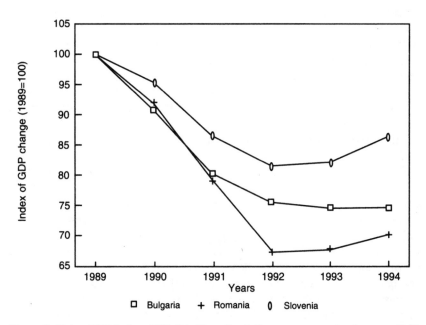

Figure 7.4(c) *GDP index, 1989–94: East South European countries (source: Table A.2 (b))*

The trends

Did something go wrong? Most experts and policy-makers acknowledged that they were baffled or disappointed with the outcomes, especially with the sharp decline in output. Does this mean that what has happened is not what should have happened? Let us quote the 1992 *World Economic Outlook* published by the IMF: 'In some Eastern European countries there were substantial budget and current account surpluses in the early stages of the reform programmes, which might, ex post, suggest that macro-economic policies could have been less restrictive' (IMF, 1992, p. 66).

The decline in GNP for the countries reviewed in Statistical Appendix , Table A.2 is of about 20 per cent for the years 1990–2 in the best cases. Figures also show a dramatic fall in investment. The downtrend in consumption was brought about by the decrease in real wages. Hungary was the only country which managed to keep its real wages more or less stable in 1990–2, an achievement which has been seen as an asset in terms of political and social stability (ECE/UN, 1993, pp. 3–38) or conversely as a weakness in terms of competitiveness (PlanEcon, April 1993).

Unemployment was not extremely high (by Western standards) even end–1993, taking into account the slump in production (see Figures 7.5 and 7.6; also Statistical Appendix , Table A.3.). This is not a positive trend; it shows that the enterprises do not adjust to recession by cutting their work force, but rather by maintaining some activity albeit at a reduced pace and with a low productivity. It also shows that despite the bankruptcy legislation in force, the governments are reluctant to provoke a large wave of bankruptcies, for political reasons. In a situation when a satisfactory social safety net cannot be put in place because of budgetary constraints, the easiest way for the governments to cushion the effects of the austerity policy is to refrain from closing large state enterprises and to implicitly endorse their social protection functions, inherited from the old regime. (For a general discussion of unemployment in transition, see Boeri, 1994; OECD, 1993b and 1994a).

However, even admitting that the completion of structural adjustment needs yet more lay-offs, it is paradoxical that while the whole developed world is searching for ways of reducing unemployment, the countries in transition are the only areas in the world where unemployment is almost looked upon as a blessing by Western, and often domestic experts (the World Bank Newsletter *Transition* asked the question in a dramatic form in a front-page title (December 1993): 'Unemployment in Eastern Europe: Social Disease or Economic Necessity?'). What is the bottom-out level of unemployment? Once it is reached, how can an acceptable rate of unemployment be restored (not accelerating inflation and allowing for growth)? Why should market forces be expected to solve the problem in these countries when they do not in the developed world?

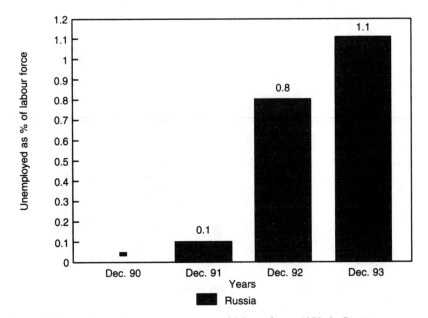

Figure 7.5(a)   *Unemployment as per cent of labour force, 1990–3: Russia*

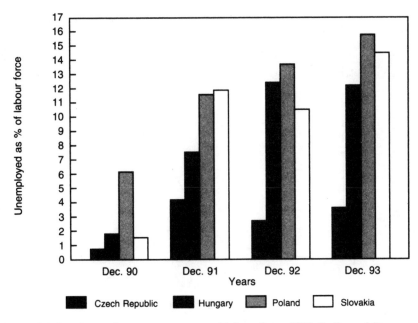

Figure 7.5(b)   *Unemployment as per cent of labour force, 1990–3: Central European countries*

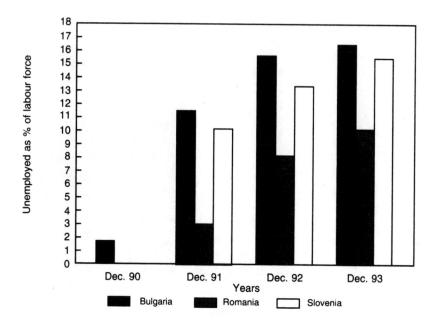

Figure 7.5(c)   *Unemployment as per cent of labour force, 1990–3: East South European countries*

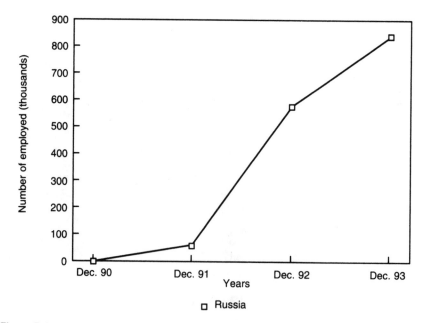

Figure 7.6(a)   *Number of unemployed, 1990–3: Russia*

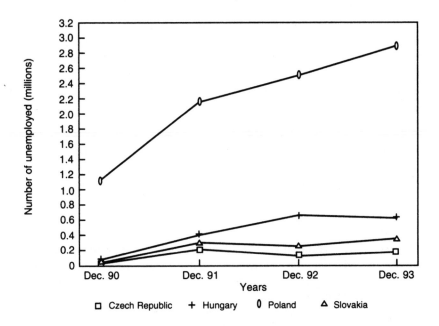

Figure 7.6(b)   *Number of unemployed, 1990–3: Central European countries*

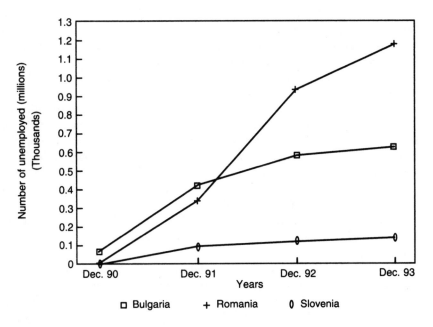

Figure 7.6(c)   *Number of unemployed, 1990–3: East South European countries*

The real growth issue is tackled in similar terms. Resumption of a growth path is largely seen as automatic once the bottom has been reached. What is a subject of worry is the large decline observed. It is very disturbing to the experts who advised the Central European governments, and to the international institutions which made their assistance conditional on the meeting of stabilisation targets – not to mention the main actors involved, i.e. the governments and their people.

Soon a large debate erupted among experts, (see Bruno, 1992; Girard, 1992; Kolodko, 1993a; Köves, 1992a; Nuti, 1993; Portes, 1992b; Williamson, 1992b; among others). We borrow from Nuti, (1993) a classification of the reactions into three groups: incredulity, complacency, 'gradualism'.

Nothing went wrong

The 'incredulity' reaction is the following: true, the situation is bad, but this is only an illusion. The recession mainly means that a large share of production, now rapidly declining, was formerly produced without any demand just to meet the requirements of the plan, according to Kornai's scheme of a resource-constrained economy (Kornai, 1980). Not only is this decline explainable now that market reactions begin to appear, but in addition it is useful because such activities in fact generated a negative value-added (see McKinnon, 1991b; Hughes and Hare, 1991). Moreover, as statistical recording is inaccurate for the new private sector, the output of this sector is grossly undervalued, and the actual reduction in output might turn out to be much less than the official figures show. Thus, the architect of the stabilisation programme in Poland, Leszek Balcerowicz, argues that once the correction is made Polish GDP appears to have declined not by 18 per cent as official statistics show but by 5–10 per cent (Balcerowicz, 1994). This is a double-edged argument. True, on the one hand, the contribution of the private sector may well be under-recorded, especially in the field of services for which the statistical offices have very little experience. On the other hand, 'negative value-added' production is still manufactured in many state-owned enterprises, with a still lower productivity than in the past. Logically, if it is argued that the removal of negative value-added production means an addition to the GNP, then one should admit that its continuation means that the recorded GNP is above its actual level. Unfortunately none of the two sides of the argument can be proved with the statistical tools available.

The same incredulity reaction also relates to other real indicators. For instance, the fall in real wages as an outcome of deflationary policies has been questioned. It has been said that the computing of an index of real wages as the nominal wage index deflated by the consumers' price index did not yield an accurate picture because it did not take into account the variety of consumption patterns. Secondly and more important, a statistical real wage index does not take into account qualitative factors such as the reduction of the time spent in queues, which amounts to an increase in welfare (ECE/UN 1994b, p. 79; for Russia, Koen and Phillips, 1993). Finally, to compare real wages before and after the stabilisation shock is faulty, the same line of argument runs, because real wages were artificially high due to an artificially low consumer price index deflator (because prices were administered and because inflation was hidden).

Some of these considerations have to be retained, but certainly not to the point of denying the very decline in real wages. Those authors who call up housewives in support of their argument should remember that while it is certainly frustrating to stand in queues, it is frustrating as well not to be able to go out shopping because your purse is empty. In the first stage of the transition real wages did fall, perhaps to a lesser extent than shown by the figures. They display a similar trend to that of output. In the countries which are bottoming out, real wages stop declining or start rising (see Statistical Appendix, Table A.2) while in the countries that did not succeed in stabilising their economy and resuming growth, real wages go on deteriorating. Is this because wage earners more successfully resist wage cuts when the economy looks healthier, or because the growth in output, itself the result of productivity gains, allows for some wage increases? It is hard to tell.

Output had to fall, if not that deeply

The 'complacency' attitude means that the situation is bad, but should be so. This is by far the most common attitude. Not surprisingly: most of the actors have a vested interest in arguing that things are normal. This is the case of the policy-makers, but also of the advisers and experts.

(1) The *policy-makers* are prone to use external shocks as scapegoats. In 1991 the 'external shock' argument was predominantly quoted. The aftermath of the Gulf war which temporarily increased the price of oil, the collapse of trade with the USSR linked with the fall of Comecon, and the disintegration of the USSR itself, were supposed to be largely responsible for the recession. However, the price of oil did not remain high for long; and most of the enterprises (especially in heavy industry) which traded predominantly with the USSR were not closed – or we would have witnessed many more bankruptcies. Most of the experts also supported this argument however. It was only in 1993 that some of them began to question it (see Bofinger, 1993, challenging the conclusions of Bruno, 1992, and Rodrik, 1992).

The external shock undoubtedly mattered, though probably not to a high degree. The supporters of this view were logically induced to recommend some arrangement among Central and East European countries and among them and the USSR, a suggestion very much opposed by the policy-makers in the region (see Chapter 9). In 1992, a new external shock hit the Balkan countries, which were affected by the Western embargo on the FR of Yugoslavia: Bulgaria, Romania, Slovenia could rightly claim that it contributed to the output decline.

(2)   Western economists have usually stressed that stabilisation policies should have a deflationary effect on *domestic absorption* 'even in well-functioning market economies' (IMF, 1992, p. 67). Then the problem is mainly not to implement an excessively deflationary policy (Williamson, 1992b; Brada and King, 1992). The two most debated issues in this respect have been the initial extent of the *devaluation* (Asselain, 1994), and the 'credit crunch' (Calvo and Coricelli, 1992, and 1994 on the second topic). Initial *over-devaluations* (such as in Poland or Czechoslovakia, which were based on the rate of the black market) brought the real wages down to an excessively low level, and fuelled imported inflation which had then to be fought with still more restrictive policies. The *credit crunch* achieved through high interest rates did not hit the state-owned enterprises and mostly fuelled the growth of inter-enterprise indebtedness; it did hit the nascent private sector and the small enterprises, as well as the agricultural sector, and hampered their development.

Excessive *liberalisation* has also been criticised: in particular, domestic markets have been opened too early and too strongly, and a protective policy should be in order, perhaps in the form of import surcharges as new tariffs might be difficult to reimpose in light of the agreements with the EC (Nuti and Portes, 1993, p. 15).

When the *supply side* is considered, we have the 'J-curve effect': as in the case of a devaluation, the introduction of a stabilisation programme brings about a reduction in supply not just as an effect of the demand shock, but because of rigidities in the supply response. This is linked by Gomulka (1991) with a Schumpeterian-like process of 'creative destruction': resources allocated to unproductive uses in the past are no longer used, and thus become available for future, more productive uses, once the economy fully responds to the market signals: then there will be an upward movement along the right side of the 'J'.

Unfortunately what we observe is, rather, an L-curve, with a protracted though decelerating recession. We are then back to a theory based on the excesses of stabilisation which decrease demand (Brada and King, 1992), or to stressing the rigidities in the supply, which are inherited from the past (Linotte, 1992) or due to the slowness of structural reforms (Bofinger, 1993).

It is remarkable that in all these analyses, the return to a growth path is not discussed. Of course a Keynesian type of macro-economic policy is out of the question, as it would contradict the essence of the deflationist packages applied. As summed up by Stanislaw Gomulka (1994, p. 100): according to these theses, 'the [post-transition] recessions are created on the demand side, but must be solved on the supply side'. This dominant view has been criticised by Alec Nove as a 'gap' in transition models. The standard model assumes that investment will generate growth as soon as free market forces are able to operate fully in a stabilised context. But 'investment in what, financed how, by whom?' (Nove, 1994, p. 865). How should the state be involved? These are indeed questions left open, and we shall return to them in the next chapter. Meanwhile, the general attitude is to rejoice every time growth begins to resume, disregarding the fact that even in the best cases it might take several years just to return to the level reached before the beginning of the transition.

There were alternatives

The 'gradualistic' argument tends to support an alternative policy opposed to the shock therapy concept. The obvious case is Hungary, which explains why the 'gradualists' are frequently Hungarian authors (Köves, 1992a; Ábel and Bonin, 1992; Szamuely, 1993). Gradualistic views may be expressed in 'big bang' countries by authors who do not share their government's views (Vintrová, 1993, for the Czech Republic), or who caution against over-optimism (Minassian, 1994, for Bulgaria). The problem with gradualism is that it gets its supporters nowhere. 'Gradualism' is a vague concept, tainted with politics (suggesting that its advocates are close to die-hard commu-nists), and totally lacks credibility. In addition, either nobody is gradualist, or everybody is. To focus on the Hungarian case, Hungary applied the same package of stabilisation as the other countries, except of course it did not have to do overnight what had already been done, such as liberalising trade and prices. One might certainly argue that Hungary had a more lax fiscal policy than Czechoslovakia, but not more than Poland, with identical problems facing the Hungarian and Polish governments, i.e. weak political support and the growing fatigue of the population, which emerged into protests on social protection issues.

The gradualistic line of thought usually stresses two arguments. The first is obviously that shock therapy cannot apply to structural reforms: one cannot privatise overnight, even in the most radical give-away schemes; one cannot reform the banking system overnight. The second is that the beneficial outcomes attributed to shock therapy might have been obtained at a lesser social cost. Both arguments are rejected by the 'shock therapists'. Structural transformation does require time, they admit, but its efficiency is enhanced by a quickly conducted stabilisation. Nobody can tell whether the social costs of transformation would have been lower under an alternative policy, and in any case these costs may be alleviated by proper compensation schemes.

The stabilisation packages experienced until now have all been very similar. The only significant difference among them has been the political resolve of their implementation. The extreme case is Ukraine where the reforms packages never really took off the ground.

There is another good reason for why there were no alternative solutions. The model that has inspired the transition process is the IMF–World Bank structural adjustment package (dubbed the 'Washington consensus'; see John Williamson, 1994). It has to be followed not just because it commands the conditionality of the Fund and the Bank and hence the support of the governments of developed countries and of international business. It is credible because it works, or rather because nothing else has been convincing enough in the long run. The strength of the model finally lies in its simplicity and short-term aims. All the long-term issues are left open, including the methods and outcome of structural transformation and the role to be attributed to the post-transition state, as an alternative not to shock therapy, but to an excessive faith in market forces for ensuring structural transformation and sustainable growth. The main problem is thus to overcome what has been called the supply inertia (Nuti, 1993) through greater progress of the structural reform.

8 Privatisation and Structural Reforms

Structural transformation is supposed to begin at the same time as the 'stabilisation-cum-liberalisation' programmes. Its main building block is privatisation, which means creating a greenfield private sector, and changing formerly state-owned enterprises into privately owned ones. Privatisation may also mean making existing state enterprises, either earmarked for further privatisation or remaining in state property, work as commercial enterprises; however, in Central East European countries this process is, rather, called marketisation. Reforms of the banking and tax system, and creation of capital markets, are also among the first priorities of the policy-makers and advisers. Though most of the advisers also advocate the creation of a social safety net, which is meant to replace the former state 'paternalism', this is often seen as a 'luxury' in the East, as well as the safeguard of the environment. Developing an industrial policy meant to organise an orderly dismantling of obsolete branches while providing for the growth of new sectors is very low on the scale of priorities as it is generally identified with nostalgia for the old system.

This chapter will deal first with the privatisation policies, then with the other first-priority targets of the structural transformation. The last section will explore the neglected if not suspicious areas of state intervention, in the form of welfare or industrial policies.

PRIVATISATION

The concepts and practice of privatisation turned out to be much more complex than was thought in the beginning of transition. We shall look at the definitions of privatisation, its aims, its mechanisms, the main difficulties that were encountered, and finally the outcomes in the early stages of the transformation. Table 8.1 summarises these issues.

Definitions

In a narrow sense privatisation may be defined as a legal transfer of property rights from the state to private agents. State property includes what belonged to the state itself, and also to the socialist cooperatives. Does it include 'social ownership' as well, in the sense used in self-management, Yugoslav style? This is indeed a difficult question, and before the break-up

Table 8.1   *The main issues of the privatisation process in the countries in transition*

A. Main ways of creating a private sector

Greenfield privatisation (the setting up of new enterprises).	Transfer of state enterprises into the hands of new owners or lease of state property.	Corporatisation along with state ownership of assets and market-type management.

B. Privatisation institutions

Ministry of privatisation (Cz, Slk, Pld, Baltic states, Ukraine) or Minister without portfolio (H) or special department within a Ministry of Economic Reform (Rom)	State Property Agency (H); (National) Privatisation Agency (B, Rom, Sln) State Committee for the Management of State Property (Russia, Uzbekistan)	State Assets Management Co (H; to be merged with State Property Agency in 1995); State (or National) Ownership (Property) Fund (B, Cz, Slk, Rom, Ukraine, Russia); Treasury ministry (Pol, 1995) Development Fund (Sln).
Applies the general policy of privatisation under the government's control; selects the objects to privatise; examines the privatisation projects submitted by the enterprises; participates in setting up legal rules for privatisation.	Supplements the ministry of privatisation or acts as the main agency of privatisation. Protects state property during the process, oversees privatisation programs, implementation of process; assists in negotiations with foreign investors; evaluates the outcomes.	Management of state assets, either not yet privatised or due to remain in state property; restructuring of state-owned enterprises.

C. 'Small-scale' privatisation *(small enterprises, mainly in the services sector and in construction; housing; land)*

Restitution to former owners: – in kind or with attribution of an equivalent asset : Cz, Slk, B; (for land:R); – in form of a compensation in cash: when otherwise impossible (Cz, Slk, B); – in privatisation vouchers: B, H (for land), Baltic states, Sln. – No restitution in CIS countries. – Restitution does not apply to non-residents as a rule.	Divestment of state assets: – closing down of enterprises; – sale by parts and redeployment of physical assets (in Pol, procedure of 'liquidation'); – sale by auctions (in most countries); – leasing, also by auctions; – buy-out by employees or by management (H, Pol, Russia), sometimes financed with vouchers for 'large' privatisation; – give-away schemes (for land (B, R), and housing).	Financing of privatisation – domestic capital; – foreign capital (in principle not allowed, or allowed under restrictive conditions; in fact largely resorted to, through straw-men)

D. 'Large-scale' privatisation (large industrial or service enterprises, banks)

Methods not implying revenues for the state.	Methods based on domestic capital.	Methods based on foreign capital.
Give-away schemes (so called 'mass privatisation'). Main method applied in Cz; in Slk before partition of Czechoslovakia; in Rom (in principle) and in Russia.	'Spontaneous privatisation': usually not recognised as a privatisation method; is in fact the indirect outcome of give-away schemes, and the direct outcome of 'liquidation' procedures (Pol), of direct sales to the public, or of management buy-out schemes (Russia). Case-by-case sales on the capital market: has really been practised mainly in H.	Direct sale to foreign investors which detain the majority of the capital. Desired method everywhere; practised mainly in H.

Abbreviations: B = Bulgaria, Cz = Czech Republic, H = Hungary, Pol = Poland, Rom = Romania, Slk = Slovakia, Sln = Slovenia.
Source: Various reports and sources on privatisation (see text).

of Yugoslavia the 1989 Law on the Circulation and Disposal of Social Capital amounted to an implicit nationalisation prior to divestiture (Uvalic, 1992, p. 184). Private owners may be individuals as well as legal persons, including foreigners.

A broader definition includes all measures contributing to the de-statisation of economic activity. In this sense privatisation may be consistent with a large state-owned sector, provided state enterprises are managed according to market rules and exposed to competition. Accordingly most of the present state sector in developed economies, with the possible exception of public utilities, would qualify as already 'privatised'. 'Marketisation' or 'commercialisation' (corporatisation) of state-owned enterprises would thus mean privatisation; similarly, the transformation of standard socialist cooperatives into market-type genuine cooperatives would also mean a shift toward privatisation.

Private property does not necessarily mean full ownership; transfers in the form of long-term leases, for instance (provided they genuinely transferred property rights, which was not the case with the Soviet *arenda* Gorbachev-style) may also qualify.

Finally, privatisation should also include creating entirely new enterprises. In this sense privatisation is tantamount to liberalisation; it means that anybody might engage in any kind of legal activity provided he/she complies with a minimum of rules.

In what follows we concentrate on the de-statisation of state-owned assets, which is the main problem in all the transition countries.

The Aims of Privatisation

In transition economies, privatisation understood in a broad sense may pursue different aims (Bornstein, 1992; Jackson, 1992a). *Politically* it means taking away property from the state and creating a new class of capitalists and entrepreneurs. *Equity considerations* suggest returning property to those who have been forcibly deprived of it during the nationalisation process, or giving priority to employees for buying shares in their enterprises; or even giving away state assets to the citizens. Privatisation may be pursued for *efficiency* reasons. If the latter are dominant, privatisation is no longer an aim *per se*. Better management of existing state enterprises, on the basis of a hard budgetary constraint following their marketisation, may increase productive static efficiency, if these enterprises are subject to competitive pressure. Allocative efficiency will be increased through privatisation only if there is a market environment with many buyers and sellers, the least possible barriers to entry and exit of the market, and a low degree of external protection. As in market economies entering into a privatisation process, the aims may be *financial*. If conducted through capital markets privatisation generates revenues to the state. Finally the governments may want to use privatisation as an additional *instrument of stabilisation*, and offer state assets for sale so as to eliminate the 'monetary overhang' whenever the savings of the population are large at the beginning of transition.

Whatever the initial illusions, the last two aims soon receded. Inflation has wiped out the monetary overhang wherever it existed, and weakened the propensity to save. Hungary was the only country to have had some concept of the *fiscal potential* of privatisation, and this is why the government initially decided upon not giving away, but selling off state property. Experience has shown that far from bringing revenues to the state, privatisation is costly even when assets are sold rather than given away. The most striking example is that of the German *Treuhand* which wound up activities (end-1994) with accumulated debts of DM 270 billion, to be met by the federal budget of Germany, while receipts from sales amounted only to DM 53 billion. In the privatising countries, the costs incurred consist of various items: fees to the foreign accounting and consulting companies for estimating the value of the assets sold; expenditures of the privatisation agencies; recapitalising or debt consolidation. Costs are minimised, but far from nullified, when the assets are given away; but in that case receipts are nil. Sell-off procures revenues, but at the expense of greater costs in restructuring.

In Poland *equity* considerations have been dominant in allowing the most extensive workers' preferential share in the assets of privatising companies. The tripartite 'enterprise pact' signed in February 1993 by the government with trade unions and employers allows workers to decide on the form of privatisation for their enterprise, and to be represented in top management (with one-third of the seats). The workers are also granted 10 per cent of the shares of their enterprises at privatisation. However the Parliament had not yet approved in 1994 the laws allowing the pact to come into force.

In Czechoslovakia *political* goals have turned the privatisation process into an aim *per se*. The government wanted to take state property away from its former Communist management, which had largely survived the change in the political regime. Hence the speed of privatisation was crucial, and it was impossible to resort to sell-offs. Thus Czechoslovakia was the first country to launch a 'voucher-type' programme which allows citizens to obtain shares in state companies at a symbolic nominal price. For the same reason, Czechoslovakia is the only country providing for physical restitution of non-agricultural assets nationalised after February 1948.

The privatisation in Russia may also be explained by *social and political motives* above all, though efficiency was mentioned as an important aim in the privatisation programme. In the recurring conflict between the government and the parliament a quick transfer of property rights to millions of voters was meant to generate political support for the government and the presidency.

Looking at the aims of privatisation one also has to examine why there may be resistance to it, which is the case in Bulgaria and Romania. In both countries, while small-scale privatisation proceeded rather quickly, the privatisation of the large firms has stalled, due both to the lack of political will from the authorities and to the lack of support from the public, in both cases despite the existence of a legal framework.

The Mechanisms of Privatisation

As has been noted, privatisation *in a broad sense* is tantamount to liberalisation. As soon as it was allowed to engage in retail trade and other small business activities, private enterprise emerged spontaneously. It generally began with 'street sales', which were a striking feature of the post-big-bang Poland in January 1990. Then all kinds of service activities developed, especially those for which the main input was human capital: consulting, private teaching, engineering and computer services. Very often such activities had already long been conducted in the framework of the 'parallel economy'. Later on this type of entrepreneurship was supported by laws on 'small privatisation', meant to transfer small state assets to private persons, mainly in trade and services, truck transport, construction, through sales of assets, by direct trade sales, by auctions officially not open to foreigners, and through leasing arrangements.

Large-scale privatisation of big enterprises is, on the contrary, very slow everywhere. The methods differed initially but are converging, out of necessity, toward the same model, i.e. the free or quasi-free distribution of assets. But in turn this kind of privatisation is mainly 'on the surface' (Hunya 1993) or 'cosmetic' (Nuti, 1993 and 1994a). The main problem lies in the management and the governance of the firms, and is twofold. How are former state enterprises turned into efficient capitalist firms? How to manage the remaining (temporarily or permanently) state sector along market methods?

In a very simplified view, the main methods of privatising big state-owned enterprises amount to four variants: sale to foreign investors, sale to domestic capital, give-away schemes, and spontaneous privatisation. These methods may be combined in the privatisation process. Before going through these variants, we shall briefly describe the institutional framework of the process.

The institutional framework

In all countries, even the most committed to 'laissez-faire', the state or a parastatal agency have to organise and monitor the process. In most cases changes are to be made in the legal status and/or in the economic situation of the enterprise to be privatised.

The governments of the countries in transition are usually reluctant to involve themselves deeply in the privatisation process. Hence the institutional framework has been kept to the minimum in most countries. The powerful *Treuhandanstalt*, the agency which has conducted the East German privatisation with extensive financial and legal means including ownership and control functions, has not been a model. Instead, the privatisation process has been dispersed among various bodies, according to the issues to be addressed (Table 8.1):

(1) The *government* as a whole supervises the process. Decisions involving very big enterprises are taken at the council of ministers level. Current supervision is ensured by privatisation ministries, committees or agencies. According to the country considered, these agencies must launch the privatisation, monitor it, and endorse the plans proposed by the enterprises themselves. In some cases local governments are entitled to similar functions; these authorities are generally in charge of conducting small privatisation.

(2) The question of the *ownership* of state enterprises has raised many difficulties. In the past, under the principle of 'socialist ownership of the means of production', the state was the owner of these means. Was it the individual owner of each state enterprise? This was never clarified, and actually did not need to be, as what mattered was party control and administrative direction, the latter being done by the branch ministries. As both the party and the branch ministerial framework were suppressed, decisions had to be taken about the ownership of the enterprises during the privatisation process. Ownership rights were given either to the same

agencies as the ones conducting the privatisation process, or to special agencies or funds. In Hungary, this body (the State Asset Management Company) retained the largest set of rights, extending well beyond privatisation proper. It was decided in November 1994 to merge it with the State Property Agency. In Poland, in 1994, the government decided to transform the existing ministry of privatisation into a treasury ministry which would not only sell but also control and direct state assets.

(3) Prior to privatisation, in most cases the state enterprises were *transformed into joint-stock* companies or companies with limited liability, a process called 'marketisation', 'commercialisation', or corporatisation' according to the cases. In some countries this had happened under the communist regime, as in 1988–90 in Hungary, 1988–9 in Poland. Until privatisation is completed, the state remains the sole shareholder, under various schemes depending on the agencies which exercise the ownership rights.

(4) In a comprehensive and centralised concept of privatisation, the process should not be initiated without several far-reaching economic and financial measures. The assets of the firms should be *valued*. The process is costly and lengthy. This is why, in the mass privatisation variant applied in Czechoslovakia, the giving away of the enterprises to be privatised and their valuation was realised in the same process, through the auctioning of the shares in several rounds: a time-saving and money-saving procedure, but which was very close to a lottery-like scheme as the prospective shareholders had very little information on the performance and market potential of the enterprises. Whenever privatisation starts with a valuation process assessing the liabilities and assets of an enterprise, it should lead to a *liquidation* (winding up) if necessary. In this case the enterprise should be closed and its assets sold at scrap value. The governments have shunned such actions, because this approach would have led to a great number of closures, and would also start from the assumption that the market, not the government, should decide about the winding up of enterprises. What is called liquidation in Poland, a very widely applied procedure since 1990, is the sale of some viable parts of an enterprise to a new private company usually set up by the former managers and employees, and is in fact a legalisation of 'spontaneous privatisation' (see below).

Related decisions might imply a *restructuring* and a *recapitalising* of the firm before or during privatising, in the case of large state-owned enterprises. This was not readily envisioned, both because of lack of funds and because of the reluctance to implement anything resembling an industrial policy. However, all countries had to address and solve these issues. *Industrial, or organisational, restructuring* was a by-product of the privatisation process, as enterprises to be privatised had everywhere to submit plans which defined their future internal structure, often implying a splitting-up of the enterprise into several parts, and outlined the industrial strategy for the future. This was done by the institution(s) in charge of privatisation, or by special agencies such as the State Assets Management Company in Hungary or the Industrial Development Agency in Poland. *Financial restructuring* could not be ignored as soon as the bankruptcy legislation was introduced and implemented. Because many, if not most, of the enterprises were loss-making, and as large inter-enterprises arrears had built up, a strict implementation of bankruptcy procedures would have a domino effect and generate chains of bankruptcies. At the same time, because the banks, themselves still mainly state-owned, are the creditors of the enterprises, and increasingly their shareholders through the privatisation process, they find themselves burdened with bad loans. The bad debts problems may be tackled at the bank level through a financial consolidation procedure (as was done in Czechoslovakia and Hungary), and/or at the enterprise level (through the writing off of debts, as in Russia in 1992) or through additional financing, a better solution, but which is more costly (as in Hungary in 1992–3).

The institutional setting thus provides a minimum framework for conducting privatisation. The only clear policy is to try and manage a quick divestiture.

Privatisation with the help of foreign capital

In the beginning of the transition there were hopes of a large involvement of foreign capital in privatisation. As early as 1988 the Hungarian minister of foreign trade was touring Western countries offering 50 state firms for sale, without much success.

A legal framework for foreign investment had been created in all countries: in the 1960s in Yugoslavia (1967), in the 1970s in Hungary, Romania (beginning in 1972) and Poland (1976), in the eighties in Bulgaria (1980), Russia (1987), and Czechoslovakia (1989). Once the transition had begun, ambiguous attitudes developed about foreign direct investment. On the one hand, the new governments hoped very much to attract foreign investors, and the legislation was accordingly made much more favourable than it was before. On the other hand, the authorities had to take care of nationalistic feelings and dispel the idea that foreigners would select the best choices so as to make big profits. The sensitiveness of public opinion is particularly high when ownership of land is concerned. Even in Hungary, the country which may be seen as the most open to foreign capital, the land law passed in April 1994 severely limited foreign investment in agriculture by banning new purchases of land by foreigners (*Financial Times*, 7 April 1994). Nevertheless Hungary attracted most of the foreign investment flowing into Central Europe; Czechoslovakia ranked second after a slow start; Poland was only third, mainly because of the uncertainties fuelled by its political instability (see Hunya, 1993, and Hammid, 1994). Other countries got a trickle of the capital inflows. Russia and some of the ex-Soviet republics such as Kazakhstan will potentially attract large Western investment flows especially in the field of mineral resources and energy, provided the economic and political situation stabilises. In Russia, the policy toward foreign investments has been very contradictory. A tax on foreign loans was 'accidentally' introduced in December 1993, and was repealed only a few months later. The restrictions on foreign bank activities in Russia have been lifted only in June 1994 to allow the signature of the partnership agreement between Russia and the European Union. The law on oil and gas investment was not yet passed by the parliament by end-1994, and though both sectors are open to foreign investment, issues such as land and sub-soil ownership are not clarified, and export duties on oil deter potential investors. Table 8.2 assesses the flows of foreign direct investment for the period 1990–3.

Foreign investment is certainly not a solution for achieving overall privatisation. True, in Hungary foreign investment accounted for between

Table 8.2   *Foreign investment in countries in transition (number of projects; million US$)*

Countries	Joint ventures[a] (number of projects)		Net flows of FDI (portfolio investment included) (million US$)					
	1992	*1993*	*1990*	*1991*	*1992*	*1993 estimate*	*1990–3 cumulated*	*1993 per capita in US$*
Bulgaria	1200	2300	4	56	42	48	150	5
Czech Republic	3120	5000	360	710	1160	720	2950	73
Hungary	17182	21500	311	1459	1471	2328	5569	226
Poland	5740	6800	88	117	284	380	869	11
Romania	20684	29115	−18	37	73	48	140	2
Slovakia	2875	4350	53	82	72	120	327	28
Slovenia	2815	3300	−2	41	113	110	262	55
Eastern Europe	53616	72365	796	2502	3215	3754	10267	33
Russia	3252	7989	100	800	400	1300	3	
Total	56868	80354	796	2602	4015	4154	11567	

[a] Number of projects registered, end of period.
For Hungary, Poland, and Slovakia: operational projects only.
For the Czech Republic, the 1993 figure for the net flow of FDI does not include portfolio investment (amounting to $942 million); other countries include portfolio investment in FDI data.
Source: ECE/UN (1994a).

80 and 90 per cent of the proceeds received by the State Property Agency in 1991 (Marrese, 1992, p. 33). However, in 1992, foreign capital accounted for 3 per cent of business assets, while in Austria the foreign share amounts to 25–30 per cent (Hunya, 1992, p. 507). It seems doubtful that in any of the transition countries foreign capital might account for more than 10–15 per cent of the total capital. In addition, as has been evidenced in 1992 and 1993, foreign-owned companies pursue aims of their own, which may contradict the home country's policy objectives. Foreign firms have pressed the governments to provide them greater protection, through increased tariffs on imported competing goods (such as cars) or a more depressed exchange rate so as to encourage exports and prevent imports. These demands may reduce the willingness of the countries in transition to open their economies, so as to increase competition on the domestic market and to respond to the lowering of tariffs granted by the EC in the framework of the association or other agreements negotiated or in negotiation (see Chapter 9). Some clashes between national governments and multinational firms had great visibility, such as the cancellation in 1993 of part of an investment package by the German firm Volkswagen for its subsidiary the Czech car manufacturer Skoda, which strongly reduced the expectations raised in 1991 when the joint venture was concluded (*Financial Times*, 17 September 1993). The joint venture concluded in 1989 between the US General Electric and the Hungarian firm of lighting products Tungsram turned into a near 99 per cent GE ownership in 1994 after several increases in the US company's stake, large lay-offs, and disputes with the Hungarian government about the rate of exchange of the forint when the increase in the real exchange rate threatened to wipe out the initial attractiveness of the deal to GE, namely low Hungarian dollar wages.

As an instrument of privatisation, foreign direct investment has definite qualitative advantages. It solves the restructuring problems by passing them on to foreign firms – however, as foreign capital selects the best enterprises these are also the least in need of restructuring (as compared with other candidates for privatisation). Along with capital, management skills and modern technology are transferred. But the motivations of foreign investors may contradict the long-term aims of national governments. When the foreign investor primarily looks at his gains in terms of lower costs, an increase in these costs may prompt him to settle in another location, and here the competition between the developing countries and the countries in transition is high; the latter are exceedingly confident in their specific advantages (geographical closeness to Western Europe, skills of the labour force) which are easily eroded in a context of industrial globalisation: distances matter less, human technical skills matter less. When the investor looks at market expansion, often he tries to buy a monopoly position, at a time when the national governments try to de-monopolise (ECE/UN, 1994b, Chapter 5 'Restructuring of state-owned enterprises in Eastern Europe').

Foreign investment is thus difficult to control by national governments, and not only difficult to lure into the country. In addition the best deals have been made at the beginning of the transition; the privileged sectors in Central and Eastern Europe have been the car-making industry, food processing, pharmaceuticals, and hotels. The service sector is still promising, especially banking and insurance activities, and public utilities (power distribution, telephone).

In addition to foreign direct investment, foreign capital may be involved in portfolio investment, which supposes the existence of capital markets. There is little information on the topic, as the Czech Republic is the only country where portfolio investment is reported separately. Taking the Czech example, one has witnessed a large expansion of portfolio investment in 1993, coinciding with the opening of the Prague Stock Exchange and the first wave of voucher privatisation (see Table 9.5). Portfolio investment adds financial resources to the domestic capital and avoids the drawbacks of foreign direct investment in terms of corporate control. It has its drawbacks, of which the volatility of emerging stock markets is the most critical.

Sale of assets to domestic capitalists

In some cases this method is tantamount to the former one. Even though small-scale privatisation was officially not open to foreign capital, in fact in many cases (especially in Czechoslovakia and Hungary) foreign funds were extensively used, through family or other informal connections, to privatise hotels, restaurants, and other personal services.

The lack of domestic capital soon emerged as the major stumbling block of overall privatisation. Most of the available domestic savings were quickly absorbed by the small privatisation. Poland and especially Hungary tried to sell big state enterprises through public offerings, tenders, or individual sales. In both countries only a few hundred companies could be sold that way. Each transaction took a long time, delays being caused by the need for financial and management restructuring, and emerged as quite costly in terms of assets evaluation (involving foreign accounting companies and consultants charging high fees). The experiences were even less conclusive in other Eastern European countries. Ultimately most of the countries evolved toward the 'free distribution' model which was devised in Czechoslovakia as the main privatisation method.

To avoid the requirement for domestic capital some authors have suggested privatisation through non-cash bids. The state enterprises would be first converted into joint stock companies, then their shares would be allocated to their creditors, among which the banks would appear as the main creditors and hence the core owners. The core owners would then solicit cash and non-cash bids (the latter may be based on reorganisation projects submitted by a new management team) (see Aghion, 1993).

Does the recent emergence of booming capital markets in Eastern Europe (see pp. 182–3) reverse the picture? It may seem that there is a lack of stock rather than capital; for instance, when the second large state-owned bank, the Bank Slaski, was privatised in Poland in December 1993, the issue was massively oversubscribed several times (Bossak, 1994, p. 116). But it must be remembered that the stock market is very narrow; that the public offerings procedures lack transparency (and in this particular case led to a financial scandal and to a plunge of the Warsaw Stock Exchange in the beginning of 1994); and finally that households lack financial experience and see stock deals rather as a form of gambling than as a form of investment.

Mass privatisation schemes

Free transfers of shares to the public may involve two main variants: (i) distribution of vouchers, or coupons, to be converted into shares in operating companies; (ii) distribution of shares in investment funds or holding companies that in turn have shares in companies. A combination of both occurs when the citizens are permitted to ask an investment fund to auction their vouchers for them.

Czechoslovakia opted for variant (i) as the main method for privatising large enterprises; the process was launched in the beginning of 1992, involving about 2,000 enterprises of which almost 1,500 were auctioned (PlanEcon, 1993a). After the partition of the country, while Slovakia was waiting before launching the second wave, the Czech Republic decided in 1993 on a go-ahead for nearly 1,000 companies; this second wave began in April 1994. (For a detailed account of voucher privatisation in the Czech Republic, see Leeds, 1993; Svejnar and Singer, 1994.)

Poland chose, within its 'Mass Privatisation Programme' to experiment with method (ii) for a significant number of state enterprises (400, then 600). The programme was announced in June 1991 and prepared during the year 1992, with great delays due to difficulties in setting up investment funds. The final version of the programme was ultimately approved by the Polish parliament in April 1993, following a government/parliament conflict which expressed frustrations as to the many uncertainties surrounding the programme. But the actual sell-offs were to start only in 1995.

In 1993 the Hungarian government first contemplated a shift toward a mass privatisation plan, due to the delays in implementing privatisation by sell-offs. The new plan, decided on in April 1994, will however include a higher contribution from the public than in Poland and Czechoslovakia, which would be financed through cheap credit. It will also be less 'massive' as only 70 companies have been included in the first round, to begin end–1994. Due to the fact that the scheme was approved in view of the approaching general elections (held in May 1994), which were lost by the government, the developments of this scheme are very uncertain.

Other countries have launched mass privatisation schemes. Slovakia, once separated from the Czech Republic, decided to temporarily stop the programme in 1994, then relaunched it in the end of 1994. Romania has officially launched its mass privatisation programme in 1992 by distributing privatisation vouchers to about 17 million citizens so as to let them acquire 30 per cent of the capital of the 6,300 companies to be privatised, but nothing followed. A new programme was decided on in July 1994, probably to comply with the government's commitment to the IMF, according to which half of the industrial enterprises should be privatised in 1994. Bulgaria amended its 1992 law on privatisation in June 1994 to pave the way for mass privatisation. All Bulgarian citizens will be able to acquire investment coupons paying a symbolic fee; these bonds will not be tradable but will be used to buy shares in enterprises or in investment funds. Table 8.3 summarises the different variants.

The Baltic countries and the former CIS countries have also launched or at least decreed privatisation programmes. The Russian scheme is based on the privatisation law of 1991 amended in 1992. *All* Russian citizens each

Table 8.3 *Mass privatisation schemes*

Methods	Advantages	Drawbacks
Issue of vouchers that are used to buy enterprise shares or may be entrusted to investment funds (Cz; Slk before partition; B since 1994). Distribution of shares on subsidised credit (H). Issue of certificates of investment funds set up by the state, which have a stake in the companies to be privatised (Pol, Rom, Sln). Issue of vouchers which may be exchanged against shares or certificates of investment, freely traded on the market, or used for employee buy-back schemes (Russia).	Moral compensation for Communist past injustice, which deprived the people of what belonged to them in principle. Swiftness of the procedure; the valuation problem is suppressed; no need for restructuring. No need for capital. Political support.	No revenues for the state Inflationary when vouchers are freely transferable. Risk of speculation from investment funds (Cz, Russia). Time-consuming procedure when investment funds are involved from the outset (Pol). Actual use of the procedure to foster employee ownership, openly (Russia) or unintendedly (in most countries). The procedure leaves open corporate governance problems.

Abbreviations: B = Bulgaria; Cz = Czech Republic; H = Hungary; Pol = Poland; Rom = Romania; Sln = Slovenia; Slk = Slovakia.

received 10,000 rubles' worth of privatisation vouchers, beginning in October 1992, immediately tradable in cash or exchangeable against shares in enterprises selected for privatisation. Enterprises, after being transformed into joint-stock companies at the initiative of their management of employees, and being selected for participation in the programme, were auctioned at direct public auctions opened to nationals and foreigners. Three variants could be selected by the staff of the enterprises to be auctioned. Variant 1 provided for free allocation of 25 per cent of the charter capital to all employees, in non-voting shares. Variant 2 allocated 51 per cent of the shares to the employees at 1.7 times their book value on 1 January 1992 (a gift, in a situation of high inflation) and with voting rights, plus an option of a further percentage of voting shares. Variant 3 allowed a group of employees to get 20 per cent of the voting shares at book value under the commitment to restructure the enterprise within a year, plus a further 20 per cent if the restructuring was successful. The rest of the shares were auctioned in all three variants. Bidders could pay in cash, or in vouchers. Of the large state enterprises 70 per cent were thus privatised by end-June 1994; past that deadline the vouchers were no longer valid. A second wave was to follow, to auction the rest of the enterprises to be privatised, on commercial conditions.

It seems thus obvious that whatever the initially preferred methods, all countries moved toward mass privatisation schemes, generally combined with other forms of divestiture, for the following main reasons: (i) it was quicker than any other (but still could take time if technical constraints and political obstacles interfered, as in the Polish case); (ii) it was politically appealing as it amounted to a massive gift to the electoral constituency; (iii) it appeared as an irreversible commitment to capitalism (Nuti, 1994a).

Spontaneous privatisation

Spontaneous privatisation is often defined as the way for members of the former communist *nomenklatura* to become owners of the companies they managed before (or of the best parts of these companies), in a more or less illegal manner. This happened first in Poland and Hungary, in fact under a legal cover. In both countries, still under the communist regime, state enterprises were first granted more rights, with enterprise or workers' councils getting involved in management and even (in Hungary) in the selection of the enterprises' directors. Then state enterprises were transformed into joint-stock companies as has been mentioned. The managers used the new legal framework to split up state companies, and transform the best sections into limited liability companies or joint ventures, securing jobs for themselves and the most skilled of their employees, and leaving in state ownership only the non-profitable parts of the previous state enterprise (Marrese, 1992). In Czechoslovakia the process was prevented by the fact that there was no adequate legal framework in the beginning of the new regime, and also because of a greater social and political intolerance toward the former *nomenklatura*. Since 1990 such deals are no longer possible legally; whereas in Poland there were attempts to cancel them due to the pressure of public opinion, a greater tolerance was displayed in Hungary. In other countries spontaneous privatisation has developed as well, though generally denied, or else acknowledged as a deformation of the legal process.

In principle, this kind of privatisation should not be confused with privatisation initiated by the state companies themselves. This takes place when the companies are allowed or encouraged to present 'privatisation plans' submitted to the state authority in charge of the process. However, one cannot exclude that 'insider information' leads, in this case as well, to some kind of 'spontaneous privatisation'. In the Russian schemes, spontaneous privatisation thus appears as 'semi-legal' because the employees have to prepare a privatisation plan (to be approved by either the State Committee for Management of State Assets, or by local authorities), and because the preferred scheme among the three variants outlined above has been 'variant 2' transferring 51 per cent of the shares to 'insiders'.

It is very difficult to reach a sober assessment on this issue. Eastern governments and Western experts alike are very much against this form of privatisation. It looks too much like Western insider trading and legacies of communist *nomenklatura*'s privileges combined. Few people openly acknowledge that this might be in fact the most common way of privatising, and in any case an unavoidable one. Thus the Hungarian economist Péter Mihályi boldly makes the equation ' "Large" privatisation = Spontaneous privatisation', and cautions against an ideological condemnation of the phenomenon (Mihályi, 1993, p. 34). In the Hungarian case, this has led to a complex corporate structure linked by cross-ownership; 'this shift,' Mihályi argues, 'from a relatively monolithical structure of state ownership toward the cross-ownership model is a spontaneous evolution fed by the energy of the Hungarian managerial class and made possible by the benign neglect of the country's political masters' (Mihályi, 1993, p. 38). Is the process bad *per se*? The question is hardly relevant as there is no real choice on a large scale. The countries in transition each need thousands of managers. While it was relatively easy to find a few dozen experts among former dissidents or quasi-dissidents to take jobs in the new state administration, it is impossible to find enough good managers to replace the previous managerial class. This class may be trained. The former communist managers are able to act with a view to maximising their own economic interests, which they did in the past, and which is after all the quintessence of capitalism. As most of them (if not all) never really believed in communism but just pretended to, there is no risk that they would help to bring the old regime back. And if not them, who else? If they are excluded on political grounds, then the alternative would be political appointees of the opposite side, lacking experience and probably less apt as the few apt people are already in business.

Is there a link between spontaneous privatisation and the return to power of the parties originating from the former communist parties? By mid-1994 all countries in transition except a few (the exceptions were Albania, Armenia, the Czech Republic, Estonia and Latvia) were ruled by governments supported by coalitions led by the former communist parties. These governments all declare themselves committed to market reforms, sometimes just paying lip-service to the reforms, in any case lagging behind in implementation. In contrast, the 'ex-nomenklaturists' that in fact manage the enterprises, both state and privatised, are certainly more earnestly committed to the market as their aim is to maximise their gains. There are links between the political power and the industrial managers, as is very obvious, for example, in Russia. One may guess that when the political leadership is very adverse to the former nomenklaturists the latter have to be much more efficient still because they cannot count on political favour.

The privatisation process has encountered many difficulties, of which some have been mentioned already, such as:

- *economic* constraints, of which the lack of domestic capital is the most substantial, especially under deflationary macro-economic policies which affect investment still more than consumption;
- *technical* constraints, and among them the lack of proper accounting rules and experience. All the big accounting and consulting companies have opened offices in Eastern Europe, as well as a host of smaller companies, often set up as joint ventures. These institutions absorb a significant share of the revenues of privatisation (up to 25 per cent according to some statements), and also a large share of the technical assistance granted to the countries in transition;
- *institutional* problems, related to the central and local government involvement in the process. The specific institutions which have been set up are constantly criticised for their action, overcommitted, and unable to meet the deadlines; often they are accused of conflict of interests and insider trading.

All these difficulties, however serious, are solved while the process develops. Some issues remain open and still under discussion.

The Lasting Difficulties of Privatisation

There are some difficult issues that reflect the political nature of privatisation itself. We have selected the following: the speed and sequencing of privatisation; the restitution problem; the benefits to be extended, if any, to the former employees; the special case of privatisation in agriculture.

The speed and sequencing

The issues of speed and sequencing have been raised first in relation to the stabilisation programme. As we have seen earlier, they were not very relevant as the stabilisation packages had to be put in force swiftly and virtually at once.

Should the transformation process be quick or gradual? As obviously it is slow, a reality acknowledged even by supporters of fast-track privatisation (Sachs, 1992, p. 43), the question becomes whether it is possible and suitable to accelerate the process. Most of the authors recommend that from the very beginning there should be a firm commitment of the government toward privatisation. Should one then immediately move to 'instant' models of privatisation? The early literature favoured such an option (Blanchard *et al.*, 1991, Chapter 2). Most Western economists and experts have grown cautious. Even those who favour quick privatisation recognise that there is a risk of going too fast in a voluntarist approach (Aghion and Blanchard, 1993. and Aghion, 1993). And anyhow, even 'instant capitalism' may be slow, as we have seen above. The swifter case is the Czech one, where mass privatisation is conducted without any prior restructuring or valuation of the enterprises, and where an electronic device allows for fixing the prices of the shares in several 'rounds' (for a detailed explanation of this device, see PlanEcon, 1993a, and Frydman *et al.*, 1993d).

If privatisation is to last a long time, then the issue of sequencing becomes essential. In the early debates the order of liberalising and privatising measures was deemed important. Should one liberalise prices first so as to get a new price structure allowing for the valuation of assets? Or should one privatise first to allow for a proper market response to free prices? Whatever the arguments price liberalisation has proceeded first, in line with trade liberalisation. Later the debate shifted towards the selection of the proper order in privatising, restructuring, creating capital markets, reforming the banking system, and reforming the tax system. It was generally found that no ideal linear reform path could be defined; instead, the reform package should be announced and launched at once, with a clear commitment and a schedule; at any given moment some parts of the package would be pursued with a greater intensity than the others (for instance, during Year 1 and Year 2 of the reform, macroeconomic stabilisation should be conducted with greatest intensity, small-scale privatisation should be implemented, large-scale privatisation should be prepared; in Year 3 macrostabilisation might be more flexible, large-scale privatisation would have gained momentum, banking reform would be on track, etc.). Clearly this is what is happening; however one cannot derive firm guidelines from such a framework, which allows for as many variants as there are individual countries (see Fisher and Gelb, 1991).

Restitution

Equity considerations point to the need, prior to privatisation, to restitute what has been taken away by the communist power from the former owners, or at least to compensate the latter (or their heirs) for the loss of property. Once the principle is admitted (which has been the case in Central and Eastern Europe and in the Baltic States), the implementation is difficult. Former owners have to be identified, many of whom are deceased or have emigrated abroad. Even in the case of resident, and still alive, former owners, their identification may raise problems especially if the same asset is claimed by several persons. It is necessary to establish the date of the nationalisations that are to be compensated. In most cases only communist nationalisations were taken into consideration, which excluded earlier cases of confiscation by post-war non-communist governments. This provision turned out to discriminate against Germans (Nazis and non-Nazis alike) and against Jews, as mentioned in Chapter 2 (Slovakia in 1993 decided to compensate the Jews expropriated between 1945 and 1990). A decision also has to be made about whether the restitution will be made in kind or in terms of a compensation (through cash payments, privatisation vouchers or securities), and in the latter case whether it will amount to a hundred per cent compensation or whether there will be some discount. Compensation in turn raises the problem of the proper evaluation of the asset, especially in countries where there was no land cadastre, and where the book value of industrial assets was fictitious. Finally it must be determined who is entitled to restitution: all former owners or their heirs, only residents, and in the case of land all claimants or only farmers. For instance Hungary, the most reluctant country in Eastern Europe to espouse the principle, admitted reprivatisation of land only, and even in this case only to the benefit of recipients committing themselves to farm it for at least five years (law of 1991); in all other cases the claimants were entitled to tradable compensation vouchers. Institutions are usually not allowed to claim restitution; churches are an exception in some countries, and this has been hotly debated in particular in Czechoslovakia. Table 8.1 sums up the issues and the solutions retained. In all cases, whatever the solutions, restitution proved a very politicised issue not only domestically but also in bilateral relations (such as in the case of the Czech–German discussions on the compensation for the ethnic Germans of the *Sudetenland*).

Restitution proved a very difficult issue. It alienated many people and groups (among them peasants) in the countries in transition. It delayed small and large privatisation. Though a deadline was set for claims to be received (between end-1991 and end-1992 according to the countries), many were not yet settled by 1994. Even when the claims are formally settled, the solutions are not satisfactory. Compensation in cash is usually a small fraction of the real value of the asset. Compensation in the form of securities or privatisation vouchers has left claimants with assets difficult to use or trade at good conditions.

The claims of the former employees

Are employees of a state enterprise entitled to special rights in the privatisation process and in the management of the privatised firms? The answer is ambiguous. The new governments in the countries in transition are very resistant to any form of self-management, and in the countries where some elements of self-management had been introduced in the 1980s, such as Poland and Hungary, the regulations on the new grassroot private companies do not allow for it, even in the mild form of co-determination, German style. For the same reason, to give explicit privileges to the workers is viewed with suspicion. Such privileges are seen as unethical, economically inefficient, and allowing for collusion between former managers and their employees (on the basis of job promises), which make EBOs (employee buy-outs) and ESOP (employee share ownership programmes) schemes tantamount to spontaneous privatisation. In fact, even when no privileged rights are given to employees, a large part of the 'small privatisation' and a non-negligible part of the privatisation of medium-sized enterprises through trade sales turned out to be MBO/EBOs. One may then reach the conclusion that it is better to acknowledge the fact and specifically regulate sales to the employees, as is done in the Hungarian legislation and in the Russian mass privatisation (see OECD, 1994b).

The special case of agriculture

Privatisation in *agriculture* is a special case combining the problems of restitution and those of giving workers special rights. Only in Poland and in Yugoslavia were agricultural cooperatives dissolved (in the 1950s) and the land returned to the farmers. In other countries the process of collectivisation had generally followed a land reform which expropriated large landowners and distributed property among the peasants. Wherever the principle of land restitution has been retained (in Bulgaria, Hungary, Romania, Albania, and the Baltic States), it was coupled with redistribution to the farmers in kind (but generally not in full property of all the land confiscated) or in farming rights. In Czechoslovakia, the issue was highly complicated by the fact that the land had never formally been taken away from the peasants, and by the beginning of the transition about half of the land was actually owned by non-rural dwellers. In Russia, ownership rights have been granted to the farmers on their privately cultivated plots, but the question of buying and selling larger tracts of agricultural land was a matter of strong disagreement between the government and the parliament, the latter blocking the actual implementation of the law on land private ownership. The situation was only settled legally at the end of 1993, by means of a presidential decree allowing for a free land market (not open to foreigners, though), and entitling each member of a state or collective farm to a part of the farm property. But because of political reluctance and lack of precise rules for the implementation of the decree, no land market had yet emerged in Russia in 1994.

The privatisation in agriculture thus exemplifies an ethical and political conflict between the principle that the land should be returned to those who have been dispossessed by the communists, and the principle that the land should belong to whoever farms it.

In most of the countries in transition, and even in those most committed to the free market, property rights in agriculture remain unclear. Despite the distribution of land to private owners, and the dissolving of the cooperatives which in most countries had to turn into companies or voluntary associations and re-register as such, little has changed. The private farmers have guaranteed rights on what was in the past their personal plot and may expand it legally, but have no access to credit, and no training as managers. They have to deal with suppliers and wholesale distribution companies which are largely monopolised. The former cooperatives have on the whole better management skills, and provide some social security benefits. Capitalist farming on a large scale is so far impossible, and the forcible elimination of cooperatives would be very counterproductive. In actual fact, the legally revamped cooperatives have proved to be the segment of the former communist ownership structure the most unyielding to change. However, it should not be looked upon just as a case of political resistance to transition.

The legacies of the past are very ambiguous. Western literature has repeatedly stressed the higher performance of small private farming as opposed to collective farming, by quoting statistics showing that with a very small percentage of total cultivated land the private plots provided for a very high share of agricultural produce. We have stated earlier (Chapter 3) that this was a distorted view; the higher productivity of the private plots could be attributed to the fact that the latter 'lived on' the cooperative through diverting its human and material inputs. Nevertheless the myth of an intrinsic superiority of small private farming over large cooperative farming is still very much established; though it is not clear why in market conditions small farming should be productive in the East while it is in great difficulty in the West (Maurel, 1991). The vitality of the cooperatives might suggest a potential for the revival of the agricultural sector.

The Outcome of Privatisation: Who Controls the Enterprises?

There are two main ways of viewing the privatisation process. One is to look at the *share* of the privatised sector (in overall production or employment) assuming that a given unit of production may be considered as private as long as its *ownership* has been transferred from the state to a new owner. In this sense, the outcomes are quite impressive (Table 8.4). The statistical data lump all private property rights together, adding the production (or employment) in grassroots enterprises and in privatised enterprises (industrial firms, farms, banks, etc.).

The other way to look at privatisation is to investigate the way the privatised sector is *managed*. Here one has to distinguish between small-scale assets and large-scale units. While small-scale privatisation most often leads to family businesses, the corporate governance of the privatised large-scale state-owned enterprises is not easy to clarify.

In all transition countries, the former state-owned enterprises may now be divided into three groups. The first one is made up of the enterprises already privatised. Within this group, the only sub-group more or less easy to identify from the point of view of management and control comprises the companies under foreign control, but these are the minority. The bulk of the privatised companies is made up of commercialised (corporatised) large firms; privatisation often went along with the splitting up of the previous state-owned firms. The second group is made up of state firms preparing themselves for privatisation and submitting projects to that effect to the institutions in charge. Finally the third group is made up of state-owned enterprises either to be privatised in the future or to remain in the state sector. There is no clear policy as to what kind of enterprises should remain in the state sector, except for a small number of utilities. (Only in Romania has there been a definition of the scope of the state sector to remain; it would comprise energy distribution, mines, railways, the postal service, with a French-type status of 'regies autonomes'). Most of the enterprises in this group are, or are being, transformed into stock companies. As will be shown, all the three groups (with the exception of the 100 per cent foreign-owned firms) are evolving toward the same kind of corporate governance.

Some pioneering studies have explored the behaviour of the firms under transition conditions (Brada *et al.*, 1994, for Hungary; Pinto *et al*, 1993, for Poland; Sereghyova, 1993, for Czechoslovakia). What comes out of these studies is that there is no 'ownership frontier' as far as performance is considered – successful and unsuccessful firms are to be found on each side. What the successful firms have in common is a quick adjustment to market conditions, 'survival strategies' to secure markets and finance in the beginning, moving toward more long-term strategies with time.

Theoretical studies on corporate governance of firms in transition usually discuss the issue in terms of the principal/agent approach (see Frydman *et al.*, 1993b and c, and 1994 for a summing up of the discussion). How are the managers to be controlled? We know that in the past the system functioned on the basis of a political hierarchy without property rights. In present conditions, who is to control the managers? In capitalist firms, external control is exerted by the owners (shareholders), by the creditors, or by the

Table 8.4 *The outcomes of the privatisation programmes (1990–4)*

Criteria	Czech Republic	Hungary	Poland	Russia
Number of units privatised				
– Small-scale privatisation:				
Number (1993)	22,000	7,600	n.a.[a]	About 30,000[b]
Per cent of total	69 per cent	76 per cent	n.a.[a]	20 per cent[b]
– Large-scale privatisation: Number (1993)	– First round voucher privatisation (1993): 988 joint stock comp. – Second round (registration closed Dec.93): 860 companies – Total industrial enterprises engaged in privatisation: 3293 (Feb 94)	972 out of a total of 2300 to be privatised (industry)[c]	899 (1990–3) out of 3714 enterprises to be privatised (including state farms)	About 14,000
State enterprises in per cent of total of large enterprises	19 per cent end-1993 accounting for 1/3 of employment (industry)	80 per cent[c]	79.3 per cent end-1993	30 per cent mid-94
Share of private sector in GDP, mid-94 in per cent[d]				
Total	37 (46 per cent in Dec.)	35	50	15
Industry	17	20	37.4	12
Construction	50	50	85.8	nd
Retail trade	72	40	87.8	32
Share of private sector in total employment, in per cent	Over 60 per cent mid-1994	42 per cent in 1993	60 per cent in 1993	70 per cent in 1994

Bankruptcy law	In force April 1993	In force 1 Jan 1992	Insolvency Act of Feb. 1990 (referring to Bankruptcy Act of 1934)	In force April 1993
Number of bankruptcy procedures	A few cases[e]	1360 completed by mid-1993, on 15634 filed	1111 completed in 1990–3; in addition 700 firms 'liquidated' as a form of privatisation	A few cases initiated by mid-1994; tougher laws announced[h]
Restructuring procedures	No official restructuring policy	968 agreements reached by mid-93 on 5099 filed		
Debt consolidation	Through Konsolidacni Banka (set up in 1991). No figures on number of cases filed.	Specific procedure for 13 big firms in 1992. Several thousand firms involved in 1993[f]	11 investigations initiated by end-93 [g]	Promissory notes scheme announced to solve huge interenterprise indebtedness[i]

[a] Already in 1990 about 80 per cent of retail trade and services were in private hands. One may consider that the 'liquidation' procedure (law of 13 July 1990; see text, p. 161) amounts to small privatisation as it was mainly applied to medium-sized enterprises (939 cases initiated, about 700 completed end-1993).

[b] Figures are contradictory and incomplete. The data relate to small privatisation in the services sector (retail trade, catering, workshops). To this one has to add about 7,000 small and medium industrial enterprises (one-third of the total). All these data refer to end-1992. Mid-1994 the Russian minister of privatisation, A. Chubais, said that 84,000 small units (74 % of total) had been sold to private owners (RFE/RL News Briefs, 5–8 July 1994).

[c] The percentage relates to the state sector overall; the figure on the number of privatised units relates to industry.

[d] Including the greenfield private sector.

[e] As stated by Sharon Fisher, 'Czech Economy Presents Mixed Picture', RFE/RL Research Report, 22 July 1994.

[f] ECE/UN, Economic Survey of Europe in 1993–94, Chapter 5.

[g] ECE/UN, ibid.

[h] Financial Times, 19 August 1994.

[i] Financial Times, 24 and 25 August 1994.

Source: Economic Survey of Europe in 1992–1993, passim; OECD country economic surveys; various press reports. Specifically, Renzo Daviddi, 'Privatisation in the Transition to a Market Economy', mimeo, August 1994; special issue of Le Courrier des Pays de l'Est, Paris, La Documentation Française, 'Diversité des privatisations en Europe centrale et en Russie', June–July 1994.

market (competition leading to bankruptcy if the firm performs poorly; threat of take-over). In labour-managed firms, there is an insider control by employees. What kind of control is emerging now?

Privatisation in the West has to deal with the problem as well. One of the major concerns of the privatising authorities was how to prevent, in the conditions of an open, largely deregulated market, an excessive concentration of capital in the hands of a small number of big shareholders, who could easily buy out the shares from thousands of small, not so well informed new capitalists. This was achieved through the policy of 'hard core' stable shareholders, which in France were selected outside the market by a specific procedure conducted through the ministry in charge of the privatisations. Thus it can be said that in the French case, and more generally in developed market economies undertaking privatisation, the problem has not just been where to find capital but *what* kind of capital to use. Letting the market do the job can lead to concentration of capital in politically unwanted hands. Establishing 'hard core' shareholders can raise harsh political disputes if it is shown that the government in charge of the privatisations favoured its friends. In France, the 'hard core' (*noyau dur*) policy evolved in the second privatisation programme starting in 1993 toward a system of intricate cross-shareholdings between industry, banks and insurance companies under the control of the state.

In Eastern Europe, it was an illusion to think that under any privatisation scheme one might witness a large class of small capitalist-minded shareowners emerging spontaneously and ready for controlling the management of its assets. In mass privatisation schemes, in most cases the population was mainly interested in cashing the distributed shares. People tried to sell their shares even when no trading was allowed for some time, a provision to be found in all cases except in Russia (and in Hungary concerning the compensation vouchers allocated to claimants in the 'restitution' issue). What gradually emerges in the privatised companies is a complex ownership structure involving banks, investment funds, other enterprises, state asset management agencies, and local governments, with a network of cross-ownership. The actual managers are the former ones in many cases, due to the difficulties of finding thousands of able managers willing to do the job. There is little the new governments are able (and even willing) to do to control the whole process. In the Polish mass privatisation scheme the centrally-controlled investment funds are supposed to act as blockholders of shares to avoid insider control, but their efficiency might be questioned, as the management of the funds itself is meant to be in the hands of foreign consultants, who are hired because of their expertise and who are not supposed to run the privatised companies.

This evolution means that all forms of privatisation ultimately lead to an unwanted spontaneous privatisation model, with enterprise governance by the insiders. A solution would be to have a system of strong financial intermediaries (Frydman *et al.*, 1993a; Jackson, 1992b). How could the existing state (or newly privatised) commercial banks be transformed to perform this function, or how could new intermediaries be created? This leads us to the other areas of structural transformation, which is critical to the privatisation process.

OTHER AREAS OF STRUCTURAL TRANSFORMATION

Structural transformation means building a market environment. Liberal-ising prices and trade has been part of the stabilisation programmes as well. This does not automatically create competitive markets, especially if competition from abroad has been initially limited by the over-devaluation of the domestic currencies that made imports very expensive. Competition on the domestic market means *demonopolisation*, a very complex issue. On the one hand, clearly the huge state monopolies of the past must be dismantled, and in some countries (Hungary and Poland) the process had begun, rather unsuccessfully, even before the transition. On the other hand, the Western developed world is one of big companies. The countries in transition are introducing anti-trust legislation on the Western model, without yet having 'trusts' – in the Western sense! Such 'trusts' will emerge (and are emerging) in the sectors controlled by foreign investment, such as food processing, automobile industry, retail chains. The danger here would be to tend towards a dual industrial structure, with foreign-owned big corporations and a domestic sector made of small and medium-sized entities resulting from a forcible split of the former state monopolies.

Creating a market environment means having a modern financial and tax system. It also calls for cushioning the impact both of stabilisation and of structural transformation through building a new social security network. What is the role of the state in these emerging markets? The question of industrial policy is a very controversial one.

The Banking and Financial Sectors Reform

The *banking reform* and the setting-up of *capital markets* are generally seen as most urgent and related problems, and parts of the building blocks of stabilisation-cum-transformation (see Table 7.1).

The new banking system

In the socialist countries there was a system based on a 'monobank' endowed with all the banking functions: it was issuing money, acting as the Treasury of the state, and as the sole source of credit for the economy. The first task was thus to create a two-tier banking system, with a Central Bank and independent commercial banks. In Hungary and Poland such a two-tier system had already been established before transition began, and was emerging in the Soviet Union under the *perestroyka*. In Czechoslovakia a banking law was introduced just after the 'velvet revolution' of 1989; in Romania and Bulgaria two-tier banking emerged after the beginning of the transition. In all cases the process began with separating the Central Bank activities from those of the newly created commercial banks, and endowing the latter with the bulk of the former State Bank resources. Competition was introduced in this sector by allowing enterprises, local administration, individuals, and foreigners to set up new banks, under various provisions.

Several roles were conceivable for this new banking system: to support the stabilisation programme; to provide finance to the economy (the era of consumers' credit is yet to come); and to facilitate privatisation and enterprise control.

(1)   The banking system was supposed to manage the monetary side of the stabilisation programme. High interest rates were set. The Central Bank was to control commercial lending through the usual array of methods available in Western practice. In fact, its policy amounted to sheer quantitative credit tightening. Standard open market policies were not possible due to the lack of a financial market. Re-financing procedures work well when they are based upon a variety of high-quality corporate bills or government securities. All of this is missing. Hence the policy of the Central Bank has been to restrict commericial credit through the interest rate policy, and at the same time, in selected cases, to allow commercial banks to rescue big state companies on the verge of bankruptcy. However, this emergency credit by no means met the current needs of the enterprises. As a result, as we have seen in the previous chapter, a huge inter-enterprise indebtedness emerged everywhere, together with large payment and tax arrears. Such a situation is very damaging on three counts. First, it deprives stabilisation policy one of its main instruments; even with high interest rates, there is no adjustment on the enterprise side; enterprises survive and pay wages even when they are poorly performing, and there is a surge in inflation. Second, the banks are not in a position to exert pressure on the management of the enterprises, since they will abstain from taking action against bad debtors as they are reluctant to show a large percentage of non-performing loans (Begg and Portes, 1992). Third, while there are some (state and private) well-performing enterprises which deserve to get credit by all standard criteria, there will be an adverse selection effect; these enterprises will have to pay higher rates, as the banks will have to raise their provisions because of bad loans, and thus to seek higher profits through higher spreads (between their lending rates and the cost of their borrowing from the Central Bank). This has actually led the best Hungarian companies to borrow from foreign rather than from domestic banks.

(2)   The substitution (at least in part) of interenterprise indebtedness for banking credit in turn severely constrained the privatisation process. The choice was between privatising without financial restructuring, as in the case of mass privatisation, which gives citizens shares in debts rather than in assets, and attempting a financial restructuring (including recapitalisation of the enterprises) before privatisation. In fact financial restructuring, even when preferred (as in Hungary and Poland) was hardly affordable on a large scale (see Hunya, 1993). Lack of adequate information yields the impression that most of the enterprises are indebted both to banks and to other enterprises. This deters foreign investors, prompts shareholders in the case of mass privatisation to get rid of their shares by selling them to investment funds or on a black (grey) market, and ultimately strengthens insiders' control.

Recapitalising of banks has been resorted to as well. It has been strongly recommended in the early Western literature (see Begg and Portes, 1992), and actually implemented in the Czech Republic (in 1991, through the establishment of a special institution, the *Konsolidacni Banka)*, and in Hungary, where the bad loans have been purchased against government bonds by a state agency, the State Development and Investment Company. In both cases there was very little capital injection and thus it is rather a transfer of bad loans to the state, which amounts to sharing of the debt burden between generations (Csáki, 1993, p. 19). In 1993 the process had to be repeated in Hungary, involving bank and enterprise debt consolidation as well (ECE/UN, 1994b, Chapter 5). Western banks and international institutions such as the World Bank and the EBRD are involved in technical assistance in this field, but the process is both lengthy and costly.

Meanwhile, in all countries in transition the banking sector is fragile. Apart from the bad debts, which according to an estimate from the EBRD amount to 60 per cent of the balance sheets of the Eastern banks (Robinson and Denton, 1993), the banking business is plagued by fraud, bribery and negligence which emerge during financial scandals, which happen occasionally in Central Europe (such as the case of Banka Bohemia in Prague which issued bogus securities, April 1994) and are endemic in Russia where the new banking sector of more than 2,000 banks is plagued by overdraft with the Central Bank, fraud and money-laundering linked with Mafia control, and by open crime.

(3)   The reform blueprints did not explicitly assign to the banking system the function of controlling the privatised enterprises. The banks were expected to assist the cleaning-up of the enterprise sector through bankruptcy procedures, but it was soon acknowledged that they would avoid triggering bankruptcies so as not to expose their bad loans. They were not expected to become major stakeholders in the enterprises. Out of the two basic Western models, the reformers in the countries in transition by and large preferred the US–UK model, where banks perform savings and

lending activities but are not involved in corporate activities, to the 'German–Japanese' model where banks have close equity links with enterprises (see Corbett and Mayer, 1991; Steinherr and Gilibert, 1994). The first model is associated with a developed securities market and with networks of financial intermediaries such as investment and pension funds. The second model involves much closer links between banks and the management of corporations. It has also led to an expansion of financial intermediation by the banks themselves, increasingly in association with the insurance sector.

What emerged in fact was the worst of both worlds. Banks became major shareholders in privatised companies, either directly or through the investment funds they had set up. They also remained major stakeholders in state-owned companies, either through the debts owed to them or through personal links inherited from the past. At the same time, capital markets developed in a volatile way. Non-controlled financial intermediaries expanded as well, and often turned out to be very fragile financially.

The emerging capital market

The need for *capital markets* has often been quoted as a precondition for privatisation. The lack of capital markets, even in the countries which have introduced a stock exchange, is indeed obvious, and prevents large-scale privatisation through public offerings, which is the dominant method used in the West. One should nevertheless remark that even in the Western economies it took many decades to turn the national stock exchanges into a sophisticated global network, and that a stock exchange can hardly operate without capital, which is the case now in the East.

The countries in transition have begun with symbols rather than with realities. In most countries a stock exchange has been set up, or revived, with a very small level of activity even in the earliest to operate, i.e. the Budapest Stock Exchange (set up in 1990) (see Table 7.1). Such institutions are certainly useful in helping people to become familiar with the notion of a capital market, but they play a very small role and do not assist the privatisation process in the way capital markets do in the West. These emerging markets were booming in 1993, especially the Polish market which registered a gain of 783 per cent in dollar terms (PlanEcon, 1994; also PlanEcon 1993c). The Czech Republic has, in addition to the Prague Stock Exchange, an over-the-counter electronic RM-system that trades the shares of the privatised companies through the voucher system, and organises auctions of these shares. These emerging stock markets are small – a few dozen stocks are quoted – and very volatile. After the 1993 boom, all Central European stock exchanges experienced a fall in the first part of 1994. They are vulnerable to financial scandals, which are likely to occur often due to the lack of experience of the operators, and the control established by the new mafias on these activities. The MMM scandal in Russia, where a finance house collapsed after having issued, with a dramatic advertisement campaign, bogus shares whose value had risen in three months by eight times, epitomises the gullibility of the public (*Financial Times*, 1 August 1994), and so does a similar case in Romania, where in 22 months a pyramid scheme called Caritas managed to attract deposits from four million Romanians for a total amount of $1 billion! (*Financial Times*, 22 February 1994).

There is a great deal of confusion and misunderstanding as to the role of the new investment funds created in the wake of privatisation. In mass privatisation schemes, they facilitate the distribution of vouchers and the auctioning off because beneficiaries prefer to entrust their vouchers to these funds. In Poland, the Mass Privatisation Programme went further; the national investment funds instituted by the law of 1993 will have to manage, restructure and increase the value of the assets of the state-owned companies to be privatised; 33 per cent of the shares of each such company will be attributed to one of the twenty or so funds to be set up, and 27 per cent of its shares will be distributed among the other funds in approximately equal parts (Bossak, 1994). Each of the funds will thus own a bulk of the shares of about twenty companies of the 400 or so to participate in the scheme. The shares of the funds will be owned by the citizens, who will receive them against a nominal payment. The idea was thus to create strong financial intermediaries. Who is to manage the funds? The initial idea was to have foreign experts (preferably of Polish descent). But it turned out to be very difficult to get good professionals to come to Poland, even for a high salary (however inferior to Western standards). The managers of the funds, appointed by the Polish administration, will thus probably be taken from the enterprises to be privatised – thus restoring the risk of insider control.

In the absence of developed financial market institutions (one has in particular to mention here that the potential role of insurance companies is far from understood as yet), the investment funds are thus bound to be managed by three categories of people: imaginative individuals with a more or less clean (politically and ethically) background, who will soon master the rules of the financial games and develop speculation on their account (the notorious MMM fund which collapsed in August 1994 in Moscow and its chairman, a former researcher in applied mathematics, are an example); bank or state-owned firms' managers, who will strengthen 'spontaneous' privatisation; and political appointees. A combination of two or three of these options is no less possible.

The Tax Reform

Reforming the tax system is a part of the structural transformation but is also crucial to the stabilisation programme. The new tax system should provide resources to the budget, be transparent, as simple as possible, and not too heavy on enterprises and individuals so as to avoid stifling entrepreneurship. Most of all, the levying of the taxes by the governments should be perceived not as an arbitrary charge imposed on taxpayers, but a just contribution to collective expenses. In the past, enterprises used to bargain about the taxes they paid and negotiate them with the state authorities, an attitude which was replaced by sheer evasion and avoidance.

During the transition, the state sector has been discriminated against in the field of taxation. For instance, in Poland state enterprises have been subjected to high taxation in the form of a 'dividend' on profits unrelated to actual profits, exactly as in the former system. At the same time, 'hidden subsidies' allowed the state enterprises to survive though unprofitable. The implicit subsidisation is embodied in the reluctant implementation of the bankruptcy regulations, as we have seen.

Tax reforms are being implemented as a part of the structural transformation process, while taxes are of course used in the stabilisation programme, with mixed results because of tax evasion (see Table 7.2). The evasion factor may explain why many countries moved toward the introduction of a value added tax, not only because this is part of the approximation of their tax regulations with those of the European Community. VAT is less painful for the public than income tax, and less easy to evade. The rates are higher than in Western Europe, averaging 22–25 per cent for most items. But VAT is not easy to monitor, and in market economies it took several years to master it: for instance in France it was formally introduced in 1958, and generalised only in 1966.

A new system of personal income taxes and corporate profit taxes is gradually introduced. Specific taxes on excess wage payments have been levied as a part of the incomes control policy.

The tax reforms are however very slow to implement. The tax administration is not sufficiently trained to manage a complex tax system. The accounting systems do not allow for a precise monitoring of the corporate profit tax. Finally as the foreign investments have large tax benefits the domestic taxpayers feel that the burden of the tax payments falls on them (see Kodrzycki, 1993).

The failure in implementing large-scale tax reforms has of course an impact on the expenditures to be financed by the budget. The lack of resources is the main obstacle to building an efficient social safety net.

Building a New Social Safety Network

The need for a new *social safety net* is widely recognised by governments and Western experts, both to cushion the impact of the stabilisation and structural transformation, and to shape new attitudes, away from the former overall protection system provided by the Communist state.

Hungary was already altering its social security model in the 1980s; the other countries in transition have tackled this task after the beginning of the transition. Contrary to a widely held assumption in the West, the main problem is not unemployment. Growing unemployment is still a recent phenomenon, and still manageable insofar as it first hits women or young people who have some support in their family. Unemployment benefits have been introduced; they are generally rather low and allocated for a short period. The social transfers in nature (i.e. free health services) are still provided but at a very low-quality level while paying health care is developing. The main problem is that of the pension system. Retirement age is generally low, the population is ageing, and retired people form the bulk of the 'new poor' as inflation has eroded their very low pensions.

Social expenditures are financed from the budget, and through contributions from the enterprises (and the employees, as in Hungary) in proportion to the wages. The pressing requests for a balanced budget urged by the IMF may clash with the needs for expanding social expenditures, as was the case in Poland in the beginning of 1993. Private insurance schemes are not quite realistic. They would require a developed general insurance market which does not exist (and could also provide much needed financial intermediaries: see section on the emerging capital market above). They impose a heavy load on the enterprises which would have to finance the major share of it for their employees. The local governments are also involved in covering social expenditures, with still less resources. Table 8.5 surveys the existing system in selected countries.

Is an Industrial Policy Necessary?

In view of the constraints on the budgets, the *industrial policies* issue was quite controversial from the outset. The problem is not only that there is no money to finance it, but also that national governments are very much against it – it strongly resembles central planning. At the same time there is no clear idea of what an industrial policy might encompass.

(1) In the standard definition, an industrial policy is meant to involve the state in *long-term strategic development* of a given activity. In the countries in transition, there was initially no scheme for organising the decline of whole sectors, for promoting small and medium enterprises, for encouraging R&D or modernisation, or for 'picking winners' for future growth. Initial devaluations have acted as an incentive for exports, and a protection against imports. Tariffs were increased in 1992, after their dramatic lowering in all countries in 1991, so as to protect 'nascent industries' or on the other hand 'ageing industries' that could provide export earnings. However this amounts to very little in terms of an active industrial policy (Fath, 1992).

Table 8.5 The social safety network (1993 unless otherwise stated)

Issues	Czech Republic	Hungary	Poland	Russia
Objectives: reorient public attitudes away from guaranteed protection by state 'from cradle to grave' (1) limit public spending (2)	Mix of (1) and (2)	Mainly (2)	Mainly (2)	Mainly (1)
Constraints: to do with a low level of resources (budget deficit) (1) to avoid inflation fuelled by public spending (2) to avoid too high taxation of firms (3)	Mainly (3)	Mainly (1) and (2)	Mainly (1) and (3)	Mainly (1)
Administrative body	Social Security Administration, with strong decentralisation	Social Security Administration	Social Insurance Office (ZUS in Polish) Labour Fund for unemployment	Pension fund Social Insurance Fund, managed by the Independent Federation of Trade Unions
Sources of funding	No payroll tax specifically allocated to social security (the payroll tax of 50 per cent goes into the budget, which finances social security with non-affected resources)	44 per cent employer payroll tax + employee contribution of 10 per cent gross salary; some budget transfers. Unemployment benefits: 7 per cent payroll tax, 2 per cent employee contrib.	45 per cent payroll tax + 3 per cent for Labour Fund; deficit of Social security covered by budget (about 30 per cent of state budget expenditures for 1993, from 15 per cent in 1991). Social assistance and health care covered by budget (5–6 per cent of budget goes to health care).	Pension Fund: 31.6 payroll tax and 1 per cent employee contribution; Social Insurance Fund: 5.4 per cent payroll tax

Areas: social insurance (pensions, disability payments, family payments, illness compensation)	*Pensions* paid to 3 million. Retirement age: 60 for men; between 53 and 57 for women. Minimum pensions are indexed to inflation. *Family benefits* for children up to 26 years (if children are supported by their parents).	*Pensions* paid to 2.8 million. Retirement age: 60 for men; 55 for women, to be raised gradually from 1995. Basis: wages during the last years of employment. Pensions are partly indexed to inflation. *Maternity benefits*: 24 weeks at full previous wage; 2 years at 75 per cent + another year of child allowance. Job retained for 3 years.	*Pensions* paid to 8.7 million people, of which 3.5 disability pensions. To qualify for old-age pensions: 65 years men, 60 women; 25 years employment for men required (20 for women). 2 components: 24 per cent of current average wage + 'base sum' for each year of employment. Pensions indexed to average wage (percentage of indexation decreasing from 100 per cent in 1991 to 90 in 1993.	Pensions paid to 35 million. Retirement age: 60 for men; 55 for women. Minimum pensions are indexed to inflation since 1993. *Sick pay*: 100 per cent wage for work-related illness; between 100 and 60 per cent of wage depending on number of years of service, for non-work-related illness. *Family benefits* for children up to 6 years. Maternity benefit for women on maternity leave, for 126 days.
unemployment	Standard benefit: 65 per cent of last wage for 6 months, 60 per cent for the following 6 months. After one year, minimal allowance of about 25 per cent of the average wage (1993). In 1994 duration of benefit reduced to 6 months.	Standard benefit: 50 per cent of previous average wage. Maximum period of receipt: 18 months reduced to 12 months in 1994.	Standard benefit: 36 per cent of average wage. Maximum period of receipt: 12 months. To qualify: six months work required in the preceding year.	Standard benefit: 75 per cent of last wage for 3 months, 60 per cent for the next 4 months, 45 per cent for the following five months. In fact end-94 the average benefit was 10 per cent of average wage.
Share of unemployed receiving benefits (1993)	38 per cent (1992)	52 per cent	48 per cent	66 per cent.
public assistance	Some poverty allowances to compensate for the suppression of subsidies to food and energy.	Poverty line: 11509 ft in Jn 1993; 1.5 to 2 million people below poverty line. Assistance: child education programme for poor families of 3 children and over; income support after end of unemployment benefit; home maintenance assistance	'last-resort' cash benefit: 28 per cent of average wage; poverty line in case of income lower than minimum pension.	Some emergency assistance through the Fund for the Social Support of the Population (refugees, disable or orphaned children; large families; homeless people)

Table 8.5 continued

Issues	Czech Republic	Hungary	Poland	Russia
Areas (continued) health care	Free health care in state hospitals.	Mix of state and private health care.	Free of charge; low quality due to lack of funds. Private clinics available. Basic medicines free.	Free health care in state hospitals, at a very low quality level. An obligatory medical insurance scheme is being introduced, financed by employer contributions to a medical insurance fund.
Level of funding	Average pension: about 50 per cent of average wage.	Average pension: 80 per cent of minimum income in Jan. 1993.	Average monthly pension: 1.8 million zloty in 1992 (average monthly wage: 2.5 million)	Average pension: about 50 per cent of minimum wage.
Trends for the future	Privatisation of health care. Introduction of insurance schemes.	Introduction of private insurance schemes. Distribution of benefits to be managed more by local governments. Allowing the SSA to be financed on transfers of state property. Increasing retirement age.	Introduction of medical insurance debated and controversial.	Privatisation of health care. Introduction of insurance schemes.
Country specifics	The social security network was particularly extensive during the Communist rule, probably the best in the East. It is both too costly and too much state-managed now.	Significant role of local authorities in supporting social costs.	Conflict over the pension financing erupted between government and Parliament, and caused postponement of IMF deal in 1992–1993.	The social security network was very extensive during the Communist rule. It was also largely corrupt, a continuing trend during the transition.

Source: OECD country studies on Poland, Hungary and the CSFR; various press reports; Sheila Marnie, 'Economic Reform and the Social Safety Net', *RFL/RL Research Report*, vol. 2, no. 17, 23 April 1993 (in the same volume, country reports on Poland and Hungary by Louise Vinton and Karoly Okolicsanyi). Sheila Marnie, 'The Social Safety Net in Russia', *RFL/RL Research Report*, vol. 2, no. 17, 23 April 1993, various press reports.

In fact most of the industrial policy has been involuntary. As van Brabant (1994) states, privatisation was a surrogate for industrial policy as many state-owned enterprises have been kept afloat through subsidies or through deferred bankruptcies. The constraint of reorienting exports to the West has also acted as a substitute to open industrial policy, with the result that less-competitive-than-average sectors have been supported (Hughes and Hare, 1992). This issue is part of a broader one, which is the role of the state in the transition economies, and which we revert to in the last chapter.

(2)   A narrower definition of the industrial policy links it to *restructuring*. Restructuring policies may imply closing firms judged unprofitable, or sections of firms, and laying off workers (Aghion and Blanchard, 1993); reorganising the production process as a whole; recapitalising the enterprises; pursuing an anti-monopoly policy and splitting up the enterprises (see Charap and Zemplinerova, 1993, and Carlin and Mayer, 1992, for a clear statement of the issues). The range of opinions goes from a minimalist approach, advocating the maintenance of the state-owned assets until actual privatisation can take place (Aghion, 1993) to the 'restructuring first' proposal, on the model of the *Treuhandanstalt* in East Germany (Carlin and Mayer, 1992). A fine-tuning in sequencing is suggested by Roland (1993), with best firms being privatised first, restructuring following before privatisation for the others.

Under the pressure of circumstances, the Central European countries have ultimately resorted, if not to an openly defined industrial policy, at least to a more positive approach to restructuring, as a substitute for what the 'market' was not doing spontaneously (the cleaning up through bankruptcies), or could not be left doing if a massive winding up was to be avoided. Hungary began in 1992 with a special programme for 13 big enterprises in trouble (see ECE/UN, 1994b, Chapter 5), and in 1993 expanded the programme to a more comprehensive scheme. Poland is applying a more piecemeal, sectoral scheme combined with privatisation. In the Czech government, where the very concept of industrial policy is rejected, there have been individual cases of rescuing large enterprises so as to avoid a domino effect.

(3)   Finally one has to mention the difficult issue of the *agricultural policy*. Early liberalisation has left the agricultural sector in a very difficult position. This sector did not benefit from the end of price subsidies on food as the profits from higher prices were appropriated by the retail distribution chains. It endured the full impact of increased interest rates, which stifled investment. It also had to pay higher taxes than in the past. The land reform and the restitution programmes disorganised the sector. The farmers to whom land was attributed (for instance in Romania and Bulgaria) often could not get their rights implemented. In most countries cooperatives remained, often unwanted. At the same time, farm exports were a strong component of the export basket to the West.

The farm constituencies began to ask for support, especially as, since the opening up of the economy, food imports had increased, in particular from the European Union, using the subsidisation mechanisms of the CAP (Common Agricultural Policy). Since 1992 there has been increased pressure for import protection and subsidies, using a CAP-like format. Obviously the Central and Eastern European countries cannot afford a CAP-equivalent level of subsidisation, as evidenced in a 1994 report commissioned by the House of Lords, which would amount to over $19,000 per person working in agriculture – having in mind that the average GDP per head is a quarter of the EU level even at the most favourable estimates, and that the number of persons working in agriculture is much higher than in Western Europe (House of Lords, 1994). Even a much lower support would be very costly. In addition, it is bound to have an impact on the agricultural relations between the EU and the transition countries, and even more – on the future of the CAP itself, as we shall see in the next chapter.

9 Reintegrating the World Economy

The countries in transition wish to be reintegrated in the world economy as market economies, after decades of 'bloc autarky' within the CMEA. This has readily been accepted in principle in the West. It was expected that these countries would take action to abandon their past behaviour as 'state-trading' countries and become 'normal' partners.

Misunderstanding developed as to these claims and acknowledgements, with mounting disillusion and acrimony on both sides. The European countries in transition, including the former USSR, expected a preferential reintegration: as parts of Europe, to which they profess to belong, due to long-lasting historical links and to geographical connections. The Central and Eastern European countries demanded firm commitments as to future membership in the European Community (European Union since November 1993), and the ex-Soviet states, first of all Russia, asked to be treated as partners if not associates in the first stage. Outrage was felt when the Western countries recommended that, notwithstanding these claims, some steps should be taken to restore mutual links and trade within Eastern Europe and between this region and the former USSR. Frustration was expressed when it became obvious that the new 'Europe Agreements' did not open the European markets for a whole range of sensitive products.

The Western world has promised to extend assistance in various forms. Here too disappointment gathered, on both sides. The donors felt that their commitments were high, while the beneficiaries claimed that assistance was small in size and scope, and inefficiently managed. Ultimately the countries in transition claim more openness from the West to their goods and to their workers, rather than financial aid.

HOW TO RECONSTRUCT REGIONAL ARRANGEMENTS IN THE EAST

In this section we are going to discuss two related though substantially different issues. The first is the way of promoting trade and payments arrangements in Eastern Europe. The second is the way of stopping the disintegration of the former Soviet space. What unites these issues is the historical reference to the experience of post-war Europe, which is often put forward in the West to suggest comparable solutions.

191

The collapse of foreign trade among the countries in transition, which was already obvious in the very beginning of the transition (see Chapter 6), persisted in the following years. 'Eastern' trade, i.e. trade among Eastern European countries as well as between them and the successor states to the USSR, fell on average by 60 per cent in three years, the share of this trade in the total trade of the region with the world reaching an average of 30 per cent. Trade among the successor states to the USSR, once the USSR was dissolved, fell still more steeply. Table 9.1 sums up these developments.

Table 9.1   *Patterns of foreign trade of the countries in transition (1991–3)*

	1991	1992	1993	1993
	Growth rates in per cent			Structure by direction
Bulgaria				
Total trade: exports	−34.2	1.6	−13.4	100.0
Transition countries	−27.8	−25.7	−12.2	23.6
of which Russia[b]	−80.2	−50.0	−20.0	14.9
Developed West	−36.3	61.6	−17.2	43.1
Third World	−47.6	14.2	−8.9	18.5
Total trade: imports	−51.5	27.5	0.2	100.0
Transition countries	−43.1	−4.3	18.3	14.9
Russia[b]	−84.3	9.2	26.0	29.9
Developed West	−59.8	79.3	−11.7	42.4
Third World	−54.4	26.7	−10.0	12.8
Czech Republic[a]				
Total trade: exports	5.6	3.2	15.5	100.0
Transition countries	6.8	−33.0	−0.6	11.9
Russia[b]	−6.0	−43.5	−2.0	7.5
Developed West	6.9	26.4	19.5	69.9
Third World	−6.0	27.4	24.2	10.7
Total trade: imports	−7.2	14.6	0.5	100.0
Transition countries	0.3	−10.2	−14.2	6.9
Russia[b]	−11.4	−6.0	−23.0	14.0
Developed West	−13.7	39.6	5.2	73.1
Third World	4.4	−20.4	6.5	6.0
Hungary				
Total trade: exports	5.1	4.1	−16.8	100.0
Transition countries	−26.8	3.2	−6.0	9.8
Russia[b]	−41.0	3.2	−13.0	16.5
Developed West	21.4	8.9	−21.0	66.3
Third World	21.8	−23.9	−8.0	7.3
Total trade: imports	30.2	−3.2	13.2	100.0
Transition countries	2.8	1.8	32.9	8.5
Russia[b]	5.9	6.9	6.6	15.4
Developed West	44.3	−1.7	5.9	69.1
Third World	29.0	−46.5	15.3	7.0

	1991	*1992*	*1993*	*1993*
	Growth rates in per cent			*Structure by direction*
Poland				
Total trade: exports	−18.5	−11.6	6.9	100.0
Transition countries	−62.0	−18.9	−19.2	5.1
Russia[b]	−56.3	−24.0	−3.0	8.6
Developed West	13.7	−13.8	12.1	75.3
Third World	−15.5	26.8	13.9	10.9
Total trade: imports	24.3	1.8	24.9	100.0
Transition countries	−42.8	−10.3	−20.0	4.3
Russia[b]	−26.0	−13.0	1.0	10.2
Developed West	71.7	6.9	29.8	76.3
Third World	151.0	−8.5	75.9	9.2
Romania				
Total trade: exports	−7.1	5.2	6.4	100.0
Transition countries	29.2	−16.3	−3.0	8.3
Russia[b]	40.0	20.0	−43.0	9.5
Developed West	−23.0	1.3	7.3	64.4
Third World	−11.9	55.4	14.4	17.8
Total trade: imports	−17.6	8.2	6.1	100.0
Transition countries	−8.9	−8.5	−0.9	6.2
Russia[b]	41.0	−5.0	18.0	17.1
Developed West	−9.4	40.3	15.6	61.9
Third World	−32.7	−17.2	11.5	14.9
Russia[b]				
Total trade: exports	−24.6	−25.2	1.4	100.0
Transition countries	−35.1	−25.8	−12.6	7.9
East Europe	−40.8	−32.7	−7.9	17.0
Developed West	−16.2	−20.3	4.6	59.8
Third World	−29.0	−44.0	23.1	15.3
Total trade: imports	−35.9	−21.3	−27.1	100.0
Transition countries	−35.9	−42.8	−14.7	10.4
East Europe	−51.6	−49.7	−46.0	14.8
Developed West	−31.0	−13.0	−36.9	59.3
Third World	−35.8	−2.6	−4.5	15.6

[a] Czechoslovakia, for 1991 and 1992. Trade with Slovakia is not included in 1993.
[b] Former Soviet Union for 1991 and 1992. In 1993 trade with the CIS and Baltic countries is not included.

Notes:
'Transition countries' refers to the ex-socialist countries, including the CMEA members, former Yugoslavia, and China. Growth rates are calculated including Russia (in the case of the Eastern European countries) and East Europe (in the case of Russia). For the structure of trade calculations the entry is taken as 'other transition countries' (than Russia, for the Eastern European countries, or than Eastern Europe, in the case of Russia).

Sources: Calculations from ECE/UN, *Economic Survey of Europe in 1993–1994*, and *PlanEcon Report*, country monthly economic monitor issues.

The collapse of the former 'communist trade' raises many questions. Could and should one try to avoid it? Is it the normal outcome of the transition process? Is it more urgent to revive the links among the successor states of the USSR than among Central European countries?

One has to look differently at the two areas, Central and Eastern Europe on the one hand, and the former USSR on the other. The reorientation of the Central European countries toward the West is irreversible. It is sustained by the willingness of these countries to join the EC, and though the EC countries are increasingly worried about the surge of sensitive imports from the East, the political setting is such that the European Commission has to accelerate the integration process, beyond what was stipulated in the 'Europe agreements'.

The collapse of intra-USSR (CIS) trade is of a different nature. It has been provoked by the economic collapse of the USSR, by political conflicts, and by the inability of Russia to solve the monetary problems of the area with its partners. It is not only advisable but necessary to stop the disintegration of this economic space, and there is no analogy here with the impact of the CMEA collapse. The CMEA was not really an economic union, or a supranational organisation: its very weaknesses have in a sense alleviated the consequences of its dissolving. Trade flows among its members were geared to the needs and interests of the Soviet Union. Despite significant trade interdependencies between the Central and Eastern European countries on the one hand, and the USSR on the other, the national economies were not deeply connected, and all endeavours to increase intra-branch and intra-product industrial cooperation in the area have failed. This specific weakness of the CMEA scheme greatly helped Central and Eastern European countries to sever their mutual links, despite the blow caused by the fall in trade.

The USSR was a single state under the cover of a Federation. Its industries were interdependent not in the Western, market sense of intra-industry links, but out of political decisions which had created intricate networks of administrative links. If these relations are not replaced with a new, normalised foreign trade, the recovery of the CIS economies may take much more time than expected.

The Rationale for a Central and Eastern European Regional Grouping

There is a definite pressure from the West to convince Eastern Europe that a regional arrangement would suit the interests of the region and is not just a way of diverting to other Eastern countries some sensitive exports presently directed to Western countries. Lessons from history are invoked, as well as economic and political arguments.

Lessons from Eastern history

Eastern European countries claim that they have been forced into the Soviet bloc since the Second World War, while before the war they mostly traded with 'the West'. But was 1938, for instance, a significant year? In 1938, following almost a decade of Nazi rule in Germany, Central European countries were tied to their powerful neighbour through a whole set of political arrangements, including a system of settlements in clearing aimed not just at facilitating trade but at exploiting these countries and isolating them from Western democracies as well as from the Soviet enemy.

Precisely for this reason, a study published by the Institute for International Economics in Washington (Collins and Rodrik, 1991) has decided upon the year 1928 as the last pre-war 'normal' year for investigating trade patterns. The conclusion is that 'although suggestive, the 1928 composition of trade is far from being a reliable guide for future trade patterns' (p. 41), especially because of the shifting role of individual Western countries in world trade. Accounting for that, the authors propose a model which provides a projection of pre-war trends assuming that East Central European countries would not have become 'socialist', and would have behaved in line with several 'comparator' countries in Europe. This exercise leads to several conclusions: (i) there should be a very strong reorientation of trade to the West and especially toward EC countries; (ii) trade with the Soviet Union should decline dramatically; and (iii) trade among the Eastern countries might stabilise and even increase (in proportion to total trade). The authors acknowledge that the model has not fully taken into account some variables and hypotheses, such as the impact of past specialisation in the region, the consequences of EC trade policies, or the event of a recovery of the Soviet market, the latter not being considered as plausible.

Lessons from Western history

An extensive literature has been published on the relevancy of the Marshall plan and the post-war Western cooperation to the present situation of Eastern Europe. The Marshall plan was proposed in June 1947 by the US Secretary of State, offering US help for the economic reconstruction of war-devastated Europe. In July 1947 the European Committee for Economic Cooperation was set up; this was the precursor of the OEEC (Organisation for European Economic Cooperation) which itself evolved into the OECD. The European countries developed their cooperation under the direct pressure of the United States. The Marshall plan supported the creation of the EPU (European Payments Union) along with the commitment to liberalise trade in Europe. The EPU was set up in 1950 so as to facilitate a gradual and coordinated transition to convertibility of the European currencies. In 1951 the Marshall plan transfers came to an end. In the same year the ECSC (the European Community for Steel and Coal) was created. In 1957 the Rome Treaty instituting the Common Market was signed. In 1958 the EPU had achieved its task as all the European currencies were convertible, and was dissolved.

This story was used both by supporters of an Eastern EPU or trade union (among them, Jozef van Brabant was the most enthusiastic; see van Brabant, 1993; Bakos, 1993), and by its critics. The difficulty lies in establishing a link between the Plan and the post-war economic events. Within a ten-year period, the European countries reconstructed their infrastructures, resumed growth, successfully fought inflation, balanced their budgets, liberalised their trade, made their currencies convertible, and launched a common market, at the same time healing political wounds among nations which had fought each other during the war. How can one separate the impact of the Marshall plan, of the political game between the United States and the European countries, of the national policies, of the drive toward European cooperation? Was the Marshall plan 'the most successful structural adjustment programme in history', as claimed in de Long and Eichengreen (1992), or the catalyst of economic cooperation as former French Prime Minister Raymond Barre, who worked in the European Cooperation Administration, sees it (Barre *et al.*, 1992b)? There are strong analogies in the initial situations in 1947 and in 1989: countries that are devastated by the war or by decades of communist economic management; strong enmities among the nations, due to war or to history; readiness of a rich partner to help against some conditionality, in his own interests.

However the differences are considerable. In 1947 the European economies were developed market economies, which normal way of operating had been suspended for a few years only. Before the war these countries already dominated the world scene and already conducted about 40 per cent of their foreign trade among themselves. This is not to say that a trade arrangement or a payment union is not to be advocated for Eastern Europe. If they are, this ought not necessarily be based on the post-war experience.

Economic arguments

In international economic theory various approaches may be selected to support one view or the other. Gravity models suggest that neighbours are prone to trade together, though economists generally distrust them. The Heckscher-Ohlin model and the derived theories would support the rationale for Russia–Eastern Europe trade relations as these are based on complementary factor endowments, but would not so much advocate an expansion of intra-Eastern European trade, as the economic structures and endowments of Central and Eastern European countries are very similar. However, countries with similar industries may well trade among themselves according to an intra-branch trade pattern, or trade similar goods in an imperfect competition approach.

Anyhow, applied international economics are devised for market economies. Thus one may well assert that countries in transition should first turn into market economies. Trade among them will develop according to a market rationale only if this initial condition is fulfilled; no artificial grouping can be a substitute for the market. In this neo-classical spirit the EPU scheme is strongly criticised. A payments union, it is argued, may enhance trade if the latter is impaired mainly by lack of convertible currencies. If the causes of the stalemate are different and due to structural supply rigidities, absence of a fully-fledged demand market, or economic recession, no payments union could generate trade *per se*. It would only be inefficient, and very costly (see Kenen, 1991).

One may also question any model aiming at establishing what should be the 'normal' level of trade among the former CMEA countries. Using a gravity model, Dariusz Rosati (1993b) shows that 'normal' trade among the countries of Central and Eastern Europe and with the USSR would be rather below the (already depressed) levels of 1989–90. Harriet Matejka (1994) challenges any such approach. First the statistical distortions are such, before and after the collapse of the CMEA, that it is virtually impossible to claim robust results. Second, to assume that a 'normal' state would be the intensity of trade among countries displaying comparable economic characteristics, is to ignore that the transition economies are not only moving to a market system but are, at the same time, undergoing a formidable upheaval which is changing all economic relationships. Thus, to apply to them parameters calculated for established market economies or for them at an earlier stage is simply meaningless.

Political arguments

The political arguments are the most compelling. Eastern European countries do not want any arrangement resembling the former CMEA. They are still more opposed to any conditionality linking assistance with the commitment to regional cooperation.

They also interpret Western arguments that are in favour of a regional arrangement as motivated by political afterthoughts. While the Western world is ready to 'reintegrate' the East, it may not be ready to absorb the shock. The President of the European Commission, Jacques Delors, very early urged on the Central European countries not to compete among themselves for a faster membership but to look for mutual cooperation. Even in such mild terms the advice is suspect to the countries which are engaged in the procedure of accession. These countries believe, in which they are right, that behind this urge there is a desire to delay their accession. They are wrong on three points: (i) even without specific pressure for delaying their accession this will be a long way off, due to all the conditions to be met, and to the accession queue; (ii) the European governments will not move faster whatever the demand for quick accession; (iii) a regional arrangement cannot harm.

The sheer weight of the former USSR and specifically of Russia is a disturbing element. Before the collapse of the USSR it was obvious that any arrangement not including the USSR would hardly help, because of the small amounts of trade involved, and that an arrangement including the USSR would be a source of imbalance. Once the USSR collapsed the debate shifted to another issue, that of an intra-CIS arrangement. It looks almost impossible to solve both issues at once.

The Actual Arrangements in Eastern and Central Europe

Central European countries form what the West is calling 'the Visegrád group', a phrase not very popular among them. The Visegrád agreement was indeed signed in February 1991 among Poland, Hungary and the CSFR. The Final Declaration recommended 'free movement of capital and labour', to be promoted by 'the development of market-based *economic cooperation*', cooperation in infrastructure development, and in the ecological sphere. But no explicit mechanism or regulations were to ensure that the goal be met (Visegrád, 1991). The concept of a *free-trade area* surfaced again in 1992. The 'Europe agreements' had been signed by each Central European country with the EC on 16 December 1991. These agreements established a free trade area, again between each of them and the EC. It was thus just paradoxical that these countries should maintain among themselves the kind of barriers which were dismantled vis-à-vis the EC members. Ultimately, a free-trade-area agreement was signed between four members (the Czech and Slovak republics being split as of January 1993) of the 'Visegrád group' in Cracow, on 21 December 1992, to be in force as of 1 March 1993, i.e. exactly one year following the enforcement of the 'Interim Agreements' whereby the 'Europe Agreements' were implemented pending their ratification. Slovenia signed bilateral free trade agreements with each of the Visegrád countries (except Poland) in 1994.

Though the new CEFTA (Central European Free Trade Area) was hailed in the West as creating a market of 64 million, the main outcome of the new agreement is to level the playing-field. Mutual concessions have been devised so as to ensure that mutual trade will not be discriminated against by comparison with trade with the EC. There is a striking parallelism between the Association agreements, on the one hand, and the CEFTA agreement, on the other, regarding deadlines, and the categorisation of goods traded. In both cases goods are divided among non-sensitive products on which duties are abolished immediately; 'normal' products on which duties are to be reduced over a period of three to four years; and sensitive goods on which duties are to be reduced over eight years (steel and textiles are included in the last category). The only significant difference with the Association agreements is that within the Visegrád group concessions are symmetrical, in contrast to the asymmetrical format of the EC–Central European countries. As with the EC, the most thorny point was the question of agricultural goods, for which a quota system is to remain in force. It could be expected that the new CEFTA would have some difficulties, with four signatories but three custom zones as the Czech and Slovak republics form a customs union (Okolicsanyi, 1993; Hoen, 1994).

The concept of the Central European grouping thus clearly appears as a facilitating device for joining the EC. Not surprisingly, the pressure from the Central European countries on the EC mounted following the signature of the CEFTA agreement, as if to stress that the CEFTA countries had fulfilled a precondition, and proved that they were able to work together. In the CEFTA countries, those economists who are most in favour of the development of intra-regional trade, or rather the less opposed to it, would advocate liberalising mutual trade (beyond what is provided for in the agreement), dismantling the existing barriers to the regional flows of investment, and eliminating the unnecessary costs of mutual trade and in particular the use of Western intermediaries. In turn, the EU should support more actively regional trade and cooperation by aid packages (in particular to expand trade with the former Soviet Union) and co-financing of regional infrastructural projects (Inotai and Sass, 1994).

Other attempts are still less substantial. On 14 February 1993 in Debrecen (Hungary) a Euroregion linking the local communities in Poland, Hungary, Ukraine, and Slovakia (without the Czech Republic) was established. This new Euroregion follows a model initiated in 1963 among three border regions of France, Germany and Switzerland; by the end of 1992 there were about 30 registered Euroregions in Western Europe, with cultural and economic purposes (Weydenthal, 1993a). A few 'East–West' Euroregions have been set up since the transition. The Carpathian Euroregion is the first one totally 'Eastern'. It has already provoked controversy, especially in Poland, on nationalistic grounds. The Western experience shows that Euroregions add little to development opportunities, even though they are supported by EC funding, and that local transborder cooperation is generally much more actively fostered by the initiatives of the states involved. At best they may have encouraged cultural and good-neighbourly relations among local communities. The future of the Carpathian Euroregion does not look too promising. In the best case it will not be able to solve economic problems though contributing to some stability in the area. In the worst case it might exacerbate nationalistic feelings and stir unrest.

One should mention a larger grouping which was meant to bring together Eastern and Western countries. This is the *Pentagonale* (later *Hexagonale*) which started as a statement on future cooperation among Austria, Hungary, Italy and Yugoslavia on 12 November 1989. The Quadrangle was joined by the ČSFR (in May 1990) then by Poland (July 1991). The Yugoslav crisis of course greatly affected the scheme. In the field of economics the organisation was to focus heavily on telecommunications, transport and tourism. It had no specific financing and depended on foreign assistance, which stopped with the flaring up of the Yugoslav conflict. It then evolved into a Central European Initiative (CEI), with separate membership for the Czech and the Slovak Republics, and for Croatia, Slovenia, Bosnia and Hercegovina, and Macedonia. The CEI Summit held in Budapest in July 1993 stated the political aims of the organisation, and discussed the construction of a Baltic–Adriatic highway among the economic issues (Hoen, 1994).

New Trade and Payments Arrangements in the CIS Space

The Commonwealth of Independent States which links Russia and, according to the Russian-coined word, its 'near-abroad', is neither a customs union, nor a payments union. The disaggregation of the Soviet Union compelled the successor states to look for an arrangement whereby some of the links uniting them in the past could be maintained. The most worrying, and yet unresolved, problem is that of the currency. No clear option has been retained out of the two possible ones, a ruble zone or a payments union.

The attempts to form an economic union

The CIS was established in December 1991 as a loose arrangement between the former Republics of the USSR, except the Baltic states and Georgia (which decided to join the organisation in October 1993 to prevent its own internal disaggregation). Several moves took place in 1992–94:

- In Minsk in February 1992, the heads of state of the CIS agreed to preserve mutual trade, to abstain from quantitative restrictions on licensing exports or imports, except for strategic goods specified in bilateral protocols, and to accept the ruble as the sole payments unit.
- In October 1992 in Bishkek, the capital of Kyrgyzstan, eight countries (Russia, Belarus, Moldova, Armenia and the Central Asian countries except Turkmenistan) agreed to remain in a common currency zone and to set up an Interstate Bank to ensure their settlements. They also agreed to coordinate the issue of money in the area.
- On 22 January 1993 in Minsk seven states (the eight mentioned above minus Moldova) endorsed a Charter to be ratified within a year. Ukraine, Turkmenistan and Moldova signed an agreement which left

open the possibility for them to sign the agreement later. The Charter draft provided for cooperation in the establishment of a common economic space with free movement of goods, capital, labour, and services, and in the promotion of mutual trade.

- On 24 September 1993, just on the eve of the political crisis in Russia that erupted between the parliament and the presidency, nine countries (the 'Bishkek' eight plus Azerbaijan), met to sign a treaty setting up an economic union. Georgia signed some of the provisions; Ukraine claimed the status of an associate member; Turkmenistan opted out but did not rule out signing later if its claims were fulfilled as regards taxation, company law, and finance. It was announced that some 35 other agreements would be needed to implement the treaty. The main provisions of this treaty include the abolition of trade barriers, equal legal status for one another's companies and promotion of jointly owned companies, and finally a payments union along with a ruble zone for those countries staying in it.
- On 15 April 1994, all CIS leaders agreed to participate in the economic union, to work towards a customs union, and to create an Interstate Economic Commission. These commitments were repeated on 21 October 1994, along with the decision to create a payments union.

These arrangements have been purely declarative, and largely repetitive. Overall in 1992–4, about 20 meetings were held, and over 400 documents signed; none of these texts was actually implemented. Along with these moves, integration is also sought on a sub-regional level.

A summit of the *Central Asian states* was held in Tashkent in January 1993 to discuss the possibility of a Central Asian Common market. On 1 February 1994, an agreement went into effect between Kazakhstan, Uzbekistan, and Kyrgyzstan on the creation of a less ambitious 'common economic space'. Free circulation of capital, goods, and labour will be allowed, and common policies on credit, prices, taxes, customs, and currency should be set. As a first move, customs posts were removed on the common borders of the three states. However, it is difficult to see how the three states will be able to coordinate their economic policies, as Uzbekistan is far less advanced in reform than its two partners, and it was only in February 1994 that it regulated private property (Brown, 1994).

In addition, the Central Asian countries all became members of the *Economic Cooperation Organisation* (ECO), with the last country, Tajikistan, to join in February 1993. ECO was established in 1985 by Iran, Pakistan and Turkey, and joined in 1992 by Azerbaijan and Afghanistan. In July 1993 the heads of state of ECO agreed to establish a trade and investment bank, a reinsurance firm and a shipping company.

The *Black Sea Economic Cooperation* was established in June 1992 between 6 CIS members (Armenia, Azerbaijan, Georgia, Moldova, Russia,

Ukraine), Turkey, Bulgaria, Romania, Greece and Albania. This Turkish initiative is meant to develop economic cooperation in various areas (transportation, communications, tourism, statistics, agriculture, energy, environment, health care, and R&D). The organisation lacks the institutional structure needed to enforce its directives, and is affected by the military and political tensions in the Black Sea region. A Black Sea trade and investment bank was to be set up in Thessaloniki, Greece, but it was unclear how it may function without international support and funding. The BSEC has a symbolic potential in offering cooperation between CIS states, South Eastern Europe, and two Western states. It has yet to establish itself politically, institutionally, and economically (Connelly, 1994).

The concept of a *Slavic Union*, which had emerged as early as December 1991 (it was then the first move that led to the creation of the CIS) surfaced again. Russia, Ukraine and Belarus proclaimed a Slavic economic union in July 1993, as declarative as any of the other similar attempts. But in April 1994 Belarus and Russia went further by signing a monetary union, which also provided for the establishment of a free-trade zone (Markus, 1994). The elections held in Ukraine and Belarus in June 1994 brought to power new government leaders closer to the idea of a Slavic association, if not integration. The prospects were still very fuzzy end-1994.

The *Baltic states* set up a free trade zone and sent a message to the European Community expressing their willingness to sign free trade agreements with it, on 12 September 1993. The cooperation strategy was thus a signal directed to the European Union, and indeed three trade pacts were signed in July 1994. 'Europe Agreements' were signed between the EU and each of the Baltic states in April 1995.

Intra-CIS trade issues

The description of the various attempts to set up a trade arrangement is daunting. But supposing that these attempts were to get some reality, would a trade arrangement help? The answer seems obvious as trade within the former Soviet area fell about 15–20 per cent in 1991 and 25–40 per cent in 1992; these are very rough figures provided in the Annual Report of the EBRD for 1992 (EBRD, 1993). In 1993 and 1994 the same trend continued although it is impossible to state exact figures (ECE/UN, 1994b, p. 105). In this trade Russia had a large surplus which tends to shrink as exports contract more than imports. The reality of a trade collapse is undisputable. There may be several explanations:

Explanation 1. Trade has fallen as a result of the decline in *overall production*. Thus the key to a resumption in trade would be a resumption of growth. The latter would be rather achieved by macro-economic and structural measures in the domestic policy than by the formal setting up of a union.

Explanation 2. Trade has fallen as the result of the *disaggregation* of the Soviet Union. If this explanation is the main one, the Commonwealth should of course be strengthened, but a definite political willingness is required.

Explanation 3. Trade has fallen due to specific *restrictions in bilateral trade*. Trade is conducted among the CIS states on the basis of trade agreements very similar to the institutional arrangements which characterised state trading among Comecon countries in the past, with indicative and compulsory lists of products, export quotas, and controlled prices especially for energy. Thus oil and gas supplies from Russia to other CIS countries form the most critical segment of bilateral trade.

Explanation 4. The main problems are those due to *energy trade*. In 1992 the Russian oil and gas prices charged to the New Independent states were lower than world prices by 50 to 30 per cent, and in addition payments were often delayed. Overall the Russian trade subsidy to the NIS was said to amount to an equivalent of 17 billion dollars (ITAR-TASS, 13 July 1993) for the year 1992. A special arrangement on oil trade was concluded in March 1993, whereby 12 states (the CIS states except Turkmenistan, plus Georgia and Lithuania) agreed to create an 'Intergovernmental Council on Oil and Gas'. The arrangement provided for joint investments in Russia to develop oil production, while Russia committed itself to maintain its energy supplies, in a way very similar to the CMEA joint investment format in the 1970s.

The shift from the past economic relations among the republics within a single country to 'new' foreign trade is by no means clear. In principle world prices denominated in dollars were to be applied in 1993 to all energy deliveries in excess of the quantities stated in the bilateral trade agreements, aiming at a generalisation of world prices in overall intra-CIS trade in 1994. In the framework of the bilateral agreements specific prices are applied, which are higher than domestic Russian prices but still much lower than world prices. In addition trade agreements are not implemented. In 1992 the partners of Russia have supplied it with only 18 to 59 per cent of the goods committed in the agreements, while Russia claims to have supplied them with 60 to 75 per cent of the contracted deliveries (Whitlock, 1993). In 1993, the fulfilment of export quotas for oil by Russia ranged from 14 per cent (sales to Turkmenistan, an oil producer itself) to 94 per cent (Uzbekistan), with 67–69 per cent in the case of Belarus, Ukraine and Kazakhstan. Finally, the debt owed to Russia is not repaid. In 1993 several new ways of settling this debt were explored, including debt for equity swaps. For instance, Russian gas export firm Gasprom, itself undergoing privatisation, proposed to acquire pipelines and storage facilities in Belarus and Ukraine. Moldova agreed to barter its gas debt against consumer goods and foodstuffs in 1994. The 'gas' crisis developed in 1994 into gas supplies cuts to Ukraine, Belarus and Moldova to force these countries into repaying their debts. However, the customers of Russia have retaliation means. Ukraine controls the gas pipeline carrying Russian gas to Eastern Europe and to the West. Belarus threatened not to sign the monetary union treaty which was being negotiated at the beginning of 1994. Ultimately agreements were signed between Gasprom and the three Republics in August 1994. Only between Ukraine and Russia a comprehensive deal could be reached in March 1995 on debt and gas delivery issues, due to the pressure of the IMF on both countries when the stand-by loans to both Ukraine and Russia were negotiated.

Russia also attempted to get a share in oil and gas fields in Kazakhstan. Here Russia exerts pressure because it controls Kazakh oil exports through pipelines that cross Russia's territory. Kazakh oil and gas are exported to Russia; Russian oil is sent to Kazakhstan, most of it on a barter basis.

Explanation 5.　The issue of energy raises the more general question of the *costs and benefits in inter-republican trade*, in the past and in the future, and it may be contended that trade collapsed because Russia cannot afford and does not want to go on supporting the 'near abroad'. A study based on the analysis of past inter-republican links using Soviet input–output tables (Senik-Leygonie and Hughes, 1992) argues that Russia has in the past 'subsidised' the other republics – its 'satellites' – in two ways. First, Russia supplied them with underpriced raw materials and energy and at the same time allowed them to maintain a large internal 'deficit' with it, within the framework of inter-republican trade. Secondly, Russia financed the trade deficits of the other republics with the rest of the world. It may indeed be argued that, as Russia accounted for a larger share of the USSR's exports to the rest of the world than of its imports, the republic also financed the aggregate external balance of the Union as a whole. The mechanism is compared by the authors of the mentioned study (Senik-Leygonie and Hughes, 1992, p. 372) to that of intra-Comecon subsidies in the past, as interpreted by Marrese and Vanous (1983): a bargain between economic gains and political advantages, as if Russia was 'buying' the right to exercise central power through subsidising its partners.

Thus the breakup of the Soviet Union is freeing Russia from the burden of subsidising both 'deficits' of the other Republics, in trade with the rest of the world and in inter-republican trade. Russia is also in the best position to trade on its own with the rest of the world due to its size and resources, assuming that in a first stage it will rely on its present comparative advantages and mainly export raw materials, energy and intermediate goods. Nevertheless Russia is affected by the breakup of the Union, due to the disruption of intricate intra-industry links, and to the fact that many big enterprises located in the Republics had a 'federal' status and were supplying the whole Union.

To sum up, there are many reasons explaining the collapse in mutual trade among the states of the former Soviet Union. The question now is whether this trade should be revived through specific measures, such as the setting up of a free trade area (along with payments arrangements, to be elaborated upon in the next section) (Michalopoulos and Tarr, 1992).

We strongly disagree with the general view, according to which there was in the past a single economic space with a high degree of integration and specialisation, that has suddenly been broken up. This is a misrepresentation. The Soviet Union was held together by a highly integrated political and administrative structure. Economically it was far from integrated. True, huge federal firms were supplying customers all over the Union, at high transportation costs; such links bear no rationality and should be severed. The planned distribution system (*Gossnab*, see Chapter 1, p. 6) linked suppliers and buyers in such a way that often two producers located in the same area – let us say, a processing plant and a machinery firm manufacturing equipment of the kind used by the processing plant – had to trade with a supplier or a customer located thousands of kilometres away, instead of trading with each other. The idea of a high degree of specialisation must also be reconsidered. Specialisation existed mostly on paper. The deadlocks of the administrative supply system were such that the big communist firms tried to manufacture themselves all that was needed for their operation in terms of spare parts and components instead of relying on specialized deliveries. Thus, at the same time, trade links within the Soviet Union were above *and* below what economic rationality would have commanded.

The most critical issue, as has been seen, is that of energy. Production in the Soviet Union used to be very energy-intensive, both because of the importance of heavy industry, and because of the low cost of energy which induced all users to waste it. It is only desirable that the related trade flows be strongly reduced.

This brings us to a conclusion: there is no point in 'reviving' trade links. New trade flows are emerging and will develop in the course of market transformation. Thus the latter should be accelerated, but this cannot be done forcibly, especially when political disputes add to the picture. This is not to say that facilitating measures and initiatives are useless. Also, the transportation system is acting as a bottleneck and should be improved, with project-based international aid, for example for rebuilding pipelines, modernising railways and highways.

Should a new payment system be devised to help trade flows? The answer is certainly yes if one believes that trade is impaired due to the lack of payment instruments. It should be no if one believes that it is rooted in the legacies of the past.

The problem of the ruble zone

Once the break-up of the USSR was consummated, the question of the currency to be used in the former Soviet space arose. Initially the international community (independent experts and international organisations as well) favoured the variant of a ruble zone under Russia's control. Several circumstances led to a change of mind. These were the growing monetary crisis in Russia itself, the political battle between the Russian Central Bank (RCB) which was until September 1993 controlled by the parliament, and the government, and finally the moves of several states toward establishing their own currency. The ruble zone then appeared as non-feasible, and various forms of a payments agreement, or payments union, were put forward. However it has been periodically reactivated.

An extraordinary amount of literature flourished on the topic. We guess that this was due to the excitement of international monetary economics theorists and experts. The issue of the optimum currency area is one of the most interesting fields of modern monetary theory. A live experiment, with policy-making opportunities, is very seldom at hand. What Western economists could not guess, as they were used to rational economic modelling and to consistent policies, was that the former Soviet Union states would constantly vacillate from one solution to the other and ultimately chose the worst of both. The episodes of this very confused development may be summed up as follows:

(1) *Russia* is often assumed to be in favour of a ruble zone which increases its power and seignorage. In fact, the concept of a ruble zone is criticised in various circles, from the reformers to the extreme right. The main concern of the Russian authorities, both government and RCB, was to prevent the consequences of the lax monetary policy of its partners. In July 1992 it was decided to suspend the operations on the 'correspondent accounts' which each of the republican banks held at the RCB. All payments were to be made to the delivery of goods, and were no longer to be financed by automatic credit. In fact these new rules were very difficult to apply, and led to a huge trade crisis with some countries such as Ukraine, Moldova or the Baltic states (Hanson, 1992b). In May 1993 the agreement between the government and the RCB over a credit tightening programme also called for a cutback in credit to other CIS states. The agreement could only be effective if the CBR had the means of controlling the credit policy of the other members of the ruble zone, which was not the case. The next step was the decision, taken unilaterally by the RCB in July 1993, to take out of circulation the pre-1993 banknotes, as a substitute for credit control and a means of pressure on those states which had not clearly decided whether they wanted to stay in the ruble zone, and in this case to let their monetary and fiscal policy be determined by Russia, or whether they wanted to introduce their currency, at their own risk.

(2) While Russia acted initially as the leader of the ruble zone more through inertia than through a deliberate willingness, the countries that remained, officially or *de facto*, in the ruble zone, did so more by routine than through an explicit commitment to follow the monetary policy decided

in Moscow. There has been *no coordination of monetary policies*. While the RCB retained the monopoly of issuing rubles in cash, all the other Central Banks could create rubles through credit expansion, and actually have done so to ease the financial restrictions laid upon their firms. One has to mention here, however, that the cash monopoly of the RCB is an important issue. The ratio between cash/non-cash transactions is much higher in the states of the former Soviet Union than in modern monetised economies, because of the underdevelopment of monetary instruments and of the former separation of the monetary circuit into cash/non cash transactions (see Chapter 1, p. 13). It was the lack of cash that basically induced all countries to begin introducing substitutes for money, in the form of coupons of various kinds, rather than a specific desire for monetary independence.

(3)   The unilateral currency reform decided by Russia prompted *several countries, which had chosen to remain in the ruble zone, to walk out*. Still in September 1993 it seemed that the ruble zone would survive the shock of the currency reform. Russia, Belarus, Armenia, Kazakhstan, Uzbekistan, and Tajikistan signed a framework agreement on 7 September in Moscow.. Some of these countries had, however, already introduced their own interim or parallel currency or were contemplating doing so, essentially to cope with the shortage of cash as the RCB did not provide enough cash for their needs, and imposed stringent conditions for delivering cash. Two months later, in November, just after having each introduced their own currency, Kazakhstan and Uzbekistan decided to leave the ruble zone and to eventually introduce a common currency. Armenia decided as well to issue its own currency but it was not clear whether it would or would not remain in the ruble zone. The agreement of 24 September 1993 was meant to introduce *a double-track monetary system in the former Soviet space*. The countries which agreed to stay with Russia in the ruble zone were to comply with the Russian conditions. The other CIS members were to take steps to establish a payments union. The IMF, after having supported in 1992 the ruble zone concept, shifted to a preference for the payments union: only the states with a separate currency could get IMF credits.

Thus two quite different reasons explain this rejection of the ruble zone. The first one was the policy of Russia, using the ruble zone as a way of imposing monetary discipline on its partners, as was provided for in the September 1993 agreement. The second one was the policy of the IMF, at that time (end-1993) totally antagonistic to the idea of a ruble zone, which made it clear that support to the CIS countries would be conditional on their introducing their own currencies.

(4)   Even the states which were the first to introduce their *own currency* (the Baltic States) still used their ruble balances for some time, until mid-1993. This is even more so the case for their followers.

(5)   In April 1994, in the context of a strengthening of the 'Slavic Bloc', Russia and Belarus signed an agreement for a monetary union, which goes a

Table 9.2 The status of the currencies in the successor states of the USSR

State	Name of the national currency	Exchange rate regime convertibility:		Monetary operation
		in foreign currencies	in rubles	
Russia	Ruble	Floating rate; partial current account convertibility	—	Monopoly for issuing cash for all the states that use rubles. Exclusive use of the ruble as the domestic currency unit (as from 1 Jan. 1994).
Estonia	Kroon (June 1992)	Currency board regime. Current account convertibility for residents. The Kroon has a fixed exchange rate to the DM; 1DM = 8 Kroon.	No	The Kroon is the only currency in use in the country since June 1992. Trade is conducted in foreign currency with Russia; there is a transitory regime for the settlement of mutual debts.
Latvia	Latvian ruble in 1992; *lat* introduced in March 1983	Floating rate; pegged exchange rate contemplated in 1994; current account and capital account convertibility.	No	The domestic currency is the only currency in use. There is a transitory regime for the settlements with Russia and the CIS countries.
Lithuania	*Talonas* (coupons) introduced in 1992; *litas* as new currency in June 1993	Floating rate; pegged rate since April 94 on Estonian model (1$ = 4 *litai*); limited convertibility.	No	The litas is the only currency in use. Settlements are made in foreign currency with Russia, with transitory arrangements.
Ukraine	*Kupon* introduced as parallel currency in 1991; renamed *karbovanets* in November 1992; *hrynia* future national currency	Partial convertibility; no foreign exchange auctions since end-93; transactions conducted along various arrangements.	Partly	In principle the *kupon/karbovanets* is the only currency in use. Settlements in foreign currency with Russia since 1993. The ruble balances with Russia are not settled.
Azerbaijan	*Manat* introduced in August 1992 as a cash currency; the azeri ruble pegged to the Russian ruble was used for non-cash transactions until 1 Jan 94.	No convertibility.	Partly	Both currencies were used until 1 Jan 1994. Since then manat sole legal tender.

Armenia	Ruble. Introduction of *dram* in November 1993.	Fixed rate regime upon the introduction of dram; floating regime in 1994.	No	
Georgia	Ruble coupons since April 1993. *Lari* to be introduced at unspecified date; in fact belongs to ruble zone.			
Kyrgyzstan	Ruble until May 1993. *Som* official currency since then.	Floating rate regime; current account convertibility.	Limited	Only the som is used for domestic transactions. Foreign trade partners reluctant to accept it.
Kazakhstan	Ruble until Nov. 1993. Introduction of *tenge* Nov. 1993 (pegged to the DM).	No convertibility; exchange rate fixed at weekly auctions.	No	Payments arrangements with Russia. Strong disagreements over settlements and debts.
Tajikistan	Soviet ruble until Dec. 1993. Russian ruble introduced January 1994. Introduction of the Tajik ruble May 1995.	Same as ruble.	No	Payments arrangements with Russia.
Uzbekistan	*Sum*-coupons introduced Nov. 1993. Economic union (without currency union) with Kazakhstan and Kyrgyzstan agreed end-January 1994. Sum contemplated.	No convertibility.	No	Payments arrangements.
Turkmenistan	Ruble until Nov. 1993. *Manat* introduced 1 Nov. 1993.	Exchange rate fixed at weekly auctions.	No	Payments arrangements.
Belarus	Ruble until August 1993, replaced by coupon-*zaichik* (bunny). Currency union with Russia signed April 1994, to be ratified.			Payments agreements with Russia, not duly implemented.
Moldova	Ruble until Nov. 1993, replaced by *leu*.	No convertibility.	Pre-1993 rubles still used.	

Sources: *Economic Survey of Europe in 1992–93*, United Nations, Economic Commission for Europe, New York, Geneva, 1993; 'Financial Relations Among Counties of the former Soviet Union', *IMF Economic Reviews*, 1994, 1. Various press reports.

step further than a currency area. By mid-1994 it seemed doubtful that this agreement would ever be implemented. (See Table 9.2 for a picture of the troubled currency situation of the former Soviet Union countries; also see Wolf *et al.*, 1994, for a comprehensive discussion of the facts and issues.)

Lessons from theory

There has been a large theoretical literature on the monetary integration of the former USSR (to quote a very small selection, see CEPR, 1993; Bofinger and Gros, 1992; Eichengreen, 1993; Eichengreen and Uzan, 1992; Williamson, 1992a; Wolf *et al.*, 1994). The discussion focused on different issues. In the international monetary theory literature the usual departure point is the following: why should sovereign countries with a national currency abandon their currency independence and choose to form a currency area (hence the discussion of the optimal currency area deriving from the work of Mundell and McKinnon; see Bofinger *et al.*, 1993) or a payments union?

The discussion then concentrated on the advantages and drawbacks of both solutions as applied to the former Soviet union space, generally leading to a rejection of the ruble zone, both because of the internal flaws of the optimum currency area theory and because of the conditions prevailing in the CIS (the main obstacle to a monetary union being the difficulty of achieving a credible monetary policy in Russia and of having it followed by the other Republics). A variant has been suggested by John Williamson (1992a) in the form of a ruble *area,* as distinct from a ruble *zone*, which was to operate like the former sterling area: 'a group of countries with separate currencies that continue to use the currency of the former "colonial" power for international purposes, even after establishing monetary independence' (Williamson, 1992a, p. 24). According to Williamson, and apart from political conditions, the basic condition for such a scheme would be that the ruble must emerge as a relatively stable currency. This condition does not seem to be fulfilled, even if the ruble is a more stable currency than the other currencies of the CIS. Moreover, the case of the sterling area, to which one may add that of the French franc area, suggests that such a scheme requires a strong political commitment on both sides, and the willingness of the dominant partner to accept a definite financial burden in exchange for political and economic influence. Russia has neither the willingness, nor, moreover, the capacity, to sustain a 'ruble area' scheme.

Then the obvious solution is to have a monetary arrangement of some kind (either a European Payments Union type or a multilateral arrangement based on a fixed exchange rate like the initial Bretton Woods system). Such an arrangement may only work if there is some cooperation among the members in conducting the same stabilisation policies, if the bilateral deficits are not too big, and essentially if there is external financing available. If such conditions are not met, than a third solution offers better prospects: that each country pursues its own stabilisation policy with a separate currency to be ultimately made convertible.

The IMF explicitly supported the implementation of the separate currency policy. First the Fund was involved in giving technical advice in the first experiences of setting up a separate currency (in the Baltic States and in Kyrgyzstan – not in Ukraine). The Director General confirmed the Fund's balance of payment support to the next countries contemplating the introduction of their own currency, in a note of 15 November 1993 (*IMF Bulletin*, 6 December), provided these countries implemented stringent stabilisation-cum-reform policies. The example of the Baltic states was quoted, and especially that of Estonia, which established a currency board system in June 1992, pegging the kroon to the DM at a fixed exchange rate and backing it 100 per cent by its currency reserves. Lithuania introduced a similar system in April 1994. Estonia was widely praised for its performance in cutting down inflation, despite the fact that it experienced a very steep recession, which bottomed out at the end of 1993. Thus the main benefit of the separate currency was seen as the opportunity, for the international community supporting the transition, for better monitoring and control of the structural adjustment programmes. This is also the underlying reason for promoting a well-designed payments union; as was contended, the Marshall plan was in fact the best device in history to achieve a successful structural adjustment (Eichengreen and Uzan, 1992).

This section has shown how difficult it is to achieve a restructuring of the former trade areas to which the centrally planned economies belonged. Turning to the West not only expresses hopes for an improved market access. It is also a way of escaping the almost impossible task of rebuilding mutual relations out of the present chaos.

THE REORIENTATION TO THE WEST

The framework for these relations is a complex set of agreements. The 'first circle' comprises a series of 'Europe agreements', which were first signed with the Central European countries (Poland, Hungary, and the ČSFR) on 16 December 1991. These were extended in March 1993 to Bulgaria and Romania and in April 1995 to the Baltic states. A similar agreement was contemplated with Slovenia, with talks beginning at the end of 1993. The 'second circle' is the set of 'Partnership and Cooperation' agreements which began to be discussed with several successor states of the former Soviet Union in 1992. Negotiations started at the end of 1992 with Russia, and followed with Ukraine, Kyrgyzstan, Kazakhstan, and Belarus; partnership agreements were reached in June 1994 with Ukraine and Russia. The actual implementation of the partnership agreement with Russia was stalled in 1995 due to the Chechen war.

The outer circle providing for the less advantageous regime encompasses the 'Trade and Cooperation' agreements. The format for these agreements had already been established before the transition; they were the first general agreements with the socialist economies to be concluded, and were signed at the end of the 1980s with most of these countries, including the USSR. After the breakup of the USSR, they were offered to the Baltic states and signed in May 1992, with a provision mentioned in the preamble according to which they could evolve into an association agreement. A similar trade and cooperation agreement was signed with Albania in 1992. Until the Partnership agreements are finalised with the successor states of the USSR the provisions of the Trade and Cooperation agreements apply. Table 9.3 summarises the main provisions of these agreements.

Table 9.3 *Agreements involving the countries in transition and the European Community (Union)*

A. The 'first circle': the Europe (association) Agreements

Partners:	*Main provisions:*
– Poland, Hungary, the Czech and Slovak Federal Republic: ● Agreements signed between the European Commission and each of the countries, 16 December 1991; ● Interim agreements in force since 1 March 1992 (implementing only trade provisions); ● Full implementation since February 1994 (for Poland, Hungary); ● Renegotiation with Czech Republic and Slovak republic in 1993; separate agreements signed October 1993.	– Political dialogue; – Setting up of a free-trade area (for the movement of goods) in ten years maximum; – Asymmetric concessions in trade (for industrial goods the EC has agreed to suppress immediately all quantitative restrictions, and in 5 years tariff restrictions; the commitments of the partners are spread over a longer period); – Special provisions for trade in sensitive goods (food products, textile and steel); – Harmonisation of competition laws; – *No* free movement of labour; – Economic and financial cooperation; – *No* clear commitment toward full membership.
Additional concessions decided at the Copenhagen Summit of EC countries, June 1994 – Bulgaria, Romania: ● Agreements signed end-1992; ● Interim agreements in force May 1993 (Romania), January 1994 (Bulgaria). – Baltic States: agreements signed April 1995 Potential partners: Albania, Slovenia	– Clear commitment to full membership; – Quickening of implementation of trade concessions. Provisions basically the same as for the above countries. Decisions of the Copenhagen Summit not applied to Bulgaria.

B. The 'second circle': the Partnership Agreements

Potential partners: all countries of the former USSR.
Negotiations conducted with Russia, Ukraine, Belarus and Kyrgyzstan. Partnership agreements signed with Ukraine and Russia (June 1994), and Kyrgyzstan (February 1995).

Provisions of the agreements:
- Improvement of market access;
- Mutual MFN treatment;
- Possibility of creating a free-trade zone in the future;
- Separate arrangements for sensitive sectors (agriculture, textile, steel, coal);
- Special protocols for uranium, aluminium, satellite launching (Russia).

C. The 'outer circle': Trade and cooperation agreements

Partners:

Hungary (1988), Poland (1989), Czechoslovakia and Bulgaria (1990), Romania (1991). These agreements are superseded by the Europe agreements.

The USSR (1990). Being or to be superseded by Partnership agreements with the CIS members.

Slovenia (1992; unlike the standard trade and cooperation agreements, the agreement with Slovenia contains preferential provisions).

Albania (1992); Estonia, Latvia, Lithuania (1992; these accords have evolved into trade pacts signed July 1994 providing for free trade in industrial goods).

Standard provisions:
- Non-preferential trade agreement providing for MFN treatment, mutual trade concessions, removal of certain quantitative restrictions; pledge for further trade liberalisation.
- Economic cooperation monitored by joint committee.

For the Baltic states: fisheries agreements with EC (1992).

D. Related agreements

EFTA free-trade agreements with:
- Czechoslovakia (1992), renegotiated with the Czech and Slovak republics (1993);
- Poland, Romania (1992); Bulgaria, Romania (1993);
- Albania, Slovenia (negotiations in 1994).

Bilateral free-trade agreements between each of the Baltic States and each of the Nordic States (Finland, Norway, Sweden) (1992).

Provisions:
- Asymmetric concessions from the EFTA partners;
- Eventual elimination of import duties and non-tariff barriers affecting industrial goods;
- Improvement of access for agricultural goods;
- Dates of implementation arranged bilaterally for each EFTA partner with each East European partner.

Sources: ECE/UN, *Economic Survey of Europe in 1993–94*, Geneva and New York , 1994; OECD, *Integrating Emerging Market Economies into the International Trading System*, Paris, 1994; press reports.

Do the institutional agreements provide for an increased market access? There is an apparent contradiction between the advantages granted in the agreements and the growing difficulties arising in the trade of sensitive products (steel, agricultural goods) between the EC and East Central Europe, as well as in trade in services. With the former USSR states and particularly with Russia, similar difficulties are shown in the aluminium case.

Finally, is there a commitment from the EC (the European Union) to integrate the transition countries as members? A look at the 'accession queue' shows how remote this goal actually is.

The Most Advanced Framework: The Europe Agreements

One must first stress that the 'Europe agreements' as signed in 1991 were not enforced immediately in all their provisions. They had to be ratified by all the EC members. 'Interim Agreements' have applied since March 1992 (with the Central European countries), and March 1993 (with Romania; the enforcement of the interim agreement with Bulgaria was delayed until 1994) pending ratification. These Interim Agreements encompassed only trade-related measures. They did not regulate other forms of cooperation provided for in the full Europe agreements, such as the political dialogue, industrial, scientific and technological cooperation, as well as cultural cooperation (in particular in the television field). They lacked the complete institutional framework of councils or committees mentioned in the agreements, and were managed by an interim joint committee in each case. In addition, one has to mention the special case of the ČSFR. The Interim Agreement applied to both countries resulting from the partition as of 1 January 1993, but the agreement itself has been renegotiated with the Czech Republic and the Slovak Republic separately. Both countries signed the new agreements on the same day (4 October 1993). In April 1994, following the entry in force of the fully ratified Europe Agreements, Hungary and Poland officially applied for membership in the European Union.

The following comments relate to the first round of agreements which were signed with the Central European countries; the agreements with Romania and Bulgaria are basically identical, though Central European countries are meant to be closer to membership in the European Union, if and when the matter comes to fruition.

In the field of trade, the Europe Agreements (EA) provided for asymmetrical and gradual trade concessions, and foresaw the establishment of a free trade area between each Central European country and the EC. *For the goods regulated by the agreements*, i.e. industrial goods, and among them only those not regulated otherwise, the main commitments of the EC were the following:

- *Quantitative restrictions were to be removed for all industrial goods* as of March 1, 1992.
- *tariffs* were to be removed immediately as well for most of the goods. For 'semi-sensitive' or 'sensitive' goods tariffs were to be reduced gradually within quota-levels, with an increase in the quota-level, over a period not exceeding five years. 'Sensitive' goods include textile products other than those regulated by the Multi-Fibre Agreements, iron and steel other than the ECSC (European Community for Coal and Steel) products, chemicals, footwear, glassware, motor vehicles, furniture.

The reciprocal commitments for the Central European countries were spread over a longer period: seven years for Poland, and nine years for Hungary and the CSFR. In addition, these countries were allowed to resort to new restrictions or tariffs, while the standstill clause applied to the EC countries. These facilities were granted in the case of nascent industries, or activities undergoing structural transformation.

These provisions seem very generous indeed. However, this basic framework did not apply to a range of products, for which special protocols had been negotiated. These were:

- *agricultural goods*, ruled by the Common Agricultural Policy. For these goods the EC mainly confirmed provisions already included in the Generalised System of Trade Preferences (GSP), which was granted as of January 1990 (Poland and Hungary) or 1991 (the CSFR). A few additional concessions have been made. Basically future concessions will have to be negotiated case by case, and on a reciprocal basis. Some products were altogether excluded, such as beef meat, for which the global ceiling of 425,000 cattle units remains unchanged as long as the market in the EC is characterised by excess supply. This particular longstanding 'bone of contention' between Central European countries (especially Hungary) and the EC was not affected at all by the agreements.
- *textile goods regulated by the MFA* (Multifibre Arrangement). A special annex to the Europe agreements provided for a complicated schedule, because the MFA itself was to be dismantled by the completion of the Uruguay Round. The transitional period in this case was to take six years (for the abolition of duties) or at least five years, and, at most, half the time agreed in the Uruguay Round accord for the abolition of the MFA (in the case of quantitative restrictions) – note that the last phase of the MFA's phasing out is to occur in 2002–4 (Corado, 1994).
- *coal and steel* products regulated by the ECSC. Here the schedule was basically the same as for industrial sensitive products, however with additional provisions as to competition rules, and as to the transparency of public subsidies.

To sum up, the market access provided for in the Europe agreements is not so generous as it may seem:

(a) The most extensive concessions had already been granted earlier, either in the GSP, or in the trade and economic cooperation agreements concluded in 1988 with each of the Central European countries. They were then unilateral. According to the Agreements they imply a reciprocity, albeit asymmetrical.

(b) The tariff facility for nascent or restructuring industries looks very generous. One must not forget, however, that in the first stages of transition trade liberalisation was very abrupt. While they were preparing the EAs the Central European countries literally dismantled their tariffs, whose average level fell to 5 per cent in the CSFR, 8 per cent in Poland, 15 per cent in Hungary beginning 1991. Though trade liberalisation is usually part of the standard reform and stabilisation package, several Western experts had already suggested at that time that some temporary tariff protection would be useful (see McKinnon, 1991b, and the debate with Williamson, 1991b, p. 38). Such proposals became more pressing later, especially as the initial protection offered by the over-devaluation of the Central European currencies was wearing out (Nuti and Portes, 1993). Other pressures were less high-principled. Multinationals established in the East, especially in the car industry, strongly lobbied in favour of increased tariffs: in particular, Volkswagen in the Czech Republic, Fiat in Poland, General Motors in Hungary (Bobinski, 1992). This in turn angered the United States which felt discriminated against, and provoked reservations from the GATT (Dunne, 1992; Robinson, 1993a).

(c) As shown in Table 9.4, the more sensitive products, for which trade concessions are lower, amount to the dominant share in *present* Central European exports to the West. These goods are typically produced in existing capacities. These capacities, in industry and agriculture, have immediately been mobilised in the shift from East to West. In most cases these are 'negative value added' activities, which *should* be scrapped in due course. Steel industry is the best, also the most controverted, example.

(d) Both parties may use *anti-dumping* and *safeguard* procedures. In fact from the outset it was clear that such procedures were to help the EC against a surge of low-priced imports from the East. In the past, *anti-dumping* procedures have been extensively used against state trading countries, especially for chemicals. The transition countries are now considered as market economies, but their price structure and the operation of the state companies often prove to EC producers that in some particular industries market rules do not yet work.

As for the *safeguard* clause, the conditions are very extensively defined in the Agreements. Safeguard measures are authorised whenever imports from any Central European country may cause 'serious injury to domestic producers of like or directly competitive products', or 'serious disturbances

Table 9.4 *Trade in sensitive products between the EC countries and five countries in transition in 1992*

Commodity groups *(according to sections of EC Common Tariff)*	Five CEECs	Poland	CSFR	Hungary	Romania	Bulgaria
– Agricultural goods (including processed): share in total exports to EC (in percent)	12.3	13.4	5.0	20.8	5.5	20.4
– balance of the CEECs (exports minus imports), in million ECU	+301	+28	–141	+602	–248	+59
Chemical products:						
– share in total exports to EC (in per cent)	5.7	5.6	6.2	5.5	4.1	7.7
– balance of the CEECs (exports minus imports), in million ECU	–1,012	–492	–175	–234	–67	–44
Textiles:						
– share in total exports to EC (in per cent)	16.5	15.7	12.0	16.5	35.2	22.1
– balance of the CEECs (exports minus imports), in million ECU	+749	+170	+244	+104	+170	+62
Base metals and articles:						
– share in total exports to EC (in per cent)	16.1	18.9	18.2	10.4	10.7	15.2
– balance of the CEECs (exports minus imports), in million ECU	+1,869	+886	+630	+178	+78	+99
Total sensitive products:						
– share in total exports to EC (in per cent)	50.6	53.6	41.4	53.2	55.5	65.3
– balance of the CEECs (export minus imports), in million ECU	+1,907	+592	+558	+650	–67	+176
Total trade:						
– total exports to EC (in per cent)	100.0	100.0	100.0	100.0	100.0	100.0
– total balance of the CEECs (exports minus imports), in million ECU	–2,541	–1,071	–728	–74	–452	–215

EC = European Community
CEEC = Central and Eastern European countries
Source: Calculations from D. Mario Nuti, 'The Impact of Systemic Transition on the European Community (Table 7), in Stephen Martin (ed.), *The Construction of Europe – A Festschrift in Honour of Emile Noel,* Berlin: de Gruyter, 1994.

in any sector of the economy or difficulties which could bring about serious deterioration in the economic situation of a region' (quoted from the official text). This clause is very undetermined. What is 'serious' deterioration, disturbance or injury? It is quite subjective, and even more so is the potential impact of the 'difficulties'. The clause may be invoked by domestic producers, by 'sectors', or by 'regions'. Finally, special safeguard clauses apply to agricultural, and textile and clothing trade.

(e) *Rules of origin* are rather strictly defined. Products which qualify for trade concessions must have been produced in the Central European countries, and must not have more than a 40 per cent import content (in per cent of the value of the output), in terms of imports from non-EC countries. This is a powerful disincentive to non-EC foreign investment. In particular, US or Japanese computer manufacturers may find it very difficult to invest in Central Europe, as in this industry more than 40 per cent of the components are usually imported from non-EC countries. A similar statement has been made for the textile and clothing industry (Corado, 1994).

(f) All concessions included in the Europe agreements applied to trade in goods. But as Winters (1992) rightly stated, 'little as the EC desires CHP [= Czechoslovakia, Hungary, Poland] goods, it desires their workers even less' (p. 23). True, both parties granted each other national treatment in terms of establishment rights. However, exceptions were possible for up to ten years. Manpower movements are considered as a matter of national legislation. Hence the principle of non-discrimination only applies to the workers already legally employed in the EC. No new facilities are granted, and the legal rules are defined exclusively by each member state. In fact the immigration laws are increasingly restrictive in all the EC countries, and the movements, from the East to the EC, of workers other than those who are highly qualified are bound to meet a growing resistance.

Some of the provisions were revised later at the Copenhagen (June 1993) and Essen (December 1994) EC (EU) Councils. The timetable of the concessions made to the Central European countries was modified so as to accelerate the implementation of the Agreements (by six months on average). But the framework of the EAs remained unchanged (see 'Accession Queue', section below).

The Steel (and Aluminium) Case

The steel case is not the only outburst of conflict between the Central European and the EC countries. Following the steel case, an agricultural 'war' erupted in March 1993 when the EC Commission decided to impose a one-month ban on livestock, meat, milk and dairy products imports from all East European countries, because a case of foot-and-mouth disease had appeared in Italy and had been traced to imports from former Yugoslavia. Hungary, Poland, and the Czech and Slovak Republics retaliated by banning imports (including transit) of the same goods from the EC, using the same pretext. Though the ban was lifted as scheduled, as well as the retaliatory measures, it left hurt feelings and is expected to trigger further protectionist measures (Weydenthal, 1993b).

The steel case is however more serious and longlasting (Messerlin, 1993). In November 1992, after an eighteen month campaign (which thus began before the signature of the Europe agreements), the West European steel-makers won their anti-dumping case against the three Central European countries plus Croatia (the case against Croatia was later dropped). From the outset the steel-makers had feared the consequences of the Europe agreements. The previous system amounting to voluntary export restraints, which operated in the relations of the EC with state trading countries, was scrapped as of March 1992; tariffs were reduced by 20 per cent, with further yearly reductions to take place.

The anti-dumping case concerned steel pipes, for which the given countries had increased their market share from 7.8 per cent in 1988 to 13.4 per cent in 1991 due to low prices. Hence anti-dumping duties have been imposed, amounting to 10.8 per cent for Poland, 21.7 per cent for Hungary, and 30.4 per cent for the CSFR. A very confused debate then emerged over steel imports as a whole, at a time when the Western European steel industry was experiencing a deep crisis, and was itself threatened by anti-dumping actions from the United States (in November 1992 and March 1993); the United States also acted against Poland and Romania (Hindley, 1993; Wang and Winters, 1993).

The restructuring plan for the steel industry that was adopted in February 1993 in a preliminary form by the EC anticipated job cuts amounting to 50,000 over three years in Western Europe, to be matched with tariff-quotas on imports of individual steel products from Eastern countries (Poland, Czech and Slovak Republics, and Romania). These measures would allow for some increase in imports but impose higher tariffs if the limit was exceeded. There is apparently a clear logic here. One cannot impose painful restructuring measures upon Western producers and at the same time abstain from limiting imports from the East, at a time when the American market is closing.

(a) Is the East really a threat? The share of the Eastern European countries in extra-EC imports of steel into the EC soared from 16.3 per cent in 1988 to 35 per cent in the first half of 1992 (Wang and Winters, 1993, pp. 7–8). In 1992 these imports accounted for 3 per cent of total steel consumption in the EC (Hindley, 1993, p. 16). This is a modest figure, but in the context of the recession in the West and overcapacity in the EC steel industry the impact of these imports is significant, especially as the sales of the East drag the EC prices down. Moreover their share is much greater for specific categories of steel, such as, for instance, structural steel used in construction, which reached 9 per cent of EU market in 1993, triggering an anti-dumping complaint in 1994 (*Financial Times*, 2 August 1994).

(b) Can it really be said that 'dumping prices' apply in this context? The Central European countries argue that, following severe devaluations of their currencies, their costs and prices are now much lower than world prices. However, these industries are subsidised, even when subsidies have been formally abolished, just because the steel mills are loss-making enterprises but are not forced to close. Hungary used just that argument against the CSFR when it introduced quotas on 15 steel products exported by the CSFR, at the request of the Hungarian steel-makers (Gács, 1992, p. 27). But then, Western European steel mills are subsidised as well, as the chairman of the German steel industry federation, Ruprecht Vondran, said of the Italian and Spanish steel-makers (*Financial Times*, 22 February 1993).

(c) The Western producers' strategy is not altogether innocent. In some cases they themselves bought the steel products from the East, and resold them at a profit. Such practices first show that, as in the past, Eastern European producers do not market their goods efficiently. They could sell at a higher cost, retain the profit for themselves, and escape dumping allegations – especially if they themselves had a cartelised structure. Second, while public opinion in the West is mobilised against the 'invasion' by Eastern goods, which is held responsible for losses of jobs in the industry, the highly cartelised Western steel industry deliberately increases unemployment by its trade practices.

(e) The share of steel in overall Eastern exports decreased in 1991 and 1992. The increases only relate to certain products such as pipes, and certain countries such as the CSFR. This has to be assessed in view of the general decline in capacity in the East. For all Eastern Europe, including Bulgaria and Romania, steel output declined by about 50 per cent in volume in 1989–92 (though by less than one third in the CSFR). About 50,000 employees in Poland, and 40,000 in Hungary, have lost their jobs. Contrary to what happens in the West, this adjustment is made without any special assistance, let alone coordination among the countries (Robinson, 1993b).

Winters (1994) suggests that the steel industry, both in EU countries and in Central end Eastern European countries, should be slimmed down, and that it would be beneficial to both sides if it was to occur on *strictly market criteria* (Winters, 1994, p. 32; emphasised in the text). However, according to the author, such a rationalisation is not due to happen, because of the lobbying power of the heavyweights of the Western European steel industry. Ideally, according to Winters, the Central and Eastern European countries should be allowed to expand their sales of lower grade, cheaper steel to Western Europe while importing higher grade steel for their industries, during the time required for restructuring. This would only marginally harm some EU steel producers, who would have to adjust anyhow even without such a pressure. But is the present competitiveness of Eastern Europe in low-grade steel production a reality? We shall revert to the general problem of competitiveness later.

The *aluminium case*, which concerns Russian–EC relations, is still more impressive than the steel case. Press reports repeatedly talked of an aluminium 'flood' in 1993, the most significant of the overall increase in metal exports being from Russia and the CIS. The aluminium exports from the CIS to the West, most of them from Russia, went up from an annual average of 80,000 tons before the breakup of the Soviet Union, to 600,000 tons in 1992 and 1.7 million tons in 1993. The costs of producing aluminium in the Russian smelters were until October 1993 the smallest in the world, about one-half of the average European price. However, these costs have almost doubled since October 1993 when the energy prices were increased in Russia, thus pushing the Russian price up to the international level. By mid-1994 the Russian costs were expected to be even higher than Western costs, by 8 per cent (*Financial Times*, 22 July 1994). Following a longlasting dispute with the EC Commission, import curbs were imposed in August 1993 in the form of a quota of 60,000 tons per month until the end of the year 1993, as a 'safeguard action', the Commission arguing that the low Russian price was due to cheap energy and lax environmental standards (*Aluminium*, 1993). Further discussions between the EC and Russia explored the possibility of an agreement on aluminium exports. The EC unilateral action had the effect of partly redirecting Russian aluminium exports to North America. As in the case of Eastern European steel, some share of these purchases has been made by North American producers.

The aluminium dispute has been partly defused for two reasons. First, a pact has been concluded among the main aluminium producer countries (the United States, Canada, Australia, the European Union, Norway, and Russia) end-January 1994, according to which the world output should be cut by up to 2 million tons annually for two years. Russia promised to cut its production by 500,000 tons each year, with loans and investment by Western producers to restructure the industry, up to 1.5 billion dollars (*Le Figaro*, 2 February 1994). However it was well below this target in July 1994, and was expanding its exports at a level equivalent to that of 1993. Nevertheless, a second reason explains why the aluminium problem was much less important in 1994. Analysts had underestimated the demand growth, which pushed prices up in 1994 and reversed the downward trend provoked by the surge in Russian sales on the world market since 1992.

More generally, in the case of steel or aluminium as in the case of other sensitive goods, such as chemicals, agricultural goods, and to a lesser extent textiles and clothing, the present export specialisation is a 'distress strategy'. One sells what is at hand. But the sectors which produce the 'sensitive goods' are declining. The chemical industry was developed on the basis of cheap Soviet oil and has no future at normal prices for fuels. The farm sector is slowly transforming itself. Privatisation is delayed by restitution procedures, by the reluctance of the farmers who do not want to lose their social cover and chose not to dismantle the cooperatives. The small family farm model has no more future in the East than it has in the West. But the East lacks finance and skills to imitate an efficient capitalist farming model. Textile and clothing might look more promising, but basically as a subcontracting workshop for EC producers (Graziani, 1992). This is particularly the case for clothing: about two-thirds of the imports of clothing from the East by EC countries in 1992 were due to outward processing trade operations (e.g. subcontracting, whereby EC firms bring both the design and the fabrics, and re-import the finished product) (Corado, 1994).

A British study on trade in sensitive products also observes the poor performance of the sensitive products on the EC markets (in 1990 and 1991), and attributes these results more to the high levels of protection of the EC than to an inherent lack of competitiveness. The study contends that the EC has not much to lose by opening its markets, and that 'for Eastern Europe, future export earnings are likely to come from industries which are not currently important in either production or trade [within the EC countries. ML.] and where there are thus no existing rents to lose' (Rollo and Smith, 1993, p. 166). Such industries are however not identified. In any case, the authors contend, any industry in which the East is successful in expanding exports would *ipso facto* become sensitive and trigger restrictions: ' "contingent protection", which may seriously deter investment in Eastern Europe, may simply be protectionism in any sector in which Eastern Europe is successful' (p. 139).

But which are these sectors in the long term? Following a much-referred-to study (Hamilton and Winters, 1992) it has been assumed that the Eastern European countries had a comparative advantage in industries that are relatively intensive in human capital. Hughes and Hare (1992), using the DRC (domestic calculated costs) methodology, have shown that the most competitive sectors differ from one country to another, but that food processing (except in Bulgaria and to a lesser extent Poland and Hungary) is not competitive. Energy-intensive products tend to be uncompetitive. In general, the most competitive would be labour-intensive products included as sensitive in the EAs. Another author, using the revealed comparative advantage methodology (Neven, 1994), finds that the comparative advantage of Central and Eastern Europe lies in products that are both capital-intensive and unqualified labour-intensive. All these authors join in the (wishful) suggestion that the countries in transition should be allowed to export such goods (which they do in fact), without too many obstacles, and that the brunt of the adjustment should be carried by the West, for which the burden is marginal.

This might be a justified macro-economic view, but the sectoral interests in the West are bound to react negatively (and have done so), since what is marginal overall may be significant at the firm level. In addition, this may seem very disappointing for the Eastern European countries in transition themselves. In the socialist past, they were always claiming that their future lay in high-technology exports, and that the unjustified Western embargo on technology exports was preventing them from reaching this aim. Nowadays, while demanding to be integrated in the European Union, they hope to reach the Western European average level of technological development in a few years, provided there is market access for the products of their nascent advanced industries. These hopes will be dashed. Technological development is not just a matter of investment and skills, or even markets. It is also related to being part of industrial international cooperation, through the network of multinationals. At best, Central and Eastern Europe may develop into the backyard or the assembly line of such global firms (as the example of the car industry shows). Exploring the opportunities of the service sector may be more promising, especially in its most advanced branches (such as business and computer services).

In any case, for the Central and Eastern European countries, the immediate aim is to be integrated in the EU as soon as possible. The European Commission seems to move to this conclusion at well, not without strong reluctance on the part of some of the EU members.

The Accession Queue

Whereas the Europe agreements did not explicitly contain a provision committing the EC members to take steps towards membership of the Central and Eastern European countries in the EC, it was implicitly assumed that sooner or later it would be impossible to resist these countries' explicit wish. Indeed the Europe Agreements mentioned that 'the final objective of [the given country] is to become a member of the Community, and that this association, in the view of the Parties, will help to achieve this objective': a very cautious statement indeed, which did not commit the Community, and which was agreed upon after lengthy discussions. But a quick integration was not on the agenda in any way. The prospects for the countries belonging to the 'second' and 'third' circles in terms of their arrangements with the EC seemed still more remote.

By 1994, the situation had changed. For the Central European countries, prospects for EU membership seemed closer, and the conditions for admission more manageable. However a new question was emerging: was the EU itself ready to accept these new members, or would such an admission trigger far-reaching changes in the EU format itself?

The 'Europe Agreements' countries

In terms of a strategic approach to international relations, the strength of the Central and Eastern European countries lies in political pressure. In the economic field, while the exports to the EC account for a large share of these countries' total exports (40 to 50 per cent), the EC trade with the same countries is less than its trade with Switzerland alone. This asymmetry suggests that while Eastern Europe would certainly gain from a quick integration, it is not a significant trade partner for the EC. Lobbies in the EC have strongly fought liberalisation in sensitive sectors; conversely, no lobbies will fight for a greater market access for Eastern Europe to be ensured through integration.

What conditions for EU membership?   The EC itself has always experienced difficulties in defining a global vision of its international relations. The views of the Commission cannot overrule those of the member states, which have not reached a cohesion strong enough to generate such a vision (Messerlin, 1993, p. 102). Thus the position of the Commission has been initially mainly defensive, stressing the obstacles to quick integration without suggesting viable alternatives:

- The enlargement of the Community was in any case to begin with closer to the Community EFTA members (Norway, Sweden, Finland, Austria), a process completed in 1994 but for Norway.
- There are many conditions to fulfil before applying, and the prospective applicants do not yet meet them.
- Applicants should prove their ability to cooperate among themselves within a free trade area, or a customs union, or a payments union (see the first section of this chapter).
- As a variant of the previous argument, applicants should first join EFTA so as to be trained in an integration exercise (Baldwin, 1992). Though such a solution may seem sensible, it is hampered by the fact that the EFTA countries are being integrated into the European Union, and the EFTA itself is gradually turning into an empty shell.

Eastern countries have voiced a strong opposition to any of these solutions or arguments. This may be exemplified by the developments in 1992 and 1993 following the signing of the first EAs. The EC Commission prepared a proposal to the EC members for the Edinburgh European Council of December 1992, 'Towards a closer association with the countries of Central and Eastern Europe'. Without establishing a timetable, the proposal went closer to the idea of accession by stating the conditions required for full membership and offering to involve the Central European countries in EC policy-making in such fields as energy, environment, transport and telecommunications (Gardner, 1992). The idea of a 'Pan-European Free Trade Area' was also suggested.

A conference at foreign ministers level was later held in Copenhagen on 13–14 April 1993 and brought together the EC members, EFTA countries and 11 Eastern European countries including the Baltic states. The conference final declaration stressed that one should move both towards the European union as defined in the Maastricht treaty, and towards 'inter-European' cooperation through a larger free trade area. But the Eastern European countries again felt unsatisfied on two counts: pledges toward greater market access in sensitive sectors were not made; they felt again forcibly induced to revive a trade bloc among themselves as a kind of pre-condition to EC accession.

The European Council held in Copenhagen (June 1993), following the conclusions of the Edinburgh Summit in December 1992, was supposed to 'prepare the Associate countries for Accession to the Union'. It decided that the Associate countries could contemplate accession (without, again, any time-table) provided broad conditions were met. The Essen Summit in December 1994 confirmed this pledge and announced a 'pre-accession strategy' which would be spelled out in 1995 and fix the steps to be taken for future membership.

The accession conditions are established by the Rome Treaty, as modified by the European Single Act (1986; art. 8) and by the Maastricht treaty. They also follow from previous enlargements:

- any European country may apply to join the Union (art. 237 of the Treaty of Rome);
- politically the applicants must be stable pluralist democracies (this implying the existence of independent political parties) and be committed to the rule of law, to the respect for human rights, and to the protection of minorities;
- economically they must be established market economies;
- they endorse the objective of political, economic and monetary Union;
- they have to be able to assume the obligations of membership, in particular what comes under the 'acquis communautaire' (the 'Four Freedoms', free circulation of goods, services, capital and workers; the Common Agricultural Policy; the competition policy rules; fiscal harmonisation; the commitments towards developing countries). This also means that the applicants must be able to comply with all the decisions and legal provisions of any kind implemented since the relevant Treaties are in force (Nuti, 1994b).

In addition, art. 109 J of the Rome Treaty as modified by the Maastricht treaty defines the 'convergence criteria' to be met for the evolution of the EU into an EMU (Economic and Monetary Union). These are not conditions for accession but will be taken into account in the discussions over accession.

The conditions of membership are so broad that they may be considered as met by and large, and at the same time as unattainable in full before many years. The three more advanced Visegrád countries (Slovakia lagging behind) may indeed be considered as stable democracies and established market economies. They have all already taken steps to comply with the 'acquis communautaire', and the Europe agreements encompass some of them, such as the competition rules.

As to the 'Maastricht convergence criteria', these are *not* conditions for accession, but for reaching the stage of the economic and monetary union within the EU. True, the Eastern and even Central European countries do not meet them, but this is also the case of other established members. These criteria are:

- a public debt not exceeding 60 per cent of the GDP. It is very difficult to state whether the CECs move toward this target. The concept of public debt has not been clearly defined. Obviously it is a very complex issue, as in the past there has not been any clear-cut separation between state budget accounts and state enterprise accounts. The consolidation of the state enterprises and banks indebtedness is still to come, and its impact on the public debt is yet unclear;
- a public sector deficit not exceeding 3 per cent of the GDP. Only the Czech Republic would comply with this criterion in 1994 (with 0 per cent deficit estimated in 1993); Poland moved toward this target with a ratio of 6 per cent in 1992, 3.4 per cent in 1993, and 3 per cent in 1994; Hungary is still far from the target (7 per cent in 1992, 7.5 per cent in 1993, 8 per cent in 1994);
- inflation rates differentials not exceeding 1.5 per cent and interest rates differentials not exceeding 2 per cent over the respective rates of the three member states characterised by the lowest inflation. Despite the undeniable achievements in the CECs in bringing inflation under control, none of these countries meets the target, and in 1994 inflation rates are still over the 30 per cent mark in Poland, 19 per cent in Hungary, and 10 per cent in the Czech republic;
- a stable exchange rate (two years of ERM (exchange rate mechanism) membership without devaluations). Here too the Czech Republic would be the only country to comply.

A closer look at the conditions, as well as at the latest enlargement discussions, shows that the main problem is the EU's capacity to absorb new members. Unlike the EFTA three new members (since Janauary 1995), the Visegrád Three are poorer (by comparison with the average EC income level) countries; structurally they have export specialisations that are potentially damaging to the EU (in particular in agriculture); they are thus likely to claim large transfers in the framework of the CAP on the one hand and the structural funds on the other.

Is the EU ready to absorb new members? Looking at the membership criteria at large, two conclusions emerge: (i) the Central European countries (CECs), though the closest to accession, are not yet meeting all the requirements; (ii) they are moving in the right direction as far as their domestic policies are concerned.

The way membership was negotiated with the EFTA countries admitted in 1994 gives some idea of the problems that would be raised in the rather improbable case of quick membership negotiations with the CECs.

The main issue would be that of *agriculture*. The agricultural potential of the CECs and the present level of prices in these countries suggest that the present EU members would have to face increased competition, and very high costs arising from the CAP being extended to these new members, where agriculture has a much larger share in the GDP than on average in the EU (the average share for the EU is 3 per cent; is slightly less than 6 per cent in the Czech Republic, over 7 per cent in Hungary and Poland). This would probably lead to a collapse of the CAP with far-reaching consequences on several EU members.

Two reports were issued in 1994 on the agricultural question (Nallet and van Stolk, 1994; House of Lords, 1994). Their main lines are the following:

(a) Though the CECs are much more dependent on agriculture than the EU members, as may be seen from the share of agriculture in their GNP and employment, the situation of the agricultural sector is rapidly deteriorating. Privatisation has been impeded in Hungary and in the Czech and Slovak Republics by the restitution and compensation procedures to the persons who had been expropriated by the communists. When de-collectivisation is achieved, it amounts to splitting up large estates into a large number of small farms, not viable by Western standards. Small peasants do not have access to credit for modernising; credit is too expensive due to a stringent monetary policy, and anyhow not available. They could not really benefit from the increases in retail prices for food, as these increases mainly benefited state-owned wholesale distribution chains. Investment is falling.

(b) Though agricultural production declined, sales to the West increased due to the reorientation of domestic sales and of previous exports to the East (mainly to the USSR/Russia). But imports from the West increased still more. The imports from the EU are subsidised through the CAP. In 1993, for the first time, the EU moved into a surplus in food trade with Eastern Europe; it used to be in deficit in the past.

(c) Understandably, the farmers of Eastern Europe are requesting more protection from their governments. The farmers' party is within the ruling coalition in Poland, and is very influential in Hungary. The requested support would be in the form of a 'CAP for the poor'. But such a support, even at levels much lower than the EU level, could not be sustained by the CECs. In addition, it would induce them to maintain obsolete, non-competitive branches – hence the suggestion, expressed in the Nallet and van Stolk report, according to which the CECs should avoid a CAP-like format and rather opt for a policy of restructuring the agricultural sector, for which they should be helped by the EU. This help would take the form of subsidised credits to the farmers (with the support of the EBRD), and of price subsidies, *for a short period and at a level 30 to 40 per cent lower than the level of Western European CAP-guaranteed prices.*

(d) But in such a situation the CAP itself is questioned. It would be quite unsustainable to ask the CECs to refrain from introducing *their* CAP in the form of subsidised prices, and to go on subsidising EU agriculture on the same level. Thus a reform of the CAP seems unavoidable, as the report for the House of Lords recommends. This is also the conclusion of a provocative book by Richard Baldwin (1994). The same conclusion has been very carefully introduced into a report on a 'wider Europe' prepared for the December 1994 European Summit (Barber, 1994).

Another issue in the impending EU membership would be the qualification of all CECs for receiving transfers from the *structural funds*. While the recent applications are increasing the income per capita level in the EU, the membership of the CECs, even in the event of a continuing recovery, would decrease that level and ultimately jeopardise the situation of the less developed regions in the present EU. The complex system of the European structural funds pursues several aims: to assist the development of lagging regions (where GDP per capita is less than 75 per cent of the EU average) (aim no. 1); to help the conversion of regions experiencing a decline in their industry (aim no. 2); to reduce long-term unemployment (aim no. 3); to promote the social insertion of young people (aim no. 4); to help the restructuring of the agricultural sector (aim no. 5). Presently, under the criterion of GDP per capita, Greece and Ireland qualify for the most important section (no. 1) for all their regions; so do half of the regions in Spain and Portugal, the Mezzogiorno in Italy, the new Lander in Germany, Corsica and the French West Indies in France, and Northern Ireland in the UK. To this will be added the Austrian Burgenland, and under a new 'basket' (aim no. 6) the Arctic regions for the Scandinavian new members. The structural funds amounted to about a quarter of the EU budget in 1993. If the 'Visegrád' countries were to join the EU, they would all qualify for all their regions, though they would lower the average GDP per capita and thus evict some of the previous beneficiaries. If the system of the structural funds were to remain the same, this would mean larger contributions from the richest countries and would compel Greece, Portugal, Spain and Ireland to share some of the benefits with the newcomers. True, one may expect the CECs to resume growth in the coming years, but they would need several years before regaining their pre-transition level.

Finally, the problem of the European *institutions*, already substantial in the recent accession negotiations, would emerge as very acute, especially if the accession of the 'first circle' of the 'Visegrád countries' was seen as the initial step, with other waves of accession following. Namely, the 'big countries' of the EU-12 (France, Germany, Great Britain, Italy, and Spain) have a majority of votes in the Council of Ministers of the EU, with ten votes each for the first four, and eight for Spain. Thus they cannot be outvoted by a coalition of the smaller seven countries, which have four votes each. But the latter cannot be outvoted by the 'big five', because for important votes the blocking minority has been established at 23 votes. The admission of the three EFTA countries has already raised problems due to the fact that it increases the power of the smaller states. The integration of the 'Visegrád' countries, not to speak of other present 'associates', would add to this shift of power. The reform of the EU institutions in 1996 is to tackle these problems.

The 'outer' circles

Notwithstanding their limitations, the Europe agreements are a model for the countries which have not yet reached this stage. This is particularly obvious in the Russian case for the 'Partnership' agreement signed in 1994. The major contention of Russia in 1993 was that it should be treated not as a state trading country as was the case in the 'trade and cooperation agreement' signed in 1990, but as a market economy, even before its accession to GATT to which it applied in June 1993.

The lack of a global vision is still more obvious here. By the end of 1993, the European Union was mainly concerned with issues of deepening its integration, as exemplified by its new name (following the entry in force of the Maastricht Treaty on 1 November 1993), and with enlargement limited to the first three EFTA members on the list. On a larger scale, the difficulties encountered in Uruguay Round negotiations suggest that if and when Russia is admitted into the WTO (World Trade Organisation, which replaced GATT in 1995), it will be in a global context of growingly managed trade with increased protection (Ostry, 1993).

Ultimately two partnership agreements were signed, the one with Russia (24 June 1994) being preceded by a few days by a similar agreement with Ukraine (14 June 1994). In the case of Ukraine the main concern of the EU members was to obtain the shutdown of the Chernobyl nuclear complex, against aid to build alternative nuclear reactors. Russia's agreement, as Ukraine's, is not meant to be the first step toward EU membership. However it envisions a free-trade zone, only for 1998 and on the condition that market reforms continue. As in the Europe agreements, there are tariff and quotas concessions, except for sensitive products such as steel, textiles, and uranium. The agreement also covers the sphere of services, with Russia easing the restrictions on foreign banks operating on the Russian territory, and allowing them to accept deposits from Russian firms and persons.

Other CIS countries are to become 'partners' according to a comparable scheme. The EU is thus faced with several questions related to its potential enlargement. Assuming that the 'Visegrád' countries are to be integrated by the year 2000, what is the likely timetable for the other associates? What about the 'partners' of the CIS? And will it be a 'multi-speed' or 'multi-tier' Europe?

To avoid or solve such problems, Richard Baldwin (1994) envisions a complex architecture of multilateral agreements instead of the present 'hub-and-spoke' structure linking the EU with each of its associates or partners. There would be an AAA (Association of Association Agreements), which would monitor duty-free trade for industrial products among its members (what the association agreements and the Visegrád agreement are supposed to achieve separately). This AAA would regroup the existing and future partners in Association Agreements, i.e. all Eastern Europe including not only Romania and Bulgaria (partners in such agreements since 1993) but also Slovenia, Albania, and the Baltic States. A more restricted circle would be comprised of the present Visegrád countries with the EU, within an OEI (an Organisation for European Integration), which would be the framework of a single market. Thus straightforward accession could be postponed until all partners are ready, and one would not have to resort to politically unpleasant solutions such as 'second-zone' members with reduced institutional rights.

Such constructions show that the accession conditions are not just linked with the present situation of the transition countries. What is at stake is the way the EU operates now, and has planned to operate as provided for in the Maastricht treaty. The format might simply not be sustainable. There is a growing consciousness within the EU that it may have to be altered soon. The discussion about the entry of the EFTA countries has acted as a revealing factor: if a step which was in principle so much easier to achieve than the enlargement of the countries in transition has proved so difficult in fact, then the issue of future enlargement must be tackled differently.

Thus the present format of the European Union is simply not sustainable with an enlargement which could not be limited to just three countries. Transitional measures would help to postpone the impact of the accession but not solve the problem. Hence there are two main ways out: either to keep the present set of rules and policies for the existing members – including the new EFTA members – and to set up a 'multi-tier' Community into which new members could be admitted without automatically being granted the full support provided by the CAP (as reformed in 1992) and the structural funds (Nuti, 1994b); or to radically alter the existing model of integration, which is another story.

INTERNATIONAL MIGRATION ISSUES

The Europe agreements do not provide for opportunities for large East–West labour movements. The beginning of the transition immediately fuelled fears of a massive emigration to the West. These fears now appear to have been largely exaggerated, especially in light of migration pressures originating from other regions of the world (Africa for Europe, Central America for the United States).

Does One Need To Be Afraid?

Several circumstances explain the 'migration psychosis' which seized Western Europe soon after the transition:

- There had been a strong migration drive just before the transition, in some cases quite dramatic, such as the flight of East German citizens to the West through Czechoslovakia and Hungary in 1989, or the flight of Albanians to Italy in 1991.
- The Western media extrapolated from opinions polls made in the East that dozens of millions were potentially ready to emigrate.
- Eastern European citizens quickly became very conspicuous in Western European cities, as 'tourists' arriving in large parties, spending little and trying to earn some money through moonlighting or selling goods more or less legally.
- Cases of 'brain drain', especially from the former Soviet Union, were given much publicity.
- Information on unemployment in Eastern Europe, actual or potential, gave the impression that large amounts of migrants would seek jobs in the West.

The Prospects for Emigration from the East

The likely flows

It is very difficult to estimate the future flows of migrants. The past flows do not provide any clue, as the right to leave was severely restricted, and strictly regulated for some categories of the population, such as Jews. Some estimates start from the South–North flows within Europe between 1950 and 1980 (Layard *et al.*, 1992, p. 17). Finding that during this period about 6 per cent of the Southern European population moved to richer countries, and retaining a very conservative percentage of 3 per cent in the case of Eastern Europe and the European part of the former USSR, the authors of the quoted study find that the likely flows of migrants should amount to a total of 10 million.

Other estimates take into account specific factors influencing migration, such as the present economic situation and the prospects for economic recovery in individual countries, the political situation including the state of civil war in some countries, and the Western response (ECE/UN, 1992, ch. 7: 'Migration from East to West: A Framework for Analysis'). Though no figures are offered, such studies suggest that the flows of migrants will be much more diversified and on the whole much smaller than anticipated in the West:

- While the dramatic disparity in wages among Western and Eastern European countries should trigger emigration (the dollar average wage in Eastern Europe ranged from 80 to 300 dollars per month in 1993, and was as low as 15 dollars in Russia), it also limits permanent migration; to improve one's situation it is enough to work for a few weeks in the West as a 'tourist'.
- Unemployment is a pressure to emigrate. However the rates of unemployment are still either low (in the former USSR, in the Czech Republic) or manageable; unemployment affects specific categories (women, minorities).
- Poverty coupled with ethnic war or political trouble is a strong incentive to emigrate, but not necessarily to the West. Poland is unwillingly becoming an immigration country for Russians, Armenians, Romanian gypsies, Albanians.
- The Western response has to be taken into account. Though the US study quoted (Layard *et al.*, 1992) contends that Europe, which according to the authors admits virtually no refugees (p. 7) should take in an average of 300,000 people a year, this is wishful thinking. All European countries have indeed stopped entries on the basis of asylum-seeking, and entries on the basis of job permits are severely restricted.

Thus the likely flows should be smaller than anticipated. What is to be expected from such a situation?

The alternatives to emigration

The first outcome will be, and is already, an intense frustration in the East. The citizens of the former communist world were of course very naive when they believed that if and when the iron curtain was lifted, they would be warmly welcomed in all the countries which had exerted a political pressure on their governments so that the right to leave their own country was recognised on human rights grounds. They do not understand that the right to leave has nothing to do with the right to be admitted elsewhere. They do not understand either that economic liberalisation stops where labour movements are concerned.

Are these disillusions creating a potential for a crisis? The West is afraid of the social and political impact of too large an imbalance in the standards of living between East and West. Economic theory shows that trade may be a substitute for migration (through exports of labour-intensive goods), as well as foreign direct investment (which would use the cheap labour resources in the Eastern countries). We have already seen that there are strong obstacles to a surge of labour-intensive exports (see Winters and Wang, 1993, for the footwear industry case) as such branches are sensitive sectors in the West; in addition there are competitors from the developing countries. Foreign direct investment is attracted by many factors of which low wages are only one component. Thus both solutions can only alleviate the problem. If low wages are due to low efficiency, itself the consequence of legacies of the past and of a slow transformation pace, then foreign investment will be deterred, and labour-intensive exports will perpetuate a wrong specialisation.

Foreign assistance in general may also be an alternative to admitting immigrants. Layard and his co-authors (1992) acknowledge that Western Europe should be the main donor, as the region has most to lose due to the onrush of immigrants, and most to gain if the East recovers. They also claim that the ultimate arbiter is the IMF, which means that the United States has to be convinced (Layard *et al.*, p. 69). We have thus to shift to the last section of this chapter, devoted to foreign assistance to the transition.

WESTERN ASSISTANCE TO THE TRANSITION

The European Community has indeed been the forerunner of Western assistance to the East, and emerged as the main coordinator. We shall review the build-up of Western assistance, its main forms, and its difficulties and prospects.

The Early Stages of Assistance to the Transition

Foreign assistance has followed the pace of transition in a gradual build-up. In July 1989, at the G-7 Summit in Paris, it was decided to help Poland and Hungary in their transition to a market economy and to democracy. The EC Commission was to ensure the coordination of the assistance undertaken by the G-24 (the 24 OECD members taking part in the initiative). The starting point was the creation by the G-24 of the formal aid programme called PHARE (see Chapter 6). PHARE was later extended to all the countries in transition except the CIS, where a special programme TACIS is applied. (TACIS stands for Technical Assistance to the Commonwealth of Independent States.)

In December 1989 the French President François Mitterrand proposed the setting-up of the first post-cold-war international financial institution, the EBRD (European Bank for Reconstruction and Development, so called to correspond to the official name of the World Bank, the IBRD). The EBRD began to operate in April 1991. In 1994 it had 57 shareholder states (donors and recipients), including non-European, developing countries such as Mexico, Morocco, Egypt, Israel, and Korea, and two international members, the EC and the European Investment Bank. Its statutory aims were to promote democratic institutions and open market economies in Central and Eastern Europe, including the former USSR, through lending and investing, with 60 per cent funding at least being directed to private sector enterprises or to state-owned enterprises engaged in privatising.

Finally the international financial institutions became major actors in the assistance to transition. By 1992 all the Eastern and Central European countries were members of the IMF and the World Bank, as well as the Baltic States and the members of the CIS. The IMF became actively involved in assistance insofar as its help was conditional on the implementation of stabilisation programmes, and its approval of these programmes not only triggered the disbursement of IMF funding, but also conditioned other forms of public and private financing including debt relief.

The Forms of Assistance

It is very difficult to decide where to stop when identifying assistance to transition. From the most to the less obvious one can draw the following list:

- humanitarian aid, in the form of emergency supplies of food and medicine;
- technical assistance, such as training, and providing consultancy and macro-economic policy advice;
- macroeconomic multilateral financing (including the drawings on IMF facilities);
- special balance of payments financing, which comprises debt write-offs, rescheduling and concessionary restructuring;
- financing of specific projects on concessionary terms;
- providing a stabilisation fund to help establish the currency convertibility;
- granting of export credits on concessionary or non-concessionary terms (the latter may be considered as assistance, as many countries in transition would not be able to get credits on normal commercial terms due to their lack of credibility);
- the provision of investment guarantees.

In a broader concept of assistance, private investment flows and trade arrangements also qualify as aid. Private investment and private finance flows are usually recorded separately from aid flows but are intricately linked with the latter, because private finance is facilitated through specific assistance measures, and also because the global credibility of a country is enhanced by the seal of approval that it gets from the IMF. In addition, private finance and investment add to the overall external financing of the recipient country and reinforce the impact of assistance. An example will highlight how much private investment and international assistance are interconnected. In one of the biggest foreign direct investment deals concluded in Eastern Europe, Volkswagen established a joint venture with the Skoda automobile firm; the deal was finalised in 1991, involving a total investment of 9 billion DM over several years. In September 1993 Volkswagen was ready to launch a 1.4 billion DM investment with the involvement of the EBRD, the World Bank's International Finance Corporation, and a private banking consortium led by Dresdner bank. The deal was cancelled just before signing, Volkswagen arguing that due to successful restructuring of the Czech firm the inflow of new money was no longer necessary (*Financial Times*, 17 September 1993). The event does not just affect the relations between a Western multinational firm and an Eastern government but also the efforts of two international financial institutions in promoting project financing in Eastern Europe.

Are trade arrangements a form of aid or an alternative to aid? Improving the countries' market access to the West is undisputably a form of aid, and the most efficient one according to many political leaders in the East. Western experts do not deny the point but contend that the two questions must be separated; aid is granted precisely to allow the recipient countries to become internationally more competitive, and to turn into fully-fledged members of the international trade system.

The Amount of Assistance

Table 9.5 gives a very broad overview of the amounts of assistance granted in 1990–3, including foreign investment flows, with the breakdown by donors, recipients and forms of assistance. The figures are to be treated with extreme caution. Overall the assistance to transition is far from transparent. Though entitled to coordinate assistance, the EC Commission does not get all the information it needs in a comparable form. Information on bilateral assistance, and specifically on disbursements as opposed to commitments, is very patchy, not to say biased. It is available with great delay.

These gaps and delays in information explain why there is a growing disappointment over assistance both in the East and in the West. The Western public is informed of huge commitments to Eastern Europe and

Table 9.5 *Financial flows to Eastern Europe and to the former Soviet Union/Russia, 1990–3 (million $US)*

	1990	1991	1992	1993 preliminary	Cumulated 1990–3
A. Non-aid related					
1. Borrowing on capital markets (gross financial flows):					
Total Eastern Europe	1425	1661	1494	6341	10921
of which Hungary	987	1378	1446	5071	8882
Czechoslovakia (Czech Republic since 1993)	438	278	40	240	996
Total USSR (Russia since 1992)	3250	–	–	28	3278
2. Net FDI flows:					
Total Eastern Europe	573	2302	3055	3548	9478
Total USSR (Russia since 1992)	–	200	858(c)	540(c)	1598
3. Portfolio investment (net):					
Total Eastern Europe	–	–	–	962	962
of which Czech Republic	942	942			
Total USSR (Russia since 1992)	–	–	–	100	100
Total Eastern Europe	1998	3963	4549	10851	21361
Total USSR/Russia	3250	200	858	668	4976
B. Aid-related					
1. Official flows:					
a. Grants:					
Total Eastern Europe	1200	1700	1500	1500	5900
Total USSR (Russia since 1992)	–	2200	3735	3500	9435
b. Bilateral and guaranteed credits:					
Total Eastern Europe (a)	500	1000	800	800	3100
Total USSR (Russia since 1992)	7650(b)	12000	12500	5100	37250
c. Multilateral credits					
Total Eastern Europe	1774	6186	3561	1734	13255
of which to Hungary	–	–	–	–	3340
Poland	–	–	–	–	2532
the Czech Republic	–	–	–	–	2664
Total USSR (Russia since 1992)	–	–	1000	2491	3491
2. Special finance:					
Total Eastern Europe	10417	9628	7396	5644	33085
Total Soviet Union/Russia	4500	−500	13900	18200	36100
Total aid flows	26041	32223	44392	38969	141625
Total Eastern Europe	13891	18523	13257	9678	55349
Total USSR (Russia since 1992)	12150	13700	31135	29291	86276
Grand total, financial flows	31289	36386	49799	50488	167962
Total Eastern Europe	15889	22486	17806	20529	76710
Total USSR (Russia since 1992)	15400	13900	31993	29959	91252

(a) Concessionary credits only.
(b) All credits including commercial bank credit on normal terms.
(c) FDI into Russia and Estonia in 1992 and 1993.

Sources: ECE/UN, *Economic Survey of Europe in 1993–94*, ch. 4.

Russia. For instance, in the case of the latter country, a package of 24 billion dollars was announced in April 1992, then another package of 43.4 billion dollars was launched in April 1993 at the G-7 Summit in Tokyo. Very little of the first package had actually been disbursed because Russia could not meet the conditionality attached to the assistance measures; some of it was re-included in the second package, which mixed multilateral and bilateral financing of various kinds. A third package was announced in April 1994, but the arrangement with the IMF was reached in April 1995 only, (see Table 9.6). Thus, in many cases, commitments are reported twice and figures overlap. The Eastern population is very frustrated by the low share of the disbursements, and has the impression that only a trickle of the announced funding is actually available. Other frustrations add to the disappointment over the figures.

Table 9.6 *Official aid packages for Russia (billion US dollars)*

	Package I (1992)		Package II (1993)		Package III (1994)	
	Proposed	Actual	Proposed	Actual	Proposed	Actual
Bilateral credits	11.0	12.5	10.0	6.0	–	0.1
IMF facilities						
Standby	4.0	1.0	4.1	1.5	13.5	6.5 (e)
STF*	–	–	3.0	1.5	–	1.5 (f)
Stabilisation	6.0	–	6.0	–	–	–
World Bank	0.6	–	4.9 (a)	0.5	2.1	–
EBRD	–	–	0.3			
Special finance (b)	2.5	13.9 (c)	15.0	16.5	7.0	–
Deferred/rescheduled		7.1 (c)	15.0	15.0	7.0	–
Arrears		6.8 (c)	–	1.5 (d)	–	
Total	24.0	27.4	43.0	23.5	22.6	

* Systemic Transformation Facility
(a) $1 billion rehabilitation loan, and oil sector loans.
(b) From Paris Club only.
(c) Also includes relief and arrears on commercial debt (London Club)
(d) Arrears on interest payments to London Club member banks.
(e) Agreed April 1995.
(f) Relates to Package II.
Sources: IMF Press release, 1 February 1994; press reports. For 1994: ECE/UN (1995), p. 155; press reports.

The Drawbacks of Assistance

We may sum up these drawbacks under four headings:

(a) *The very concept of assistance is ambiguous.* Even if a narrow concept is retained, excluding foreign direct investment, one may ask the question:

who helps whom? Emergency food aid has been sensed as a way for the West to get rid of its surpluses, at the same time impairing the competitiveness of domestic producers (in the case of Poland) or enriching mafia networks (in the case of Russia). Technical assistance is largely considered in the East as inadequate, supplied by individuals and institutions who generally lack a serious knowledge of the countries in transition and at best only have experience of the developing countries. It is perceived as providing funds to Western consultant firms or academic institutions, and allowing foreigners to learn about business opportunities in the East. Export credit obviously helps the exporters, and engages Eastern importers in unnecessary purchases. Project finance is often directed towards areas of interest to the West more than to the East (for instance, projects focused on nuclear safety or environmental protection) (for Eastern views, see Inotai, 1993; Kiss, 1994).

(b) *Assistance is tied or conditional.* This is naturally the case for the macro-financial assistance from the IMF. Though the stabilisation packages were in all countries designed and implemented on the base of national programmes, the IMF conditionality is binding because of its lack of flexibility (even when a given country voluntarily refrains from drawing on available funds as was the case for Hungary in 1992, due to the fact that the budget deficit target was exceeded). There is an implicit conditionality in private financing as well: the multinationals which make large investments in transition countries exert a pressure on the governments to obtain increased tariff protection, to force a devaluation, and to keep domestic prices for the goods they manufacture low enough on the local market, all of which may clash with the macroeconomic policy recommended by the IMF and endorsed by the governments.

More generally, the recipients complain about all the administrative conditions and red tape required to unleash the funding. They resent the lack of coordination between the donors and the recipients. They also feel that there is no global vision over assistance. Beyond the commitments to assist transformation, no clear design emerges from the addition of numerous measures, as there is also no coordination among the donors. Eastern recipients often feel that Western assistance is dominated by a collusion among private lobbies and political interests.

(c) *The grant element in assistance is very low.* This is combined with the huge gap between commitments and disbursements. For the Central European countries, for instance, the grant component of the commitments amounted to 14 per cent in 1989–91. In addition, a large share of the assistance in form of credits generates further indebtedness (Ners and Buxell, 1995).

(d) Even when assistance is actually disbursed, its efficiency is impaired by difficulties in *absorption*. The infrastructure is inadequate, the financial institutions in the East lack experience, and the managers are unable to find the guarantees which trigger the delivery of the funds. This in turn creates the impression in the West that the assistance is not really needed as the available funds are not promptly used.

The Prospects of Assistance

The nostalgia of a Marshall Plan for the transition expresses the disappointment over actual assistance rather than a workable recommendation for the future. In 1947 the task was simpler: there was a single donor, the recipients were developed market economies, there was imposed coordination among them, and the mechanisms of disbursement were swift and strongly controlled. There was a grand design – to keep the Western world safe from communism and to strengthen it against the enemy – and there was also a clear perception of the economic interests of the donor in a quick recovery of its export markets.

As has already been mentioned, the scheme of a Marshall Plan is not feasible to-day. Recommendations are made to the effect of improving what is already done, in several directions.

(a) There should be *better coordination*. Various proposals have been formulated to that effect (see Barre *et al.*, 1992a). Unfortunately all these proposals hit built-in obstacles. *Coordination among the donors* may be improved technically but is fundamentally impossible due to the conflicts of interests among the donors and their institutions. Among the countries involved, the single biggest donor is Germany, which has its own priority – to reconstruct Eastern Germany – and its own specific interests in a region, Central Europe, where it also controls the flows of private finance. The USA is more interested in Russia and would like to assume a political leadership in Western assistance but does not support the main financial burden. Among the international institutions, there is an obvious overlapping between the coordinating functions of the Community and of the IMF. The EC is the official coordinator (for Central and Eastern Europe only; it has no coordination tasks for the CIS) but hardly goes beyond monitoring and collecting information for all the assistance efforts outside the specific PHARE programme. The IMF is not a coordinator and could not act as such. However, in fact, the impact of IMF conditionality endows the institution with an implicit governance of the assistance process. *Coordination among the recipients* is impaired by obvious conflicts of interests, which are increased by the inequality in distribution of aid (see Table 9.4). It is also hindered by the unfortunate debate over a regional arrangement in Eastern Europe, which is seen by the recipients as a way of postponing their integration into the European Community. The idea of *cooperation among the donors and the recipients*, i.e. the claim for *partnership*, shifts the debate from assistance proper to the 'trade versus aid' dispute.

(b) *Assistance should be more substantial.* This is a claim from the recipient countries, especially those which have until now received a small share of the total. This claim is sustained by overall and often vague estimates of the global needs for financing in the countries in transition (Zoethout, 1993), which range from 23 billion to over 200 billion dollars annually for Eastern Europe only. The opposite view, understandably expressed on the donor's side, is that the recipient countries already have great difficulty in absorbing the actually supplied assistance, and also that there is a large amount of capital flight from some countries in transition.

(c) Assistance should be *better geared to transformation needs, and less concentrated on macro-economic stabilisation.* This is a widely acknowledged proposal. Its feasibility is impeded by two factors. First, as the IMF is in fact the main controlling agency, it is not surprising that assistance is concentrated in the fields that the agency masters best and for which it has a mandate. Second, there is no worldwide experience of the granting of structural long-term assistance. The IBRD and the EBRD concentrate on project financing, with micro-economic criteria. There are no clear criteria by which to estimate and control the broader efficiency of this type of assistance. For instance, it had been suggested that assistance to Russia should be developed in the form of aid to unemployment benefit schemes, on the grounds that if unemployment grows, then there is a clear signal that structural transformation is under way, and no other conditionality would be needed. But the message might be not so clear, the amount of funding for such a purpose is not easy to define, and such an assistance obviously implies an intervention in domestic policies if it is to be controlled, much beyond the usual conditionality attached to IMF programmes. The proposals for long-term support for modernisation, which would be 'non-debt creating for the beneficiaries and market-creating for the donor countries' (Inotai, 1993, p. 18), are quite enticing but not easily implementable. They imply a consensus among donors and recipients over a long-term modernisation policy, which brings us back to the difficulties of an industrial policy for the transition. To be efficient, assistance to modernisation has to rely on an adequate market environment which precisely is lacking.

One has then to reckon that inadequate as it is, Western assistance to transition can only marginally be improved. IMF governance may be questioned but it is the only strong force at hand. The short-term, selfish interests of the donors, such as security concerns, environmental protection, and safeguards against the economic risks entailed by the transition process for the Western economies (in terms of undesired flows of people and goods from the East to the West, or in terms of a financial collapse), have to be reckoned with. There is little realism in suggesting a trade-off between these short-term considerations and long-term interests such as the attractiveness of huge markets if and when the transition is successfully completed. What does a successful transition mean? This is the question tentatively asked in the next chapter.

10 Towards a Theory of the Transition?

A few years after the bolshevik revolution in Russia, neo-classical economists asked whether a socialist economic system was viable. They concluded that it could not operate rationally. Other economists, socialist-oriented, attempted to show that resource allocation could be rational in a socialist economy, even if the actual Soviet regime was not functioning that way. Thus emerged in the 1930s the debate on 'market socialism'.

When a number of countries became centrally planned economies after the Second World War, various theoretical approaches were developed. Many analysts, both economists and political scientists, considered that this system unduly called itself 'socialist', and thus marred a concept which encompassed a set of positive human values. They preferred to call it 'real socialism' (or 'really existing'). This triggered a debate on the real nature of the system (or the real nature of the USSR when this country was taken as an ideal type). Many authors contributed to the debate in the West, in a political economy or a systemic approach. In the East, the most significant contributor was the Hungarian economist Janos Kornai with his *Economics of Shortage* (1980), and later *The Socialist System: Political Economy of Communism* (1992).

Do we need a theory of the transition? The answer is a straightforward 'no' when one believes that the socialist economy was a non-system now turning into a 'fully-fledged' market economy. But what if the transition is a continuing process, resulting in a specific economic regime in the East? Then it deserves a theoretical approach; otherwise, if it is only treated as a market system in limbo, some serious policy errors may be committed in managing the transition.

MARKET SOCIALISM

Marx believed that capitalism could only generate anarchy. In the Soviet literature on the political economy of capitalism this built-in anarchy (*stikhiya*) was opposed to the efficient, plan-regulated coordination of economic activities. However, the first theoretical questioning of a socialist economy was on the contrary putting market rationality in opposition to plan irrationality. Ludwig von Mises demonstrated in 1920 that in a complex socialist economy, with thousands of plants operating, it would be impossible for a government to efficiently allocate labour and producers' goods. To Mises this impossibility was due to the original sin of socialism, which had been to abolish private ownership on producers' goods. Hence the only way to an efficient economy was to get rid of socialism itself.

Other economists spoke of a practical impossibility, claiming that to solve millions of equations on the basis of thousands of statistical data obtained from millions of estimates would prove unfeasible (Robbins, 1937). What, then, if it were possible to achieve such economic calculation without having to solve millions of equations, or if modern computing techniques allowed to solve these equations almost instantly?

Oskar Lange and the Market Socialism Blueprint

Though Oskar Lange never used the phrase he is generally considered as the father of market socialism theory, having developed the model in two large studies in 1936–7. The paternity of the term *Marktsozialismus* is attributed by Nuti (1992) to a German economist, E. Heimann (1922). Reduced to its essentials, the market socialism model operates as follows. Individuals may freely choose which goods and services they want to consume, and which job they want to do in which work-place. Prices of consumer goods, as well as wages, are determined by the supply–demand mechanisms. The incomes are the sum of the wages paid by the enterprises and of a 'social dividend' allocated by the state; this yields the aggregate demand. The means of production are owned by the state. The Central Planning Board is informed of consumer preferences (through the demand prices), of the total amount of the productive resources (which it controls), and of the feasible technological combinations of factors. The managers of the public-owned enterprises are instructed to choose the combination of factors which minimises their average cost, and to increase their output to the point where marginal cost is equal to the price of the product. In doing so, they use market prices for goods and labour, and 'accounting prices' fixed for the means of production by the Central Planning Board (CPB).

Who is to ensure that these 'accounting prices' are rational? The Lange model provides for a trial-and-error procedure. Initially the CPB fixes prices at random. The enterprises then determine their production programmes. On the same basis, the CPB itself determines investment programmes (which it controls). As in the beginning prices will not be correct, at the end of the first period or production cycle the CPB will be informed that for a number of goods supply and demand were not balanced: there will be shortages, or excess inventories. The CPB will then change the prices. Gradually the process will converge to the system of equilibrium prices. The CPB will replicate the market, so as to ensure the same coordination functions with the same initial information. The so-called 'parametric function of prices' also allows the state to impose its choices in consumption and production.

Objections and New Suggestions

Lange was criticised on many technical points but the main objection to his theory had already been formulated by Friedrich von Hayek in 1935, a year before the first of Lange's two articles had been published. As editor of *Collectivist Economic Planning*, a collection of essays including the 1920 article by Ludwig von Mises, Hayek emphasised a crucial point. According to him, the difficulty was not just whether under socialism one could calculate rational prices, but mainly that an incentive was needed for the enterprises to obtain and use the information required for their decisions to conform to the wishes of the CPB. Such incentives only exist, he claimed, if there is a private ownership for producer goods.

Following the war and the establishment of a command economy on a large scale in Europe, the debate re-emerged in the early 1960s when the first waves of reforms spread in Eastern Europe and in the USSR. The phrase 'market socialism' was taboo in the East. The closest version to it was the 'socialism with a human face' model conceived during the Prague Spring (1967–8) and crushed by the Soviet armed intervention in 1968. The authors of the 'new economic mechanism' introduced in Hungary in the same year 1968 were very careful not to refer to anything that hinted of market socialism ideas. In official Soviet parlance, all the reforms aimed at 'improving the planning methods' by a recourse to 'money-market mechanisms'; Western comments spoke of the 'combination' of plan and market.

Among the theoretical contributions of this period one should mention those by Wlodzimierz Brus (1961) and Alec Nove (1983). None of them specifically refers to 'market socialism' but rather to 'central planning with regulated market mechanism' (Brus) or 'feasible socialism' with a large decentralization of decision-making and broad social guarantees (Nove). Brus later evolved toward a broader definition of market socialism where the market would include capital as well (Brus and Laski, 1989).

What do we learn from these debates and what is the point of discussing them now? Probably the main weakness of the model (which maybe was acknowledged later by Lange himself, when after the war he almost rejected his pre-war model) was that it treated economic calculation under socialism as a technical problem, and did not take into account the political features of the communist regime. Party monopoly of political power supplemented and superseded state monopoly of ownership and central planning. The managers of the state enterprises were trained to obey party orders, explicit or implicit, and therefore decentralisation and introduction of market mechanisms, even extensively as in Hungary, could not radically alter their priorities and their ways of adjusting. This was also the case in the Yugoslav self-managed system, which had been likened as well to a kind of market socialism *sui generis*, or 'market syndicalism' (Ward, 1958). It has been very convincingly shown by Milica Uvalic (1992) that 'although the institution of social property could have implied the redistribution of property rights in favour of enterprises *vis-à-vis* the state, since the political authorities continued to be responsible for a number of fundamental issues, it was the state that was the effective owner of enterprise assets' (Uvalic, 1992, p. 207).

Market socialism was thus not feasible. What has been demonstrated through the Soviet and Eastern European experience was not that the market is incompatible with central planning or state ownership, but that it is incompatible with the overall political interference of the communist party.

This requires a footnote: what about the Chinese model? It is tempting and too easy to answer that this is an entirely different world, with different traditions and different social behaviour. Is China the proof that market socialism is possible under a communist regime? Different explanations are possible. One may argue that there is no market socialism at all but a kind of social pact whereby the regime bargains dictatorship against social welfare and growth performance (Brada, 1993). Most specialists see China as a case for a semi-reformed planned economy; in the country areas collective farms still remain but the household-reponsibility system emerging within them provides incentives similar to those of private farming; in the field of services and small industry, responsibility capitalism is emerging; but the bulk of industry is still organised in large state-owned enterprises that display all the standard features of a command economy, the main one being the softness of the budget constraint (Knell and Yang, 1992; Lardy, 1991). The boom in the Chinese economy reflects several factors: genuine liberalisation and decentralisation in agriculture; the emergence of a new private sector; the opening up of the economy through quasi-convertibility of the currency; and the position of the country in the early stage of the take-off, in a Rostowian sense. Does all this mean that China is typically a Hayekian case in the sense that a spontaneous order developed among individuals freely contracting in a market setting in agriculture (McKinnon, 1992)? If we follow this line, it would be to admit that China offers an example of coexistence between pure capitalism and standard socialism, and certainly not a case of market socialism.

Could Market Socialism Offer a Workable Post-Transition Model?

In 1988, debates were conducted on market socialism in Eastern Europe – perhaps the first and the last year when this was possible (*Market Socialism*, 1989). While some expectations assumed that the transition would strengthen social-democrat orientations in politics, especially in Hungary, the 1989 revolutions actually brought to power right-wing governments in Eastern Europe. Such governments could obviously not accept any 'third way' which, according to the Minister of Finance of the Czech and Slovak

Federative Republic, Vaclav Klaus (1990) was the surest road to the Third World. Is market socialism, then, to be labelled as 'the model that might have been and never was' (Nuti, 1992)? Nuti characterises market socialism as a 'free economy' in the sense used by Kornai (1990), with the following additional features:

- The market is competitive and open, and operates for all goods and services, and for money and foreign exchange. There is no administrative allocation of producer goods. Monopolies have been dismantled, and all enterprises are allowed to diversify their output, and to move in and out of any sectors of their choice.
- Ownership is pluralist, combining state and cooperative with private ownership. As the state sector could not be curbed immediately one should experience all means of privatising the management, for instance through the leasing of state assets, or through cross-shareholdings.
- The state uses a wide range of policy instruments to implement government policies; these policies are however supplementary and not all-embracing; they are also contingent and applied only if the economy departs from a desirable course (assessed by the government, itself subject to frequent electoral checking by the people).
- There are some specifically socialist policies in the field of social security, employment, income distribution, etc. A minimum income is guaranteed. Some medical care is provided free, as well as education; the health and education sectors are however largely privatised.
- A share economy operates in various ways. There is profit sharing in cooperatives, optionally in private companies; there may be participation in capital as well.

In the post-communist world such a scheme is closer to what may be observed in some capitalist economies than in any transition country. In the latter, what dominates is 'capitalist triumphalism' to use the phrase of Peter Wiles (1992). This may easily be explained both by political aversion and by the deep recession induced by the stabilisation policies: there is no room for financing social benefits anyway. Instead, what we have is what Kornai calls 'a "*dual system*", in which many elements of the socialist and capitalist societies exist side by side' (Kornai, 1992); what is labelled by Nuti 'a necessary stage of *forced market socialism*, during which the state sector cannot just disappear but must be commercialised rapidly, reorganised, undergo financial restructuring and as much capacity restructuring as feasible, and be treated equally with the private sector in its fiscal burden and access to credit' (Nuti, 1993); what Chavance calls 'the post-socialist transition mixed economy' (1992b). Unlike the market socialism blueprint, this is not an ideal or desirable model, but rather the unfortunate consequence both of past inertia and of present political bigotry as far as the state sector is concerned.

'REAL' SOCIALISM

Why mention here the past debates on the true nature of the socialist societies? This is not just to remind us how many energies were devoted to issues that now seem hardly relevant. It also shows that the post-communist reality is very useful in revealing some features of the past.

Socialism was a Kind of Capitalism

A number of analyses viewed socialism as a kind of capitalism (state monopolist, bureaucratic, etc.). One of the most systematic representatives of this view is the French economist Charles Bettelheim, who theorised the split between the formal collective ownership of the means of production, and the real appropriation of these goods. The workers could not realise a 'social appropriation', and instead a state capitalism developed with all its negative consequences: existence of a wage-earning class, capital accumulation, confiscation of the profit by the exploiting class, made up of the true owners of the means of production, i.e. the party *nomenklatura*, and reproduction of market mechanisms. Such an analysis is essentially Marxist (Bettelheim, 1977 and 1979).

A variant of this approach may be found in the French school of *la régulation*, analysed by its founder Robert Boyer in an entry in the *New Palgrave* (1987). The approach 'combines Marxian intuitions and Kaleckian or Keynesian macro-economics in order to revive institutionalist or historical studies'. Though mainly oriented toward a critique of contemporary capitalism the theory was used for socialist economies as well, assuming they pertained to 'market logic'. Thus Jacques Sapir described the USSR as a 'mobilised economy', i.e. a market war economy in peacetime (1990). Wladimir Andreff applied to the EPCs ('economies planned from the Centre' in his wording) the concept of structural crisis which is central to the theory of *la régulation* (1993).

One may also feel there is implicit acknowledgement of the capitalist nature of socialist economies in many developments, especially in the 1980s, whereby concepts and tools of conventional macro-economics and new micro-economics may be applied to Eastern economies. Richard Portes developed the macroeconomic line (especially in his analysis of the impact of external disturbances in the West on the socialist economies; see Portes, 1980). Irena Grosfeld (1990) provides a survey of the second current. She very rightly states that, interesting as these approaches may be, they suppose a market system with private ownership of the means of production, non-existing in the East. Not surprisingly, as soon as this market environment emerged, such theories as the agency theory, the theory of incentives, and the transaction costs theory, were quickly tried in the cases of the countries in transition.

Socialism was a Specific System

Among the supporters of the specificity of socialism, are the Marxists, and of course the official theorists of the system in the socialist countries. A large debate emerged in the late 1960s to account for the fact that the economic reforms were yielding disappointing results while the socialist countries were supposed to have built socialism proper and to be heading toward communism and the age of plenty according to Marx. This was the theory of the 'advanced socialist society' (analysed in Lavigne, 1978). With the same ideological references but with opposite conclusions Gorbachev offered a theory of 'stagnation', or 'standstill' (*zastoy*). Western Marxists spoke of 'perverted' socialism (Nagels, 1990). A sophisticated approach combining the analytical tools of Marxism with those of modern micro-economics may be found in Roland (1989).

A large body of sovietologists adhered to a systemic approach, identifying and discussing the specific features of the socialist or centrally planned economies using the framework of comparative economic systems analyses (Bornstein, Holzman, Grossman, among many others; see Bornstein 1994, and Grossman 1994, for the most recent developments).

The Hungarian economist Janos Kornai provided the only non-Marxist comprehensive approach of the socialist system elaborated in the East. He did so in two stages (1980, 1992). In his *Economics of Shortage* (1980) starting from micro-economics (and even 'infra'-micro-economics), and using a non-standard disequilibrium analysis, he disclosed the main difference between planned and market economies. In the latter, firms are demand-constrained because they are producing for a market and have a hard budgetary constraint. If their costs exceed their revenue they go bankrupt, without any economic agent or authority to rescue them. In centrally planned economies the enterprise works with a view to implementing and overfulfilling the plan. The plan itself is always taut, and anticipates a volume of output higher than the production capacities would allow for, because the planning authorities expect that the enterprise will find ways of under-reporting its capacities and over-reporting its output. Thus there is no 'slack' in the system. The enterprise hits a resource constraint. It thus tries to expand its capacities in hoarding labour, inputs, and investment goods, extracted from the central allocator-planner. It is not constrained by demand as it has a soft budgetary constraint: if it does not meet its financial indicators it is always rescued by the authorities. As all the producers have a resource constraint and as the plan is taut, all the agents are always in short supply of some resource while keeping other resources in excess of their needs. Shortage and surplus coexist and cannot be netted out; the surpluses cannot be used while the shortages are a permanent constraint.

Kornai's analysis of the consumer shows that in contrast to the producer, the consumer has a hard budgetary constraint: he cannot spend more than his income. But he is also subject to the paternalistic behaviour of the state. The state decides on his consumption through explicit or implicit (through shortages) rationing, provides him with free (rationed) goods on a large scale, and with a very wide protection system including guaranteed jobs.

This analysis was immediately very appealing to the Western sovietologists because it integrated the basic stylised facts about the functioning of centrally planned economies into a coherent, simply formalised whole. However, a link was missing, because Kornai never expanded on the political setting. This link was re-established in *The Socialist System. The Political Economy of Communism* (1992). In this book, the 'anatomy' of the classical communist system begins with power, and ideology, which are the core of the system. Then the author looks at the property system, and finally discusses the coordination mechanism, thus considering the three foundations of the system, before analysing how it worked. The discussion of the external economic relations and of the 'national variations' introduces the international and comparative aspects, which were only briefly mentioned in Kornai's *Economics of Shortage*. A very important conclusion is drawn: The 'classical' socialist system had a built-in coherence and was viable – albeit at high cost. Changes that were meant to reform it resulted in contradictions which undermined its viability. But the collapse of the system was a political act, from which the transition started.

In the decade following the publication of *Economics of Shortage*, Kornai's work was widely used and referred to in the West, often supplementing the analysis with a political economy approach (see, for instance, Dembinski, 1991; Welfens, 1992), and insisting on the distortions that led to the collapse.

TOWARD A THEORY OF THE TRANSITION

Now the collapse of communism is behind us, and a new world is emerging. Can theory help? The question was asked on the panel on transition organised at the Annual Congress of the European Economic Association in 1992 (see Aghion, 1993; Roland, 1993; Weitzman, 1993). If indeed theory helps, which one?

Transition Leads to the Market and a Theory of the Market Already Exists

The answer depends on the views one has about the post-transition. In the countries first engaged in the transition process, the transition is seen as a process leading as quickly as possible to a market economy, as defined in standard textbooks. There is no third way in between the plan and the market. There is no need for a theory on transition either. Or rather, what is needed is a policy approach which should define the best strategies to create the market, in the shortest time and with the minimum costs. The debate on transition then concentrates on issues of speed and sequencing. A very systematic presentation of this stance can be found in Balcerowicz (1993).

If one adheres to this view, then all that needs to be done is to account for what, apparently, went wrong. We have already seen how the lasting recession in the transition countries was dealt with (Chapter 7). More generally, the final aim being a 'fully-fledged' market, whatever goes wrong during the process is attributed: (i) to the legacies of the past; (ii) to a wrong evaluation of the reality due to imperfect statistics; (iii) to the external constraint; (iv) to technical errors in policies; and ultimately (v) to the inadequate assistance of the West (this last point has been emphatically underlined by Jeffrey Sachs in many statements: for instance, Sachs, 1994; other representative evaluations include Åslund, 1994; Balcerowicz and Gelb, 1994).

This commitment to the quickest possible move to the market preceded by stabilisation does not suffer critics. Any objection, even any question, is then deemed to come from an opponent of the market, i.e. a die-hard communist. (I personally remember attending a symposium on privatisation in 1990, where I asked a presenter, involved in the privatisation process of his country, whether the scheme he outlined would have the popular support that he expected, in terms of the proportion of people actually using their rights to become share-owners. The answer was: 'If you ask this question it means that you are against the privatisation in our country'.)

There is a striking similarity with the former 'general line' supported by the party. Let us remember how the protracted recession of the East European countries in the early 1980s was officially explained: (i) by the oil shock; (ii) by 'errors' in the conduct of the economic reform; (iii) by the credit squeeze from the West and by the technological embargo. At that time Western scholars who acknowledged that these factors had a certain impact but that the main problem lay in the inconsistencies of the system itself were considered as political opponents.

Most of the Western analysts, even when convinced of the accuracy of the standard transition package, doubt that one can ignore the difficulties and duration of the process, and offer relevant explanations and suggestions.

Transition Leads to the Market, But Slowly

The emerging market will display failures as in the existing market economies. In addition, the legacies of the past and the shock of the 'stabilisation-cum-transformation' are leading to specific distortions and failures.

Hence one has to analyse the logic of the transformation in the micro-economic sphere. Because transformation is obviously very much affected by political factors, one tempting orientation is to use the framework of the public choice theory, which applies the tools of the economist to non-market decision-making (see Murrell, 1991, and the whole issue of the *Journal of Comparative Economics*, June 1991, devoted to this topic).

As enterprise is often viewed as the core element of the transformation process, the contemporary developments of the theory of the firm are called upon (property rights, transaction costs, industrial organisation theory, incentives theory, principal/agent, etc.; see Frydman and Rapaczynski, 1993b; Yavlinsky and Braguinsky, 1994). Problems of decision-making within organisations in a context of bounded rationality are typically faced by Eastern European and Russian managers. Strategic behaviour, and asymmetric access to information are investigated through case studies (Charap and Webster, 1993) and are theorised (Mayhew and Seabright, 1992; Frydman *et al.*, 1993a; Wijnbergen, 1993), usually with policy recommendations.

The institutional approach takes a broader view (see Jackson, 1992a). Within this current, the evolutionary theory appears the most controverted, first because it already raises much argument within the capitalist context, and second because it is wrongly confused with a standard 'gradualist' approach.

The evolutionary theory as applied to transition economy has been elaborated by Peter Murrell in numerous articles. The author indeed recommends a piecemeal approach to privatisation, and opposes this approach to 'radicalism'. However, he does not criticise the stabilisation part of the radical programmes (actually he does not discuss that part in its macro-economic policy component), except for the fact that these policies are relying solely on market-based instruments. Instead, he advocates strict direct controls on the non-market sphere, i.e. on state-owned enterprises, so as not to hinder the market response from the nascent market (private) sector, and therefore joins Kornai (1990). Thus slow privatisation might no longer appear as a weakness of the transformation process but rather as a positive way of managing the transition.

The ambiguity of the evolutionary approach is illustrated by Irena Grosfeld (1992). She asserts that it needs a radical step (privatisation through quick divestiture of the state) so as to establish a new institutional and organisational order, in the sense given to that phrase by Douglass North (1990), and only then can an evolutionary process be initiated. Thus what Grosfeld calls 'radical', or 'pure' evolutionists *à la* Murrell, may conflict with her own 'evolutionary gradualism' beginning with a mass privatisation big bang (see also Pelikan, 1993).

Both approaches have the same drawback. They do not provide clear insights into what will happen next, once the market structures are established (probably because they assume that these structures will allow the market to operate as in standard developed market systems). Nor do they say what is going to happen during the supposedly short (Grosfeld), or rather long (Murrell) time when the state-owned enterprises will be in operation. Hopefully, as mentioned in IFC (1993) or Brada (1993), these enterprises will not behave exactly as the former communist enterprises; though maintaining some legacies from the past in their behaviour, they will display some adaptative features, so that the conflict between the old and the new will perhaps not be so drastic as assumed by the evolutionary theorists. Is it possible to look at the transition not only as a lasting process, but also as a specific, mixed economy?

A Country in Transition Is a Mixed Economy, Whether It Likes It or Not

Such an assertion is usually seen as insulting to these countries. Alternatively, it is a judgement over the uncompletedness of the process in the countries which have not yet wholly disengaged themselves from the old system (for example, Romania, Ukraine, the Central Asian states, etc.). The idea of a mixed economy is rooted in that of market socialism, which is seen as an unacceptable or unrealistic concept. However, as we have seen earlier in this chapter, one can hardly question the fact that for the time being these economies are 'mixed' in the sense that they carry on a specific inertia of the former system (Nuti, 1993).

The main difficulty is that the state is still there, and unwanted. There is 'state desertion' (Nuti and Portes, 1993): state-owned enterprises are left floundering, which leaves the road open to spontaneous privatisation and *nomenklatura* management. Should one then apply the solution recommended by the evolutionists and strictly control them? Even assuming that the governments would agree to such a policy, they could not in practice re-establish central control for lack of institutional means and political will, and would certainly be prevented from doing that by the assistance-providing organisations.

How should this kind of economy be managed? No detailed solutions are provided. Most proposals boil down to managing gradual bankruptcies, financial restructuring and solving the problem of the bad debts. Some interesting suggestions are to be found in Wijnbergen (1993) on the management of non-privatisable state enterprises before definitive closure through 'workfare firms'. The same author outlines the role of the state in the post-transition economy as organising training programmes (though acknowledging that in the West this is a very partial solution to unemployment), crediting restructuring plans, financing public infrastructure investment (in roads, access to electricity, education facilities) and selectively supporting regions.

A French economist, Bernard Chavance (1992b) is rather pessimistic about 'the mixed post-socialist transition economy'. His 'grey scenario' foresees a rather inert state sector, with a stagnant production, low modernisation and continuous disinvestment. The government tries to avoid bankruptcies for fear of social explosion. The private sector is burdened by the existence of the public sector which crowds it out. Social expenditures are decreasing except for unemployment benefits. Investment is low and deterred by high taxes. International competitiveness is weakened. A more 'rosy' scenario should, according to the author, imply a more interventionist role for the state, with an active industrial and agricultural policy, a voluntarist employment and regional policy. The state should also actively deal with the remaining state sector.

An increasing number of authors have been calling for a greater role for the state – along with a feeling that the transformation process turned out to be more complicated than expected (Ellman, 1994) – when the first evaluations of the transformation process on several years have shown the damage caused by the non-benign neglect of the state. More generally, the importance of institutions is underlined (Taylor, 1994), which leads to a more general 'political economy' approach to the reform (Williamson, 1994; Roland, 1994a).

However, it is difficult to advocate interventionism when all over the world the state disengages itself both from ownership of enterprises, and from active economic policy other than monetary. Are there convincing historical experiences? One may refer to the revamping of the state sector in France which took place in the early 1970s, so as to strengthen the international competitiveness of the country when the Common Market entered into its last stage of completion. The restructuring scheme was elaborated in an official report called *Rapport Nora* (1967) from the name of the drafting committee chairman. The Report answered several questions: what the mission of the public sector should be; how to finance the large state enterprises; how to control them. It started from the claim that 'the command economy is no longer adapted to the new needs' (p. 24), while 'the nationalisation developed in a climate of shortage, when it was more important to produce than to be competitive' (p. 24). The new mission of the public sector called for an 'organised market' and 'flexible planning', the task of the state enterprise being to achieve efficiency, and the task of the state being to create the conditions for the autonomy of these enterprises.

How should the public sector be financed? The priority should be given, stated the *Rapport Nora*, to the increase in prices and tariffs, and if it proved insufficient, to limited subsidies and to long-term borrowing; detailed suggestions were then given for the major state monopolies (electricity and gas distribution, railways, the Paris underground, and the coal authority). The most interesting part of the report is related to the *control* of the state enterprises, with a differentiation among the enterprises with high public constraints (i.e. the utilities mentioned above) and the enterprises of the 'market sector'. The first group should be controlled by the state mainly *a posteriori*, on the base of contractual policies between the state and the enterprises. For the 'market sector' state enterprises, the government should restructure them (through a breaking-down and merger policy), and intervene through a policy of 'holdings', in any case getting rid of the 'lame ducks'.

It is not the purpose of this book to relate how the French state sector was revamped following these recommendations. Let us simply state that more than twenty years later, the post-socialist French government had a state sector in rather good shape for privatising, and that the public enterprises (and banks) of the 'market sector' fared quite well (or no worse than their private counterparts). True, the reform of the state sector took place in a market environment. Nevertheless in 1968 France was still an administered and rather underdeveloped economy. The government which decided to modernise the state sector without 'getting rid' of it was not a socialist or social-democrat one; it was the government of the very anti-communist General de Gaulle.

This scheme belongs to policy-making rather than to theory. In any case we believe that what is missing in the countries in transition is a clear perception of the role of the state at large (see Kornai, 1994, p. 60). The economists or policy-makers of these countries are not to be blamed; if they so disregarded the matter, this is not only because of prejudices rooted in their own past, but maybe also because the West has not equipped them with the proper analytical tools and policy instruments to tackle the issue.

Conclusion

Salt is good; but if the salt have lost his savour, wherewith shall it be seasoned?   (Holy Bible, King James Version, St Luke 14:34)

What is the impact of the transition on *us*? Isn't it indecent to ask the question when the transition directly and direly affects millions of people in their everyday lives? But isn't it also an implicit question that goes beyond the assistance programmes to the countries involved, the moral support, and the interest of the general public? We have to reconsider our own system, our values, our future. It also leads to a reconsideration of the relations between the developed and the developing world. North–South (i.e. West–South) relations were simpler when communism ruled a part of the world. Inadequate as these relations were, it could always be pointed out that East–South relations did not bring about a better solution for enhancing development. The transition is the end of a war, which was described as 'cold'. A symposium in 1992 was aptly devoted to the *Economic Consequences of the East* (CEPR, 1992a), an allusion to the famous book by Keynes published in 1919, *The Economic Consequences of the Peace*. How will the world look following the transition? Is it the *End of History* (Fukuyama, 1991), or the beginning of a new Middle Ages while the second millennium is ending, as suggested by a French author (Minc, 1993)? This conclusory chapter will limit itself to the economic impact, which itself is interrelated with political and ideological developments.

A SMALL ECONOMIC IMPACT

The change of regime has had immediate *ideological* consequences (Chirot, 1991). It has discredited the Left all over the word, and turned socialism into a dirty word. While communism is still strong in some Asiatic countries and in Cuba, the African-type Marxist ideologies have promptly collapsed – true, the latter were a camouflage for personal or tribal dictatorship still very much alive. In the West, the communist parties had to adapt through restructuring and renaming, and could not avoid losing ground. The non-communist left lost credibility as well though endorsing many of the right-wing policy schemes. The right-wing parties and ideas benefited in the short term, but quickly realised that the loss of their main opponent and scapegoat might entail some perils in the future.

254

In *international politics*, the transition has led to a reconsideration of the whole security system. It has weakened the defensive international organisations and first of all NATO, which is debating whether or not to admit some of the countries in transition and devising alternative arrangements such as the 'Partnership for Peace' offered to East Central Europe in 1994. The transition has shaken the military–industrial complexes in all big countries. The foreign policy schemes which had been developed with a view to fighting, deterring or containing communism were suddenly out of date. The new ethnic or nationalistic conflicts have taken the West by surprise and have not triggered an adequate response.

By comparison, the economic impact has been very weak. Prospects are dim, in terms of opportunities, threats or risks. Foreign investors expect large potential returns but have committed little capital in terms of overall world foreign direct investment. Exporters have lost their routines; those who were familiar with state-trading ways had to adjust and find new partners; they mainly tried to secure their positions. New exporters, among them small and medium enterprises, found they could take advantage of new niches, and sometimes struck very good deals. As a whole the Western world has maintained surpluses in trade with the countries in transition. Assistance to transition did not hurt the Western taxpayer much except in Germany, and it benefited a host of suppliers of goods and services, non-profit institutions, advice-givers, and money-makers of all kinds. Losses from transition were small in the West. Some sectoral interests claimed they were hurt, such as farmers or steelmakers; in fact losses directly due to Eastern exports were compounded with the impact of global recession and growing structural inefficiencies in these sensitive sectors in the West itself; besides, these losses were alleviated by restrictive measures or compensation against the export surge. The West did not suffer from a large-scale influx of immigrants from the East despite its fears. The only exception is Germany, but in this case the first wave was migration from Eastern to Western Germany before and after reunification, and from 'ethnic Germans' from further East. The transition process only began to alter the balance between the three main countries, the United States, Germany and Japan, in terms of economic power.

Did the South lose from the transition? The 'crowding out' effect is dubious. It is not evidenced that assistance to the East reduced funding available to the South (Laux, 1994). The argument is used on both sides: by the developing countries, to support the claims for help, and by the donors, as an excuse for not granting enough assistance.

The international economic organisations were given increased responsibilities in the process. The European Community was the most involved as an overall coordinator of assistance, and as a negotiator of new trade relations between its members and the countries in transition. It had to alter earlier visions about its own evolution in terms of deepening and especially enlargement. The IMF strengthened its role in economic governance of the world.

The main 'economic consequences of the East' are still ahead, and ambivalent. The optimists contend that the recession in the East has bottomed out or is soon to do so. Growth in these countries will stimulate the end of recession in the West. The market will be successfully implemented. The 'green shoots' of the private sector are visible everywhere and will soon be blooming. The pessimists see a protracted recession, little structural change, and seeds of conflict and disorganisation on top of open wars in some areas of the CIS and in Yugoslavia. Capitalism has won; moreover, it is now free from critics, as the questioning of its failures, in terms of social injustice or inequality in income distribution, can immediately be discarded as a resurgence of communist ideology.

THERE IS ONLY ONE WORLD

The new post-communist world is divided among developed and developing countries. The countries in transition implicitly belong to the second group. Some may grow into members of the first, as well as the East Asian developing countries which are heading for the most successful performance in the 1990s.

The global market economy is regulated by a small number of countries or groups of countries which influence the domestic developments in the others through the enforcement of adjustment programmes drafted on a similar model, under the guidance of the leading international economic organisations. Within the industrialised countries, governments, big business and big finance interact; among them, conflicts are solved by the same decision-making forces through cooperative or non-cooperative strategies.

Global capitalism is increasingly insecure. It is pervaded by economic crime, financial volatility, environmental deterioration, and social threats as sluggish growth fuels unemployment and poverty. All these suddenly loom very large now that the threat of global confrontation between communism and the free world has vanished. Against these high risks, the transition in the East has created a kind of diversion, though remaining marginal enough on a world scale to be treated as 'all things being equal': as if the standard free-market model operated as usual. What if this model itself is not so clearcut as it looks like in textbooks (Stiglitz, 1994)? What if this limited (in time and space) transition was but the prelude to a worldwide transition? The countries in transition do know where they want to go: where we stand now. But where do *we* want to go now?

Statistical Appendix

Table A.1. *Eastern Europe and the USSR: Exports and Imports by Direction, 1975, 1980, 1986, 1989*

	1975 (values, billion US $)	1975 (per cent)	1980 (values, billion US$)	1980 (per cent)	1986 (values, billion US$)	1986 (per cent)	1989 (values, billion US$)	1989 (per cent)
Bulgaria								
Total exports	4.7	100.0	10.4	100.0	14.1	100.0	16.0	100.0
East	3.5	74.6	6.9	66.4	11.3	79.6	13.3	83.0
West	0.6	11.7	1.9	18.5	1.1	7.8	1.3	8.2
Other	0.6	13.6	1.6	15.1	1.8	12.6	1.4	8.7
Total imports	5.4	100.0	9.7	100.0	15.2	100.0	15.2	100.0
East	3.7	68.7	7.3	75.4	11.3	74.1	10.9	71.5
West	1.4	25.0	1.8	18.5	2.5	16.4	2.7	18.1
Other	0.3	6.3	0.6	6.1	1.4	9.5	1.6	10.3
Czechoslovakia								
Total exports	8.4	100.0	14.9	100.0	‖ 12.2	100.0	14.5	100.0
East	5.5	65.4	9.5	63.4	6.7	55.1	7.8	53.7
West	2.0	23.6	3.8	25.6	3.8	30.6	5.0	34.4
Other	0.9	11.0	1.6	11.0	1.8	14.3	1.7	11.9
Total imports	9.1	100.0	15.2	100.0	‖ 12.4	100.0	14.3	100.0
East	5.9	64.4	9.8	64.8	7.2	58.3	7.8	54.8
West	2.5	27.7	4.2	27.7	3.9	31.3	4.9	34.2
Other	0.7	7.8	1.1	7.5	1.3	10.4	1.6	11.0
GDR								
Total exports	10.4	100.0	18.6	100.0	‖ 16.4	100.0	17.3	100.0
East	6.8	65.5	11.1	59.4	7.0	42.9	7.2	41.7
West	2.9	27.4	5.9	31.5	7.7	46.9	8.7	50.1
Other	0.7	7.1	1.7	7.1	1.7	10.2	1.4	8.2
Total imports	11.7	100.0	20.3	100.0	‖ 16.1	100.0	17.8	100.0
East	7.1	60.5	11.3	55.5	7.6	47.0	6.8	38.1
West	3.9	33.4	7.5	36.9	7.1	44.0	9.8	54.8
Other	0.7	6.0	1.5	7.6	1.5	9.1	1.2	7.0
Hungary								
Total exports	6.1	100.0	‖ 8.6	100.0	9.2	100.0	9.7	100.0
East	4.1	67.7	4.3	50.3	5.0	54.0	4.0	41.0
West	1.5	23.9	3.3	38.0	3.2	34.8	4.6	48.0
Other	0.5	8.6	1.0	11.7	1.0	11.3	1.1	11.1
Total imports	7.2	100.0	‖ 9.2	100.0	9.6	100.0	8.9	100.0
East	4.5	62.7	4.3	46.9	4.9	50.8	3.5	39.2
West	2.0	28.4	3.9	42.2	3.9	40.4	4.7	52.9
Other	0.6	9.0	1.0	11.0	0.9	8.9	0.7	7.8

Table continued overleaf

257

Table A.1 continued

	1975 (values, billion US $)	1975 (per cent)	1980 (values, billion US$)	1980 (per cent)	1986 (values, billion US$)	1986 (per cent)	1989 (values, billion US$)	1989 (per cent)
Poland								
Total exports	10.3	100.0	17.0	100.0	‖ 12.1	100.0	12.9	100.0
East	5.8	56.6	8.9	52.3	5.6	46.1	4.5	34.8
West	3.5	33.9	6.2	36.5	4.6	37.7	6.8	52.7
Other	1.0	9.5	1.9	11.2	2.0	16.2	1.6	12.5
Total imports	12.6	100.0	19.1	100.0	‖ 11.2	100.0	11.3	100.0
East	5.5	43.4	12.1	63.2	6.1	54.3	3.6	32.1
West	6.3	50.3	6.9	36.2	4.1	36.4	6.4	56.5
Other	0.8	6.2	2.1	11.0	1.0	9.3	1.3	11.4
Romania								
Total exports	5.3	100.0	11.4	100.0	‖ 9.8	100.0	11.3	100.0
East	2.0	38.2	4.2	37.2	4.0	41.4	4.6	40.5
West	2.0	38.0	4.4	38.5	3.4	35.1	4.3	37.7
Other	1.3	23.8	2.8	24.3	2.3	23.5	2.5	22.0
Total imports	5.3	100.0	13.2	100.0	‖ 8.1	100.0	10.5	100.0
East	2.0	36.9	4.1	30.7	4.4	55.0	4.0	38.5
West	2.4	44.8	4.4	33.0	1.6	19.9	4.3	41.2
Other	1.0	18.5	4.8	36.3	2.0	25.1	2.1	20.2
Eastern Europe								
Total exports	45.2	100.0	80.9	100.0	74.7	100.0	81.1	100.0
East	27.8	61.5	44.9	55.5	39.6	52.9	40.8	50.4
West	12.3	27.3	25.5	31.5	23.7	31.7	31.0	38.2
Other	5.1	11.2	10.6	13.1	10.7	14.3	9.5	11.7
Total imports	51.2	100.0	86.7	100.0	72.6	100.0	75.9	100.0
East	28.6	55.7	46.8	54.0	41.5	57.1	37.0	48.8
West	18.5	36.1	28.6	33.1	23.0	31.7	29.6	39.0
Other	4.2	8.1	11.2	12.9	8.1	11.2	9.3	12.2
USSR								
Total exports	33.3	100.0	76.5	100.0	96.9	100.0	‖ 109.1	100.0
East	16.4	49.4	32.2	42.1	51.0	52.6	50.4	46.2
West	9.6	28.9	28.1	36.8	21.2	21.9	29.6	27.1
Other	7.2	21.7	16.1	21.1	24.8	25.5	29.2	26.7
Total imports	36.9	100.0	68.5	100.0	88.9	100.0	‖ 114.5	100.0
East	15.7	42.4	29.4	42.9	47.3	53.2	56.8	49.6
West	14.1	38.2	25.7	37.5	25.6	28.8	36.0	31.4
Other	7.2	19.4	13.4	19.6	16.0	18.0	21.7	18.9

It is usually said that Eastern European countries had an extremely large share of their total trade within the CMEA, expressing their 'block autarky' (see Lavigne, 1991, p. 14). The average usually quoted is 60 per cent of that total. Table A.1 shows that in 1989 the average share of the 'East' (mainly Comecon) for Eastern Europe was 50 per cent, and was still lower for the USSR. The only country with an overwhelming share (over 70 per cent) was Bulgaria. Also, the table shows that for most countries at some point the share of trade with the CMEA suddenly decreased (it would have been still more obvious over a continuous sequence of years).

The reason why it is so difficult to estimate the shares of the CMEA (hence the share of the West) and moreover to compare the countries from this point of view, is that trade was not measured in comparable units.

Non-socialist trade was conducted in convertible currencies. As socialist trade was mainly conducted within the CMEA, it was expressed in transferable rubles, a unit of account which one may, with some approximation, equate to the Soviet foreign trade unit of account, i.e. the 'devisa-ruble'. The devisa-ruble was linked to the dollar and other convertible currencies by an official exchange rate. This exchange rate was initially derived from the official gold parity of the ruble, an arbitrary figure last set up in 1961 in order to convey the idea that the ruble was 'stronger' than the dollar (in 1961, 1 'devisa-ruble' = 1.11 dollars). Later, when the official gold parity of the dollar was terminated, this official exchange rate was calculated on the basis of a basket of Western currencies. It had no relation to the domestic purchasing power of the ruble; it was a pure unit of account. As the official ruble/dollar rate was overvaluing the ruble, it follows that the share of the trade flows conducted in rubles was significantly overestimated.

Each socialist country had foreign trade statistics denominated in its own, non-convertible currency. These currencies also had official exchange rates against the Western currencies and against the ruble. Gradually Eastern European countries moved toward more 'realistic' exchange rates, calculated as the export purchasing power parity, i.e. the average amount of domestic currency (in domestic wholesale prices) which had to be spent in production costs in order to obtain one unit of a convertible currency, or a 'devisa' (transferable) ruble. These rates were fixed by the Eastern European countries without any coordination among them, which brought about increasing difficulties in comparing foreign trade statistics, as the resulting ruble/ dollar cross-rates were widely diverging. In addition, these new rates were introduced at different periods. Their introduction immediately brought about a discontinuity in statistics, expressed by the sign ‖ in the table. The discontinuity is due to the fact that the new 'commercial rates' amounted to a strong 'devaluation' of the ruble against the dollar (and all other convertible currencies) which immediately led to an increase in the share of trade with the 'West' and a fall in trade with the 'East'. No attempt was made to correct the previous trade figures.

Source: Calculations from ECE/UN, Economic Survey of Europe in 1990–1991, appendix tables C.4 and C.5.

'East' refers to East European country members of the CMEA and the Soviet Union; 'West' refers to Western European countries, North America and Japan.

Notes and source for Table A.2(a)

*For 1989 and 1990: Jan–Dec rate of change (annual rate of change: 251 in 89, 586 in 90, in per cent).

We chose to measure the rate of change in consumer prices, for the years 1989–90, rather as the change between January and December than the change in the average price level against preceding year. In a situation of wide fluctuations between January and December, with the monthly rate of inflation peaking in December 1989 and again in January 1990 (as a result of the freeing of prices on January 1st, 1990), this way of computing price changes better expresses how inflation accelerated in 1989 and decelerated in 1990, while the average change index gives the impression that inflation indeed accelerated instead of decelerating in 1990.

**The initial estimate for 1992 was 0.5 bn \$ surplus. Trade Ministry's figures announced in March yielded a deficit (see *Financial Times*, 9 March 1993).

***Figures do not take into account the reduction of the official debt of Poland (32 bn \$) due to be reduced by 50 per cent in instalments according to the agreement reached with the Paris Club in 1991. In March 1994, the London Club of creditor commercial banks cut 45 per cent from the 13 billion \$ owed to them by Poland.

(a) World Economy Research Institute, Warsaw, Poland: *International Economic Report 1993/94*.

Source: ECE/UN, *Economic Survey of Europe*, various issues; WIIW (Wiener Institut fur internationale Wirtschaftsvergleiche) reports; *PlanEcon Report*, various issues; for GNP per capita, *World Bank Atlas* and WIIW.

Table A.2(a) *Macro-economic indicators of countries in transition, 1989–94: Central European countries*

	1989	1990	1991	1992	1993	1994 (preliminary)
Poland						
GDP (average annual rate of change, in per cent)	0.2	–11.6	–7.6	1.5	4.5	5.0
GDP per capita in US$	1890		1790	1960	2200	
Gross industrial output (average annual rate of change, in per cent)	–0.5	–24.2	–11.9	4.2	7.4	13.0
Gross investment (average annual rate of change, in per cent)	–2.4	–10.1	–4.4	0.7	2.0	8.0
Consumer prices (average annual rate of change, in per cent)*	640.0	250.0	70.3	43.0	36.0	33.3
Real wages (average annual rate of change, in per cent)	8.3	–24.4	–0.3	–2.7	–1.5	2.0
Average monthly US dollar wages (in US $)		108.4	166.0	214.0	220.0	
Budget balance (in % of the GNP)	–6.1	0.7	–3.5	–6.1	3.4	–2.8
Current account balance in convertible currencies (bn $)**	0.2	1.4	–0.8	–0.3	–2.3	–0.9
Gross debt in convertible currencies (bn $, end-year)***	40.8	48.5	48.4	47.0	47.4	41.9
Debt service due/exports (per cent) (a)		78.6	69.1	46.6	39.1	
Debt service paid/exports (per cent) (a)		6.8	9.7	11.0	13.2	
Hungary						
GDP (average annual rate of change, in per cent)	–0.2	–3.3	–11.9	–4.2	2.3	2.0
GDP per capita in US$	2630		2750	3010	3500	
Gross industrial production (average annual rate of change, in per cent)	–1.0	–5.0	–19.1	–10.0	4.0	9.1
Gross investment (average annual rate of change, in percent)	4.3	–8.8	–11.7	–6.3	0.2	3.5
Consumer prices (average annual rate of change, in per cent)	17.0	28.9	36.0	23.0	22.5	19.1
Real wages (average annual rate of change, in per cent)	0.7	–1.2	–3.7	–4.0	–1.6	7.0
Average monthly US dollar wages (in US $)		217.7	240.0	278.0	320.0	
Budget balance (in % of the GNP)	–1.3	–0.1	–4.6	–7.4	–7.5	–7.9
Current account balance in convertible currencies (bn $)	0.5	0.3	0.2	–0.1	–3.6	–3.9
Gross debt in convertible currencies (bn $, end-year)	19.2	21.3	22.7	21.4	24.6	28.5

Czechoslovakia

GDP (average annual rate of change, in per cent)	1.4	-1.4	-14.3	-6.5		
Czech Republic		-1.2	-14.2	-6.6	-0.3	2.7
Slovakia		-2.5	-14.5	-6.1	-4.7	4.8
GDP per capita in US$						
Czech Republic				2700	2440	3000
Slovakia				2220	1920	2070
Gross industrial production (average annual rate of change, in per cent)	0.7	-3.5	-24.7	-11.0		
Czech Republic		-3.5	-24.4	-10.6	-5.3	2.3
Slovakia		-4.0	-25.4	-13.7	-10.6	6.4
Gross investment (average annual rate of change, in per cent)	1.6	6.1	-27.2	3.0		
Czech Republic		6.5	-26.8	3.8	4.2	6.0
Slovakia		5.3	-28.1	1.0	16.0	-14.0
Consumer prices (average annual rate of change, in per cent)	1.4	10.1	57.9	11.0		
Czech Republic		9.9	56.7	11.1	20.8	10.0
Slovakia		10.6	61.2	10.0	23.2	13.4
Real wages (average annual rate of change, in per cent)	0.1	-4.7	-27.0			
Czech Republic				10.1	5.0	5.1
Slovakia				10.0	-3.0	3.0
Average monthly US dollar wages (in US $)		188.4	128.0	163.0	235.0 (Czech R)	
Budget balance (in % of the GNP)	-2.4	-0.3	-1.9	-1.8		
Czech Republic				0.0	0.1	1.0
Slovakia				-2.8	-5.5	-5.7
Current account balance in convertible currencies (bn $)	0.1	-1.5	-0.3	-1.6		
Czech Republic				-1.4	0.3	0.7
Slovakia				-0.2	-1.2	0.5
Gross debt in convertible currencies (bn $, end-year)	7.9	10.0	11.4	12.0		
Czech Republic				7.5	8.7	9.3
Slovakia				2.3	2.9	4.2

Sources: See page 259.

Table A.2(b) *Macroeconomic indicators of countries in transition, 1989–94: South Eastern European countries*

	1989	1990	1991	1992	1993	1994 preliminary
Bulgaria						
GDP (average annual rate of change, in per cent)	-0.3	-9.1	-11.7	-5.7	-1.5	0.2
GDP per capita in US$ (World Bank)	2680		1840	1330	1200	
Gross industrial output (average annual rate of change, in per cent)	2.2	-17.6	-23.3	-21.9	-9.2	2.0
Gross investment (average annual rate of change, in per cent)	n.a.	-18.5	-19.9	-23.2	-29.7	-20.2
Consumer prices (average annual rate of change, in per cent)	6.2	23.8	338.5	91.3	74.0	96.0
Real wages (average annual rate of change, in per cent)	3.0	6.9	-39.4	19.2	-11.7	-19.0
Average monthly US dollar wages (in US $)			58.0	70.0	122.0	
Budget balance (in % of the GNP)	-0.6	-4.9	-3.5	-6.1	-11.9	-8.0
Current account balance in convertible currencies (bn $)	-1.2	-0.7	0.7	-0.5	-0.7	-0.1
Gross debt in convertible currencies (bn $, end-year)	10.6	10.4	11.9	12.9	12.7	11.0
Romania						
GDP (average annual rate of change, in per cent)	-5.8	-8.2	-13.7	-15.4	1.0	3.4
GDP per capita in US$ (World Bank)	1730		1400	1090		
Gross industrial production (average annual rate of change, in per cent)	-2.1	-19.0	-18.7	-22.1	1.3	3.1
Gross investment (average annual rate of change, in per cent)	-1.6	-38.3	-26.0	-1.1	0.8	8.0
Consumer prices (average annual rate of change, in per cent)	0.9	5.7	165.5	210.9	257.4	137.0
Real wages (average annual rate of changhe, in per cent)	2.7	5.5	-16.6	-13.2	-15.8	-10.0
Average monthly US dollar wages (in US $)			98.0	66.0	85.0	
Budget balance (in % of the GNP)	8.2	1.0	-2.4	-4.8	-1.6	-4.5

Current account balance in convertible currencies (bn $)	2.9	-1.7	-1.4	-1.4	-1.2	0.1
Gross debt in convertible currencies (bn $, end-year)	0.6	0.3	2.2	3.5	4.5	5.0
Slovenia						
GDP (average annual rate of change, in per cent)	-0.5	-4.7	-9.3	-6.0	1.0	5.0
Gross industrial production (average annual rate of change, in per cent)	0.7	-10.5	-12.4	-13.2	-2.8	6.4
Gross investment (average annual rate of change, in per cent)	-10.1	-9.8	-14.8	-14.5	11.0	15.0
Consumer prices (average annual rate of change, in per cent)	1306.0	549.7	246.0	92.0	32.7	19.9
Real wages (average annual rate of change, in per cent)	15.2	-25.7	-15.5	-2.8	14.4	6.8
Average monthly US dollar wages (in US $)		506.0	426.0	377.0	415.0	
Budget balance (in % of the GNP)	n.a.	n.a.	2.6	0.2	0.5	0.0
Current account balance in convertible currencies (bn $)	0.1	-0.6	-0.3	0.5	0.1	0.5
Gross debt in convertible currencies (bn $, end-year)	n.a.	n.a.	1.8	1.7	1.8	2.2

Source: Same as Table A.2(a).

Table A.2(c) *Macroeconomic indicators of countries in transition, 1989–94: the successor states of the USSR: the cases of Russia and Ukraine*

	1989	1990	1991	1992	1993	1994
USSR						
GDP (average annual rate of change, in per cent)	3.0	-2.3	-17.0			
Gross industrial output (average annual rate of change, in per cent)	1.7	-1.2	-7.8			
Gross investment (average annual rate of change, in per cent)	4.7	0.6	-12.0			
Consumer prices (average annual rate of change, in per cent)	1.9	5.3	96.0			
Real wages (average annual rate of change, in per cent)	7.3	9.1	10.0			
Budget balance (in % of the GNP)	-8.6	-4.1	-20.0			
Trade balance in convertible currencies (bn $)	-6.5	-5.1	0.0			
Gross debt in convertible currencies (bn $, end-year)	58.5	61.0	65.3			
Russia						
GDP (average annual rate of change, in per cent)	1.6	-4.0	-12.9	-18.5	-12.0	-15.0
Gross industrial production (average annual rate of change, in per cent)	1.4	-0.1	-8.0	-18.8	-16.2	-20.9
Gross investment (average annual rate of change, in per cent)	4.1	0.1	-15.5	-40.0	-15.0	-25.0
Consumer prices (average annual rate of change, in per cent)		5.2	91.8	1750.0	911.0	303.0
Real wages (average annual rate of change, in per cent)	8.7	-7.2	-29.8	-1.7	-3.5	-16.0
Average monthly US dollar wages (in US $)			8.9	44.3	121.1	150.0
Budget balance (in % of the GNP)	-15.3	-10.0	-5.7	-10.4	-9.4	-10.4
Trade balance in convertible currencies (bn $)			1.5	11.1	16.0	19.8
Gross debt in convertible currencies (bn $, end-year)			61.1	65.3	83.7	91.0

Ukraine

GDP (average annual rate of change, in per cent)	5.0	-3.6	-11.2	-16.0	-16.0	-20.0
Gross industrial production (average annual rate of change, in per cent)	2.8	-0.1	-4.8	-9.0	-22.4	-27.7
Gross investment (average annual rate of change, in per cent)	3.7	1.9	-7.1	-36.9	-30.0	-25.0
Consumer prices (average annual rate of change, in per cent)			84.6	1240.0	4474.0	876.0
Real wages (average annual rate of change, in per cent)	6.9	7.9	1.9	-18.2	-49.1	-22.0
Average monthly US dollar wages (in US $)				32.6	16.4	
Budget balance (in % of the GNP)			-20.0	-32.0	-19.0	-11.0
Trade balance in convertible currencies (bn $)				1.5	0.7	1.9
Gross debt in convertible currencies (bn $, end-year)				3.5	4.1	7.1

Source: Same as Table A.2(a).

Table A.3 *Unemployment in the transition countries, 1990–3*

	Dec. 90	Dec. 91	Dec. 92	Dec. 93
Bulgaria				
number of unemployed (thous.)	65.1	419.0	577.0	626.1
in per cent of the labour force	1.7	11.5	15.6	16.4
Czech Republic				
number of unemployed (thous.)	39.0	221.7	134.8	185.2
in per cent of the labour force	0.7	4.1	2.6	3.5
Hungary				
number of unemployed (thous.)	79.5	406.1	663.0	632.1
in per cent of the labour force	1.7	7.4	12.3	12.1
Poland				
number of unemployed (thous.)	1126.1	2155.6	2509.3	2889.6
in per cent of the labour force	6.1	11.5	13.6	15.7
Romania				
number of unemployed (thous.)	–	337.4	929.0	1170.0
in per cent of the labour force	–	3.0	8.2	10.1
Slovakia				
number of unemployed (thous.)	37.0	302.0	260.3	368.1
in per cent of the labour force	1.5	11.8	10.4	14.4
Slovenia				
number of unemployed (thous.)	–	91.2	118.2	137.1
in per cent of the labour force	–	10.1	13.3	15.4
Russia				
number of unemployed (thous.)	–	60.0	577.7	835.5
in per cent of the labour force	–	0.1	0.8	1.1

Sources: ECE/UN, *Economic Survey of Europe*, 1991–2, 1992–3, 1993–4.

Suggestions for Further Reading

It may seem strange to provide suggestions for further reading as the bibliography includes almost 500 entries. However, some guidance is in order to help the non-specialist reader to find his or her way in a huge amount of literature on transition. The indications that follow will deal separately with Part I and Part II of the present volume, as the former relates to history, while the latter is concerned with the moving target of transition. What follows is by no means a comprehensive guide. Rather, this is a personal selection, reflecting my own experience as a teacher and a tutor.

PART I

For this section of the reading guidance I would first recommend as an *introduction* the last edition (and also the previous editions which are to be found in libraries) of Bornstein (1994), a classic in comparative economics, to which one should add Campbell (1991), which despite its title is more concerned with pre-transition systems, and is a very accessible text on the socialist economies as they were entering the path of transition. Both books also provide reading guidance.

On the *bases of the socialist system*, Kornai (1980 and 1992) presents the most coherent and comprehensive view as seen from the East. An easier but no less accurate introduction, however, focused on the Soviet model, is Nove (1987). Wiles (1968) and Holzman (1976) approach these fundamentals through their impact on international trade.

For an introduction to the *history* of the system, Nove (1992) for the USSR and Kaser (1985, 1986) are classic references. Zaleski (1980) is an extremely comprehensive book on Stalinist planning. There are many books on the history of the socialist systems; Swain and Swain (1993) and White *et al.* (1993) look at this history from the viewpoint of transition in progress.

A large number of books have been devoted to the *reforms* within the socialist system. To orient oneself in the maze of these sources one may use the very convenient guide of Jeffries (1993), of which more than half is devoted to the socialist past of the countries in transition. Another approach would be to refer to the series of volumes edited for the Joint Economic Committee of the Congress of the United States since the end of the 1960s, covering China, Eastern Europe, and the USSR. The general bibliography quotes two of them (Hardt and Kaufman, 1989 and 1993); these volumes are an invaluable source as they cover both general issues and country cases, and have attracted over the years all the significant experts in the field in the Western world. Since the 1950s the UN Economic Commission for Europe has devoted a large share of the annual *Economic Survey of Europe* to a systematic coverage of Soviet and Eastern European economies, always based on national statistical data (though discussing their inconsistencies when needed), in a scholarly approach combining cooperation with Eastern economists and a professional, unprejudiced treatment of the issues.

On the record of *economic performance and growth*, Bergson and Kuznets (1963) and Gregory and Stuart (1990) should be starting points.

International trade issues have been best covered by Franklyn Holzman (see the references to his quoted books and articles). Also see Brabant (1980), Wolf (1988), and Brada (1991).

PART II

The chapters of Part II contain a large number of bibliographical references. I have selected only a part of a very large literature. A convenient way to follow on is to refer to the *Journal of Economic Literature* (particularly section *P, Economic Systems*). Rather than repeating them I would like to provide a guidance to institutions, journals and series dealing with transition economies.

(a) National Institutes

The *institutes* and centres that dealt with the socialist planned economies usually continued, sometimes under different names. New ones emerged. It is impossible to mention them all. In addition, new centres appeared in the countries in transition themselves.

In the *United Kingdom*, the *CEPR* (Centre for Economic Policy Research) is undoubtedly the largest think-tank and contributor of discussion papers on transition (of which a significant part later appears in a more or less modified form in other publications). The Birmingham *CREES* (Centre on Russian and East European Studies) has been publishing papers both on economic history and on contemporary issues, and has in particular explored issues linked with foreign trade and technological progress.

In *Belgium*, the *LICEES* (Leuven Institute for Central and Eastern European Studies) has expanded since 1991 and has published a number of discussion and working papers, in many cases with the contribution of Eastern European scholars.

In *Germany*, the main specialised research institutes (*BIOST* in Cologne – the acronym of the Federal Institute for international and East-European studies; the *Ost-Europa Institut* and the *Sudosteuropa Institut* in Munich) essentially publish in German. There is a similar situation in *France*, where the *ROSES* (Réforme et ouverture des systèmes économiques (post)-socialistes) and the *IRSES* (Institutions et Régulation dans les Systèmes économiques (post)-socialistes) issues working papers mainly in French.

In *Austria*, the *WIIW* (the acronym for the Vienna Institute for Comparative Economic Studies) is a major source of statistical information and research reports.

In the United States, a significant share of the Policy Analyses in International Economics published by the *Institute for International Economics* in Washington are devoted to transition.

In *Central and East European countries* and in *Russia*, there are a great number of institutes publishing working papers. It is impossible to list them all. A sample would include, for *Hungary*, the series of the *Institute for World Economics* of the Hungarian Academy of Sciences, *Trends in World Economy*, and the *Working Papers* of the same institute, as well as the *Discussion Papers* of the Kopint-Datong Institute, and the *Research Summaries* of the GKI Institute; for the *Czech Republic*, the series of working papers of the *CERGE/EI* (Centre for Economic Research and Graduate Education of the Charles University and Economics Institute of the Academy of Sciences), and of the *Institute of Economics* of the Czech National Bank, as well as the *Economic Trends* of the Komercní Banka; for *Poland*, the *Working Papers* of the *Institute of Finance* in Warsaw; for *Russia, the Russian Economic Barometer* of the Institute for World Economy and International Relations of the Russian Academy of Sciences.

(b) International Organisations

The major international organisations became increasingly involved in research on the countries in transition. We have already mentioned the *United Nations Economic Commission for Europe*; to the annual *Economic Survey of Europe* one should add the *Economic Bulletin for Europe*, also annual, devoted to international economic relations issues. The *IMF Bulletin* and *Staff Papers* have increased their coverage of transition issues. The *World Bank*, often jointly with the IMF, has published a number of volumes (often conference papers) on transition issues. It also publishes statistical updates on what is called *Historically Planned Economies*, and a newsletter about reforming economies, *Transition*.

The *OECD* (Organisation for Economic Co-operation and Development) has set up a *Centre for Co-operation with the Economies in Transition* (CCET), which publishes country studies on Central and East European countries (see bibliography, under the heading of OECD), as well as some periodicals such as *Trends and Policies in Privatisation* and *Short Term Economic Indicators, Transition Countries*.

The *Commission of the European Communities* (now Union) has produced a large number of papers on the countries in transition, in many cases restricted. The journal of the Directorate General for Economic and Financial Affairs, *European Economy*, has devoted several special issues to the countries in transition. In addition, a great number of studies has been generated by the ACE (Action for Cooperation in Economics) programmes subsidised by the EU. Most of these studies are in mimeo form; some are published, especially when large Western Institutes such as the CEPR or the LICEES have been acting as coordinators of the programmes.

The *EBRD* (European Bank for Reconstruction and Development) has been publishing working papers since 1993, and a journal, *The Economics of Transition* as well as an annual *Transition Report* (first vol. 1994).

(c) Journals

Most of the academic journals in the field of economics have been devoting a growing space to articles dealing with transition issues. More generally, the economic and business magazines and newspapers have extended their coverage of these countries. In the personal view of the author the best source in the newspaper category is the British *Financial Times*, in terms of frequency and accuracy of information. Among the magazines, one may mention *The Economist* (along with the *Country Reports* of the Economist Intelligence Unit).

The list below only includes the specialised journals, and does not pretend to be exhaustive. Most have been published for many years on planned economies; some have changed their titles. A few have been set up since the beginning of the transition.

Communist Economies and Economic Transformation, quarterly; 1989 →; edited by the Centre for Research into Communist Economies, London; Abingdon, Oxford: Carfax Publishing Co.

Comparative Economic Studies, quarterly, 1958 →, Association for Comparative Economic Studies, East Lansing: Michigan State University.

Le Courrier des Pats de l'Est (summary in English); monthly; 1964 →; edited by the Centre d'Etudes et de Documentation sur l'ex-URSS, la Chine et l'Europe de l'Est; Paris: La Documentation Française.

Eastern European Economics, a journal of translations, quarterly, bimonthly since 1994; 1962 →, Armonk, NY: M.E. Sharpe.

Economic Systems, (formerly *Jahrbuch der Wirtschaft Osteuropas*), quarterly, 1976 →, Munich: Osteuropa Institute (in association with the European Association for Comparative Economic Studies).

The Economics of Transition, quarterly, 1993 →, European Bank for Reconstruction and Development, Oxford: Oxford University Press.

Europe-Asia Studies (formerly *Soviet Studies*), quarterly, since 1993 published six times a year; 1949 →; Glasgow: The University of Glasgow.

Joice, Journal of International and Comparative Economics, quarterly, 1992 →, European Association for Comparative Economic Studies, Heidelberg: Physica-Verlag.

Journal of Comparative Economics, quarterly, 1976 →, Association for Comparative Economic Studies, San Diego: Academic Press.

Moct-Most, Economic journal on Eastern Europe and the Soviet Union, three times a year, 1991 →; Bologna, Italy: Nomisma.

PlanEcon Report, weekly; 1985 →; Washington: PlanEcon, Inc.

Problems of Economic Transition (formerly *Problems of Economics*), a journal of Translations from the Russian, quarterly, 1958 →, Armonk, NY: M.E. Sharpe.

Revue d'Etudes Comparatives Est-Quest (summary in English); quarterly; 1970 →; Paris: CNRS.

RFE/RL Research Report, 1992–4; publication stopped August 1994. Munich: Radio Free Europe, Radio Liberty Inc. (successor to separate research publications by Radio Liberty and Radio Free Europe); from January 1995, replaced by *Transition*, semi-monthly; Prague: Open Media Research Institute.

Russian and East European Finance and Trade, successor to *Soviet and East European Foreign Trade*, a journal of translations, in 1991–3 edited at the Leuven Institute for Central and East European Studies, Belgium; published in Armonk, NY: M.E. Sharpe.

Transitions, successor to *Revne des Pays de l'Est* (partly in English), bi-annual journal; 1960 →; Brussels: Université Libre de Bruxelles.

Trends and Policies in Privatisation, bi-annual journal, 1993 →, Paris: Centre for Co-operation with European Economies in Transition, Advisory Group on Privatisation, OECD.

Bibliography

Abel, István and John P. Bonin (1992), *The 'Big Bang' versus 'Slow but Steady': A Comparison of the Hungarian and the Polish Transformations*. London: CEPR (Centre for Economic Policy Research, no. 626).

Aghion, Philippe (1993), 'Economic Reform in Eastern Europe: Can Theory Help?' *European Economic Review*, vol. 37, nos 2/3, pp. 525–32.

Aghion, Philippe and Olivier Jean Blanchard (1993), *On the Speed of Transition in Central Europe*. London: EBRD, Working Paper no. 6, July.

Aluminium (1993), *Financial Times* survey, 19 October.

Andreff, Wladimir (1993), *La Crise des économies socialistes, La rupture d'un système*. Grenoble: Presses Universitaires de Grenoble.

Artisien, Patrick, Matija Rojic and Marjan Svetlicic (1993), *Foreign Investment in Central and Eastern Europe*. London: Macmillan.

Åslund, Anders (1992a), *The Post-Soviet Economy, Soviet and Western Perspectives*. London: Pinter Publishers.

Åslund, Anders (1994), 'Lessons of the First Four Years of Systemic Change in Eastern Europe', *Journal of Comparative Economics*, vol. 19, no. 1, August, pp. 22–38.

Åslund, Anders and Richard Layard (eds) (1993), *Changing the Economic System in Russia*. New York: St Martin's Press.

Asselain, Jean-Charles (1994), 'Convertibilité précoce et protection par le change: un premier bilan de la réinsertion internationale des pays de l'Est', *Revue Economique*, vol. 45, no. 3, pp. 833–44.

Bahro, Rudolf (1978), *The Alternative in Eastern Europe*. London: New Left Books.

Bakos, Gabor (1993), 'After Comecon: A Free Trade Area in Central Europe', *Europe-Asia Studies*, vol. 45, no. 6, pp. 1025–44.

Balcerowicz, Leszek (1993), *Common Fallacies in the Debate on the Economic transition in Central and Eastern Europe*. London: EBRD, Working Paper no. 11, October.

Balcerowicz, Leszek (1994), *Eastern Europe: Economic, Social and Political Dynamics*, the Sixth M.B. Grabowski Memorial Lecture. London: School of Slavonic and East European Studies.

Balcerowicz, Leszek and Alan Gelb (1994), 'How to Stabilize – Policy Lessons from Early Reformers', *Transition*, vol. 5, no. 6, (May-June) pp. 3–4.

Baldwin, Richard (1992), *An Eastern Enlargement of EFTA: Why the East Europeans Should Join and the Eftans Should Want Them*. London: Centre for Economic Policy Research, CEPR Occasional Paper no. 10, November.

Baldwin, Richard E. (1994), *Towards an Integrated Europe*. London: CEPR.

Barber, Lionel (1994) 'Brussels Paves Way for Wider Europe', *Financial Times*, 28 July.

Barre, Raymond, William H. Luers, Anthony Solomon and Krzysztof J. Ners (1992a), *Moving Beyond Assistance*, Final Report of the IEWS Task Force on Western Assistance to Transition in the Czech and Slovak Federal Republic, Hungary and Poland. New York and Prague: Institute for EastWest Studies.

Barre, Raymond *et al.* (1992b), '*La coexistence pacifique' 20 ans après, La Transition des économies de l'Est à l'économie de marché*, Fondation F. Perroux. Paris: Editions de l'Epargne.

271

Begg, David and Richard Portes (1992), *Enterprise Debt and Economic Transformation: Financial Restructuring of the State Sector in Central and Eastern Europe*. London: CEPR, Discussion Paper no. 695, June.

Begg, David and Richard Portes (1993), 'Enterprise Debt and Financial Restructuring in Central and Eastern Europe', *European Economic Review*, vol. 37, no. 2/3 (April) pp. 396–407.

Bergson, Abram (1994), 'The Communist Efficiency Gap: Alternative Measures', *Comparative Economic Studies*, vol. 36, no. 1 (Spring) pp. 1–12.

Bergson, Abram and Simon Kuznets (1963), *Economic Trends in the Soviet Union*. Cambridge, Mass.: Harvard University Press.

Bergson, Abram and Herbert S. Levine (eds) (1983), *The Soviet Economy: Toward the Year 2000*. London: George Allen & Unwin.

Beliner, Joseph (1976), *The Innovation Decision in Soviet Industry*. Cambridge, Mass.: MIT Press.

Berliner, Joseph (1983), 'Planning and Management', in Bergson and Levine (eds) pp. 350–90.

Bettelheim, Charles (1977 and 1979), *Class Struggles in the USSR (1917–23 and 1924–30)*, 2 vols. London: Harvester Press.

Blanchard, Olivier, Rodiger Dornbusch, Paul Krugman, Richard Layard and Lawrence Summers (1991), *Reform in Eastern Europe*. Cambridge, Mass: MIT Press.

Blanchard, Olivier, Kenneth A. Froot and Jeffrey D. Sachs (1994), *The Transition in Eastern Europe*, vol. 1 *Country Studies*, vol. 2 *Restructuring*. NBER, University of Chicago Press.

Bobinski, Christopher (1992), 'West Hides Behind Polish Tariffs. Car Makers Show Protective Instincts', *Financial Times*, 10 March.

Boeri, Tito (1994), 'Transitional Unemployment', *The Economics of Transition*, vol. 2, no. 1 (March) pp. 1–25.

Bofinger, Peter (1993), *The Output Decline in Central and Eastern Europe: A Classical Explanation*. London: CEPR, Discussion Paper, no. 784, May.

Bofinger, Peter and Daniel Gros (1992), *A Payments Union for the Commonwealth of Independent States: Why and How*. London: CEPR, Discussion Paper Series, no. 654.

Bofinger, Peter, Eirik Svindland and Benedikt Thanner (1993) 'Prospects of the Monetary Order in the Republics of the FSU', in CEPR (1993) pp. 9–33.

Bornstein, Morris (1992), 'Privatisation in Eastern Europe', *Communist Economies and Economic Transformation*, vol. 4, no. 3, pp. 283–320; revised in Bornstein (1994) pp. 468–510.

Bornstein, Morris (ed.) (1994), *Comparative Economic Systems, Models and Cases*, 7th edn. Burr Ridge and Boston: Irwin.

Bornstein, Morris (1995), 'Russia's Mass Privatisation Programme', *Communist Economies and Economic Transformation*, vol. 6, No. 4, pp. 419–56.

Bossak, Jan W. (ed.) (1994), *Poland, International Economic Report 1993/94*. Warsaw: World Economy Research Institute, Warsaw School of Economics.

Boyer, Robert (1987), '*Régulation*', entry in *The New Palgrave, A Dictionary of Economics*, ed. by John Eatwell, Murray Milgate and Peter Newman, vol. 4. London: Macmillan.

Brabant, Jozef M. van (1980), *Socialist Economic Integration, Aspects of Contemporary Economic Problems in Eastern Europe*. Cambridge: Cambridge University Press.

Brabant, Jozef M. van (ed.) (1991a), *Economic Reforms in Centrally Planned Economies and Their Impact on the Global Economy*, in association with the United Nations. London and Basingstoke: Macmillan.

Brabant, Jozef M. van (1991b), 'Convertibility in Eastern Europe through a Payments Union', in *Currency Convertibility in Eastern Europe*, edited by John Williamson. Washington, DC: Institute for International Economics.

Brabant, Jozef M. van (1992a), 'The New East and Old Problems – About Neighborly Trade and Payment Relations', *Economies et Sociétés*, série G, *Economie planifiée*, vol. 44 (April-June) pp. 287–314.

Brabant, Jozef M. van (1992b), *Unravelling the Ruble Regime*. London: European Policy Forum.

Brabant, Jozef M. van (1993), 'Economic Recession in the East: The Impact of Changing External Regimes', *Joice*, vol. 2, no. 3, pp. 165–89.

Brabant, Jozef M. (1994), *Industrial Policy in Eastern Europe, Governing the Transition*. Dordrecht: Kluwer Academic Publishers.

Brada, Josef C. (1988), 'Interpreting the Soviet Subsidization of Eastern Europe', *International Organization*, vol. 42, no. 4 (Autumn) pp. 639–58.

Brada, Josef C. (1991) 'The Political Economy of Communist Foreign Trade Institutions and Policies', *Journal of Comparative Economics*, vol.15, no. 2 (June) pp. 211–38.

Brada, Josef C. (1993), 'The Transformation from Communism to Capitalism: How Far? How Fast?', *Post-Soviet Affairs*, vol. 9, no. 2, pp. 87–110.

Brada, Josef C., Ed A. Hewett and Thomas A. Wolf (eds) (1988), *Economic Adjustment and Reform in Eastern Europe and the Soviet Union*, Essays in Honor of Franklyn D. Holman. Durham and London: Duke University Press.

Brada, Josef C. and Arthur E. King (1992), 'Is There a J-Curve for the Economic Transition from Socialism to Capitalism?', *Economics of Planning*, January.

Brada, Josef C., Inderjit Singh and Adám Török (1994), *Firms Afloat and Firms Adrift: Hungarian Industry and the Economic Transition*, series 'The Microeconomics of Transition Economies', vol. 1. Armonk, New York: M. E. Sharpe.

Brezinski, Horst (1991), 'Economic Reforms in Asia and Europe and Co-operation With the Less Developed Centrally Planned Economies', in Brabant (ed.) (1991a) pp. 243–65.

Brown, Bess (1994), 'Three Central Asian States Form Economic Union', *RFE/RL Research Report*, vol. 3, no. 13 (1 April) pp. 33–5.

Bruno, Michael (1992), 'Stabilization and Reform in Eastern Europe: A Preliminary Evaluation', *IMF Staff Papers*, vol. 39, no. 4 (December) pp. 741–77.

Bruno, Michael (1993), *Chrisis, Stabilization and Economic Reform. Therapy by Consensus*. Oxford: Clarendon Press.

Brus, Wlodzimierz (1961) *Ogólne Problemy Funkcjonowania Gospodarki Socjalistycznej* (General problems of functioning of a socialist economy). Translated as *The Market in a Socialist Economy* (1972). London: Routledge and Kegan Paul.

Brus, Wlodzimierz (1987), 'Market Socialism', entry in *The New Palgrave, A Dictionary of Economics*, ed. by John Eatwell. London: Macmillan. Murray Milgate and Peter Newman, vol. 3.

Brus, Wlodzimierz and Kazimierz Laski (1989), *From Marx to the Market: Socialism in Search of an Economic System*, Oxford: Clarendon Press.

Calvo, Guillermo A. (1991), 'Are High Interest Rates Effective for Stopping High Inflation?', in Commander (ed.) (1991) pp. 247–59.

Calvo, Guillermo and Fabrizio Coricelli (1992), 'Output Collapse in Eastern Europe: The Role of Credit', IMF Working Paper.

Calvo, Guillermo A. and Fabrizio Coricelli (1994), 'Credit Market Imperfections and Output Response in Previously Centrally Planned Economies', in Caprio *et al.* (eds) pp. 257–94.

Calvo, Guillermo A. and Jacob A. Frenkel (1991), 'From Centrally Planned to Market Economy, The Road from CPE to PCPE', *IMF Staff Papers*, vol. 38, no. 2 (June) pp. 268–99.

Campbell, Robert W. (1991), *The Socialist Economies in Transition: A Primer on Semi-Reformed Systems*. Bloomington and Indianapolis: Indiana University Press.

Caprio, Gerard, David Folkerts-Landau and Timothy D. Lane (eds) (1994), *Building Sound Finance in Emerging Market Economies*, proceedings of a conference held in Washington, DC, June 10–11, 1993. Washington, DC: IMF and World Bank.

Carlin, Wendy and Colin Mayer (1992), 'Restructuring Enterprises in Central and Eastern Europe', *Economic Policy*, vol. 15 (October) pp. 311–52.

Carrère d'Encausse, Hélène (1979), *Decline of an Empire: The Soviet Socialist Republics in Revolt*. New York: Newsweek Books.

Caselli, Gian Paolo and Gabriele Pastrello (1992), 'The Transition From Hell to Bliss: A Model', *Moct-Most*, no. 3, pp. 43–53.

CEPR (1992a), *The Economic Consequences of the East*, Proceedings of a conference organised by the Centre for Economic Policy Research and hosted by the Deutsche Bundesbank in Frankfurt-am-Main, March 1992. London: CEPR.

CEPR (1992b), *Is Bigger Better? The Economics of EC Enlargement*, A CEPR Annual Report. London: Centre for Economic Policy Research.

CEPR (1993), *The Economics of the New Currencies*. London: Centre for Economic Policy Research, June.

Charap, Joshua and Leila Webster (1993), 'Constraints on the Development of Private Manufacturing in St. Petersburg', *Economics of Transition*, vol. 1, no. 3 (September) pp. 299–316.

Charap, Joshua and Alena Zemplinerova (1993) *Restructuring in the Czech Economy*. London: EBRD, Working Paper, no. 2, March.

Chavance, Bernard (1992a), 'Transition et Dépression en Europe de l'Est', Juillet, document de travail du Centre d'Etudes des Modes d'Industrialisation.

Chavance, Bernard (1992b), 'L'économie mixte de transition post-socialiste (Première approche)', rapport au colloque 'Transition politique et transition économique dans les pays d'Europe centrale et orientale', 3–4 décembre, Centre français de recherche en sciences sociales, Prague.

Chavance, Bernard (1994), *La fin des Systèmes Socialistes. Crise, Réforme et Transformation*. Paris: L'Harmattan.

Chirot, Daniel (ed.) (1989), *The Origins of Backwardness in Eastern Europe: Economics and Politics from the Middle Ages Until the Early Twentieth Century*. Berkeley: University of California Press.

Chirot, Daniel (ed.) (1991), *The Crisis of Leninism and the Decline of the Left. The Revolutions of 1989*. Seattle and London: University of Washington Press.

Claassen, Emil (ed.) (1991), *Exchange Rate Policies in Developing and Post-socialist Countries*. San Francisco: International Center for Economic Growth.

Clarke, Simon (1994), 'The Politics of Privatization in Russia', paper presented at the BASEES Conference, Cambridge (March) mimeo.

Clarke, Simon *et al.* (1994), 'The Privatisation of Industrial Enterprises in Russia: Four Case-studies', *Europe-Asia Studies*, vol. 46, no. 2, pp. 179–214.

Collins, Susan M. and Dani Rodrik (1991), *Eastern Europe and the Soviet Union in the World Economy*, Institute for International Economics, Policy Analyses in International Economics, no. 32, Washington, DC, May.

Commander, Simon (ed.) (1991), *Managing Inflation in Socialist Economies in Transition*. Washington DC: The World Bank, Economic Development Institute (EDI) seminar series.

Connelly, Daniel A. (1994), 'Black Sea Economic Cooperation', *RFE/RL Research Report*, vol. 3, no. 26 (1 July) pp. 31–8.

Cooper, Julian (1991), *The Soviet Defence Industry: Conversion and Economic Reform*. London: Royal Institute of Economic Affairs.

Corado, Cristina (1994), *Textiles and Clothing Trade With Central and Eastern Europe: Impact on Members of the EC*. London: CEPR, Discussion Paper, no. 1004, August.

Corbett, Jenny and Colin Mayer (1991), 'Financial Reform in Eastern Europe: Progress with the Wrong Model', *Oxford Review of Economic Policy*, vol. 7, no. 4, pp. 57–75.

Corbo, Vittorio, Fabrizio Coricelli and Jan Bossak (1991), *Reforming Central and Eastern European Economies, Initial Results and Challenges*. Washington, DC: The World Bank.

Coricelli, Fabrizio and Gian Maria Milesi-Ferretti (1993), 'On the Credibility of "Big Bang" Constraints in Economies in Transition', *European Economic Review*, vol. 37, no. 2/3 (April) pp. 387–95.

Csaba, László (1990), *Eastern Europe and the World Economy*, Soviet and East European Studies, vol. 68. Cambridge: Cambridge University Press.

Csaba, László (ed.) (1991), *Systemic Change and Stabilization in Eastern Europe*. Aldershot: Dartmouth.

Csáki, György (1993), *Recent Improvements in Hungarian Banking*, Budapest: Institute for World Economics, Working Paper, no. 27, December.

Dallin, Alexander and Gail Lapidus (eds) (1991), *The Soviet System in Crisis: A Reader of Western and Soviet Views*. Boulder: Westview Press.

Daviddi, Renzo (1994), *Property Rights and Privatization in the Transition to a Market Economy: A Comparative Review*. Maastricht: European Institute of Public Administration, August, mimeo.

Daviddi, Renzo and Efisio Espa (1993), 'External Financing, Conditionality and Trade in Central Eastern Europe', *Transitions*, vol. 34, no. 2, pp. 27–45.

Davies, Robert W. (1980), *The Socialist Offensive: The Collectivization of Soviet Agriculture, 1929–1930*. London: Macmillan.

Dembinski, Pavel H. (1991), *The Logic of the Planned Economy. The Seeds of the Collapse*. Oxford: Clarendon Press.

Desai, Padma (1986), 'Is the Soviet Union Subsidizing Eastern Europe?' *European Economic Review*, vol. 30, no. 1, pp. 107–16.

Dobosiewicz, Zbigniew (1992), *Foreign Investment in Eastern Europe*. London and New York: Routledge.

Dunne, Nancy (1992), 'Polish Tariffs Biased to the EC, Says US', *Financial Times*, 15 August.

Earle, John S., Roman Frydman and Andrzej Rapaczynski (eds) (1993), *Privatization in the Transition to a Market Economy: Studies of Preconditions and Policies in Eastern Europe*, in association with the Central European University. New York: St. Martin's Press.

Earle, John S., Roman Frydman, Andrzej Rapaczynski and Joel Turkewitz (eds) (1994), *Small Privatization*. CEU Privatization Reports vol. 3, Budapest. London: Central European University Press.

Easterly, William and Stanley Fisher (1994), *The Soviet Economic Decline: Historical and Republican Data*, World Bank Working Paper, no. 1284. Washington: World Bank.

Eatwell, John, Murray Milgate and Peter Newman (eds) (1990), *Problems of the Planned Economy*, reprinted entries from *The New Palgrave: A Dictionary of Economics*. London and Basingstoke: Macmillan.

EBRD (1993) *Annual Economic Review 1992*. London: European Bank for Reconstruction and Development. (Special reports included, namely: Bankruptcy legislation; Voucher privatization.)

ECE/UN (1955), *Economic Survey of Europe in 1954*, Economic Commission for Europe. New York: United Nations.

ECE/UN (1991), *Economic Survey of Europe in 1990–1991*, Economic Commission for Europe. New York: United Nations.

ECE/UN (1992), *Economic Survey of Europe in 1991–1992*, Economic Commission for Europe. New York: United Nations.

ECE/UN (1993), *Economic Survey of Europe in 1992–1993*, Economic Commission for Europe. New York: United Nations.

ECE/UN (1994a), *Economic Bulletin for Europe*, vol. 45 (1993). New York and Geneva.

ECE/UN (1994b), *Economic Survey of Europe in 1993–1994*. New York and Geneva.

Eichengreen, Barry (1993), 'A Payments Mechanism for the Former Soviet Union: Is the EPU a Relevant Precedent?', *Economic Policy*, no. 17, pp. 309–54.

Eichengreen, Barry and Marc Uzan (1992), 'The Marshall Plan: Economic Effects and Implications for Eastern Europe and the Former USSR', *Economic Policy*, no. 14 (April) pp. 13–76.

Ellman, Michael (1992), 'Shock Therapy in Russia: Failure or Partial Success?' *RFE/RL Research Report*, vol. 1, no. 34 (28 August) pp. 48–61.

Ellman, Michael (1994), 'Transformation, Depression and Economics: Some Lessons', *Journal of Comparative Economics*, vol. 19, no. 1 (August) pp. 1–21.

Erlich, Alexander (1960), *The Soviet Industrialization Debate, 1924–1928*. Cambridge, Mass: Harvard University Press.

Estrin, Saul, ed. (1994), *Privatization in Central and Eastern Europe*. London and New York: Longman.

Fallenbuchl, Zbigniew (1988), 'Present State of the Economic Reform', in P. Marer and W. Siwinski (eds) *Creditworthiness and Reform in Poland*. Bloomington: Indiana University Press, pp. 115–30.

Fath, Janos (1992), *Industrial Policies for Countries in Transition?*, WIIW, Vienna Institute for Comparative Economic Studies, *Forschungsberichte*, no. 187 (November).

Fisher, Stanley and Alan Gelb (1991), 'Issues in the Reform of Socialist Economies', in Corbo *et al.* pp. 67–82.

Fry, Maxwell and D. Mario Nuti (1991), 'Monetary and Exchange Rate Policies During Eastern Europe's Transition: Some Lessons from Further East', *Oxford Review of Economic Policy*, pp. 27–43.

Frydman, Roman, Edmond S. Phelps, Andrzej Rapaczynski and Andrei Shleifer (1993a), 'Needed Mechanisms of Corporate Governance and Finance in Eastern Europe', *Economics of Transition*, vol. 1, no. 2 (June) pp. 171–207.

Frydman, Roman and Andrzej Rapaczynski (1993b), 'Insiders and the State: Overview of Responses to Agency Problems in East European Privatization', *Economics of Transition*, vol. 1, no. 1, pp. 39–59.

Frydman, Roman and Andrzej Rapaczynski (1993c), *Privatization in Eastern Europe: Is the State Withering Away?*, Budapest, London and New York: Central European University Press.

Frydman, Roman, Andrzej Rapaczynski, John S. Earle *et al.* (1993d), *The Privatization Process in Central Europe*. Budapest, London and New York: Central European University Press.

Fukuyama, Francis (1992), *The End of History and the Last Man*. New York: The Free Press.

Gács, Janos (1992), 'Trade Liberalization in Eastern Europe: Rush and Reconsideration – Experiences of the CSFR, Hungary and Poland', paper prepared for the Conference organised by the International Institute for Applied Systems Analysis, 'International Trade and Restructuring in Eastern Europe', Vienna, 19–21 November 1992, mimeo.

Gardner, David (1992), 'EC Seeks Closer Policy Ties with Eastern Europe', *Financial Times*, 10 December.

Girard, Jacques (1992), 'De la récession à la reprise en Europe centrale et orientale: bilan et perspectives', *Cahiers de la Banque Européenne d'Investissement*, no. 18 (novembre) pp. 9–22.

Goldman, Josef and Karel Kouba (1967), *Economic Growth in Czechoslovakia*. Prague: Academia.

Gomulka, Stanislaw (1991), 'The Causes of Recession Following Stabilization', *Comparative Economic Studies*, vol. 33, no. 2 (Summer) pp. 71–89.

Gomulka, Stanislaw (1992), 'Polish Economic Reform, 1990–91: Principles, Policies and Outcomes', *Cambridge Journal of Economics*, vol. 16, pp. 355–72.

Gomulka, Stanislaw (1993), 'Poland: Glass Half Full', in Portes (ed.) (1993) pp. 187–210.

Gomulka, Stanislaw (1994), 'Economic and Political Constraints During Transition', *Europe-Asia Studies*, vol. 46, no. 1, pp. 89–106.

Granick, David (1954), *The Red Executive*. New York: Columbia University Press.

Graziani, Giovanni (1992) 'Trade Patterns and Specialization of Central-Eastern Europe in EC Markets', paper presented at the symposium organised by the International Institute for Applied Systems Analysis, 'International Trade and Restructuring in Eastern Europe', Vienna, 19–21 November 1992, mimeo.

Gregory, Paul and Robert Stuart (1990), *Soviet Economic Structure and Performance*, 4th edn. New York: Harper & Row.

Grosfeld, Irena (1990), 'Reform Economics and Western Economic Theory: Unexploited Opportunities', *Economics of Planning*, vol. 23, no. 1.

Grosfeld, Irena (1992), 'The Paradox of Transformation: An Evolutionary Case for Privatization Breakthrough', *Delta Working Paper* (Paris) no. 92–94.

Grosser, Ilse *et al.* (1993), 'Shared Aspirations, Diverging Results', Part I, Overview, Part II, Country Reports, *WIIW Forschungsberichte*, Vienna Institute for Comparative Economic Studies, no. 192, February.

Grossman, Gregory (1992), 'Comparative Study of Economic Systems After the Great Collapse', paper presented at the Conference on 'Assets and Liabilities of Independence', Trento, 10–11 December.

Grossman, Gregory (1994), 'What Was – Is, Will Be – the Command Economy?', *Moct-Most*, vol. 4, no. 1, pp. 5–22.

Hamilton, C. B. and L. Alan Winters (1992), 'Opening up Trade in Eastern Europe', *Economic Policy*, no. 14.

Hammid, Christine (1994), 'Les Investissements directs étrangers dans les pays d'Europe Centrale et Orientale'. Paris: Caisse des Dépôts et Consignations, mimeo.

Hanke, Steve H., Lars Jonung and Kurt Schuler (1993), *Russian Currency and Finance: A Currency Board Approach to Reform*. London and New York: Routledge.

Hanson, Philip (1982), 'The End of Import-Led Growth? Some Observations on Soviet, Polish and Hungarian Experience in the 1970's', *Journal of Comparative Economics*, vol. 6, no. 2, pp. 130–47.

Hanson, Philip (1992a), *From Stagnation to Catastroika: Commentaries on the Soviet Economy, 1983–91*, Centre For Strategic and International Studies, in cooperation with Radio Free Europe, The Washington Papers, no. 155. New York: Praeger.

Hanson, Philip (1992b), 'The End of the Ruble Zone?' *RFE/RL Research Report*, vol. 1, no. 30 (24 July).

Hanson, Philip (1994), 'The Russian Provinces and Economic Change in Russia'. London: The Royal Institute for International Affairs, Chatham House, 14 July, mimeo.

Hardt, John P. and Richard F. Kaufman (eds) (1989), *Pressures for Reform in the East European Economies*, 2 vols, Study Papers submitted to the Joint Economic Committee, Congress of the United States. Washington, DC: US Government Printing Office.

Hardt, John P. and Richard F Kaufman (eds) (1993), *The Former Soviet Union in Transition*, 2 vols, Study Papers Submitted to the Joint Economic Committee, Congress of the United States. Washington, DC: US Government Printing Office.

Hardt, John P. and Richard F. Kaufman (eds) (1994), *East-Central European Economies in Transition*. Study Papers submitted to the Joint Economic Committee, Congress of the United States. Washington: USGPO.

Hayek, Friedrich von (ed.) (1935), *Collectivist Economic Planning: Critical Studies on the Possibilities of Socialism*. London: Routledge & Sons.

Heimann, E. (1922), *Mehrwert und Gemeinwirtschaft*. Berlin: H.R. Hengelmann.

Hewett, Ed A. (1974), *Foreign Trade Prices in the Council for Mutual Economic Assistance*. Cambridge: Cambridge University Press.

Hewett, E. (1988), *Reforming the Soviet Economy. Equality versus Efficiency*. Washington, DC: Brookings Institution.

Hewett, Ed A. (1989), 'Eastern Europe and the International Economy: An Overview', in *Pressures for Reform in the East European Countries*, Study papers submitted to the Joint Economic Committee, Congress of the United States, vol. 1. Washington, DC: USGPO, pp. 1–6.

Hindley, Brian (1993), *Helping Transition Through Trade? EC and US Policy Towards Exports From Eastern and Central Europe*. London: EBRD, Working Paper, no. 4, March.

Hoen, Herman W. (1994) 'Regional Economic Integration in Central Europe', *Most-Most*, no. 4, pp. 115–31.

Holzman, Franklyn D. (1962), 'Soviet Foreign Trade Pricing and the Question of Discrimination: A "Customs Union" Approach', *Review of Economics and Statistics*, vol. 44, no. 2 (May) pp. 134–47.

Holzman, Franklyn D. (1965), 'More on Soviet Bloc Trade Discrimination', *Soviet Studies*, vol. 17, no. 1, pp. 44–65.

Holzman, Franklyn D. (1974), *Foreign Trade Under Central Planning*. Cambridge, Mass: Harvard University Press.

Holzman, Franklyn D. (1976), *International Trade Under Communism, Politics and Economics*. New York: Basic Books.

Holzman, Franklyn D. (1985), 'A "Trade-Destroying" Customs Union?', *Journal of Comparative Economics*, vol. 9, no. 4 (December) pp. 410–23.

Holzman, Franklyn D., (1986), 'The Significance of Soviet Subsidies to Eastern Europe', *Comparative Economic Studies*, vol. 28, no. 1 (Spring) pp. 54–65.

House of Lords (1994), *The Implications for Agriculture of the Europe Agreements*, House of Lords Select Committee on the European Communities (June) 2 vols. London: HMSO.

Hughes, Gordon and Paul Hare (1991), 'Competitiveness and Industrial Restructuring in Czechoslovakia, Hungary and Poland', *European Economy*, special issue, no. 2, pp. 83–110.

Hughes, Gordon and Paul Hare (1992), 'Industrial Policy and Restructuring in Eastern Europe', CEPR Discussion Paper, no. 653.

Hunya, Gábor (1992), 'Foreign Direct Investment and Privatization in Central and Eastern Europe', *Communist Economies and Economic Transformation*, vol. 4, no. 4, pp. 501–11 (*WIIW Reprint-Serie*, no. 145, February 1993).

Hunya, Gábor (1993), 'Frictions in the Economic Transformation of Czechoslovakia, Hungary and Poland', *WIIW Forschungsberichte*, Vienna Institute for Comparative Economic Studies, no. 190, February.

IFC (International Finance Corporation) (1993), *Coping With Capitalism: The New Polish Entrepreneurs.* Washington, DC.

IMF (1992), *World Economic Outlook,* Washington, DC, September.

Inotai, Andras (1993), *Western Economic Support for Central and Eastern Europe: A Hungarian View.* Budapest: Institute for World Economics, Working Paper Series, no. 25.

Inotai, András and Magdolna Sass (1994), *Economic Integration of the Visegrád Countries: Facts and Scenarios.* Budapest: Institute for World Economics, Working Papers, no. 33, May.

Islam, Shafiqul and Michael Mandelbaum (eds) (1993), *Making Markets: Economic Transformation in Eastern Europe and the Post-Soviet States.* New York: Council on Foreign Relations Press.

Iwasaki, Teruyuki, Takeshi Mori and Hiroichi Yamaguchi (eds) (1992), *Development Strategies for the 21st Century.* Tokyo: Institute of Development Economics.

Jackson, Marvin (1991), 'Promoting Efficient Privatization: The Benefits of Small Enterprises Versus Large Ones', *Eastern European Economics*, vol. 30, no. 1 (Fall) pp. 3–21.

Jackson, Marvin (1992a), 'Constraints on Systemic Transformation and Their Policy Implications', *Oxford Review of Economic Policy*, vol. 7, no. 4, pp. 16–25.

Jackson, Marvin (1992b) 'Company Management and Capital Development in the Transition', in Lampe (ed.) pp. 57–74.

Janacek, Kamil (1994), 'La transformation de l'économie tchèque et le traité d'association avec la Communauté Européenne', in Lavigne (ed.) (1994) pp. 212–17.

Jeffries, Ian (1993), *Socialist Economies and the Transition to the Market. A Guide.* London and New York: Routledge.

Kantorovich, Leonid (1959), *Ekonomicheskiy raschet nailuchshego ispol'zovaniya resursov.* Moscow: Gosizdat.

Kantorovich, Leonid (1965), *The Best Use of Economic Resources.* Oxford: Clarendon Press; Cambridge: Harvard University Press.

Karp, Larry and Spiro Stephanou (1993), *Domestic and Trade Policy for Central and East European Agriculture.* London: CEPR Discussion Paper, no. 814, November.

Kaser, Michael (ed.) (1985, 1986), *The Economic History of Eastern Europe 1919–1975.* Oxford: Clarendon Press.

Katsenelinboigen, Aron (1977), 'Coloured Markets in the Soviet Union', *Soviet Studies*, vol. 29, no. 1 (January) pp. 62–85.

Kenen, Peter B. (1991), 'Transitional Arrangements for Trade and Payments Among the CMEA Countries', *IMF Staff Papers*, vol. 38 no. 2 (June) pp. 235–67.

Khanin, Gregoriy and Vassiliy Selyunin (1987), 'Lukavaya tsifra' ('Wicked Figure'), *Novyi Mir*, no. 3.

Kiguel, Miguel A. and Nissan Liviatan (1991), 'Stopping Inflation: The Experience of Latin America and Israel and the Implications for Central and Eastern Europe', in Corbo *et al.*, pp. 85–100.

Kimura, Tetsusaburo (1989), *The Vietnamese Economy 1975–86, Reforms and International Relations.* Tokyo: Institute of Developing Economies, IDE Occasional Papers Series, no. 23.

Kimura, Tetsusaburo (1992), 'Economic Reform in Vietnam: Coming to the Crucial Point', in Iwasaki, Mori and Yamaguchi (eds) pp. 248–69.

King, Timoty (1991), 'Requirements for Participation in the International Monetary Fund and the World Bank' in Brabant (1991a) pp. 279–300.

Kiss, Karoly (1993), 'Western Prescriptions for Eastern Transition. A Comparative Analysis of the Different Economic Schools and Issues', *Trends in World Economy*, no. 72. Budapest: Hungarian Council for World Economy.

Kiss, Judit (1994), *Who Pays the Piper? Financial Resource Mobilization for Transformation and Development*. Budapest: Institute for World Economics, Working Papers, no. 29, February.

Klaus, Vaclav (1990), *A Road to a Market Economy (Selected Articles, Speeches and Lectures Held Abroad)*. Prague: Top Agency.

Knell, Mark and Christine Rider (eds) (1992), *Socialist Economies in Transition. Appraisals of the Market Mechanism*, Aldershot, Edward Elgar.

Knell, Mark and Wenyan Yang (1992), 'Lessons From China on a Strategy for the Socialist Economies in Transition', in Knell and Rider (eds) pp. 216–35.

Kodrzycki, Yolanda K. (1993)'Tax Reform in Newly Emerging Market Economies', *New England Economic Review*, November-December, pp. 3–17.

Koen, Vincent and Steven Phillips (1993), *Price Liberalization in Russia, Behavior of Prices, Household Incomes and Consumption During the First Year*. Washington, DC: International Monetary Fund, Occasional Paper, no. 104, July.

Kolodko, Grzegorz W. (1993a), 'Stabilization, Recession and Growth in a Post-Socialist Economy', *Moct/Most*, Nomisma, January, no. 1, pp. 3–38.

Kolodko, Grzegorz W. (1993b), 'Perverse Effects of Fiscal Adjustment in Transition Economies', *Economics of Transition*. (London: EBRD) vol. 1, no. 3 (September) pp. 345–55.

Komarek, Valtr (1993), 'Czech and Slovak Federal Republic: A New Approach', in Portes (ed.) (1993) pp. 58–106.

Kornai, János (1980), *Economics of Shortage*. Amsterdam: North Holland, 2 vols.

Kornai, János (1990), *The Road to a Free Economy. Shifting from a Socialist System: The Example of Hungary*. New York: W. W. Norton.

Kornai, János (1992), *The Socialist System. The Political Economy of Communism*. Oxford: Clarendon Press.

Kornai, János (1994), 'Transformational Recession: The Main Causes', *Journal of Comparative Economics*, vol. 19, no. 1 (August) pp. 39–63.

Köves, Andras (1983), ' "Implicit Subsidies" and Some Issues of Economic Relations Within the CMEA (Remarks on the Analyses Made by Michael Marrese and Jan Vanous)', *Acta Oeconomica*, vol. 31, no. 1–2, pp. 125–36.

Köves, Andras (1992a), 'Shock-Therapy versus Gradual Change: Economic Problems and Policies in Central and Eastern Europe (1989–1991)', *Acta Oeconomica*, vol. 44, no. 1–2, pp. 13–36.

Köves, Andras (1992b), *Central and East European Economies in Transition, The International Dimension*. Boulder, Co: Westview Press.

Kupka, Martin (1992), 'Transformation of Ownership in Czechoslovakia', *Soviet Studies*, vol. 44, no. 2, pp. 297–311.

Lampe, John R. (ed.) (1992), *Creating Capital Markets in Eastern Europe*. Washington DC: The Woodrow Wilson Center Press.

Landesmann, Michael (1993), 'Industrial Policy and the Transition in East-Central Europe', *WIIW Forschungsberichte*, Vienna Institute for Comparative Economic Studies, no. 196, April.

Lange, Oskar (1936), 'On the Economic Theory of Socialism', *Review of Economic Studies*, vol. 4, no. 1, pp. 53–71.

Lapidus, Gail (1991), 'State and Society: Towards the Emergence of Civil Society in the Soviet Union', in Dallin and Lapidus (1991) pp. 130–50.

Lardy, Nicholas R. (1991), 'Is China Different? The Fate of Its Economic Reform', in D. Chirot (ed.) (1991) pp. 147–62.

Laux, Jean Kirk (1994), 'From South To East? Financing the Transition in Central and Eastern Europe', in *Canada Among Nations 1994, A Part of the Peace*, ed. by Maureen Appel Molot and Harald von Riekhoff, pp. 173–94.

Lavigne, Marie (1974), *The Socialist Economies of the Soviet Union and Europe*. London: Martin Robertson.

Lavigne, Marie (1978), 'The Advanced Socialist Society', *Economy and Society*, vol. 7, no. 4 (November) pp. 367–94.

Lavigne, Marie (ed.) (1988) *East-South Relations in the World Economy*. Boulder and London: Westview Press.

Lavigne, Marie (1991), *International Political Economy and Socialism*. Cambridge: Cambridge University Press.

Lavigne, Marie (ed.) (1994), *Capitalismes à l'Est: un accouchement difficile*. Paris: Economica, coll. Grands Débats.

Layard, Richard, Olivier Blanchard, Rudiger Dornbusch and Paul Krugman (1992), *East West Migration. The Alternatives*. Cambridge, Mass. and London: MIT Press.

Leeds, Eva Marikova (1993), 'Voucher Privatization in Czechoslovakia', *Comparative Economic Studies*, vol. 35, no. 3 (Fall) pp. 19–37.

Lemoine, Françoise (1986), *L'économie chinoise*. Paris: La Découverte, Repères, no. 39.

Lemoine, Françoise (1994), *La nouvelle économie chinoise*. Paris: La Découverte.

Lhomel, Edith (1990), 'Les mutations des structures agricoles à l'Est', *Le Courrier des Pays de l'Est*, no. 347 (February) pp. 3–32.

Linotte, Daniel (1992), 'The Fall in Industrial Output in Transition Economies: A New Interpretation', Working Paper. Leuven: Leuven Institute for Central and East European Studies.

Liska, Tibor and Antal Marias (1955), 'Optimal Returns and International Division of Labour', in ECE/UN (1955).

de Long, J. Bradford and Barry Eichengreen (1992), 'The Marshall Plan: History's Most Successful Structural Adjustment Program', *CEPR Discussion Paper Series*, No. 634; also published in R. Dornbush, W. Nolling and R. Layard (eds) *Postwar Economic Reconstruction and Lessons for the East Today*. Cambridge, Mass: MIT Press.

Lucron, Claude-Pierre (1992), 'Contenu et portée des accords entre la Communauté et la Hongrie, la Pologne et la Tchécoslovaquie', *Revue du Marché Commun et de l'Union Européenne*, no. 357 (April) pp. 293–9.

Malle, Silvana (1985), *The Economic Organisation of War Communism*. Cambridge University Press.

Marer, Paul (1985), *Dollar GNPs of the USSR and Eastern Europe*. Baltimore: The Johns Hopkins University Press.

Market Socialism (1989), special issue of *Acta Oeconomica*, vol. 40 (3–4) pp. 179–283.

Markus, Ustina (1994), 'The Russian-Belarussian Monetary Union', *RFE/RL Research Report*, vol. 3, no. 20 (20 May) pp. 28–32.

Marrese, Michael (1992), 'Hungary Emphasizes Foreign Partners', *RFE/RL Research Report*, special issue on privatization, vol. 1, no. 17 (24 April) pp. 25–33.

Marrese, Michael and Jan Vanous (1983), *Soviet Subsidization of Trade With Eastern Europe: A Soviet Perspective*. Berkeley: University of California, Institute of International Studies.

Matejka, Harriet (1993), 'Post-CMEA Trade and Payments Arrangements in Eastern Europe', in *Eastern Europe in the World Economy*, edited by Jozef van Brabant. Boulder: Westview Press, pp. 63–78.

Matejka, Harriet (1994), 'La dégradation des statistiques commerciales des pays de l'Europe de l'Est et sa signification pour l'analyse de l'évolution de leurs échanges', *Le Courrier des pays de l'Est*, September, pp. 3–10.

Maurel, Marie-Claude (1991), 'Les agricultures d'Europe centrale face au défi européen: la transition peut-elle se résoudre à un transfert de modèle?', in *Les défis de l'an 2000*, Proceedings of a symposium organized at the University of Warsaw, June 1991.

Mayhew, Ken and Paul Seabright (1992), 'Incentives and the Management of Enterprises in Economic Transition: Capital Markets Are Not Enough', *CEPR Discussion Paper Series*, No. 640.

McKinnon, Ronald I.(1991a), *The Order of Economic Liberalization: Financial Control in the Transition to a Market Economy*. Baltimore: Johns Hopkins University Press.

McKinnon, Ronald I. (1991b), 'Liberalizing Foreign Trade in a Socialist Economy: The Problem of Negative Value Added', in John Williamson (ed.), *Currency Convertibility in Eastern Europe*. Washington: Institute for International Economics, pp. 96–115.

McKinnon, Ronald I. (1992), 'Spontaneous Order on the Road Back From Socialism: An Asian Perspective', *The American Economic Review*, vol. 82, no. 2 (May) pp. 31–6.

Mendershausen, Horst (1959), 'Terms of Trade Between the Soviet Union and Smaller Communist Countries, 1955–957', *Review of Economics and Statistics*, vol. 51, no. 2 (May) pp. 106–18.

Mendershausen, Horst (1960), 'The Terms of Soviet-Satellite Trade: A Broadened Analysis', *Review of Economics and Statistics*, vol. 52, no. 2 (May) pp. 152–63.

Menshikov, Stanislav (1994), 'State Enterprises in Transition', *Transitions*, vol. 35, no. 1, pp. 125–48.

Messerlin, Patrick (1993), 'The EC and Central Europe: the Missed Rendez-Vous of 1992?', *Economics of Transition*, vol. 1, no. 1, pp. 89–109.

Michalopoulos, Constantine and David Tarr (1992), *Trade and Payments Arrangements for States of the Former USSR*. Washington, DC: The World Bank, Studies of Economics in Transformation, Paper, no. 2.

Mihályi, Péter (1993), 'Property Rights and Privatization, The Three-Agent Model (A Case Study on Hungary)', *Eastern European Economics*, vol. 31, no. 2 (Winter 1992–93) pp. 5–64.

Minassian, Garabed (1994), 'The Bulgarian Economy in Transition: Is There Anything Wrong With Macroeconomic Policy?', *Europe-Asia Studies*, vol. 46, no. 2, pp. 337–51.

Minc, Alain (1993), *Le Nouveau Moyen Âge*. Paris: Gallimard.

Mises, Ludvig von (1920), 'Economic Calculation in the Socialist Commonwealth', in Hayek (ed.) (1935) pp. 87–30.

Mizsei, Kalman (1993), 'Hungary: Gradualism Needs A Strategy', in Portes (ed.) (1993) pp. 131–86.

Murrell, Peter (1990), *The Nature of Socialist Economies: Lessons From Eastern European Foreign Trade*. Princeton: Princeton University Press.

Murrell, Peter (1991), 'Public Choice and the Transformation of Socialism', *Journal of Comparative Economics*, vol. 15, no. 2 (June) pp. 203–10.

Murrell, Peter (1992), 'Conservative Political Philosophy and the Strategy of Economic Transition', *Eastern European Politics and Societies*, vol. 6, no. 1, pp. 3–6.

Murrell, Peter and Yijiang Wang (1993), 'When Privatization Should be Delayed: The Effect of Communist Legacies on Organizational and Institutional Reforms', *Journal of Comparative Economics*, vol. 17, no. 2, pp. 385–406.

Nagels, Jacques (1990), *Du Socialisme perverti au capitalisme sauvage*. Bruxelles: Université Libre de Bruxelles.

Nallet, Henri, and Adrian van Stolk (1994), *Relations Between the European Union and the Central and Eastern European Countries in Matters Concerning Agriculture and Food Production*. Brussels: European Commission, 15 June.

Ners, Krzysztof (1994), *Privatization (From Above, Below, or Mass Privatization) versus Generic Private Enterprise Building*. Warsaw: Policy Education Centre on Assistance to Transition, IEWS, January, mimeo.

Ners, Krzysztof, and Ingrid T. Buxell (1995), *Assistance to Transition, Survey 1995*. New York: IEWS.

Neuberger, Egon and Laura d'Andrea Tyson (eds) (1980), *The Impact of International Economic Disturbances on the Soviet Union and Eastern Europe, Transmission and Response*. New York: Pergamon Press.

Neven, Damien (1994), *Trade Liberalization with Eastern Nations, How Sensitive?*. London: CEPR, Discussion Paper, no. 1000, July.

Newbery, David (1993), 'Tax and Expenditure Policy in Hungary', *The Economics of Transition*, vol. 1, no. 2 (June) pp. 245–72.

North, Douglass (1990), *Institutions, Institutional Change and Economic Performance*. Cambridge: Cambridge University Press.

Nove, Alec (1964), *Was Stalin Really Necessary? Economic Rationality and Soviet Politics*. London: George Allen & Unwin.

Nove, Alec (1983), *The Economics of Feasible Socialism*. London: Allen & Unwin. (Revised edition in 1991: *The Economics of Feasible Socialism Revisited*.)

Nove, Alec (1987), *The Soviet Economic System*. London: Allen & Unwin.

Nove, Alec (1992), *An Economic History of the USSR 1917–1991*. Harmondsworth: Penguin Books.

Nove, Alec (1994), 'A Gap in Transition Models? A Comment on Gomulka', *Europe-Asia Studies*, vol. 46, no. 5, pp. 863–9.

Nuti, D. Mario (1986), 'Hidden and Repressed Inflation in Soviet-Type Economies: Definitions, Measurements and Stabilisation', *Contributions to Political Economy*, vol. 5, pp. 37–82.

Nuti, D. Mario (1991), 'Stabilization and Reform Sequencing in the Reform of Central Eastern Europe', in Simon Commander (ed.), *Managing Inflation in Socialist Economies in Transition*. Washington: EDI-World Bank, pp. 155–74.

Nuti, D. Mario (1992), 'Market Socialism: The Model that Might Have Been but Never Was', in Anders Åslund (ed.), *Market Socialism or the Restoration of Capitalism?*. Cambridge: Cambridge University Press, pp. 17–31.

Nuti, D. Mario (1993), 'Economic Inertia in the Transitional Economies of Eastern Europe', in M. Uvalić, E. Espa and J. Lorentzen (eds), *Impediments to the Transition in Eastern Europe*. Florence: European University Institute, pp. 25–49.

Nuti, D. Mario (1994a), *Mass Privatisation: Costs and Benefits of Instant Capitalism*. London: London Business School, CIS – Middle Europe Centre, May.

Nuti, D. Mario (1994b), 'The Impact of Systemic Transition on the European Community', in Stephen Martin (ed.), *The Construction of Europe – A Festschrift in Honour of Emile Noel*. Berlin: de Gruyter.

Nuti, D. Mario (1994c), 'Russia: The Unfinished Revolution', *International Economic Outlook*, June, pp. 3–8.

Nuti, D. Mario and Richard Portes (1993), 'Central Europe: The Way Forward', in R. Portes (ed.) (1993) pp. 1–20.

OECD (1991a), *Transformation of Planned Economies: Property Rights Reform and Macroeconomic Stability*, eds. Hans Blommestein and Michael Marrese. Paris: Center for Co-operation with European Economies in Transition, OECD.

OECD (1991b), *The Czech and Slovak Federal Republic*, Economic Survey. Paris: Center for Co-operation with European Economies in Transition, OECD.

OECD (1991c), *Hungary*, Economic Survey. Paris: Center for Co-operation with European Economies in Transition, OECD.

OECD (1992a), *Poland*, Economic Survey. Paris: Center for Co-operation with European Economies in Transition, OECD.

OECD (1992b), *Bulgaria: An Economic Assessment*. Paris: Center for Co-operation with European Economies in Transition, OECD.

OECD (1993a), *Agricultural Policies, Markets and Trade: Monitoring and Outlook 1993*. Paris: OECD.

OECD (1993b), *Employment and Unemployment in Economies in Transition: Conceptual and Measurement Problems*. Paris: Center for Co-operation with European Economies in Transition, OECD.

OECD (1993c), *Transformation of the Banking System: Portfolio Restructuring, Privatisation and the Payment System*. Paris: OECD, Centre for Co-operation with the European Economies in Transition.

OECD (1993d), *Hungary*, Economic Survey. Paris: Center for Co-operation with European Economies in Transition, OECD.

OECD (1994a), *Unemployment in Central and Eastern Europe: Transient or Persistent?*. Paris.

OECD (1994b), 'Management and Employee Buy-Outs in the Context of Privatisation', special feature, *Trends and Policies in Privatisation*, vol. 1, no. 3.

OECD (1994c), *The Czech and Slovak Republics*, Economic Survey. Paris: Center for Co-operation with European Economies in Transition, OECD.

OECD (1994d), *Integrating Emerging Market Economies into the International Trading System*. Paris: Center for Co-operation with European Economies in Transition, OECD.

Okolicsanyi, Karoly (1993), 'The Visegrad Triangle's Free-Trade Zone', *RFE/RL Research Report*, vol. 2, no. 3, 15 January.

Ostry, Sylvia (1993), 'The Threat of Managed Trade to Transforming Economies'. London: EBRD, *Working Paper*, no. 3, March.

Pelikan, Pavel (1993), *Lessons of Evolutionary Economics for Transformation Policies*. Stockholm: The Industrial Institute for Economic and Social Research, January, mimeo.

Perotti, Enrico C. (1994), 'A Taxonomy of Post-Socialist Financial Systems: Decentralized Enforcement and the Creation of Inside Money', *Economics of Transition*, vol. 2, no. 1 (March) pp. 71–81.

Pinto, B., M. Belka and S. Krajewski (1993), *Transforming State Enterprises in Poland: Microeconomic Evidence on Adjustment*. Washington, DC: Brookings Papers on Economic Activity, no. 1993/1.

PlanEcon (1993a), 'Results of Czechoslovak Voucher Privatization', 'Part I: Overall Review and Statistical Data', 25 January (dated 31 December, 1992), 'Part II: Sectoral and Industry Branch Reviews', 16 February, *PlanEcon Report*, vol. 8, nos 50–51–52, vol. 9, nos 3–4.

PlanEcon (1993b), 'Hungarian Monthly Economic Monitor: Most Indicators Point to Economic Recovery Starting From September 1992', *PlanEcon Report*, vol. 9, nos 11–12 (April).

PlanEcon (1993c), 'East European Stock Market Report: Polish, Hungarian and Czech Stock Markets Outperform Most Other Emerging Markets By a Wide Margin', *PlanEcon Report*, vol. 9, no. 40–41 (19 November).

PlanEcon (1994), 'Czech Stock Market Review: The Market Collapses, Returning Many Czech Stocks to Bargain Levels', *PlanEcon Report*, vol. 10, no. 12–13 (7 June).

Plowiec, Urszula (1994), 'Réformes en Pologne et association avec la Communauté Européenne', in Lavigne (ed.) (1994) pp. 218–27.

Portes, Richard (1980), 'Effects of the World Economic Crisis on the East European Economies', *The World Economy*, no. 3, pp. 13–52.

Portes, Richard (1992a), 'The European Community's Response to Eastern Europe', in CEPR (1992).

Portes, Richard (1992b), 'The Contraction of Eastern Europe's Economies', IMF-World Bank Conference, 4–5 June, mimeo.

Portes, Richard (ed.) (1993), *Economic Transformation in Central Europe. A Progress Report*. London: CEPR, Luxembourg: Office for Official Publications of the European Communities.

Pryor, Frederic L. (1985), *A Guidebook to the Comparative Study of Economic Systems*. Englewood Cliffs: Prentice-Hall Inc.

Qian, Yingyi and Chenggang Xu (1993), 'The M-form Hierarchy and China's Economic Reform', *European Economic Review*, vol. 37, no. 2/3 (April) pp. 541–8.

Rapport Nora (1967), *Rapport sur les entreprises publiques*. Paris: Groupe de travail du Comité interministériel des entreprises publiques présidé par Simon Nora, La Documentation française, avril.

Remington, Thomas (1991), 'A Socialist Pluralism of Opinions: *Glasnost* and Policy-Making Under Gorbachev', in Dallin and Lapidus (1991) pp. 97–115.

Revue du Marché Commun et de l'Union Européenne (1993), special issue, 'Les Relations CEE-Europe centrale: problématique de l'adhésion', no. 369, June.

Robbins, Lionel (1937), *Economic Planning and International Order*. London: Macmillan.

Robinson, Anthony (1993a), 'Tariffs creeping back in Poland', *Financial Times*, 13 January.

Robinson, Anthony (1993b), 'Europe's other steel industry reels', *Financial Times*, 19 February.

Robinson, Anthony and Nicholas Denton (1993), 'Clean-Up Prior to Going on Sale', *Financial Times*, 15 September.

Rodrik, Dani (1992), *Making Sense of the Soviet Trade Shock in Eastern Europe: A Framework and Some Estimates*. CEPR, Discussion Paper, no. 705.

Roland, Gérard (1989), *Economie politique du système soviétique*. Paris: L'Harmattan.

Roland, Gérard (1992), 'Issues in the Political economies of Transition', in CEPR (1992).

Roland, Gérard (1993), 'The Political Economy of Restructuring and Privatization in Eastern Europe', *European Economic Review*, vol. 37, no. 2/3 (April) pp. 533–40.

Roland, Gérard (1994a), 'The Role of Political Constraints in Transition Economies', *Economics of Transition*, vol. 2, no. 1 (March) pp. 27–41.

Roland, Gérard (1994b), *On the Speed and Sequencing of Privatization and Restructuring*. London: CEPR, Discussion Paper, no. 942, April.

Rollo, Jim and Alastair Smith (1993), 'EC trade with Eastern Europe', *Economic Policy*, no. 16 (April) pp. 139–81.

Rosati, Dariusz K. (1993a), 'Poland: Glass Half Empty', in Portes (ed.) (1993) pp. 211–73.

Rosati, Dariusz (1993b), 'East European Trade in the Post-CMEA Era', in Uvalic *et al.* (1993) pp. 66–103.

Rusinow, Dennison (1989), 'Yugoslavia: Enduring Crisis and Delayed Reforms', in *Pressures for Reform in the East European Countries*, Study papers submitted to the Joint Economic Committee, Congress of the United States, vol. 2. Washington, DC: USGPO, pp. 52–69.

Sachs, Jeffrey D. (1992), 'Privatization in Russia: Lessons from Eastern Europe', *The American Economic Review*, vol. 82, no. 2 (May) pp. 43–8.

Sachs, Jeffrey D. (1994), 'Russia's Struggle with Stabilization', *Transition*, vol. 5, no. 5, pp. 7–10.

Sachs, Jeffrey D. and David Lipton (1991), '"Shock Therapy" and Real Incomes', *Financial Times*, 29 January.

Sapir, Jacques (1990), *L'économie mobilisée, essai sur les économies de type soviétique*. Paris: Agalma – La Découverte.

Scalapino, Robert A. (1992) 'Asian Politics and Economics: The Challenges of the 1990s', in Iwasaki, Mori and Yamagushi (eds.) pp. 229–47.

Schiavone, Giuseppe (1992), *International Organizations, A Dictionary and Directory*, 3rd edn. London and Basingstoke: Macmillan.

Schmitter, Philippe C. and Terry Lynn Karl (1994), 'The Conceptual Travels of Transitologists and Consolidologists: How Far to the East Should They Attempt To Go?', *Slavic Review*, vol. 53, no. 1 (Spring) pp. 173–85.

Schroeder, Gertrude (1979), 'The Soviet Economy on a Treadmill of "Reforms"', in *The Soviet Economy in a Time of Change*, Joint Economic Committee, Congress of the United States. Washington, DC: USGPO, pp. 312–40.

Schuller, A. and H. Hamel (1985), 'On the Membership of Socialist Countries in the International Monetary Fund', *Acta Oeconomica*, vol. 34, no. 1–2, pp. 113–30.

Senik-Leygonie, Claudia and Gordon Hughes (1992), 'Industrial Profitability and Trade Among the Former Soviet Republics', *Economic Policy*, vol. 15 (October) pp. 353–86.

Sereghyova, Jana (ed.) (1993), *Entrepreneurship in CentralEast Europe*. Heidelberg: Physica Verlag.

Simonetti, Marko (1993), 'A Comparative Review of Privatization Strategies in Four Former Socialist Countries', *Europe-Asia Studies*, vol. 45, no. 1, pp. 79–102.

Slay, Ben (1994), *The Polish Economy, Crisis, Reform, and Transformation*. Princeton: Princeton University Press.

Smith, Alan (1993), *Russia and the World Economy: Problems of Integration*. London and New York: Routledge.

Sobell, Vlad (1984), *The Red Market, Industrial Co-operation and Specialisation in Comecon*. Aldershot: Gower.

Steinherr, Alfred, and Pier-Luigi Gilibert (1994), 'Six Proposals in Search of Financial Sector Reform in Eastern Europe', *Moct-Most*, vol. 4, no. 1, pp. 101–14.

Stiglitz, Joseph E. (1994), *Wither Socialism?*. Cambridge, Mass.: The MIT Press.

Sutela, Pekka (ed.) (1993), *The Russian Economy in Crisis and Transition*. Helsinki: Bank of Finland, A:86.

Sutela, Pekka (1994), *Socialism, Planning and Optimality. A Study in Soviet Economic Thought*. Helsinki: The Finnish Society of Sciences and Letters, vol. 25.

Svejnar, Jan and Miroslav Singer (1994), 'Using Vouchers to Privatize an Economy: the Czech and Slovak Case', *Economics of Transition*, vol. 2, no. 1 (March) pp. 43–69.

Swain, Geoffrey and Nigel Swain (1993), *Eastern Europe Since 1945*. London and Basingstoke: Macmillan.

Szamuely, László (1993), *Transition from State Socialism: Whereto and How?*. Budapest: Kopint-Datorg Discussion papers, no. 12.

Szpringer, Zofia (1993), *Assessment of Price Liberalization Effects in Selected Post-Socialist Economies*. Warsaw: Institute of Finance, Working Papers, no. 34, 28 pp.

Taylor, Lance (1994), 'The Market Met Its Match: Lessons for the Future from the Transition's Initial Years', *Journal of Comparative Economics*, vol. 19, no. 1 (August) pp. 64–87.

Tinbergen, Jan (1961), 'Do Communist and Free Economies Show a Convergent Pattern?', *Soviet Studies*, vol. 12, no. 4, pp. 333–41.

Trzeciakowski, Witold (1978), *Indirect Management in a Centrally Planned Economy: Systems Constructions in Foreign Trade*. Amsterdam: North Holland.

Uvalić, Milica (1992), *Investment and Property Rights in Yugoslavia. The Long Transition to a Market Economy*. Cambridge: Cambridge University Press.

Uvalić, Milica, Efisio Espa and Jochen Lorentzen (eds) (1993), *Impediments to the Transition in Eastern Europe*. Florence: European University Institute, European Policy Studies, no. 1.

Vacic, Aleksandar M. (1992), 'Systemic Transformation in Central and Eastern Europe: General Framework, Specific Features and Prospects', in 'Transition en Europe de l'Est: les nouveaux rivages du marché', *Economies et Sociétés*, série G 'Economie Planifiée', special issue, vol. 44.

Várhegyi, Eva (1993), *Key Elements of the Reform of the Hungarian Banking System: Privatization and Portfolio Cleaning*. London: CEPR, Discussion Paper, no. 826, September.

Vintrová, Ružena (1993), 'Macroeconomic Analysis of Transformation in the CSFR', WIIW, Vienna Institute for Comparative Economic Studies, *Forschungsberichte*, no. 188, January.

Visegrád (1991), Visegrad Summit Declaration, *Report on Eastern Europe*, Radio Free Europe/RL Research Institute, 1 March, 1991, pp. 31–2.

Wang, Zhen Kun and L Alan Winters (1993), *EC Imports from Eastern Europe: Iron and Steel*. London: CEPR Discussion Paper Series, no. 825, October.

Ward, Benjamin (1958), 'The Firm in Illyria: Market Syndicalism', *American Economic Review*, vol. 48, no. 4 (September) pp. 566–89.

Webster, Leila and Joshua Charap (1993), *A Survey of Private Manufacturers in St Petersburg*. London: EBRD, Working Paper, no. 5, July.

Weitzman, Martin L. (1993), 'Economic Transition: Can Theory Help?' *European Economic Review*, vol. 37, no. 2/3 (April) pp. 549–55.

Welfens, Paul J.J. (1992), *Market-Oriented Systemic Transformations in Eastern Europe, Problems, Theoretical Issues and Policy Options*. Berlin: Springer Verlag.

Weydenthal, Jan B. de (1993a), 'Controversy in Poland Over 'Euroregions'', *RFE/RL Research Report*, vol. 2, no. 16 (16 April).

Weydenthal, Jan B. de (1993b), 'The EC and Central Europe: A Difficult Relationship', *RFE/RL Research Report*, vol. 2, no. 21 (21 May).

White, Stephen, Judy Batt and Paul G. Lewis (eds) (1993), *Developments in East European Politics*. London: Macmillan.

Whitlock, Erik (1993), 'Obstacles to CIS Economic Integration', *RFE/RL Research Report*, vol. 2, no. 27 (2 July).

Wijnbergen, Sweder van (1993), 'Enterprise Reform in Eastern Europe', *Economics of Transition*, vol. 1, no. 1 (January) pp. 21–59.

Wiles, Peter (1968), *Communist International Economics*. Oxford: Basil Blackwell.

Wiles, Peter (ed.) (1982), *The New Communist Third World*. London: Croom Helm.

Wiles, Peter (1992), 'Capitalist Triumphalism in Eastern Europe, or the Economics of Transition: An Interim Report', in A. Clesse and R. Tökes (eds) *Preventing a New East-West Divide: The Economic and Social Imperatives of the Future Europe*. Baden-Baden: Nomos Verlagsgesellschaft.

Williamson, John (ed.) (1991a), *Currency Convertibility in Eastern Europe*. Washington, DC: Institute for International Economics.

Williamson John (1991b), *The Economic Opening of Eastern Europe*. Washington, DC: Institute for International Economics, May, vol. 31.

Williamson, John (1992a), *Trade and Payments After Soviet Disintegration*, Washington, Institute for International Economics, June, vol. 37.

Williamson, John (1992b), 'Why Did Output Fall in Eastern Europe?', Paper prepared for the Arne Ryde Symposium on 'The Transition Problem', Denmark, Rungsted Kyst, 11–12 June.

Williamson, John (ed.) (1994), *The Political Economy of Policy Reform*. Washington, DC: Institute for International Economics.

Winiecki, Jan (1993a), *Post-Soviet-Type Economies in Transition*. Aldershot: Avebury.

Winiecki, Jan (1993b), *'Heterodox' Stabilisation in Eastern Europe*. London: European Bank for Reconstruction and Development, Working papers, no. 8, July.

Winters, L Alan (1992), 'The Europe Agreements: With a Little Help From Our Friends', in *The Association Process: Making it Work, Central Europe and the European Community*, CEPR Occasional Paper, no. 11, November 1992.

Winters, L Alan (1994), *The Liberalization of European Steel Trade*. London: CEPR, Discussion Paper, no. 1002, August.

Winters, L Alan and Zhen Kun Wang (1993), *Liberalizing EC Imports of Footwear From Eastern Europe*. London: CEPR Discussion Paper series, no. 836, September.

Winters, L Alan and Zhen Kun Wang (1994), *Eastern Europe's International Trade*. Manchester: Manchester University Press.

Wolf, Thomas A. (1988), *Foreign Trade in the Centrally Planned Economy*. New York: Harwood Academic Publishers.

Wolf, Thomas, Warren Coats, Daniel Citrin and Adrienne Cheasty (1994), *Financial Relations Among Countries of the Former Soviet Union*. Washington, DC: International Monetary Fund, IMF Economic Reviews, February.

Wyplosz, Charles (1993), 'After the Honeymoon. On the Economics and the Politics of Economic Transformation', *European Economic Review*, vol. 37, no. 2/3 (April) pp. 379–86.

Yavlinsky, Grigory and Serguey Braguinsky (1994), 'The Inefficiency of *Laissez-Faire* in Russia: Hysteresis Effects and the Need for Policy-Led Transformation', *Journal of Comparative Economics*, vol. 19, no. 1 (August) pp. 88–116.

Zaleski, Eugene (1980), *Stalinist Planning for Economic Growth, 1933–1952*. London: Macmillan; and Chapel Hill: University of North Carolina Press.

Zoethout, Tseard (1993), 'Financing Eastern Europe's Capital Requirements', *RFE/RL Research Report*, vol. 2, no. 7 (12 February) pp. 38–43.

Index